THE
READER'S
DIGEST
QUICK FIX

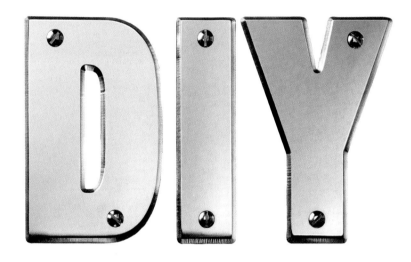

THE READER'S DIGEST QUICK FIX DIY

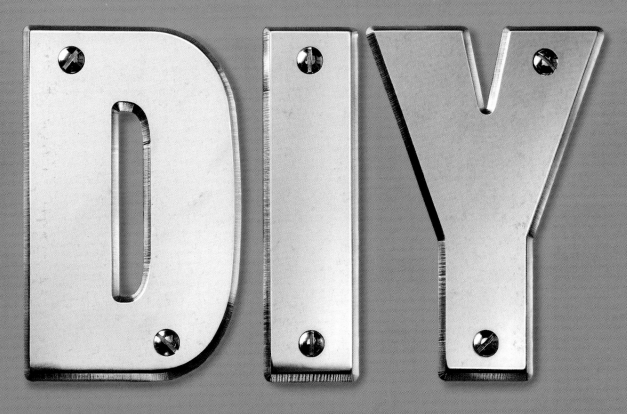

Published by The Reader's Digest Association Limited
LONDON • NEW YORK • SYDNEY • MONTREAL

contents

order of work

12 construction
Discovering how your home is built

15 home survey
Identifying faults needing action
Diagnosing damp and rot

21 inspirations
Planning internal alterations

24 solutions
Dealing with major problems

27 safety first
Avoiding accidents with DIY

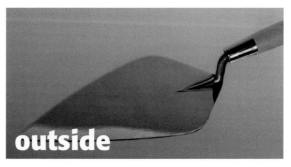

outside

32 ladders
Using access equipment safely

35 roofs
Assessing what needs doing
Replacing damaged tiles and slates
Repairing flat and corrugated roofs

44 gutters
Maintaining the rainwater system

47 brickwork
Restoring and repointing walls

50 rendering
Patching and restoring the coating

53 cladding
Fixing and replacing boards

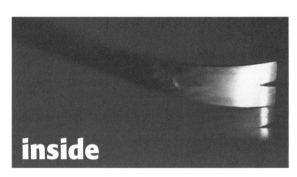

inside

doors & windows

58 floors
Keeping floors in good order
Lifting and replacing boards
Choosing new floorcoverings
Laying new floorcoverings

70 plastering
Working on walls and ceilings

73 stud walls
Planning and building the framework

76 plasterboard
Choosing and handling boards
Fixing and finishing boards

82 staircases
Repairing treads and balustrades

85 mouldings
Working with skirting boards
Fixing and repair techniques

92 fitting
Freeing jams and fixing joints

95 hardware
Curing hinge and lock problems
Fitting locks to external doors
Improving window and door security

104 glazing
Choosing glass and double glazing
Cutting and fitting new panes

110 sliding sashes
Replacing cords and curing rattles

113 repairs
Detecting and treating rot

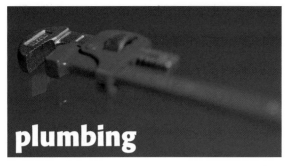

plumbing

118 systems
Locating and testing the controls

121 pipes
Working with copper and plastic pipes
Making connections and fixing leaks

127 taps
Replacing tap washers and O-rings
Fitting new taps indoors and outside

133 overflows
Curing problems with valves and tanks

136 blockages
Clearing waste pipes, toilets and drains

139 new fittings
Replacing existing plumbing equipment

142 baths
Installing and repairing baths

145 toilets
Repairing the flush and fixing leaks

148 showers
Picking the right hardware

151 appliances
Providing supply and waste connections

154 boilers
Tackling simple adjustments

157 radiators
Fixing valves and curing cold radiators
Draining systems and fitting new parts

163 heating controls
Valves, thermostats and programmers

166 noisy plumbing
Curing noises in pipes, tanks and boilers

169 insulation
Keeping tanks and pipework warm

electrics

174 systems
Investigating your house wiring

177 faultfinding
Tracing problems and using testers

180 flex
Preparing cores and making connections

183 cable
Choosing and routing cables

186 fittings
Replacing switches and socket outlets

189 extra sockets
Providing more connections for
appliances

192 lighting
Providing extra light fittings
Installing wall lights
Adding track lights and recessed fittings

201 outdoors
Providing light and power in the garden

204 services
Installing phone and aerial outlets

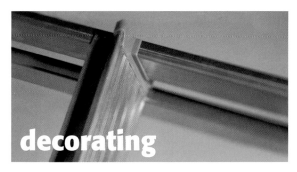

decorating

208 **preparation**
Cleaning surfaces and stripping paint

211 **sanding floors**
Stripping and sealing floorboards

214 **painting**
Outdoor walls, wood and metalwork
Types of equipment for applying paint
Working in sequence and curing flaws
Keeping equipment in good condition

226 **tiling**
Planning how to set out the tiles
Cutting, fixing and drilling tiles
Grouting joints and restoring old tiles

235 **wallpaper**
Estimating, measuring and marking out
Pasting and folding paper
Techniques for obstacles and ceilings

fittings

246 **shelving**
Getting shelves level and secure

249 **storage**
Ideas for every room in the house

252 **pictures**
Creating a professional picture show

255 **window dressing**
Hanging curtains and blinds

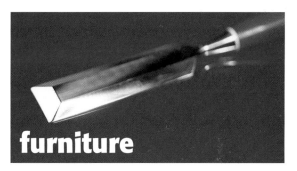

furniture

260 **blemishes**
Curing faults in surface finishes

263 **repairs**
Filling holes and cracks
Dismantling and reassembling furniture

269 **stripping**
Removing old finishes

272 **metalware**
Restoring and attaching fittings

275 **veneers**
Tackling bubbles and fitting patches

278 **finishes**
Using varnishes and lacquers
Working with oils and waxes
Colouring with dyes and stains
Using traditional french polish

garden

292 outbuildings
Shed, greenhouse and garage care

295 tools
Maintaining hand and power tools

298 lawnmowers
Safety, maintenance and storage tips

301 fences
Positioning and fixing fence posts
Tackling rot and hanging gates

307 walls
Building with bricks and blocks

310 paths
Creating walkways down the garden

314 steps
Building on a slope or against a wall

316 drives
Laying different drive surfaces

319 ponds
Positioning ponds, fountains and lights
Using rigid and flexible liners

equipment

326 selecting
Workbenches, drills and screwdrivers
Hammers and measuring tools
Hand and power saws and chisels
Routers, sanders and planers
Hiring tools and choosing materials

341 techniques
Making fixings with nails and screws
Measuring, marking and cramping
Sawing, planing and routing

350 fixings
Choosing nails and screws
Fasteners, wall plugs and sealants

356 maintenance
Keeping tools in good condition

358 index
368 acknowledgments

about this book

If you are an enthusiastic do-it-yourselfer, but sometimes wish for a friendly professional at your elbow to offer some extra advice or a handy tip, you'll find all the assistance you need in the pages of *The Reader's Digest Quick Fix DIY.*

This is not a step-by-step DIY manual. Rather than telling you how to do a job from start to finish, the book points out pitfalls and lends a helping hand, enabling you to do the job effectively and quickly. It can do this because it distils the vast experience of experts–people who have done every job in the book over and over–to gather together a wide range of short cuts, practical hints and trade tips that give great results every time.

The Reader's Digest Quick Fix DIY has 11 chapters. The first, *Order of Work*, shows you how to identify areas of your home that need attention or improvement and offers suggestions to help you to plan major projects.

The chapters that follow deal with everything you might consider doing yourself, including exterior and interior repairs, plumbing and electrical alterations, and those vital finishing touches, including painting, wallpapering and furniture repair.

Outdoor do-it-yourselfers will find lots of good advice on looking after sheds, greenhouses and garages, keeping garden equipment in good order, and a series of useful projects from building a wall to installing a pond.

No one can do a good job without the right tools and materials, so the book concludes with an invaluable chapter on selecting and using all kinds of hand and power tools and fixings, and on looking after your tool kit.

Throughout, you will find edge-of-page summary panels to remind you of the various stages involved in a range of key jobs and techniques. These also provide a quick overview of a job, so you can see at a glance whether you have the skills, tools or materials to take it on.

The Reader's Digest Quick Fix DIY is a treasure chest of advice to help you to keep all areas of your home and garden looking good and working well. We are confident you'll find it a good friend for years to come.

order of work

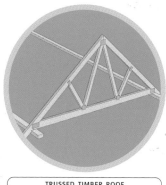

TRADITIONAL TIMBER ROOF

Generation of change
The age of your home will dictate how it has been built. The construction of houses built in the past half-century differs markedly from those put up before about 1920. Houses built during the intervening generation of change incorporate both traditional house-building techniques and some of the new methods of construction that were being introduced.

Before picking up the tools
Knowing how your home is built before embarking on DIY jobs can save you time and money. Understanding how the roof, walls and floors are put together and what they're made of will help you to plan improvements and alterations, and to deal with any faults that may develop as time goes by.

TRUSSED TIMBER ROOF

Look in the loft
A glance in the loft will tell you what sort of roof you have. Traditional timber roofs, assembled on site, have open space below the rafters for storage. Roofs constructed in the past 50 years usually have roof trusses—prefabricated timber frames incorporating rafters and ceiling joists. These are factory-made so the roof structure can be erected quickly, but the design and number of the trusses leaves little room for storage.

Save boarding on a roof
If you live in an older house with a boarded roof—one with planking laid across the tops of the rafters—don't have it stripped off if you ever have a new roof put on the property. The boarding insulates the roof space far better than a layer of roofing felt alone, and areas which are rotten can be replaced easily with sections of new pressure-treated wood.

Strong enough to bear the weight?
Old roofs are usually covered with natural slates or clay tiles, and were designed to take the weight of these. Before you replace them with concrete tiles, which are usually much heavier, ask an expert whether the roof timbers will need to be strengthened. If the timbers do need reinforcing, the cost is likely to cancel out any saving you might make by re-roofing with manufactured tiles—in which case, you're better off leaving the roof structure alone and replacing like with like.

Two kinds of external brick walls

SOLID WALL CONSTRUCTION

Solid all the way through

The bricks in solid walls are laid in patterns known as bonds. What they all have in common are headers–bricks laid end-on so that they pass right through the wall to give it strength. A solid wall will be as thick as the length of a brick (215 mm) plus the thickness of plaster inside and any rendering outside. You can measure the wall at a door or window opening.

A cavity in the middle

Only the long faces of bricks, known as stretchers, are on view if your house has cavity walls. The walls are a minimum of 255 mm thick (two single leaves of brickwork, each 102.5 mm thick, separated by a 50 mm wide cavity) and more if the cavity is wider or the internal leaf is built of thicker blockwork.

CAVITY WALL CONSTRUCTION

Drier and warmer

Cavity walls have several advantages over solid ones. Any rain that penetrates the outer leaf of brickwork cannot bridge the cavity and instead runs down its inner face to ground level, so that the inner leaf stays dry. Interior wall surfaces are warmer because the air in the cavity acts as an insulator, and extra insulation placed in the cavity during or after building makes them warmer still. **Timber-framed houses** have an inner leaf consisting of load-bearing wooden wall panels clad with external plywood sheathing and filled with insulation.

construction

13

construction Suspended and solid ground floors

SUSPENDED TIMBER FLOOR

SOLID CONCRETE FLOOR

What lies beneath your feet?

Ground floors in houses built before about 1950 are usually covered with floorboards laid over timber joists which are suspended over an underfloor airspace. In the past 50 years solid concrete ground floors have become the norm, although they may be overlaid with timber strip flooring or chipboard. **Accessing and altering plumbing** and heating pipework under a timber floor is a relatively simple matter; getting at pipes buried in concrete is much more difficult.

No more damp and better insulation

Concrete floors in the kitchens and sculleries of old houses are prone to rising damp because they were laid straight onto the earth, with no separating damp-proof membrane (DPM). Inherent dampness in a solid floor also makes it cold and so liable to condensation. Where concrete floors have been laid next to wooden ones, they can hinder ventilation of the underfloor space, increasing the risk of rot in the wood floor. Nowadays, Building Regulations ensure that concrete ground floors are underlaid with a DPM of heavy-grade polythene, and since 1990 they have also had to be insulated.

Prone to rot and draughts

In older homes, the ends of the joists supporting timber ground floors are embedded in external walls, making them prone to rot if the walls are damp. The square-edge floorboards used until the 1930s let in underfloor draughts—a problem largely cured by the use of tongue-and-groove boards, although at the cost of making the boards more difficult to lift (see page 58).

home survey Assessing the condition of your property

Get your priorities right

Carry out a survey to make sure your home is weathertight, safe and thief-proof before you do anything else. There's no point in decorating if the roof is letting in rain, or installing new light fittings if the wiring is dangerous and needs replacing. And if the house isn't secure, filling it with expensive fixtures and fittings before making sure that all the exterior doors and windows have good locks is also getting your priorities wrong.

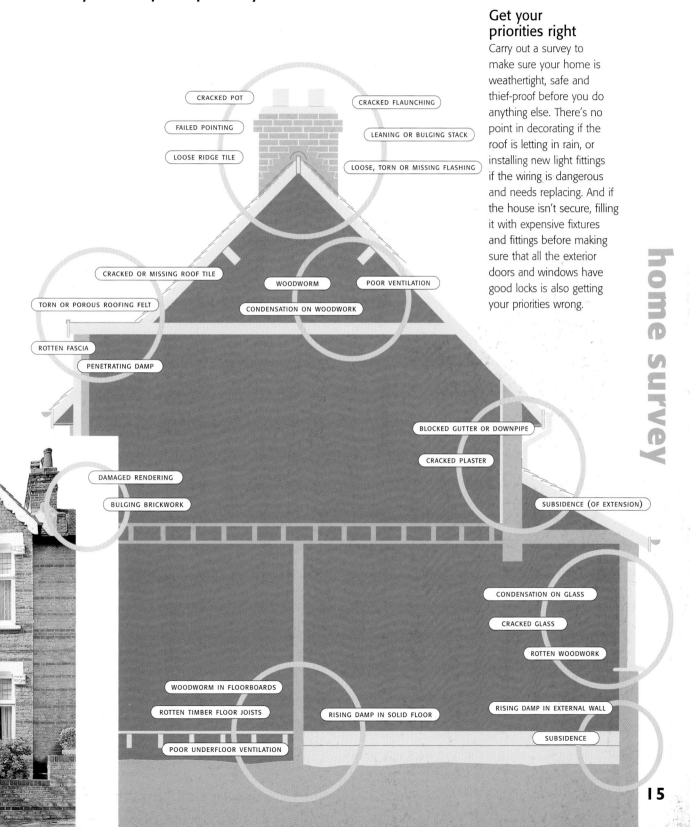

CRACKED POT

CRACKED FLAUNCHING

FAILED POINTING

LEANING OR BULGING STACK

LOOSE RIDGE TILE

LOOSE, TORN OR MISSING FLASHING

CRACKED OR MISSING ROOF TILE

WOODWORM

POOR VENTILATION

TORN OR POROUS ROOFING FELT

CONDENSATION ON WOODWORK

ROTTEN FASCIA

PENETRATING DAMP

BLOCKED GUTTER OR DOWNPIPE

CRACKED PLASTER

DAMAGED RENDERING

BULGING BRICKWORK

SUBSIDENCE (OF EXTENSION)

CONDENSATION ON GLASS

CRACKED GLASS

ROTTEN WOODWORK

WOODWORM IN FLOORBOARDS

ROTTEN TIMBER FLOOR JOISTS

RISING DAMP IN SOLID FLOOR

RISING DAMP IN EXTERNAL WALL

SUBSIDENCE

POOR UNDERFLOOR VENTILATION

15

home survey Assessing the condition of your property

Take it from the top

Start your home survey with the roof. A pair of binoculars is useful for inspecting it without having to climb a ladder. If you can't see the whole roof surface from your garden or the street, ask to view it from a neighbour's property.

Stacks of trouble

Chimneys are the most exposed part of your house, so check them closely for signs of damage. Look for cracks in the pots and in the flaunching–the mortar bed in which the pots are embedded. If a stack is built against an outside wall, examine it for straightness. The combination of coal gases condensing inside the flue and rain soaking through the mortar joints can set up a chemical reaction which makes the brickwork bulge outwards. Repointing the brickwork (see page 49) and lining the flue can arrest the problem, but a severely damaged stack may have to be completely rebuilt.

Check the controls

Before you start any DIY, make sure you know where the water and gas stoptaps and main electricity supply switch are located. Keep a torch by the electricity meter, plus some fuse wire if the system has fuses (see page 174). Locate all drain inspection chambers (manholes) and check that the covers can be lifted easily if a drain becomes blocked (see page 138).

Look for overflows

Check the gutters and downpipes for blockages (see page 44). Stains on the house walls can reveal where previous overflows have occurred. The next time it rains, check where gutters are overflowing or where water is leaking from downpipe joints.

Include the garden

Remember to survey the garden at the same time as the rest of your home. Fences may be in poor condition, a shed roof may be leaking, garden paths may need lighting, and nearby trees may be undermining boundary walls. A gate or door into the garden might need a lock ftting to it.

Inspect the loft

Go into the loft to inspect the underside of the roof. Look for water stains on the timbers, or wait until there's a heavy downpour and then look for signs of rain getting in. There should be ventilators along the eaves, at the ridge, in gable walls or on the roof slope. Shine a light along the eaves if there are none to be seen, because a badly ventilated roof space can be liable to dry rot, and this often sets in along the eaves. Lastly, examine the roof timbers for woodworm.

Is the woodwork sound?

Prod the external woodwork with a bradawl to detect rot under the paintwork (see page 82) and look round the edges of door and window frames for gaps where rainwater can penetrate—especially on north and west-facing walls, which are the most exposed to the weather.

That sinking feeling

Subsidence is the most serious problem you might detect. It occurs most commonly on clay soil, which expands when wet and then contracts as it dries out. Look at the corners of your house and at the door and window openings. Are they vertical and square?

Zigzag cracks running down the walls from the corners of door and window frames, and between the main house and an extension, are signs of possible subsidence. Inside, doors and windows may start jamming for no apparent reason, and wallpaper can crease or tear.

Barriers to rising damp

Look for a damp-proof course (DPC)—visible outside between the second and third courses of brickwork above ground level. This is a horizontal band of slate, bituminous felt or black polythene. In an older house built before DPCs were introduced, you may see a row of small mortar or rubber plugs indicating that a chemical DPC has been injected into the walls in recent years.

Where the air gets in

Airbricks or grilles are built into the outside walls, just above ground level, in houses with suspended timber ground floors. These allow air to circulate in the underfloor space, helping to keep it dry and to discourage rot. Make sure they are not blocked or obstructed in any way.

Testing timber floors

Jump up and down on timber ground floors. If they sag noticeably, the joists may be rotten because their ends are built into walls suffering from rising damp. Prod the skirting boards with a bradawl to see if they're rotten—another indication that there may be problems beneath the floor.

Safe and secure

As you work your way around the house checking the woodwork, look at how windows and external doors are secured. You may need to fit new locks or upgrade existing ones (see pages 98–103).

MOULD GROWTH IN BUILT-IN WARDROBE

PENETRATING DAMP ABOVE WINDOW

CONDENSATION ON SINGLE GLAZING

home survey
Diagnosing damp and tracing the causes

Find the reason before trying a remedy

Damp problems in a house can be due to a number of causes–rain getting through the walls or roof, moisture being absorbed from the ground, condensation settling on cold surfaces, or a mixture of these. Make sure you know what the cause of dampness is before trying to cure it, otherwise you may be dealing only with part of the problem, or even adopting the wrong remedy for the sort of damp involved.

Spot the tell-tale semicircles

In an old house with a slate damp-proof course (DPC), slight movement of the building can crack the slates, allowing damp from the ground to rise into the masonry above the crack. A single point failure will cause a semicircular patch of damp up to 1m (3 ft 3 in) or so across, while multiple cracks will lead to an almost continuous band across the affected wall.

Try the foil test

If you're not sure of the cause of a damp patch on a wall, try the foil test. Dry the wall surface with a fan heater, then tape some kitchen foil tightly over the damp area. If the surface of the foil is wet after 24 hours, you have condensation. If the foil is dry but the wall surface beneath it is damp, you have rising or penetrating damp. Discount rising damp if the moisture is more than 1m above outside ground level.

Getting through the gaps

Patches of dampness on walls around windows and doors are usually caused by rain getting through gaps between their frames and the surrounding masonry. Where the damp is below the opening, it may be because there is no drip groove to stop the water creeping under a projecting sill or threshold. If there is a drip groove, make sure the rain is not crossing it because it is blocked with paint or mortar (see page 51).

Suspect condensation

If the roof isn't leaking but the timbers and loft insulation are damp, the likely culprit is condensation. This is caused by warm moisture-laden air rising into the loft from the rooms below and condensing on cold surfaces within the loft space. In serious cases, roof timbers can start to rot and saturated insulation materials can stain ceilings.

Looking for a leak in the roof

Discovering exactly where a pitched roof is leaking can be difficult. Rain can trickle down the roofing felt and then along the sides of rafters before it drips onto the loft floor. Look for clues such as dampness on a party wall or chimney stack in the loft, which might indicate that flashings are defective or missing (see page 35). Getting someone to play a hose on the roof, area by area, while you remain inside the loft can also help to reveal where the water is getting in.

Woodworm at work

At the same time as checking lofts, underfloor spaces and built-in cupboards for signs of dampness, inspect structural timbers and joinery for evidence of woodworm, which thrives in slightly damp environments. Look for the small flight holes made by the beetles when they emerge from the wood and the fine wood dust created by the pest. Check the untreated backs of all freestanding chests and wardrobes, and the unpainted top and bottom edges of doors at the same time.

home survey Diagnosing damp and tracing the causes

Prod the paintwork

Use a bradawl to test the soundness of skirting boards if there are signs of damp in downstairs walls or the underfloor space. The backs of skirting boards are usually left unpainted, so they readily absorb moisture from the masonry. However, severe deterioration of the boards is often not apparent because of paint applied to their face sides.

Crossing the bridge

If you think you have rising damp in your house, locate the damp-proof course (DPC) and make sure it isn't covered by a flowerbed, path, drive or patio. Look for rendering that has been applied over the DPC. Check whether there is a vertical DPC sandwiched between the house wall and the end of a garden wall built up against it. Curing these common causes of rising damp will solve the problem for little or no cost, saving you from incurring an expensive bill from a professional damp-proofing firm.

Check out the plumbing

Leaks in plumbing and central-heating pipework can cause damp patches which could be misinterpreted as rising or penetrating damp. This is especially common where the pipes are run beneath a floor or are buried in wall plaster. Here a pinhole leak or a weeping fitting can release surprisingly large volumes of water as time goes by, especially if it has no chance to dry out naturally.

If this is the cause of the problem, you have two possible courses of action. You can either expose the fault and then replace the affected pipes, which will cause a lot of disruption. Alternatively, you can simply leave them where they are and bypass them by installing new ones.

Letting off steam

The kitchen and bathroom are the main sources of condensation in the home. Bathing, cooking and washing up, and washing and drying clothes all pour large volumes of steam into the air. Portable gas space heaters and paraffin stoves also create a lot of moisture.

The problem is made worse by poor room ventilation and over-efficient draught-proofng, both of which stop warm moisture-laden air inside the house being replaced with cooler drier air from outside.

Unventilated fitted cupboards built against outside walls can suffer badly from condensation. This can lead to unsightly mould growth, which will quickly spoil clothes stored there.

inspirations Prepare a plan and visualise your options

Measure and draw

Experiment with ideas for alterations by drawing a floor plan on graph paper. An ultrasonic estimator (see page 331) is the most accurate tool for quickly taking measurements. The larger the scale of the drawing, the more detail can be included on it, so use the whole sheet of graph paper, or tape a couple of sheets together if necessary. Then take lots of photocopies before you start sketching out and modifying your ideas.

Mark which way doors open—it has a vital effect on the positioning of light switches—and include other features on your plan such as radiators, light fittings and socket outlets too.

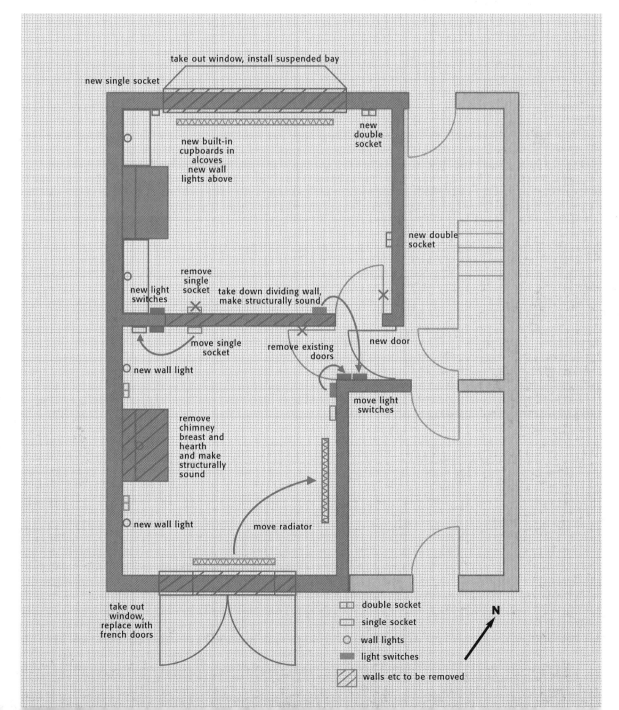

take out window, install suspended bay

new single socket

new double socket

new built-in cupboards in alcoves
new wall lights above

new double socket

remove single socket

new light switches

take down dividing wall, make structurally sound

new door

move single socket

remove existing doors

new wall light

move light switches

remove chimney breast and hearth and make structurally sound

new wall light

move radiator

take out window, replace with french doors

⊏⊐ double socket

⊏⊐ single socket

○ wall lights

▬ light switches

▨ walls etc to be removed

N

inspirations Prepare a plan and visualise your options

A sense of direction

Find out in which direction north lies and mark it on your plan. Aspect can be vital if you're thinking of building a conservatory, or having skylights or new windows put in the house—all of which need to face south or west to get most sunshine and daylight.

Envisage the impact

If you decide to have new openings made in a wall, or an existing one enlarged, you can get an idea of the overall impact by sketching them full-size on sheets of lining paper, then taping these in position on the wall surface.

Illusions of space

Several design tricks can be used to make a room feel bigger than it really is. For example, brightly lit rooms with pale walls, bare floors, simple furniture and sheer curtains feel spacious. Strategically hung mirrors also add an illusion of extra space, reflecting what lies through a window, around a corner or beyond an open doorway.

That shrinking feeling

A room can be made to feel smaller too. Dark walls and ceilings seem to advance. A picture rail also makes a ceiling feel lower, especially if the wall above the rail is painted to match the ceiling colour. Heavy, patterned fabrics, dark furniture and focused lighting emphasise the shrinking effect.

Change without disruption

Instead of altering the dimensions of rooms by knocking them into one another to create bigger spaces or putting up stud walls to make them smaller, consider creating change by illusion. Using colour, lighting, furniture and furnishings to create different effects is cheaper and less disruptive than undertaking building work.

Consider the alternatives before you start making changes

Structural considerations
Make sure a dividing wall is non-loadbearing before you knock it down to turn two rooms into one. One way to tell is to look at floorboards in the room above–if they run parallel to the wall, the joists they're laid on must be supported by the wall–but seek expert advice if you're in any doubt.

Counting the potential costs
One room made from two will have more light if both the originals had windows, but the bigger area will be more expensive to heat. A sense of comfort may be lost if the enlarged room feels too long, too narrow or too low. In addition, there will now be space where there were two surfaces to stand furniture against and hang things on.

New uses for existing areas
You can make your home suit your lifestyle better by changing the way you use rooms. For example, an understairs cupboard could be converted into a downstairs toilet. You could house the washing machine, tumble drier and airer in an old walk-in larder and increase food storage in the kitchen.

An integral garage is an obvious candidate for conversion into a playroom, a home office or a teenager's room if you're prepared to leave the car on the drive or street.

Rooms with a view
Glass creates an impression of space. Glazing a solid door at the end of a claustrophobic hall introduces a view of the outside or into a room, lets in light and makes the hall feel more spacious. Creating or emphasising a view of the garden through a window or french doors makes a room appear larger, especially if tall plants are kept away from the other side of the glass.

Lofty thoughts
Don't forget the loft when you're looking for extra space. Although the roof trusses used in most houses since about 1950 usually involve too much structural work to make loft conversion practical, the roof spaces in older properties can often be turned into an extra room (see page 12).

inspirations

23

Risks not worth the saving

Always err on the side of caution if you're not confident about your DIY skills–especially if the job involves working at height. All the equipment needed for carrying out roof repairs and alterations can be hired (see page 32), but if you are unsure about whether you can do the job safely, paying professional contractors is preferable to risking injury or worse.

Opportunity to tackle other tasks

Scaffolding forms a substantial part of the total cost of having a house re-roofed. Try to take advantage of it by having other jobs, such as painting the outside woodwork or repointing the brickwork, carried out while the scaffolding is in place. It will have to satisfy the requirements of different tradespeople (for example, providing planking and access ladders for painters). **You will probably have to pay extra** to keep the scaffolding beyond the four weeks usually negotiated by roofers. Remember that you will not be covered by the contractor's insurance if you work from the scaffolding yourself.

A sensible division of labour

Many building jobs involve an element of unskilled work. For example, having a room replastered involves hacking off and carting away the old plaster. Tradespeople will often agree to you doing this sort of work yourself to save money before they come in to carry out the skilled part of the job.

Time and patience

Before you tackle a large project yourself, estimate how long it will take and how disruptive it will be. Can you and others living in the house put up with a long period of disorder if you're able to devote only weekends to the project? **Nothing kills enthusiasm** more quickly than apparent lack of progress. You may conclude that the solution is to employ others to do the major disruptive work while devoting your input to just the finishing stages.

Get an expert opinion

Consult a professional surveyor or building engineer if your home survey alerts you to a serious problem—subsidence, for example— that could require major structural work. An expert will assess whether the problem has stabilised and requires no action, can be arrested without major building work, or requires extensive remedial work.

Strategies to combat damp problems

Let your house breathe

There are a number of simple but effective remedies for condensation. Open windows when the weather is suitable so that drier air can get in. Fit extractor fans with humidity detectors in kitchens and bathrooms to remove moist air automatically, or else plug in a dehumidifier. Lastly, remember that sealing up doors, windows and unused flues to eliminate draughts will increase the likelihood of condensation.

Is a guarantee required?

Installing a damp-proof course (DPC) in an older house usually involves drilling holes into the second or third course of brickwork above outdoor ground level, then pumping a chemical waterproofer into the walls. You can hire the equipment and do the job yourself if you don't need the guarantee.

Easy ways to cut humidity

Create less moisture by drying clothes outdoors whenever possible. If you have a tumble drier, vent it to the outside. **Keep lids on boiling saucepans** and shut bathroom and kitchen doors to stop steam spreading through the house. **Use dehumidifiers** in damp, enclosed areas and avoid heaters that run on paraffin or oil—both fuels produce large quantities of water vapour when they are burned.

solutions

solutions Strategies to combat damp problems

Allow time for drying out
If your home needs a DPC, schedule it into the order of work as early as possible. The plaster on damp walls will have absorbed salts from the masonry and will have to be hacked off to a height of about 1m (3 ft 3 in) before the DPC is installed. Then the masonry will need to be left bare for several months so that it can dry out before the walls are re-covered—either with a traditional sand and cement plaster, or with one recommended by the damp-proofing company.

Raising the floor
Always seek advice about the best way to tackle rising damp in a solid floor, which is caused by the absence or failure of a damp-proof membrane (DPM) between the floor and the ground beneath.

Low levels of damp can be tackled by coating the floor with a heavy-duty damp-proofing liquid to create a new DPM, then applying a thin sand and cement screed on top.

If you cannot afford to raise the floor level much, you can lay a self-levelling compound instead of a traditional screed to provide a new floor surface. If, however, the damp problem is very severe, you may be advised to have the whole floor lifted and replaced.

Made to absorb moisture
Decorate kitchens and bathrooms with paint specially made for these rooms. Ordinary emulsion paint will flake or develop mould if it gets damp frequently, but anti-condensation paint is designed to absorb moisture from damp air and release it back into the atmosphere when the air is drier.

Damp-proof plaster
If condensation is severe, on north-facing walls for example, have them replastered with an anti-condensation plaster. Like kitchen and bathroom paint, this product absorbs moisture when the atmosphere is damp and releases it when it is dry. The plaster also contains small air bubbles which insulate the surface, helping to further reduce the risk of condensation.

Try small adjustments first
You can hold condensation at bay by spending more on keeping the house warm—turning up the central heating and improving the insulation. Often, however, marginal adjustments—slightly more ventilation combined with a low but constant level of background heat—are just as effective, and cheaper.

safety first Solutions for accident black spots

Minimise fire danger
Buy a fire blanket and keep it somewhere accessible in the kitchen, which is where most fires start. Fit smoke detectors in the hall and on landings. Don't store tins of paint or other flammable materials under the stairs; move them to a garage or shed so they won't pose a risk to a main line of escape if you're unlucky enough to have a fire. Finally, if there are locks fitted to patio doors or upstairs windows, keep the keys nearby and make sure that everyone knows where they are.

Lighting the way
Falls tend to occur at entrance doorways, on stairs and in kitchens and bathrooms, often because people cannot see clearly where they are going.
Wire in two-way light switches so that nobody has to negotiate the stairs in the dark (see page 195). Put up a hand rail if necessary (see page 83) and if there are babies or toddlers in the house, fit stair gates at the top and bottom of the flight. Fit outside lights to illuminate the route to your front door at night (see page 201).

Stop slipping and sliding
Put down non-slip mats in shower cubicles and in baths used for showering. Fit wall-mounted grab handles in the bathroom for extra safety, especially if you have someone elderly or disabled living in the house.
A fabric bath mat soaks up water and stops the bathroom floor from being slippery when wet. If you are replacing the bathroom flooring, choose a slip-resistant material.

Warning sticker
Place a colourful label at eye level on patio doors to warn people of their existence. It's easy to walk into the glass, especially in fine weather when you might expect the doors to be open. Replace ordinary glass with toughened or laminated glass in all full-length glazed timber doors (see page 105). Then, if someone should fall against a pane, it won't break into lethal shards.

safety first Solutions for accident black spots

Wear the right gear
Assemble a safety kit before embarking on DIY. For many jobs you'll need safety goggles, a face mask, a hard hat, a pair of tough gloves and some sturdy footwear. Different items offer varying degrees of protection. A dust mask, for example, won't protect you against solvent vapours and fine droplets of paint in the air, so buy a specialist spray mask or a respirator made to at least approved standard EN405 if you're going to tackle jobs such as respraying car bodywork. If you anticipate using noisy power tools such as a concrete breaker or floor sander for long periods, buy some ear defenders too.

Invest in a first-aid kit for your workshop that meets Health and Safety Executive standards for workplace use. These are available from tool and equipment hire shops.

Remove or tape down
Loose rugs laid on polished wooden hall floors and landings pose a serious hazard, especially near the top of stairs. Either remove them, or fix special non-slip tape to the underside.

Fit castor cups
Move chairs and sofas fitted with castors away from patio doors and other low-level glazing, so there's no chance of them being propelled through the glass when people sit down on them. Alternatively, fit castor cups beneath the castors to stop the furniture from moving so easily.

Secure shelves
If you have an adjustable shelving system on an open wall, rather than in an alcove, secure the shelves to their brackets with screws. This will stop an accidental collision from dislodging a shelf or its contents. It is also a good idea to round off any sharp shelf corners in this situation.

Use tools safely
Many DIY tools need sharp blades or powerful motors to be able to do their jobs properly. This means that they can cause injury if they are not used correctly and with care. When using bladed tools, keep them sharp so they will cut without effort, and make sure that your hands are behind the cutting direction and out of the cutting line. Read the instructions before using any power tool for the first time, and never bypass or de-activate any safety guard that is fitted to the tool.

Backs against the wall
Secure the tops of tall bookcases and display units to the wall with L-shaped brackets so they cannot topple over if they are unevenly loaded or if a child tries to climb up the shelves.

Reducing the risks from power in the home

Make an appointment
If you have no record of when a gas or oil-fired central-heating boiler or water heater was last serviced, arrange for a service straightaway. This will ensure that the appliance burns its fuel properly and is adequately ventilated.
If you experience drowsiness or headaches in the room when an appliance is on, don't use it until it's been checked.

Choose coiled leads
Swap long flexes on kettles, toasters and other appliances for coiled or short straight leads that cannot dangle over the edge of worktops where a small child could reach and pull them.

Baby-safe sockets
Plug socket guards into all unused electric sockets if you have small children in the family; this prevents tiny fingers or metal objects from being poked into socket holes. It is also worth making sure that all plugs have sleeved live and neutral pins, so they are safe even if partly pulled out of their sockets.

Prevent a heat surge
The water temperature in a shower can rise suddenly and cause scalding if a cold tap is turned on elsewhere in the house. You can eliminate the risk by replacing the shower mixer with a thermostatically controlled model or by fitting a mains-fed electric shower unit (see page 148).

Fully bonded
For total electrical safety, all exposed metalwork in the bathroom and kitchen should be linked (bonded) to earth by special cables covered in green-and-yellow PVC insulation (see page 124). If there is no evidence of these vital links in your home (they may have been concealed under the floor, for example), call in an electrician to find out and to install them if necessary.

safety first

29

outside

ladders Make safety your top priority

Get a good grip
Hold the rungs, not the ladder sides, when you climb or descend a ladder. If you miss your footing, you will automatically grab them and so avoid a fall. If you hold the sides and you slip, you will get skin burns from a metal ladder and splinters from a wooden one. Don't hug the ladder; climb with your arms straight and your body upright.

Stand well away
Fit a stand-off to the top of your ladder to hold it away from overhanging eaves and allow you to work on the gutters. You may crack a plastic gutter if you rest a ladder against it.

Change to cordless
Power cables hanging from ladders are a potential safety hazard; use cordless power tools whenever you can.

Don't climb too high
Use the top four rungs of a ladder as handholds only. If you try to stand on them and grab something higher up for support, such as a gutter or sill, you are quite likely to fall.

Secure a firm foothold

If a ladder is going to be in one position for a lengthy job, tie it to sturdy pegs driven into the ground on each side of the uprights to prevent it slipping. On hard surfaces, or when you need to move the ladder frequently, get someone to stand on the bottom rung of the ladder and anchor it in place. On soft ground, stand the ladder on a board to stop it from sinking. Screw a batten to the board to prevent the ladder from sliding outwards, then tie and stake it. Alternatively, you can hire a ladder safety foot, which has a high-friction base.

Get an extra pair of hands

Someone of average height can push up the top section of an extension ladder by only about 2m (6 ft 6 in) once it is in position. To extend the ladder further, lay it on the ground with its foot braced against the wall, then pull out the extension to the required length. Don't forget to turn the ladder over before raising it, so the right side faces outwards. Triple extension ladders are available with cord-and-pulley operation. These can be extended single-handed, but you will need help to control the ladder while setting it in position.

Dress for comfort and safety

Wear thick-soled shoes with a good grip and, if you're going to be standing on one rung for long periods, fit a hook-on platform to the ladder to prevent sore feet. Trousers and long-sleeved tops protect you from knocks and scratches, and a safety helmet protects your head.

Keep off the glass

Lash a length of timber at least 75 x 50 mm across the top of a ladder to enable you to paint or glaze a window. The timber rests on the masonry at each side of the opening and holds the ladder safely away from the glass.

1 Carry ladder upright to work site unless there are overhead electricity cables or other obstacles in the way

2 To erect ladder, jam its feet against base of wall, then lift top end over your head and walk towards wall

3 Ladder is at correct angle when, with toes touching bottom of ladder and arms and back straight, you can grasp rung at shoulder height

ladders

ladders Stepladders and platforms

A prop to stop a topple
Clamp or screw a 50 x 25 mm batten, long enough to reach the ground, to the back of a stepladder at an angle of around 45°, to make it more stable.

A grip to stop a drop
Stretch strong elastic bands round the platform of a stepladder so you can tuck tools under them and prevent them rolling off. A magnetic strip stuck to the platform edge will do the same job for loose nails and screws.

Improvise a platform
Use the components of a slot-together platform tower to make a mobile low-level work platform. Lock the wheels once the platform is in position.

Handy holdall
Never climb a ladder with your hands full. Instead, raise and lower tools and other items in a small bucket tied to a length of rope, making sure the load is well balanced and not too heavy. Then hang the bucket on an S-hook—available from hardware shops and DIY stores—suspended from a rung.

Check before you climb

The three-rung test
With the ladder set up, climb three rungs and jump up and down, then lean out to each side to check that it won't settle. Reposition the ladder on firmer ground or on a board if it moves.

Look for the label
By law a new ladder must carry a label stating its safe load rating. Many also have a sticker, designed to be used with a spirit level, that enables you to set up the ladder at a safe angle.

Ladder health check
Before using an aluminium ladder, check that all the rungs are secure and that it is not dented or deformed. Inspect a wooden ladder for splits, broken rungs, missing or damaged reinforcing stays under the rungs, and rot and woodworm. Protect it with varnish or clear wood preservative. Do not use paint, which hides defects. Check that hinges and stays on stepladders are securely attached. If a stepladder is an old wooden one, make sure the restraint cords are sound.

roofs Giving your roof the once-over

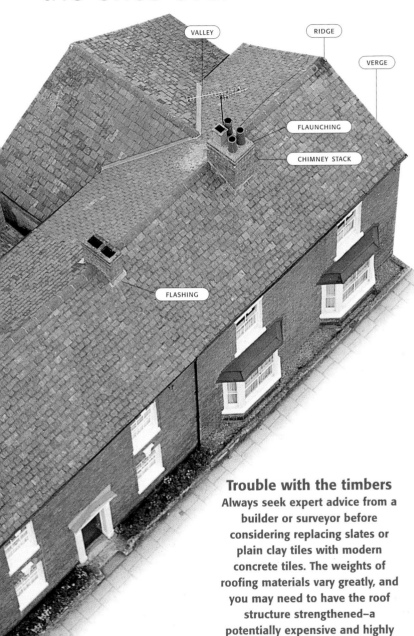

VALLEY

RIDGE

VERGE

FLAUNCHING

CHIMNEY STACK

FLASHING

Looking for faults

Carry out a thorough inspection of the roof surface and any chimney stacks on a regular basis, looking for the faults described here, then problems can be fixed before they cause serious damage. However, unless you are happy to work on your roof and to carry out necessary repairs yourself, it's best to call in a builder or a specialist roofing contractor to do the work for you.

Stacks of trouble

Start at the top of each chimney stack, checking that the pots and the mortar layer (flaunching) holding them in place on the stack is intact. Then inspect the brickwork and the pointing, noting any frost-damaged bricks or missing mortar. Consider having unused flues capped.

Keep flashings flat

Lead or aluminium flashings waterproof the join between a chimney stack and the roof surface. Make sure their upper edges are held securely in the mortar between the bricks, and that their lower edges lie flat on the roof; if they're not, rain can get behind and the roof will leak. Replace mortar fillets with metal flashings because mortar cracks.

Ridge tile healthcheck

Most houses have ridge and hip tiles set in a continuous mortar bed, and when this cracks up the tiles can be dislodged by high winds, allowing water to get in and rot the timbers. Check that yours are all secure, and identify any loose ones with a chalk cross so they can be lifted and re-bedded securely.

Trouble with the timbers
Always seek expert advice from a builder or surveyor before considering replacing slates or plain clay tiles with modern concrete tiles. The weights of roofing materials vary greatly, and you may need to have the roof structure strengthened–a potentially expensive and highly disruptive job.

Slipping slates mean rusty nails

Large numbers of slates slipping out of position indicate that the nails securing them to the battens have rusted through. The slates themselves may be sound enough to be re-fixed, but you will probably find some that need replacing. Secure the slates with copper nails that will not rust.

Stay off the tiles

Roof tiles can be lifted and cracked, or even removed completely, by high winds. However, a more likely cause of damage is someone climbing onto the roof and standing directly on the tiles. Never do this yourself; one slip could be fatal. Use a roof ladder or crawl boards at all times.

roofs

roofs Getting on top of the problem

Sound ring test
Test a secondhand slate by tapping it lightly with a hammer. You'll hear a ringing sound if it's in good condition, and a dull sound if it's cracked. Look at the underside, too; it's usually the first surface to powder and crumble.

Inspect the valleys
Valleys—the internal angles where two roof slopes meet—are usually lined with a metal tray secured to wooden boards that are themselves supported by the roof rafters. Keep them clear of wind-blown debris so they can't overflow and soak the woodwork. Check them for splits or tears too; any you find can be waterproofed temporarily by sticking on some self-adhesive flashing tape.

Watch the verges
At gables, the end tiles of each row may project beyond the face of the wall to form what is known as a verge. This overhang is supported on plain tiles, slates or strips of fibre cement sheet bedded on top of the sloping masonry. Check that the mortar forming the verge is intact. If it's cracked or missing, high winds could lift and dislodge the tiles.

Spread the load safely
Convert your ladder for roof work with a ridge hook, if you can obtain one which fits it. For extensive work on a roof, however, hire crawl boards, which are much more comfortable than an ordinary ladder. They also spread weight more evenly and reduce the risk of tiles or slates being cracked.

Wear the right safety gear
For maximum safety, wear a hard hat when working on a roof. Strong work gloves will protect your hands from sharp edges. A tool pouch makes sure you have both hands free and reduces the chances of tools sliding down the roof. Always wear stout boots with solid soles, so the rungs don't cut into your feet, and add knee pads if you wish for extra comfort.

Safe and secure

When you've built the tower up to the required height, fit a handrail and a set of toe boards all around the platform. Hire stabilisers for towers with platform heights up to 6 m (20 ft), or tie them securely to the building at eaves level.

Using an access tower

A slot-together access tower is the safest way to reach the roof. You'll need one with a platform height of about 5 m (16 ft) to reach the eaves of a two-storey building. Choose a narrow-width tower (above) if space is restricted, such as between houses. Make sure the base of the tower is standing level and square, and spread the load on soft ground by putting boards under the legs. Fit lockable castors if the tower is on hard level ground, to make it secure, but easily moved.

Firm base for the feet

One of the most useful accessories for improving ladder safety is a base stabiliser, which can be bought or hired. The high-friction base resists slipping when the ladder is standing on a hard surface. It also spreads the load and stops the feet of the ladder from sinking into soft ground.

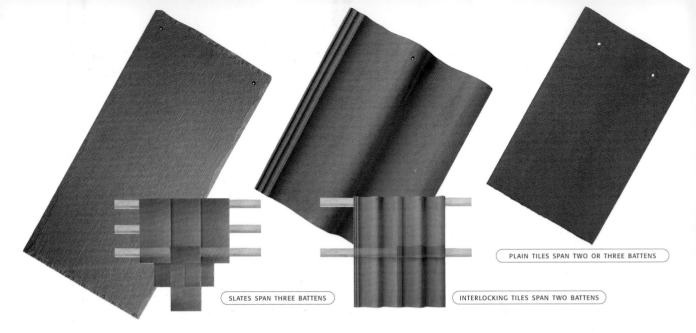

SLATES SPAN THREE BATTENS

INTERLOCKING TILES SPAN TWO BATTENS

PLAIN TILES SPAN TWO OR THREE BATTENS

roofs Replacing damaged tiles and slates

Nibs, nails or clips

How you replace a broken tile depends on how it is fixed to the underlying batten. Most plain tiles are made with nibs projecting from their top back edge, that hook over the batten and are nailed in place every fourth or fifth row. Interlocking tiles are often held with nails, or by clips nailed to the batten. But you won't be able to tell just by looking, unless you can see the underside of the tiles from the loft space.

Ripping through rusty nails

Hire a tool called a slate ripper to hook round and cut through the nails that secure slates and tiles to their battens. Most tiles are not nailed in place but all slates are fixed with two nails—usually around half-way up, but sometimes at the top.

Work from the underside

Hire a slate cutter if you need to trim a lot of slates to size. Work with the top surface of the slate downwards, so that the edges break away slightly along the cutting line. This creates a bevel like the weathered edges of the existing slates on the roof surface.

Alternatively, hold the slate bevelled side down on your workbench and align the cutting line with the bench edge. Then chop it with a bricklayer's trowel, using the bench edge as a guide.

Release single lap tiles

Try to push up the tiles in the course above the broken one (far left). Then lift the edge of the tile overlapping one neighbour and twist it to disengage the interlock with the other.

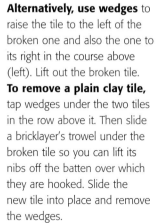

Alternatively, use wedges to raise the tile to the left of the broken one and also the one to its right in the course above (left). Lift out the broken tile.

To remove a plain clay tile, tap wedges under the two tiles in the row above it. Then slide a bricklayer's trowel under the broken tile so you can lift its nibs off the batten over which they are hooked. Slide the new tile into place and remove the wedges.

If any of the tiles are nailed, free them first with a slate ripper (above centre).

1 Slide slate ripper under damaged slate, hook barb round nail and give tool a sharp blow to cut through nail. Remove slate

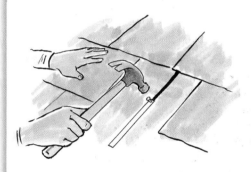

2 Locate timber batten visible between slates exposed by removed slate, and fix tingle with galvanised nail

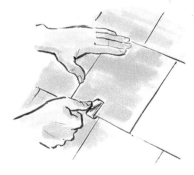

3 Slide new slate into place. Fold end of tingle over bottom edge of slate, then double it back on itself to stop snow and ice forcing clip open

roofs

roofs Replacing damaged tiles and slates

Cut and fit a tingle

As you can't nail a replacement slate in place, use a tingle—a narrow strip of lead or zinc—instead. Cut it to the length of the exposed area of slate plus about 50 mm (2 in), and nail it to the tiling batten between the exposed slates. Its lower end is then folded up to hold the replacement slate in place.

Drill holes for nails

Use a masonry bit to make nail holes in a new slate. Lay the slate on a scrap of board or a bed of sand and drill from the underside. When the bit breaks through, it will chip off a bit of slate and form a countersink for the nail head.

More grip for ridge tiles

Before you bed a loose ridge tile on fresh mortar, brush on some PVA adhesive to improve the bond. If you can't chip off the old mortar that bedded the loose tile without damaging the tiles beneath, stick it back to the old mortar with roof and gutter sealant. Don't fill the gap at the apex of the roof with mortar. This space ensures that air can circulate round the ridge board and keep the timber dry.

Hide conspicuous replacements

If you're replacing a slate or tile on a conspicuous part of the roof and the new one is a poor match, borrow an existing one from an unobtrusive part of the roof and use that instead. Fit the new tile in place of the borrowed one.

Sealing cracked slates

Squeeze roof-and-gutter sealant from a cartridge gun into cracks in slates or tiles (far left). Alternatively, cover them with self-adhesive flashing tape. Brush some flashing primer onto the slate first. Then cut the tape to size, peel off the backing paper and press it in place. Run an old wallpaper seam roller over the tape to bed it down firmly (left).

A new lease of life

Extend the life of an old flat roof with a repair kit. There are several available, all of which involve sandwiching a layer of reinforcement fabric between coats of liquid waterproofer. The roof surface must be dry and as dust-free as possible. Apply a generous coat of waterproofer with an old soft-bristled broom. Then unroll the fabric, overlapping the edges of adjoining lengths, and brush on a second coat of waterproofer. Let this dry before applying a third coat (and a fourth one if it's recommended). Wear old shoes for the job—along with the broom, they'll only be fit for throwing away afterwards.

roofs Fast fixes for felt roofs

Save the stone chippings

The chippings on a flat roof protect the felt from overheating in the sun and the degradation caused by sunlight. Over time they tend to get washed into the gutter and then down the drain. Cover the top of the downpipe with a fine mesh to prevent this, and rescue chippings from the gutter to scatter over any bald patches on the roof surface.
Solar-reflective coating is an alternative to chippings, but needs renewing periodically to maintain its effectiveness.

Stand on boards

Flat roofs are generally not designed for access. If you have to climb onto one to clean windows or to paint an exterior wall, lay boards down to spread your weight. Don't walk on the unprotected roof–your weight will push the chippings through the felt—and take care not to drop heavy tools. If you stand a ladder on a flat roof, rest its feet on a board, with a batten screwed along the outside edge to stop the feet sliding outwards.

Tape over a split

Scrape chippings from the surrounding area (far left) and get rid of any moisture trapped in the split, speeding up the process with a hot-air gun if you have one. Fill the split with bituminous mastic, then prime the area round the split with a bitumen primer and allow it to dry. Cover the area with a piece of self-adhesive roofing repair tape.
Bed the tape down firmly by running an old wallpaper seam roller over it a few times (left). If you suspect that the split lies directly over a joint between underlying decking panels, continue the repair all the way to the roof edge.

41

roofs Fast fixes for felt roofs

Stick down the seams
Loose seams in roofing felt can be lifted and torn by high winds. Use roofing mastic or cold-applied felt adhesive to stick them down before this happens.

Release chippings with heat
Use a wide scraper to remove loose chippings from areas needing repair. If they are stuck to the felt, a hot-air gun will release them.

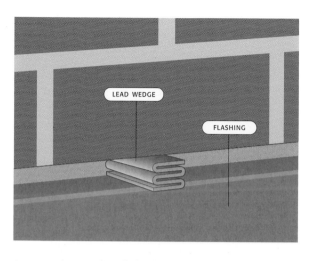

Mending blisters in felt
Use a trimming knife to make a cross-cut over the blister, taking care not to cut through the layer of felt below. Peel back the flaps and thoroughly dry the area underneath using a hot-air gun. Spread cold-applied felt adhesive to the exposed area and press the flaps back into place. When bonded, seal the cuts with a heavy-duty bituminous mastic and replace the chippings.

Secure loose lead flashings
A lead flashing waterproofs the join between, for example, a porch or lean-to and a wall. The top edge of the flashing should be wedged into a brickwork joint, then mortared in place. If a flashing needs refixing, replace any missing wedges before repointing. Cut small strips of lead and fold them concertina-fashion, then tap them into place with a mallet.

Protect a metal roof
If you live in a house with a flat roof covered in lead, zinc or copper, prevent acid attack from moss or lichen by treating it regularly with a fungicide. Patch any splits in the metal sheet with self-adhesive flashing strip.

Two ways to insulate
Flat roofs can rot from below as well as above. Warm air from the room below condenses in the ceiling space, attacking the underside of the decking panels. The solution is to insulate the roof, after carrying out any necessary remedial work to the deck, and this can be done in two ways.

A 'warm' roof is formed by laying rigid polystyrene sheet insulation over the existing decking and then adding a new layer of decking and roofing felt on top. It is the better option if the existing roof deck is still relatively sound.

A 'cold' roof has insulation beneath the roof deck, plus a ventilation gap to ensure that air can reach the underside of the deck. This can be installed only if the deck has to be completely replaced or if the ceiling below is removed.

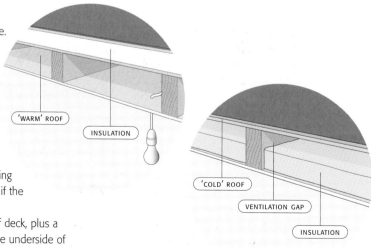

Mending a corrugated plastic roof

Cutting corrugated plastic
To hold the sheet you are sawing securely, support it on a pile of other sheets. Alternatively clamp it between two lengths of wood positioned parallel and close to the cutting line. In cold weather, bring the sheets indoors for sawing as the plastic becomes brittle and may crack in low temperatures.

Don't crack the sheet
Avoid cracking plastic sheets when you screw them down by drilling the holes a little oversize–through the corrugation ridges, not the valleys. Then make sure that the washers and any spacers are properly positioned, and don't overtighten the screws.

Making screw holes
Drilling holes for the fixings can be tricky, since the drill bit tends to slip on the curved surface of the corrugated sheet. Provide a little friction for the bit by sticking a small piece of masking tape over the drilling position.

Replacing a damaged sheet
Remove the fixings, slide the damaged sheet out and push a wooden wedge between the rafter and the adjacent sheet that overlapped it. Slide the new panel under the raised sheet, allowing an overlap of two corrugations.

Weatherproofing joints with walls
Use matching prefabricated flashing units to weatherproof the junction between the roof and a wall. Their hinged upstands can be adapted to any gradient and are designed to be lapped by a conventional metal or felt flashing (right).
Seal the eaves against draughts and water penetration by fitting flexible foam plastic filler strips between the bottom edge of the sheet and the top of the beam supporting it.

gutters Escape routes for rainwater

Don't ignore the problem

The weight of trapped water can bring a gutter crashing down—a real danger if it is a cast-iron one. Deal with blockages as soon as you see an overflow.

Make a gutter scoop by cutting the bottom from a suitably shaped plastic motor-oil container and use the spout as a handle—it will hold much more than a garden trowel. Empty debris into a bucket hung from the ladder.

Bung a rag temporarily into the top of the downpipe to prevent rubbish being swept into it as you scoop.

Reach out with a rake

To avoid having to move the ladder frequently, make a gutter rake. Cut a small piece of 9 mm or 12 mm plywood, or solid wood, to match the shape of the gutter. Use a screw to fix this to the end of a length of broom handle, about 1.2 m (4 ft) long, then attach a loop of cord to the other end to secure it to your wrist. Finally, drill some holes in the end piece of the rake for water to escape through.

Keep autumn leaves out of gutters by fitting plastic mesh leafguards if trees overhang the roof, but if you do need to put up a ladder to clean them, make sure it is fitted with a stand-off (see page 32) and do not rest it on the guttering.

Extra brackets cure a sag

Install extra support brackets if a gutter is sagging. They should be fixed about every 600–900 mm (2–3 ft). Scoop out any water lying in the gutter. Then, with the aid of a string line or straightedge, position and fix extra brackets on the fascia making sure that they are in line with the existing ones.

Test the fall by pouring water into the gutter at its highest point. If puddles form, the brackets need adjusting.

Free the downpipe

Water seeping from a joint on a section of downpipe indicates a blockage in the pipe somewhere between the affected joint and the outlet. Try unblocking the pipe from ground level first. Cover the gully to keep debris out, then push a length of stiff wire or a running garden hose up the pipe to shift the rubbish. If this doesn't work, unblock the pipe from the top using drain rods.

A wire mesh excluder fitted at the top of the downpipe will stop potential blockages such as leaves, moss and tennis balls from getting into the pipe in the first place.

Cast-iron hints and tips

Heavy metal

Cast-iron gutters and pipes are heavy—don't try to manhandle them from the top of a ladder. They also shatter if dropped, and corrode to sharp edges, so wear sturdy gloves.

Use a scaffold tower, and knock some 150 mm round wire nails into the fascia as temporary gutter supports, angling the nails so that the gutter cannot slip off them. Get help to remove and replace long lengths of gutter.

Marrying new to old

If only part of the cast-iron guttering has corroded, you can buy new—for a price—or scour architectural salvage yards for a matching replacement. Alternatively, ask a builders' merchant if a plastic adaptor is available for joining on some plastic guttering with a similar profile.

Clean and seal

Putty was traditionally used to seal the joints between sections of cast-iron and aluminium guttering, but a suitable sealant is far better for the job. If you're renovating either of these gutter types, use an old chisel to remove the putty. Then make sure the area is dry before you re-make the joint with the sealant.

Have a hacksaw handy to dismantle sections; the nuts and bolts securing them are usually rusted and seized. Saw through nuts and punch bolts out from below—but take care, cast iron is brittle. Replace them with mushroom-head plated gutter bolts and nuts.

1 Drive nail into fascia board at top end of gutter run, about 25 mm (1 in) below edge of tiles. Attach string line and allow fall of 6 mm (¼ in) for every 1 m (3 ft) of eaves length

2 Stretch string line between bracket and nail as a fixing guide for remaining brackets

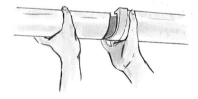

3 Fix brackets, remove line and insert gutter in brackets, back edge first. Snap-fit into retaining clips on brackets

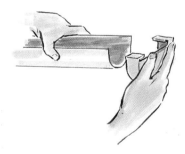

4 Cut last section of gutter so that it extends beyond end of roof by about 50 mm (2 in). Fit stop-end before fixing section in place

gutters

45

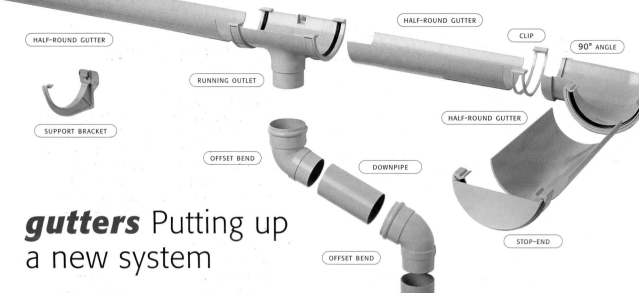

HALF-ROUND GUTTER

HALF-ROUND GUTTER

CLIP

90° ANGLE

RUNNING OUTLET

HALF-ROUND GUTTER

OFFSET BEND

DOWNPIPE

OFFSET BEND

STOP-END

gutters Putting up a new system

Centre option splits the load

On a long roof, consider placing the downpipe halfway along the eaves. This halves the weight of water that the gutter has to carry. It also halves the gap between the gutter and the edge of the tiles or slates, created by the fall of the gutter, so there is less chance of wind driving rain onto the wall in the gap between the edge of the roof and the gutter.

DOWNPIPE

PIPE CLIP

RAINWATER SHOE

Water for the garden

Diverter kits, available from garden centres and DIY stores, enable you to fill a rainwater butt from the downpipe. The diverter returns water to the downpipe before the butt overflows. **Raise the butt** on bricks or a stand, so a watering can will fit under the tap.

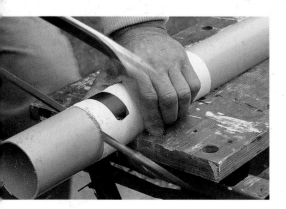

Cutting it fine

Always cut lengths of plastic guttering and downpipe at ground level. Use a hacksaw or tenon saw, and remove the burr with a file, so that it can be neatly joined to another length. To cut round pipe squarely, wrap a piece of paper around it so that the edges line up, then stick it down with tape. The edge of the paper provides a cutting guide.

Fixed and replaceable seals

The rubber seals on gutter unions eventually perish. Sometimes they are bonded and you have to buy an entire new union to stop the leak, but with some brands the seal can be detached from its groove and replaced separately.

Cure dislocated joints

Plastic gutters expand in the heat—you can hear them creaking in the sun—and sometimes sections come apart at the unions. Check the joints after a spell of hot weather. Tap the end of the gutter back into place with a mallet if it has pulled out of a union.

brickwork Facelifts for outside walls

Lock out moisture

Flakes of brick lying along the foot of a wall in winter are a sure sign of frost damage. The longer the problem is ignored the worse it will get, so as soon as the weather warms up apply a colourless, microporous water-repellent sealant, which will allow the bricks to breathe but will keep out moisture. If you're going to apply it with a spray gun, choose a still day, wear a respirator, and cover up to keep the fluid off your skin.

Treat the whole wall because the waterproofer can alter the colour of the bricks very slightly. Otherwise, the wall will look patchy, with treated areas being darker.

Water works

You can remove years of grime from bricks with nothing more elaborate than a stiff bristle brush and a running hose. Work in horizontal bands from the top to the bottom of a wall, inspecting the pointing as you go. Use a solution of household ammonia—about half a cup in a bucket of water—on really grimy areas. Wear goggles and rubber gloves to protect your eyes and hands.

Turn a damaged brick about-face

Frost-damaged bricks should be replaced, but if you cannot find a matching one turn the damaged brick around. Use a power drill, on hammer action, and a masonry bit to make holes in the joint all around the brick to its full depth. Chip away the remaining mortar with a plugging chisel, prise the brick out, then mortar it back into the hole, back to front.

Give salt the brush-off

A white powdery deposit, called efflorescence, is common on new brick walls. It is caused by salts in the bricks reacting with rainwater. Don't try to wash it off or you will make the problem last longer. Instead, brush the affected area with a dry bristle brush until it stops recurring.

Draw stains with a paste

Remove stubborn stains like tar and oil with a paste made from fuller's earth or ground chalk, mixed with paraffin or white spirit. Wipe over the stain with a little of the solvent used to make the paste, then spread a layer of paste over it (below left). Finally, tape a plastic bag or a piece of aluminium foil on top to stop the poultice drying out (below right). Over a few days the paste will draw the stain out and you can wash the bricks clean.

Avoid harsh measures

Think hard before you have the outside of your home sandblasted or cleaned with acidic chemicals. Although the results can look effective, both methods are harsh because they remove a layer from the surface of the walls. Like a piece of old furniture that has been rubbed down and lost its patina, your house could lose some of its character if you try to make the old bricks look like new.

WEATHERSTRUCK JOINT

BUCKET-HANDLE JOINT

FLUSH JOINT

brickwork Patching up the joints

Make a mortarboard

A scrap of 6 mm or 9 mm external plywood makes a good mortarboard. Ideally, you want a piece about 400 x 400 mm (16 x 16 in). Drill a hole for a screw in the centre of the piece and fix it to the end of a short length of broom handle. Hold the board tight against the wall, directly below the joint being repointed. This minimises the amount of wet mortar getting on the face of the bricks or dropping on the ground.

Making a bucket-handle joint

Traditionally, bricklayers used a short piece of metal bucket handle to 'tool' a bucket-handle joint. You can imitate the effect by dragging a short piece of hosepipe along the joint.

A profile for the elements

The way pointing is finished is crucial to repelling rain. Weatherstruck and bucket-handle joints are best, although flush joints often look best when you want to disguise small areas of new pointing.

Stick to the recipe

Buy a bag of premixed mortar containing a plasticiser for a small area of repointing. Otherwise, it's more economical to make your own; mix 1 part of ordinary Portland cement or masonry cement into 6 parts of clean building sand. Add the recommended volume of a liquid mortar plasticiser or 1 part of hydrated lime if you're using Portland cement (masonry cement contains a plasticiser). Don't use washing-up liquid instead of lime or plasticiser, it is detrimental to the mortar.

Adding extra cement will make the pointing too hard, so that bricks absorb moisture more readily than the mortar, making them liable to frost damage. Adding extra water to a mix that is going dry will weaken it, although it is a good idea to flick a little water into the raked joints with a brush, to stop the mortar drying out before you can achieve a neat finish.

Fashion a frenchman

Bricklayers use a bladed tool called a frenchman to trim away wet mortar neatly from the base of weatherstruck joints. You can make one for yourself from a strip of thin metal. Bend about 25 mm (1 in) at one end over at an angle of 90°. Wear goggles in case the metal snaps.

Make a guide from a straight piece of 75 x 25 mm planed timber about 600 mm (2 ft) long to use with the frenchman. Pin two small pieces of hardboard or thin plywood on one side of the piece of wood, near the ends. These allow clearance for the tip of the frenchman between the guide and the wall. Fix a handle on the other side of the guide.

1 Rake out old mortar to a depth of about 12 mm (½ in), using a plugging chisel. Hire a hammer drill and mortar-raking chisel for large areas

2 Load mortar onto board with trowel. Wet joints, then push mortar into joints, filling vertical ones first

3 Finish joints with pointing trowel or special pointing tool

4 Before mortar dries, blend new pointing with old using a sponge. Carefully clean face of brickwork with soft dry brush

brickwork

49

rendering Repairs to a faulty coating

Tap and listen
The bond between rendering and the wall fails when moisture seeps between the two and freezes. Tap the wall with the handle of a screwdriver, to establish how large an area sounds hollow and needs stripping off and replacing.

Testing for subsidence
Cracks in rendering could be a sign of subsidence. Call in a surveyor, who will stick glass strips across the cracks at several points with epoxy adhesive. If any strips break because the crack is widening, subsidence is the likely cause.

Paint over fine cracks
Fill hairline cracks in rendering with a coat of exterior masonry paint. If the surface is powdery, brush away loose material and seal the area with stabilising primer before painting.

Improve the bond
Scratch base coats of render to provide a key for subsequent ones to bond with. You can do this with the edge of a trowel or by making a 'scratch comb'. Drive a row of nails through a short length of batten so that the points project by about 6 mm (¼ in). Allow about 20 minutes for the render to start drying before scratching it.

Undercut for a strong key
Chop loose rendering off the wall with a brick bolster and club hammer. When you reach sound material, undercut the edges so that the new render will key well with the old coating and resist fracturing along the join as it dries.

Reinforce with metal lath
If, when you remove loose rendering, the brickwork below has deteriorated, fix a piece of expanded metal lath over it with galvanised or masonry nails before applying the new render.

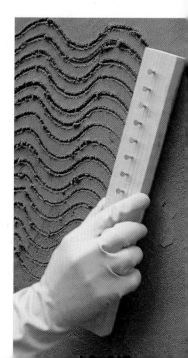

A better bond

New render will stick on the wall better if you paint on a coating made up of 1 part cement and 1 part sharp sand mixed into PVA sealer, diluted with an equal volume of water. Use a stiff brush to 'stab' the mixture onto the masonry. When it dries, the surface of the wall should feel like coarse abrasive paper, providing a key for the new render.

Repairing a bottom edge

If the bottom edge of rendering breaks away from the wall, nail a temporary batten across the gap to maintain a straight line and support the wet render while it dries. Make sure the rendering does not cover the damp-proof course (DPC), otherwise a 'bridge' will be created for moisture absorbed by the wall from the ground.

Restoring a corner

Repairing broken render around an external corner is a two-phase operation. Fix a batten to contain the edge of the wet render at the corner while you fill the gap on one wall. Then reposition the batten on the repaired side of the corner and fill the adjoining wall.

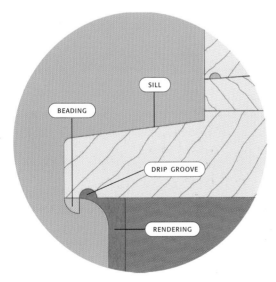

SILL

BEADING

DRIP GROOVE

RENDERING

Keep sills clean

Careless rendering can block the drip groove under projecting windowsills, allowing water to creep all the way under the frame. For a quick solution, pin a strip of quadrant beading under the front edge of the sill. In the longer term, unblock the drip groove.

1 Cut away loose material to a sound edge. Brush away dust, then prime bare brickwork with PVA adhesive sealer

2 Apply first coat using steel float, finishing about 6 mm (¼ in) below surface of the surrounding render

3 After about 20 minutes, scratch first coat with trowel or scratch comb to provide key for finishing coat

4 After 12 hours, apply finishing coat with wood float and rule off. Blend into existing surface using a damp sponge

rendering

rendering Repairs to a faulty coating

Blending new with old

Overfill the area you are patching, then use the edge of a length of timber–a piece of an old floorboard is idea–to 'rule' or scrape off the excess. Push the piece of board across the wet render with a sawing action until the repaired surface is flush with the old render, knocking the end of the board on the ground to remove the waste that gathers on it.

Use a wood float to finish the rendering; a steel one brings water and cement, and lime particles to the surface, causing fine cracks to form in the rendering as it dries.

Recipe for a successful finish

The right ratio

A good rendering mix consists of 6 parts plastering sand (also called rendering sand or fine sharp sand) to 1 part cement and 1 part hydrated lime. Mix the cement and lime together first, then blend in the sand before adding water. A liquid plasticiser is an alternative to the lime; add the recommended volume to the water. Masonry cement already contains a plasticiser. Mix it in a ratio of 1 part of cement to 5 parts sand.

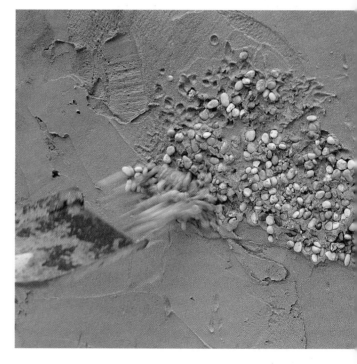

Appropriate additives

Give yourself longer to work with wet render in hot weather by adding a drying retardant to the mix. If there's a risk of freezing, add a frost-proofing additive to the mix.

Economy mix

A small bag of dry ready-mixed mortar may be adequate for a small rendering job. For larger areas, save money by buying the cement and rendering sand separately and making the mix yourself.

Colour match cement

Add a powder pigment to dry cement in a colour to match your paint to reduce the number of coats of paint required. Use white cement if you're going to paint the rendering white.

Throw on the pebbles

Pebbledashing is fairly easy to patch. Buy some matching pebbles from a builders' merchant, wash and drain them then, with a coal shovel or dustpan, throw a scoopful at the wet render. Wash any pebbles that fall off at the first attempt before reusing them. When an adequate layer is sticking to the wall, gently press the pebbles in with a wooden plasterer's float.

cladding Boarding exterior walls

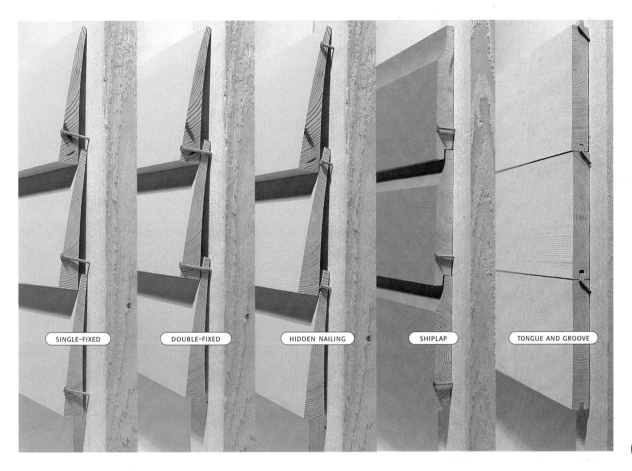

SINGLE-FIXED   DOUBLE-FIXED   HIDDEN NAILING   SHIPLAP   TONGUE AND GROOVE

Five ways to nail boards

There are several ways of nailing wood cladding to the framework of timber battens that supports it on the house wall. Which method you choose will depend on what type of cladding you're fitting and whether you want the fixings concealed or not.

Single-fixed boards are secured by nails driven through their faces and missing the board below.

Double-fixed boards are fixed by nails that pass through the board below too.

Hidden nailing involves driving the nails in close to the top edge of each board so the nail heads are hidden by the bottom edge of the next board. This technique provides good protection to the nail head but offers little resistance to the board being levered off.

Beware of moisture barriers

Wooden cladding is often used as an external wall finish on a timber-framed house, and a moisture barrier of building paper may be fitted beneath the battens to which the boards are secured. Keep an eye out for it when you are replacing damaged boards, and take care not to puncture it.

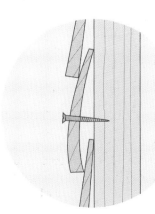

Flattening a bulge

To flatten warped and bulging boards, insert corrosion-resistant woodscrews along their centre line and into the batten behind. Drill clearance holes through the boards first to avoid splitting them. Countersink the screws and cover their heads with exterior grade filler, or with a coloured wood stopper if the boards are stained rather than painted.

53

cladding Boarding exterior walls

Doing the splits

To repair a split in timber cladding, lever the split open and squeeze in some exterior PVA woodworking adhesive (left). Tape may be strong enough to hold the split closed while the glue dries. Otherwise, screw a small block to the board below and drive a wooden wedge between it and the bottom edge of the repaired board (right).

Removing damaged timber

Reaching hidden nails

Gain access to a nail securing the board above the one you're replacing by driving in two wedges. Then slide in a mini-hacksaw and cut through the nail.

Cutting a broken board

Saw through a damaged board directly above the centre of a support batten. Drive two wooden wedges under the edge of the board on either side of the batten. This provides clearance for the saw as you cut through the board. Then wedge a piece of scrap wood into the gap so that it covers the face of the good board below, protecting it from the saw blade. **Cut as far as possible** with the tenon saw. Then wedge up the board above the cut board and finish the cut with a padsaw (keyhole saw).

'Popping' exposed nails

To remove exposed nails, use a crowbar to lever up the bottom edge of the board, resting it on a piece of scrap wood to protect the face of the board below. Then hold the crowbar blade beside the nail head and tap it to push the board back and pop out the nail.

Fixing tricks for a professional finish

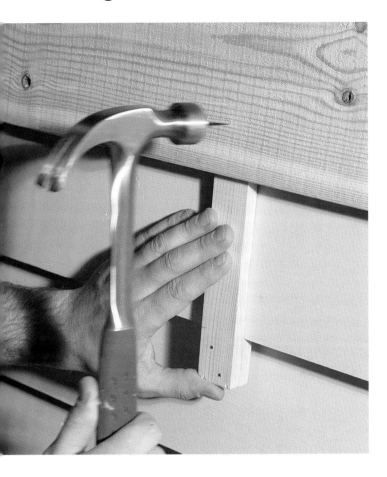

A spacer for an even overlap
Keep the overlap of the boards the same by making a spacer from a couple of pieces of scrap wood. Mark the overlap you want on the longer piece and pin the smaller offcut to it.

Avoid stains from rusty nails
Use galvanised roundhead nails to fix the boards. They won't corrode and cause rust stains as steel nails do. Punch the nail heads in slightly and fill the dimple with exterior filler.

One-handed trick
If you don't have a spare hand to hold a nail, tuck it firmly into the claw of the hammer, point facing outwards, and drive it into the board. Then unhook the claw and finish driving the nail.

Add some insulation
If you have to strip a large area of cladding, fit sheets of rigid polystyrene insulation between the battens and cover them with waterproof building paper before fitting new boards.

Avoid a patchwork look
Replace whole boards rather than small sections if rot is widespread, to avoid creating a patchwork of repairs.

Protect before fixing
Treat every surface of a new board with preservative or wood primer before fixing it in place. This will delay the onset of rot in the future.

A support while you start to nail
If you are working on your own, bend a narrow strip of soft sheet metal into an S shape and hook it over the top edge of the previous board to support one end of the next board while you nail up its other end. This will not work if you are fixing cladding between projecting masonry piers, however, as they will prevent you from slipping the hook out for re-use after nailing up each board.

Use old cut pieces of board you remove from around openings, fixtures or other obstructions as templates when cutting replacements to size.

Prevent split ends
You can stop the wood splitting when nailing near the end of a board by drilling pilot holes first. For fixings elsewhere, blunt the nails first by hammering their points on concrete.

55

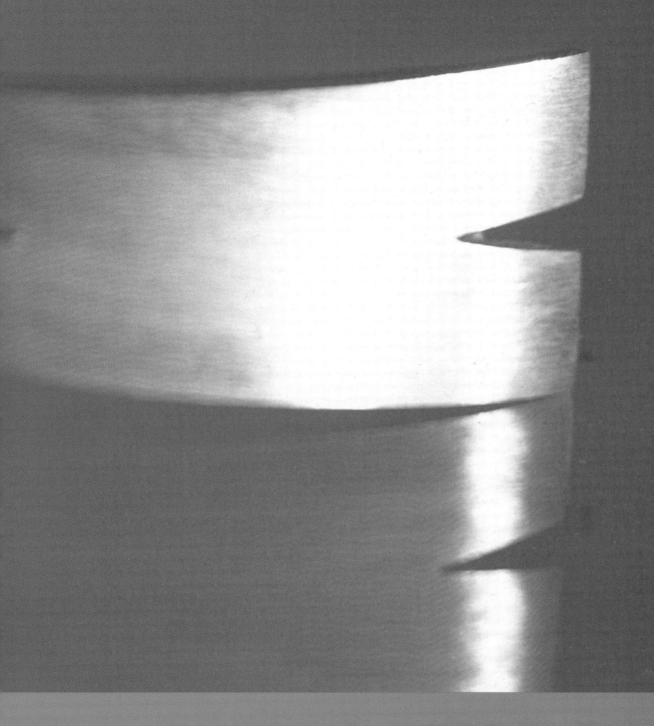

inside

floors Discover what lies underneath the boards

Are the joists dry?
Hire a moisture meter to assess the condition of the joists. If the reading is over 20 per cent, there is a risk that rot could set in or may have done so already, and underfloor ventilation should be improved as soon as possible. Use a torch to illuminate the underfloor void, and a mirror fixed to the end of a stick to spot any signs of deterioration in the timbers.

Open the airways
Clear rubbish from the crawl space beneath a suspended timber ground floor. It can block the airbricks in outside walls and obstruct the voids in the honeycombed walls that support the floor joists, preventing air from circulating freely.

Preservation in a pellet
In older houses the ends of the joists are often built into the external walls. Check their condition carefully. If the timber is sound, drill a hole in the top of each joist and insert a wood preservative pellet in it, as close to the wall as possible.

Always cover the hole
Replace floorboards loosely if you have to interrupt work. Hang a sign on the outside of the room door warning of loose boards until you have replaced them permanently.

Locate the services
Hire a cable and pipe detector to locate underfloor services before nailing or screwing down loose floorboards. Services often run immediately below the boards—in notches cut across the tops of the joists—making them very vulnerable to accidental damage.

Easy underfloor access
For access to essential fittings such as a stoptap, cross-cut the overlying board between adjacent joists. Support the replaced section on battens secured to the sides of the joists with screws.

While the carpet is up
If you're going to have a fitted carpet replaced, rip up the old one well in advance. Then you can check the condition of your floorboards before they become inaccessible again.

Marked for future reference
Take the opportunity to record the routes of cables and pipes while a floor is up. You can mark their positions straight onto the boards, unless you intend to leave them bare.

Raise the temperature

If all the boards in a downstairs room have to be lifted, take the chance to increase warmth and lower heating bills by installing underfloor insulation. There are two types available.

Lay nylon garden netting across the joists to support the same type of glass fibre insulation blanket that's used in lofts (see page 170). Wear gloves, safety goggles and a mask when working with this material. Draw the netting up tight before nailing down the boards (left), so that the blanket does not sag and allow cold air to get past it.

Cut rigid insulation, made from light polystyrene foam, to fit snugly between joists. Support the slabs on battens nailed to the sides of the joists (below).

Solutions for sagging floors

If a timber ground floor moves noticeably when you jump up and down on it, the ends of built-in floor joists may be rotten due to damp in the walls. Cure the problem by lifting the boards and sawing through the joists at least 600 mm (2 ft) beyond the last signs of rot. Bolt new preservative-treated wood to the sawn joists, using toothed timber connectors (see page 354). Support the ends in joist hangers—galvanised steel shoes secured to the walls.

Fill in dead knots

Use car body filler to block knot holes in boards before laying vinyl sheet flooring. If you don't, pressure from chair legs and similar objects could pierce and damage it.

floors

floors Ways to hide gaps and silence squeaks

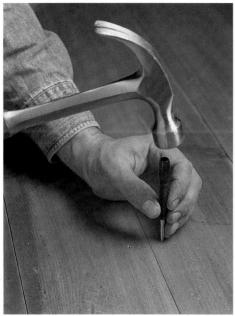

Quieten with a shim
If you can get at the underside of a squeaky board from below—to the ground floor from a cellar, for example—tap a thin wooden shim dipped in woodworking adhesive into the gap between the board and the joist, to quieten it.

Take a punch to the heads
A squeaky board can sometimes be cured by driving the nails a little deeper with a nail punch. Locate the punch carefully so it doesn't skid off the nail and scar the board when you strike it. **Talcum powder** or chalk dust, brushed into the joints between squeaky boards, usually silences them temporarily.

Tap a wedge into a gap
You can fill wide gaps between boards with thin lengths of square-edge moulding, bought at a timber merchant or DIY store. Plane them to a slight wedge shape, then apply a little woodworking adhesive before tapping them into the gaps, thin edge first. Plane them down to floor level when the adhesive has set, then stain them to match the boards.

Exchange nails for screws
Stop squeaky boards by replacing nails with screws. Use the old nail holes and choose screws the same length as the nails but thicker, so they bite into the joist but don't go any deeper. You don't want to puncture a hidden pipe or cable.

When the boards have to be taken up

Ripping off the tongues
Before lifting a tongue-and-groove (t & g) floorboard, you will need to cut through the jointed edges. The best tool for the job is a circular saw because you can set the blade depth. Lock the depth gauge to 15 mm to avoid cutting into a joist, pipe or cable. If you need to remove just a short length of board, a handsaw will do the job; hold it at a low angle so the blade does not project too far into the underfloor space.

Crosscut beside a joist
A floorboard saw is designed for cutting out a section of floorboard without marking the ones on either side. Make the cut alongside a joist (look for the nailing lines that mark the centres of the joists). Then use a straightedge and sharp trimming knife to score a guideline for the saw. Angle the saw slightly off the vertical so that the cut is bevelled; this makes the sawn line less noticeable when the board is replaced. **A jigsaw can also be used,** although you will have to drill a hole through the board to admit the saw blade. Make sure there are no cables or pipes in the way of the blade.

What sort of boards?
Find out whether you've got square-edged floorboards (butted up against one another) or tongue-and-groove ones by trying to insert the blade of a knife between the boards. With square-edged boards, there won't be any obstruction. If the knife won't go down more than about 6 mm (¼ in), it's because the blade has found a tongue.

floors

floors Laying down the floor

Mark it from the gap

When fitting a new length of board, lay it the right way up over the gap left by the old board. Mark the ends of the gap across the edges of the new board with a pencil and try square. Join the marks across the top of the board with a straightedge and trimming knife, then saw along this guideline.

The right nail for the job

Traditional cut brads are still the best nail for fixing floorboards. The shanks grip the joists better than oval or lost-head nails and the heads can be driven just below the board surface. The length of the brads should be two-and-a-half times the thickness of the floorboards.

Tiling onto a suspended floor

Ceramic tiles can be laid over old floorboards if the boards are covered first with 15 mm exterior grade plywood; otherwise the natural movement of the boards will cause the joints between the tiles to crack. Make sure that the joists are strong enough to bear the extra weight, and remember that the floor level will be raised by the thickness of the ply, adhesive and tiles.

A batten for the end

Screw battens to the joists to support the ends of the replaced board. They should fit tight under the boards on either side, to ensure the replaced board is level with its neighbours.

Grouped for effect

If you are laying new floorboards right across a room and intend to varnish them, try to group the boards so that the grain pattern and colour of the wood disguises the joins.

Tailor boards, not joists

If a replacement board is thicker than the existing ones, take the waste out of the board, not the joists. Measure the difference exactly, then use a saw and chisel to notch the underside of the board where it is supported on joists.

Driving the boards together tightly

Floor cramps can be hired for driving boards together tightly before nailing. Alternatively, a pair of wedges can be used—either wooden ones sawn from offcuts or the tough plastic sort sold in DIY stores. Lay three or four boards loose, with the grooved edge exposed if they are the tongue-and-groove type. Then nail a spare length of board across the joists to retain the wedges. Tighten the boards by driving the wedges against each other, preferably using two hammers.

Put down hardboard first

The joins between floorboards can show through the surface of floorcoverings such as linoleum, vinyl and cork, spoiling their appearance. Prevent this by covering the old floor with hardboard after first sinking any protruding nails with a nail punch. Fix the sheets down with hardboard pins, driving their diamond-shaped heads in flush with the hardboard.

Lever edge boards into place

Leave an expansion gap of about 9 mm (⅜ in)—which will be covered by the skirting board—between edge boards and walls. To get an edge board tight against the one next to it, insert a batten into the gap and use it to lever the board into place. Then maintain the tension on the batten by tapping a wooden wedge between it and the wall while you nail the board down.

Save the ceiling

Old ceilings can crack when boards are nailed down on the floor above. If yours are fragile, screw boards down instead, countersinking the screw heads and hiding them with wood plugs or dowels if the boards are being left bare.

Secret nailing for exposed floorboards

Tongue-and-groove floorboards can be secret-nailed, leaving the floor surface unmarked by fixings. If you are laying a complete new floor, hire a floor nailer (below) to help you finish the job more quickly. To drive a nail from the tool's magazine, simply strike the plunger with the mallet supplied.

floors

63

floors Laying coverings on concrete and boards

Combating rising damp

Old concrete floors were often laid straight onto the ground and can be damp as a result. If the damp is not too bad, it may be possible to keep the floor dry by coating the surface of the concrete with an epoxy resin or rubber/bitumen coating, but have the problem assessed by an expert first.

Levelling uneven concrete

An uneven concrete floor surface can be treated with a self-smoothing compound, which will raise the floor level by about 10 mm (³⁄₈ in). Remember: you need to trowel the finish out quickly to achieve good results.

Test for dampness

If you suspect that a concrete floor is damp, try this test before laying a floor covering over the top. Leave a solid object on the floor overnight so that air can't get at the area covered; if there's a dark patch when you move it the next day, there is damp in the floor.

You can hire an instrument called a hygrometer to measure the moisture content of the floor. Knowing how damp the floor is will help you to choose the appropriate treatment.

Remove with a spade

A spade is a good tool for removing old floor tiles that have been stuck to the sub-floor. File a sharp edge on the blade, then slide it under the tile edges and lever them up.

Hire a floor-tile stripper for removing large areas of flooring. The machine has a vibrating blade that can be adjusted to suit the old floor covering and the strength of the adhesive.

Incentives for hard labour

Break up an old concrete floor yourself if you are having a new floor laid and want to save money. Locate water and gas pipes before you start. Hire a concrete breaker to make the job easier; one with vibration damping will be less tiring to use and you won't get 'vibration white finger'. Wear ear defenders, work gloves, goggles and steel-toed footwear.

Conceal board edges

Cover old floorboards with hardboard sheets before laying vinyl on top. Condition the sheets by brushing 500 ml of water onto the mesh side of each one, then stacking them flat in the room, mesh sides together, for 48 hours. Then nail them mesh side up.

Stiffen floors before tiling

Cover floorboards with 15 mm exterior-grade plywood before laying ceramic or quarry tiles. Without this, the natural movement of the boards will cause the tile joints to crack. Seal the ply with wood primer first. Remember that the thickness of ply, adhesive and tile will raise the floor by up to 40 mm (1½ in).

Buy all tiles together

Purchase all the floor tiles you need at the same time, and ensure that batch numbers match, otherwise you may encounter colour variations.

The professional's tool

A notched steel trowel is well worth buying if you have a large floor to cover. It enables you to spread the adhesive much more quickly and evenly than you can with the small plastic spreader included with flooring adhesives.

STAGES IN
SETTING OUT TILES

1 Snap chalk lines between midpoints of opposite walls to find centre of room. Check that they cross at right angles

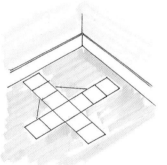

2 Dry-lay rows of tiles along chalk lines. Then adjust row positions so cut tiles at room perimeter are equal and of reasonable size. Mark chosen starting point on floor

3 Stick down tiles in pyramid pattern, beginning at centre of room and working outwards towards each wall in turn. Then cut and fit border tiles

floors Buying and storing sheet and tiles

Options in vinyl

It takes less time to lay vinyl sheet than vinyl tiles because
it doesn't need adhesive, except perhaps in doorways, or
careful measurement to find the centre of the room.
However, packs of tiles are easier to carry, there's less
wastage and cutting mistakes are usually
limited to one tile (if you make an
error when cutting vinyl
sheet, the whole piece
may be wasted).
Spare tiles are also
easier to store
than sheet
offcuts.

Storing flexible flooring

Keep vinyl and cork tiles flat in boxes and weigh down
unpacked ones to stop them curling up at the edges.
Store rolls of vinyl flat on the floor, not on end.

Cutting coverings to fit

Invisible seams

When joining vinyl sheet or lino, lay one piece over another, align the pattern and cut through both layers using a straightedge and a sharp trimming knife. Plan joins at 90° to windows; the seam will reflect less light and be less obvious than one parallel to them.

Avoid joins in doorways, where shoe heels are likely to catch, lift and tear the edges, and try not to place seams in line with the edges of floorboards or chipboard flooring panels. Any slight movement in the floor structure will immediately open up such a seam.

Tackling thick tiles

A professional tile cutter will cut most quarry tiles, but very thick ones may call for a power tile saw or angle grinder. The saw creates less dust and vibration, but the grinder is more useful for cutting irregular shapes. Remember to wear goggles, a mask and sturdy gloves when using either tool.

Patching sheet coverings

To repair damage to flexible sheet vinyl flooring, use an offcut saved from when the flooring was laid, or steal a patch from somewhere it won't be missed, such as under the fridge. Cut the patch oversize, lay it over the damaged area, align the pattern and tape it to the floor. Then cut through both layers using a straightedge and a sharp trimming knife. Lift out the damaged piece and insert the patch, which you may have to stick down with double-sided tape.

Replacing flexible tiles

Before trying to lift a damaged soft or flexible floor tile stuck to the floor, use a hot-air gun to heat the surface and soften the adhesive, or lay kitchen foil on top and heat it with an iron. Cut across the middle of the tile, then slide a scraper into the cut and lever the tile up–you'll be less likely to damage the edges of adjoining tiles. Keep the blade of the scraper hot and use it to remove the old adhesive from the floor.

floors

floors Tips for a perfect finish

Checking the gaps
Maintain even joints between hard floor tiles by using a tiling gauge marked with the right gap (see page 225), or fit tile spacers—either bought or cut from hardboard or ply. Mass-produced tiles are usually laid with a very narrow joint between them. Disguise size variations that occur in handmade floor tiles with wider joints—say, 9 –12 mm (³⁄₈–¹⁄₂ in).

Adhesive alert
Take great care when using flammable flooring adhesives. Follow instructions on the container, and don't nip into the next room to warm up beside a fire because clothing absorbs fumes and could burst into flames. Air work clothes outdoors when the job is done.

Follow curves closely
Make a paper template as a guide for fitting flexible tiles or sheet vinyl flooring around curves. Cut slits in the paper so you can fold the tongues up against the surface around the curve. Cut off tongues at the crease lines, then lay the template over the tile, mark the curve and cut it with a sharp knife.

Accurate holes for pipes
Fit vinyl flooring round radiator pipes by punching holes through it with a pipe offcut of the same diameter. Use a round file on the inside of the pipe to sharpen the cutting edge, then strike the other end with a hammer. Make a cut from the hole to the edge of the sheet so you can fit it around the pipe.

Allow for expansion
When laying wood strip or parquet flooring, leave an expansion gap round the perimeter of the room. Fill this with proprietary cork strip (usually sold along with the flooring) when you've finished, then hide it by pinning quadrant moulding to the skirting board. If you're fitting new skirting boards round the room, these will hide the cork strips.
In a very large room, extra expansion gaps may be needed at intervals across the floor. Ask your flooring supplier if this will be necessary.

Guard against staining
Seal porous quarry and terracotta tiles before laying them. This will prevent them becoming stained later on by the grout. Buy a branded sealer, or make up your own by mixing 2 parts of boiled linseed oil to 1 part of white spirit.
Once the tiles are laid and grouted, give them as many additional coats as they can absorb, allowing each to dry before applying the next one. Consult a specialist tile supplier about waxes and other preparations that will protect the seal and enhance the tile colour.

Brush vinyl flat

Use a soft-bristled broom to flatten vinyl sheet across a floor before you start to cut it to fit. This will press out any air trapped under the sheet.

Seal blocks first

Before laying a woodblock floor, seal the individual blocks. If you seal them after laying, the sealer is likely to stick the blocks together. Future shrinkage will then result in gaps opening up along the weakest joints (above).

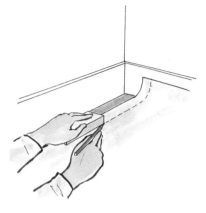

1 Pull sheet about 50 mm (2 in) away from longest wall. Then slide the block and pencil against the skirting to scribe the wall profile onto the sheet

2 Cut and fit sheet against longest wall. Draw reference mark on skirting and matching mark on edge of sheet

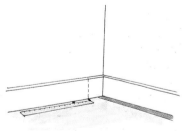

3 Pull sheet away from next wall and mark it again in line with reference mark. Measure distance between marks, cut block to match this exactly and use block and pencil to scribe edge along next wall. Repeat for other walls

floors

plastering First steps that ensure a perfect result

What sort of construction?

Repairs to plasterboard and lath-and-plaster call for different techniques, so if you're not sure what the wall or ceiling is made of, make a small hole with a bradawl. Plasterboard is either 9.5 mm or 12.5 mm thick and can be penetrated easily; lath-and-plaster is thicker, and the timber laths are not easily pierced.

Sounding the surface

Determine the extent of loose plaster before deciding whether to patch it yourself or call in a professional. Tap the surface with your knuckles, listening for the hollow sound that indicates the plaster has 'blown' (lost its adhesion to the masonry behind). Then you can mark out the full extent of the repair.

The stud detective

If you can't work out where wall studs or ceiling joists are, drill a small angled hole through the surface and feed in a length of wire until you feel it hit the timber. Grip the wire at the point where it enters the hole, then pull it out and measure the distance to the end. Studs are normally about 50 mm thick, so add 25 mm to determine the distance from the hole to the centre of the timber.

The usual measurement from the centre of one stud or joist to the centre of the next is 400 mm, but you may find other spacings in old houses.

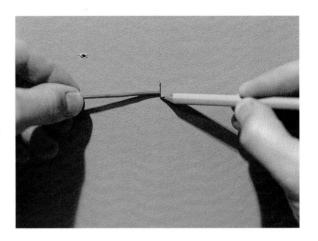

Whisk up the mix

A chef's hand whisk is the best tool for mixing up plaster. Aim for a consistency resembling thick whipped cream for the undercoat and just-melted ice cream for the finishing coat. Once it's right, don't keep on whisking; you will encourage the plaster to start drying.

Rely on the trowel

Aim to get the plaster smooth while it is still wet, rather than rubbing it down with abrasive paper after it has dried. As you apply the plaster to the wall, press the trowel hard at a shallow angle. Then spray on a fine mist of water from a garden spray gun to stop the plaster from drying too quickly, and finish off with a series of light strokes with the trowel held almost flat.

Reduce the suction

Flick some water over the area you are going to plaster. If it soaks in quickly, reduce the suction by brushing some diluted PVA sealer over the surface. This will also help the plaster to bond.

Keep it clean

The container in which you mix plaster, any implements used to mix it, and the water itself must be absolutely clean. Wash and rinse between mixes, so that no lumps of setting plaster or other impurities get into the next mix.

Add plaster to water, not the other way round. Sprinkle the plaster in gradually and keep stirring the mix until the consistency is right.

Fixing damaged wall and ceiling surfaces

Cover-up options for crumbling plaster

One way to tackle plasterwork that's in poor condition is to cover it up. You can fix new plasterboard over old, but you need to use long stainless-steel twinfast screws to fix the new sheets to the wall or ceiling timbers. A false ceiling can be suspended below the old one and walls can be covered with, for example, timber cladding fixed to battens secured to the old wall. Bear in mind that all these solutions make the room slightly smaller and lower. Even if this won't spoil the dimensions of the room, many fittings, especially electrical ones, will have to be removed and repositioned on the new wall or ceiling surface.

A patch on a string

Square off the sides of a small hole in a stud wall or ceiling using a padsaw. Then patch the damage with an offcut of board small enough to pass through the hole on the diagonal. Thread string through its face and tie it to a nail. Next, spread filler or a plasterboard adhesive on the outer face of the patch and push it through the hole. Rotate it and pull on the string so it presses against the inner face of the wallboard. Hold the string for a short while until the filler or adhesive gets a grip. Leave it to set hard, then cut off the string and plaster over the patch.

1 Hack away all loose plaster, using a club hammer and sharp brick bolster

2 Prime laths with a coat of diluted PVA sealer, then mix up undercoat plaster

3 Apply undercoat to a level about 3 mm below existing surface. Leave it to set

4 Mix up and apply finish plaster. As it dries, spray on a little water and then polish surface with steel float

plastering Fixing damaged wall and ceiling surfaces

Repair a damaged corner
The easiest way to patch a damaged external corner is to use a planed timber batten as a plastering guide. Pin the batten flush to one edge of the corner with masonry nails, leaving their heads projecting so you can remove it easily. Then plaster up to the batten. When the plaster has dried, remove the batten carefully and repeat the process from the other side of the corner. Finish by rounding off the new corner with some fine abrasive paper.

Cut back to the timbers
If you need to repair a big hole in a partition wall or ceiling, square up the damage with a multi-purpose saw, cutting back to the edges of the studs or joists on each side of the hole. Nail 50 x 25 mm battens to the joists or studs, then cut a patch of plasterboard to fit and nail it to the battens. Cover all the joints with plasterboard tape before plastering over the patch.

For a ceiling patch, skew nail 50 x 50 mm square supports between the joists at each side of the hole and nail the cut edges of the existing and new plasterboard to them.

What type of plaster?
You can apply finish plaster to minor blemishes and knocks needing a layer up to 3 mm thick. For deeper patches, apply an undercoat of browning plaster first. If there is any risk of dampness, use a render made from sand and cement with added plasticiser rather than a gypsum plaster.

Fixing bulging plaster
On a lath-and-plaster ceiling, the plaster may sag away from the laths. Vacuum up any loose plaster in the ceiling void. Push the sagging plaster back up against the laths with a piece of board and a prop. Return to ceiling void and pour a runny mix of bonding plaster over the area, leaving the board and prop in place until the plaster has set.

stud walls Planning the structure of a new wall

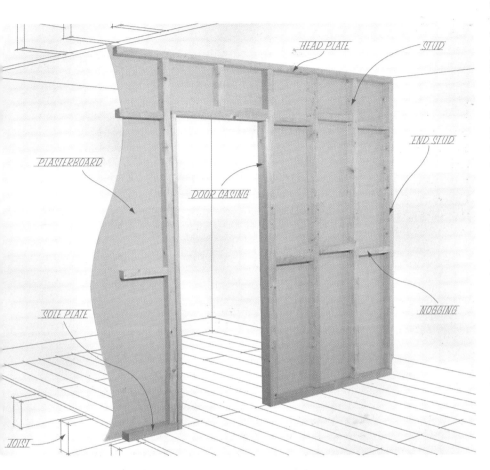

HEAD PLATE

STUD

PLASTERBOARD

DOOR CASING

END STUD

SOLE PLATE

NOGGING

JOIST

The anatomy of a stud wall

A stud wall, also known as a timber-framed partition wall, gets its name from the vertical timbers (studs) that are fitted between the horizontal head and sole plates. This simple framework provides a sturdy support for the sheets of plasterboard that are nailed to it. The only other components involved are horizontal braces called noggings fitted between the studs. These stop the studs twisting, give the plasterboard extra support and provide fixing points for shelves, wall cupboards and the like.

If the wall includes a door opening, the sole plate is cut away and an extra nogging is fitted above the door to act as a lintel. The door opening is lined with a casing, which protects the cut edges of the plasterboard. The door is then hung within the casing.

Providing light and services

If you intend to build a stud wall, plan its position with care and get your plans approved by your local authority to ensure that they comply with building regulations. Bear in mind that, although each room needs natural light (unless it is a kitchen or bathroom), regulations do not allow you to erect a wall which intersects an existing window, so a new window may be needed. You will also have to arrange lighting, heating and possibly plumbing in each new room.

Coping with high ceilings

If a room is more than 2.4 m high—the length of a sheet of plasterboard—you'll need to make up the height with cut-to-size pieces of board. Fit extra noggings between the studs to support them.

Building the new wall

Beware of cables and pipes

Before drilling any holes in your walls, ceilings and floors, use an electronic detector to check for hidden electricity cables and water or gas pipes.

stud walls Building the new wall

The right timber for the job

Use 75 x 50 mm sawn timber for walls up to about 2.4 m (8 ft) high. For rooms with higher ceilings, use 100 x 50 mm timber. Wood shrinks as it dries, so make sure your supply is well seasoned. If it is not, the resultant shrinkage in the structure can cause cracks to appear in the plaster, where the stud wall meets the adjacent wall and ceiling surfaces. Check also that all the wood you buy is straight (see page 339); you cannot build a satisfactory stud wall with warped timber.

Choose the best fixings

To minimise the risk of cracking existing ceiling plaster by hammering, use screws rather than nails to secure the head plate to the ceiling joists and the sole plate to the floor joists. No.10 screws 3½ in long are ideal.

Fasten the end studs to masonry side walls with 100 mm long frame fixings or 4 in No.10 screws and wall plugs. Then use 100 mm round wire nails to skew nail the rest of the studs to the head and sole plates, and to secure the noggings and other frame members, such as door casings.

Finding the joists

Secure the head and sole plates to each joist they cross. Locate the floor joists by looking for the lines of nails in the boards. The ceiling joists always run in the same direction as the floor joists; you can locate these initially by tapping the ceiling surface (a dead sound indicates a joist), then more accurately by making test drillings or using a joist detector.

If the new wall runs parallel to the joists, position it so it stands on top of a joist. You might need access to the ceiling void above so you can insert noggings and screw the head plate to them if ceiling and floor joists are not exactly aligned.

Beefing up the insulation

Stud walls are poor sound insulators. You can improve their performance by using 12.5 mm plasterboard instead of the standard 9.5 mm—or, better still, by using a double layer of 9.5 mm boards. Fix the second layer with 50 mm nails and stagger the joints so they don't coincide with those in the first layer. After cladding one side of the wall, jam 100 mm thick glass-fibre insulation batts between the studs, then clad the second side.

A handy block

Nail an offcut of wood temporarily to the sole plate to hold each stud in position while you skew nail it in place.

Bracing the studs with noggings

Stagger noggings that are acting solely as braces for the studs so you can nail through the side of the stud into the end of each one. If the noggings must be in line—to provide a fixing for a row of cabinets, for example—cramp a block to the stud under each nogging to support it as you skew nail it in place.

Leave clear stud marks

When all the studs are in place, mark their centre lines on the ceiling and floor along both sides of the wall as a guide when nailing on the plasterboard.

Room for manoeuvre

Don't drive the fixing screws fully home into the sole plate until the first stud is in position and you've checked whether it is truly vertical with a spirit level. If it's not, you can then adjust the sole plate position before driving in the screws.

On solid ground floors, drill clearance holes through the sole plate but don't fix it down until you've positioned the first stud on top of it and checked that it's vertical. Then you can drill and plug the holes in the floor and fix it in place.

Vary the spacing

If you are fixing 12.5 mm plasterboard, or using a double thickness of the thinner 9.5 mm board, space the studs at 600 mm (2 ft) centres. If you're using a single thickness of 9.5 mm board, space the studs at 400 mm (16 in) centres.

Supporting heavy weights

Plan the exact position of a heavy fixture, such as a wall cupboard or a washbasin, as you assemble the wall framework. Then you can include extra studs or noggings to support it before you nail up the plasterboard.

Running cables and pipes

Drill holes through the centres of the studs and noggings to run cables and pipes vertically and horizontally within the wall. Don't run cables and pipes through the same holes, though.

Mount sockets and light switches on special plastic mounting boxes that fit flush in a hole cut in the plasterboard. You can get single and double boxes.

Run electric cables inside PVC conduit clipped to the studs and noggings if the wall cavity will be filled with insulation. This will prevent them from overheating.

Cut notches for waste pipes. Drill a hole, then saw out the wedge (left). Replace the cut-out or fit bridging pieces to strengthen the wood.

STAGES IN ASSEMBLING THE FRAMEWORK

1 Use an offcut to mark position of each end of head plate on ceiling. Screw plate to joists

2 Use plumb line to position sole plate directly below, then screw it to floor. Screw end studs to side walls of room

3 Use offcut to mark stud positions. Cut and fit studs

4 Insert noggings for stiffness and casings for door openings

plasterboard Handling plasterboard

Basic requirements
There's more to plasterboard than meets the eye. For lining ceilings and cladding stud walls, you need standard plasterboard. This has one side faced with smooth ivory-coloured paper and the other with rougher grey paper. Tapered-edged boards allow you to tape and fill the joints between boards neatly (see pages 79-81). The standard thickness is 9.5 mm, but 12.5 mm boards are also available.

Special situations
There are several types of plasterboard made for special purposes. Foil-backed boards are designed to stop water vapour passing through wall and ceiling surfaces—for example, into a loft, where it could cause condensation and make the roof timbers rot. Boards backed with a layer of expanded polystyrene provide insulation for dry-lining cold external walls that are liable to condensation.

Standard board sizes
The standard 2400 x 1200 mm board size is convenient to use because the ceiling height in many houses is just under 2400 mm. However, sheets of this size are quite heavy and difficult to manoeuvre in tight spaces, and they can be easily damaged if they are knocked or bent, so get help when moving or fixing them. Smaller size boards are also available and are ideal for repair work.

Smaller for ceilings
Small boards called plasterboard lath, measuring 1200 x 400 mm, are ideal for ceilings because they are much easier to handle than full-sized boards when working overhead. The rounded edges are strengthened by the plaster skim and the joints don't need taping.

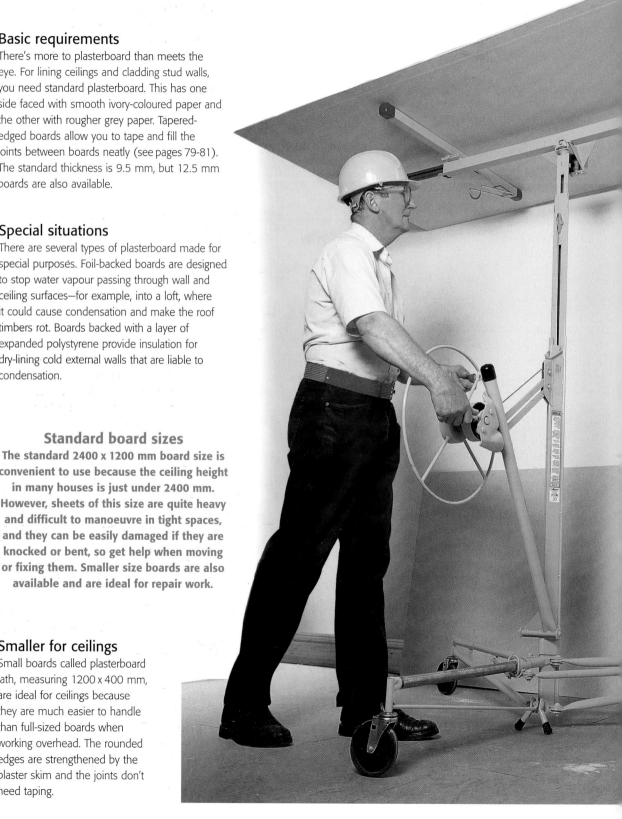

Hire a pair of extra hands

Standard-size sheets of plasterboard are too heavy and unwieldy to fix on a ceiling single-handed. If you have to work on your own, hire a panel lifter (main picture) to raise the boards into place and hold them there while you drive in the fixing nails. The machine can support panels while they are fixed to walls and sloping ceilings too.

If you have help, make a T-support from a plank and batten (left). Then use the propped plank to hold the board tightly against the ceiling joists while driving the nails into place.

Cutting it fine

Use a long straightedge and a sharp trimming knife to cut plasterboard (left). Cut through the paper and into the core of the board on the side that will face outwards. Then snap the cut open by bending the board along the cut line (below). To finish, cut through the paper on the other side.

To make a cut-out in plasterboard, drill a hole within the waste area to admit a padsaw blade, then saw carefully out to and around the cut-out line.

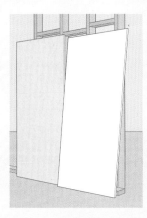

Which side is which?

The grey side of plasterboard is turned to the wall; the ivory side, covered with a higher quality paper, is designed for direct decoration with paint or wallpaper as well as skimming with plaster. The boards are fragile so store them with care. Pair ivory faces against one another to protect them, especially if you wish to decorate straight onto the board.

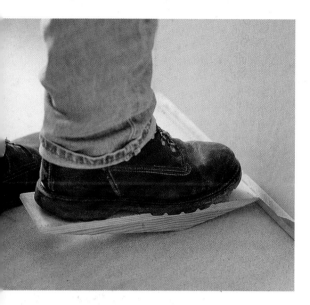

Make a rocking wedge

This simple rocking wedge or foot lifter will hold boards tightly up against the ceiling while you drive in the nails. Cut a piece of 100 x 50 mm wood about 350 mm (14 in) long, and draw a line across one face 150 mm from the end. Then draw a line on each edge, linking the ends of the first line to the opposite corners of the block, and saw off the two triangular waste sections. Slide the rocker under the base of the board and press down on it with your foot. The seesaw effect will lift the board.

Leave a narrow gap

Boards should be about 12 mm (½ in) less than room height. If this means cutting them, support cut edges on the rocking wedge and lift the boards to the ceiling. Both edge and gap will then be hidden by the skirting board.

Hammer in the nail heads

You can buy a special hammer with a domed head for nailing plasterboard. It enables you to drive in the nails until their heads dimple the surface of the board, without tearing the paper facing.

Choose the right nails

Plasterboard nails are galvanised or zinc-plated so that they won't rust and spoil decorations, slightly jagged for better grip, and countersunk so that they indent the paper surface of the board. Use 30 mm nails for 9.5 mm board and 40 mm nails for 12.5 mm board, spaced about 150 mm (6 in) apart, and at least 9 mm (⅜ in) in from the board edges. **Stick a band of insulation tape** around your hammer handle, 150 mm from the end, to make a handy nail spacing gauge.

The horizontal option

Plasterboard doesn't have to be fixed vertically. The dimensions of the wall may make it more practical to fix the boards horizontally. Work from the top downwards. Nail a temporary support to the studs to hold each board while you nail it in place, fitting the first board tight up against the ceiling.

Filling joints and turning corners

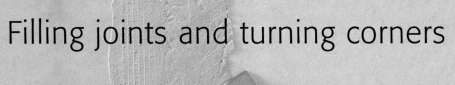

Choose mesh tape

Where plasterboard sheets meet, the joints should be sealed with tape to stop them showing through decorations. Traditional paper tape is bedded in filler along the joint lines and is difficult to apply neatly. Self-adhesive mesh tape is cleaner and easier to use. Don't overlap cut ends; just butt them together neatly, and then apply a generous band of joint filler over the tape with a filling knife.

Feather with a sponge

A damp sponge is the best tool for feathering (smoothing the edges of) joint filler so it blends smoothly with the surface of the board. When the filler is completely dry, you can smooth it further with a fine sanding block for a totally invisible joint.

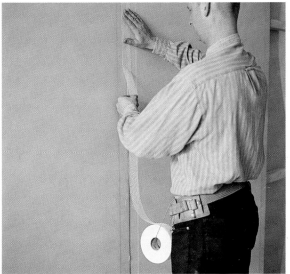

Make a tape dispenser

Once you begin taping plasterboard joints, you will find it useful to keep the roll of tape to hand, so make a simple dispenser from a wire coat hanger, bent into a V-shape and hooked onto your tool belt.

Protective seal

Leave joint filler to dry for at least two days. Then apply a coat of plaster primer to the ivory face if you plan to hang wallpaper. This evens out the suction between the raw board and the taped-and-filled joints, and also stops the board surface from tearing when the wallpaper is next stripped.

plasterboard Filling joints and turning corners

Tidy up the edges
Board edges that have been cut by hand can be rather ragged. Before applying joint tape, trim off any torn or loose paper facing and repair the board surface with filler.

Keep the filler clean
Clean the blade of your filling knife by drawing it across a piece of scrap wood rather than over the rim of the bucket in which you mixed the filler. If you scrape it on the bucket, you'll end up with a lot of gritty bits in the unused filler.

Reinforce the corners
Cover all corners with joint tape. If an external corner is especially vulnerable, use zinc-plated metal angle bead, nailed in place or bedded in with joint filler. Then skim the walls with plaster.

Plasterboard on solid walls

Give warmth to walls
A plasterboard lining on a solid outside wall provides extra insulation. Use foil-backed board to prevent condensation. Traditionally timber battens are put up first, and the boards nailed to them but so long as the wall is straight and flat, you can apply a series of dabs of plasterboard bonding compound to the wall or board (depending on the manufacturer's recommendations), then press the boards into place.

Horizontal bands of the bonding compound spread along the top and bottom of the wall reduce the airflow, improving the insulation, and provide a solid base for fixing skirting boards and cornices. Insert wedges at the bottom of the sheets of board to keep them tight to the ceiling while the compound dries.

Raid the offcuts box
You will need pieces of packing in different thicknesses to fill the gaps between the battens and the wall surface. Offcuts of hardboard and thin plywood are ideal; cut them into strips about 50 mm wide and apply a little woodworking adhesive before tapping them into place behind the battens.

Finding the high spots

If the wall is uneven, you need to put up a truly flat framework of battens to support the plasterboard. Lay a batten flat on the floor against the wall and draw a line on the floor along its outer face. Then hold the batten vertically against the wall, at intervals, and make a mark on the floor wherever its bottom end projects beyond the first line. Draw a second line parallel to the first one through the outermost of these marks. Fix the floor-level batten so its outer face is aligned with the outer line. Fix the vertical battens so their faces align with the batten at floor level, using packing where necessary. Finish off by fixing a horizontal batten at ceiling level.

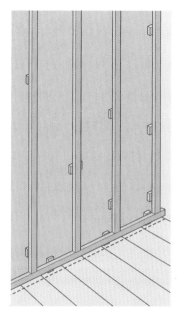

Use frame fixings

The quickest way of fixing battens is to use frame fixings—all-in-one screws and wall plugs (see page 350). Drill holes through the battens and use them as a template to drill into the wall. Insert the fixing and hammer the screw home.

Frame window reveals

Fix battens all round window and door openings to support the board edges. Make sure they align with the other battens horizontally and vertically, and use packing where necessary.

1 Cut sheet of board about 13 mm (½ in) less than floor to ceiling height. Start fixing boards in a corner

2 Fix board tight to ceiling. Nail to vertical studs, to head and sole plates and to any noggings fitted

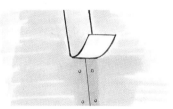

3 Drive nails in roughly every 150 mm (6 in), keeping them at least 9 mm (⅜ in) in from board edges. Tape all joints

4 Apply joint filler over tape and use it to fill nail holes too

plasterboard

8 1

HANDRAIL

BALUSTERS

NEWEL POST

STRING

QUARTER SPACE LANDING

RISER

TREAD

The weight-and-listen test

Ask someone to walk slowly up and down the stairs when you want to locate creaking steps from inside an understairs cupboard. As the other person presses down on the treads, you can often see them flex slightly, as well as hear which joints are creaking.

staircases Curing creaks from below

Replace angle blocks

Small triangular blocks of wood under the stairs stiffen the joints between treads and risers. Replace any missing ones, otherwise the stairs may creak. Apply PVA adhesive to the blocks and rub them in place until they stick. Then secure the blocks with screws long enough to pass through the blocks and into the underside of the stairs, but not right through them.

Silenced with talc

Try brushing some talcum powder or chalk dust along the tread and riser joints of stairs which creak. It often cures the problem temporarily.

Try filling the gap with foam
For a quick fix, squirt polyurethane foam filler into any gaps between treads and risers from under the stairs. The foam stops creaks by preventing the wood surfaces from chafing.

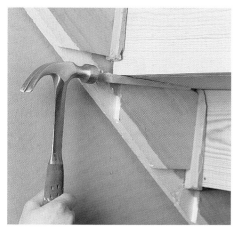

Tighten loose wedges
If there are wooden wedges under the stairs holding the treads and risers tight in the strings, check they're not loose. If any are, squeeze some glue onto the tips and tap them back into place.

Reinforcing a slack joint
To close up the joint between the back of a tread and the bottom of a riser, squeeze some PVA adhesive into the gap. Then drive three evenly spaced screws upwards, through the tread and into the riser. Position screws 12 mm (½ in) from the back edge of the tread.

TREAD

RISER

STAGES IN FITTING A HANDRAIL

1 Use spirit level to mark wall at least 900 mm (3 ft) above front edge of every tread. Join marks using a straightedge

2 Fit brackets to underside of handrail. Align top of rail with drawn line and mark fixings for top bracket

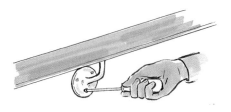

3 Secure top bracket with one wall plug and screw. Pivot rail and fix bottom bracket in same way. Mark all the screw holes. Then remove handrail and drill for wall plugs before permanent installation

mouldings
Fixes from above

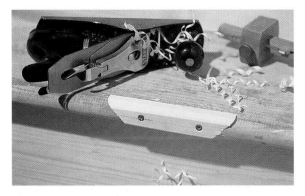

Repairing the edge of a tread

When repairing the front edge or nosing of a tread, cut the repair as shown above. The dovetail or wedge shape counteracts the weight put on it, so the repair does not depend on glue and screws alone for its strength.

Stiffen joints with brackets

When you cannot get at the underside of the staircase to reinforce loose joints, pull back the carpet and fix metal brackets into the angle between treads and risers–two on each step will be enough. The metal brackets are thin enough not to show through the carpet when it is replaced.

Remedies for broken and loose balusters

Bind up the break

If you've got all the pieces, it's possible to mend a broken baluster invisibly. Spread adhesive on the broken ends, squeeze them together and bind the repair together tightly with insulating tape. Temporarily wedge the baluster between two blocks of wood nailed to a work surface. These will keep the broken ends squeezed together while the adhesive dries. Use a fine grade abrasive paper to remove hardened glue after you have removed the tape.

Take out for stripping

Before starting to strip an intricate balustrade by hand, see if the balusters can be removed without too much trouble. If they can, take them out and pay to have them stripped. You can then concentrate on making the newel posts and handrail look like new.

Tap in a shim

Cut a shim–a slim wooden wedge–to fix a loose baluster. Spread adhesive on both sides of the shim, then use a pin hammer to tap it into the gap where the baluster is joined to the handrail or the string. When the glue has dried, use a sharp trimming knife to tidy up the repair so that the shim does not show.

Strategies for removal

Balusters are secured to the handrail and string in different ways. If they are simply nailed to the top edge of the string, free them by using a fine nail punch to drive the nails right through the ends of the balusters, rather than trying to prise them out.

If the outer string is 'open' (cut to follow the line of the treads and risers), prise off the cover moulding on the side edge of each tread. Then gently tap the bottom ends of the balusters out of their slots with a mallet.

Finding a match

Replacement balusters can be hard to find, but look around local architectural salvage yards before paying a wood turner to reproduce just one or two.

Plan ahead for best effect

Decoration and function

Mouldings are practical as well as decorative. Skirting boards save the base of walls from hard knocks. Dado rails are traditionally fixed at a height to protect walls from chair backs.

Picture rails, fixed at or above the height of door frames, support heavy pictures and mirrors securely without the need for individual wall fixings. Choose each of these mouldings in a style that reflects the overall design of the room.

Fewer joins and less waste

Measure and list the length of every stretch of wall to which you are going to attach a moulding, then add about 50 mm (2 in) as a trim allowance for every corner cut required. Visit your timber merchant or DIY store and find out what lengths they have in stock; these usually start at 1.8 m and rise in increments of 300 mm (12 in). Then choose the mouldings you're going to use and work out a cutting order that involves as little waste as possible.

Architrave mouldings for door frames are often sold in pre-cut sets—two 2.1 m lengths for the sides of the opening and a 900 mm length for the top.

Marking the height

If the skirting board is level, cut a timber rod to match the height of a proposed dado rail. Then work around the room, using a spirit level to plumb the rod before marking its height on the wall. Join up the marks with a straightedge to make a fixing line.

Alternative to timber

Mouldings made from medium-density fibreboard (MDF) are an alternative to timber so long as you're planning to paint them. They are often sold primed, ready for the final coat to be applied. Don't use MDF mouldings in bathrooms or kitchens, however, because if they absorb moisture they will swell and distort. Remember to wear a dust mask when cutting or drilling MDF.

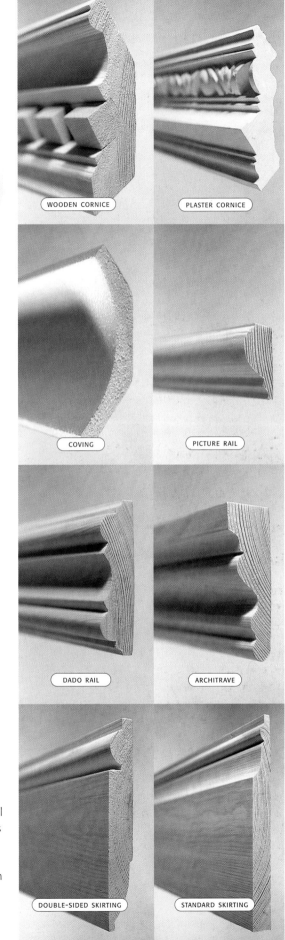

WOODEN CORNICE

PLASTER CORNICE

COVING

PICTURE RAIL

DADO RAIL

ARCHITRAVE

DOUBLE-SIDED SKIRTING

STANDARD SKIRTING

mouldings

mouldings Skilful ways at corners

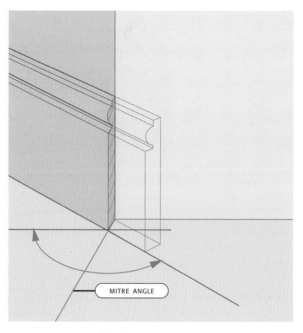

MITRE ANGLE

Draw angles on the floor

Mark the mitres where two skirting boards meet at an external corner by holding each length in turn against the wall so it overlaps the corner. Draw a line on the floor against the front edge of each board. Then hold one end of a ruler against the corner and draw a line from it through the point where the two lines on the floor intersect. This gives you the mitre angle (above).

Hold each board in place, mark its face where it crosses this mitre angle line and its back where it touches the corner of the wall. Extend the marks all round the boards and cut the mitres.

Inconspicuous joins

When you need to join two lengths of moulding along a wall, make a scarf joint by cutting the two ends at 45° angles. You can do this accurately using a jigsaw with an adjustable sole plate (top). Fix one length in place, then position and fix the other (above). Apply some woodworking adhesive to the cut ends and secure the joint with pins. Try to position it where it will not be seen—behind furniture, for example.

Guard against inaccuracy

If the floor slopes, do not match the height of a dado or picture rail to it. Either hire a laser level (see page 330), or mark the height of the moulding at one point only, then use the longest spirit level you can obtain to transfer the mark all around the room. Compensate for any slight inaccuracy in the level by turning it end over end as you go.

Plaster practice

Always saw fibrous plaster mouldings from the face side, so that any 'breaking out' occurs on the back. If the moulding has a hessian backing, cut through it with a sharp trimming knife. Mitre cut internal and external corners with a hardpoint saw, then drill clearance holes for the screws being used to secure the mouldings to the wall, otherwise they will crack the plaster when they are tightened. Seal the joints with plaster of Paris or a suitable filler, and sand smooth when dry.

Making mitres easy

A bench hook is a simple piece of equipment for holding small pieces of wood steady while you saw them. By making accurate 45° saw slots in the block screwed to its back edge, you can turn it into a mitre block that's ideal for cutting neat mitres on small panel mouldings and picture rails.

A deep mitre box is useful for cutting skirting boards. Make it up from offcuts, slightly deeper than the height of the skirting board. For accuracy, cut the 45° slots in each side of the box with a panel saw (see page 332) rather than a tenon saw. Stiffen the box by nailing or screwing a couple of battens across the top at each end.

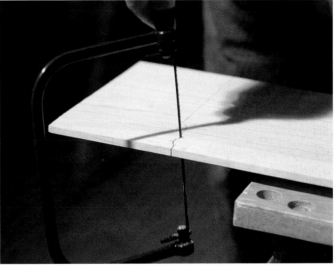

Inside knowledge

The professional way to join mouldings at inside corners is to butt one length against the wall and scribe the second one over it. Use an offcut with an accurate 90° sawn end to trace the profile of the moulding onto the back of the length you want to scribe (left). **Reverse the blade** in a coping saw to cut along the line (right). This enables it to cut on the pulling stroke, so that the face of the moulding is not spoiled by splintering. The straight section of the line can be squared onto the front of the board and cut with a tenon saw.

Ways of fixing

Wooden wedges for nails

Fix skirting board to brickwork by nailing it to wooden wedges, driven into every fourth vertical joint. Make the wedges by chopping opposing tapers on the ends of lengths of 75 x 25 mm timber, using a sharp carpenter's axe. Choose pieces of wood at least 400 mm long so your hand is well out of the way of the axe. Drive the wedges into the brick joints and saw off flush with the wall.

mouldings Ways of fixing

Too hard for masonry nails?

Masonry nails are the quickest way of fixing skirting boards, but try driving one into the wall first. They are easy to hammer into the lightweight blocks used to build the interior walls of most modern houses, but it can be hard or impossible to get them into old bricks. Make sure you wear goggles, because the nails can ricochet if they're not struck squarely with the hammer.

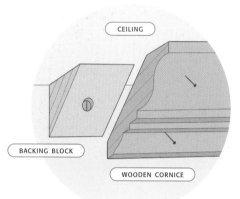

Backing blocks for cornices

Wooden cornicing is difficult to locate accurately. Rip a square-sectioned length of wood, say a 50 x 50 mm piece, diagonally to make triangular fillets.
Cut short blocks off the fillets and fix these along the junction of the wall and ceiling. Hold the cornicing in place against the blocks and nail it to them.

Nail architraves at the top

Secure the mitre joints on architraves around door and window frames by nailing them together. Drive the nails through the top piece, or head, where they won't be seen, rather than through the side pieces, or legs. It's a good idea to drill pilot holes for the nails, otherwise you're likely to split the wood when you hammer them down.

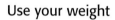

Use your weight

Press the bottom edge of new skirting board tight down to the floor before nailing it, by using a kneel board. This is simply a piece of floorboard or similar size timber, about 1.2 m (4 ft) long, propped on the top edge of the loose skirting board. Press down on it with one knee while fixing the skirting to the wall with nails or screws into wall plugs. On wooden floors that are normally covered, nail a small block into the floor against the end of the kneel board every time you move it along the wall. This traps the board so that it cannot slip off the skirting and leave you with a jarred knee.

A crafty quirk

Nail through the grooves and hollows of mouldings, especially if they're being varnished. Once the nail heads are punched in and filled over, they'll be almost invisible.

Mirror image

Before going to a timber merchant or architectural salvage yard for replacement moulding, it's a good idea to record its shape. The best tool for the job is a profile gauge, a comb-like tool composed of sliding 'needles'. Set the gauge by pressing it against the face of the moulding you want to duplicate.

Planning and care for a top-class job

Protect the decor

If a length of skirting board has to be replaced, first use a sharp trimming knife to cut through any wallpaper stuck to the top. Then find out how the board is fixed. Screws should be drilled out if they cannot be removed. Nailed boards should be eased away from the wall with a bolster chisel, until there is space to insert a nail bar, and then levered off the wall. Protect the decoration with a piece of thin ply.

Freedom of movement

Use a flexible decorator's filler to seal gaps between the tops of skirting boards and walls, and to disguise badly fitting joints in corners. The sealant is sold in cartridge form and can be painted over. It won't fall out when doors are slammed or crack because of the natural movement of the wood.

Architraving in order

When fitting architraving around a door frame, saw a 45° mitre cut on the top end of each architrave leg or upright and fix them on either side of the frame first. Then fit the head or top piece by holding it upside down across the tops of the legs, marking its length from them and cutting matching mitres.

Patching damaged skirting

The join between two pieces of skirting board butted together at 45° is less conspicuous than a square, 90° cut. If you need to patch in a piece of new skirting, tap some wedges in behind the board to ease it away from the wall slightly and create room for the saw blade. Guide the saw with a mitre block to make a 45° cut, and then use the piece you remove as a pattern when you cut the replacement to length.

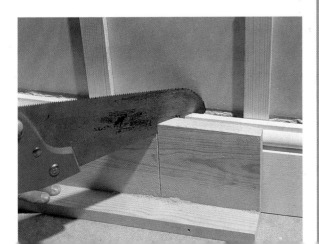

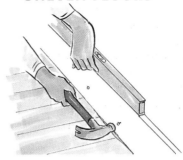

1 Cut board to length. Use a spirit level to ensure board is level. Fix temporarily to wall

2 Cut a small block of wood slightly thicker than the widest gap between board and floor

3 Use a block of wood and pencil to scribe profile of floor along skirting board

4 Remove board, saw along scribed line, then fix board permanently

mouldings

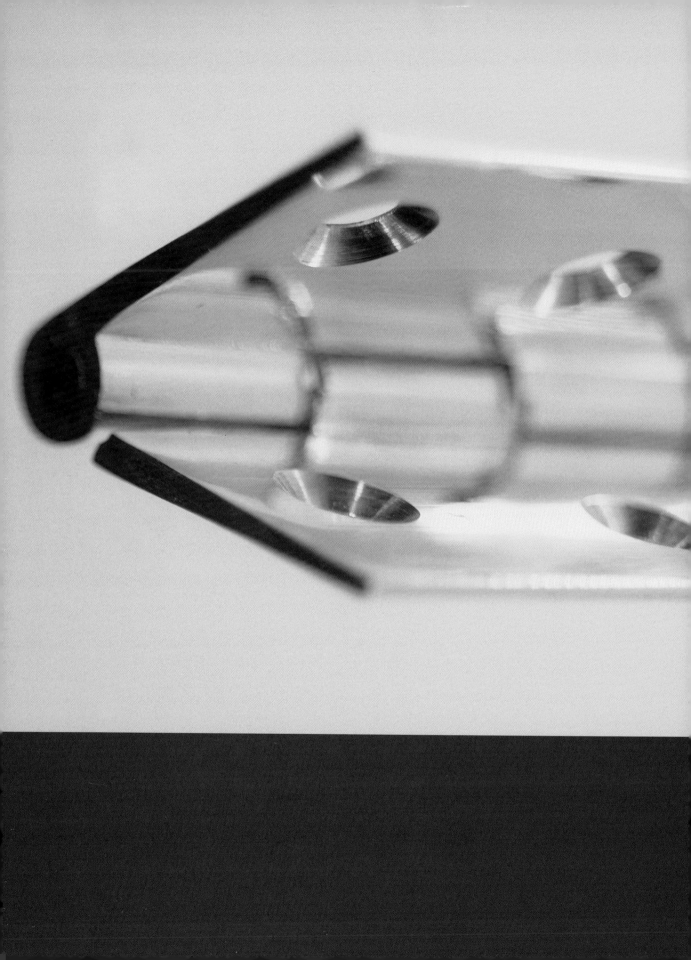

doors and windows

fitting Cures for jammed doors and windows

Wait for the swelling to go

When a door or window starts jamming in its frame with the onset of wet weather, it indicates that moisture is penetrating the paintwork, causing the wood to swell. Don't plane down the edges of the opening or you're likely to end up with too big a gap when the wood dries out. Instead, wait for a dry spell, then repaint the joinery.

Easy on the trigger

Speed up the drying process by playing heat from a hot air gun along the edges of a door or window that's swollen in its frame. The idea is to draw moisture out of the wood, so use the gun in short bursts, just warming the surface without scorching it. Take care not to crack the glass if you're working on a window.

Don't use force

Try not to force a jammed window or door open and shut repeatedly. If you do, there's a risk that the joints will be weakened and the putty loosened. You might even crack the glass.

Breaking a paint bond

Casements painted into their frames can sometimes be freed by running a trimming knife around the edge. Then release any catches and bolts before tapping the casement open from inside using a wood block and hammer.

Hold a door fast while you work

Make a clamp to hold a new door on its edge while you plane it to fit the frame. Saw a U-shaped notch in the end of a piece of 100 x 50 mm timber and fix it to the floorboards with a couple of screws. Then slide the door into the notch and jam it in place with a wooden wedge. Secure the wedge to the clamp with a length of string so it won't get lost.

No need to remove the door

You can plane the outer edge of a door if it is binding on the frame without having to take it off its hinges. To stop the door swinging as you work on it, tap in a pair of wedges beneath the door, one on top of the other (see top). Remove the lock or latch if there's a chance of the plane striking it. Plane off a little at a time, aiming for a 2 mm gap (about as thick as a 50p piece) between the door edge and the frame.

Hire an electric door trimmer (above) to shorten door bottoms so they'll clear a new fitted carpet or other floor covering. The trimmer takes off a thin sliver of wood, and it vacuums up the sawdust too.

1 Stand in front of doorway and 'walk' door up to frame. Get top of door and top of frame parallel with each other

2 Run a pencil around rebate on frame to mark door for planing. Allow an extra 2 mm all round to accept hinges

3 Plane door to fit. Check it in its frame, then sand off all sharp edges, cut recesses for hinges and hang door

fitting

fitting First aid for loose and broken joints

Metal reinforcements

Loose joints on windows and doors can be braced with metal corner plates (right). You can hide the plates by chopping out a shallow recess for them. Screw the plates in place, then paint them with a rust inhibitor before hiding them below a layer of wood filler. Once the filler has dried, sand it to blend with the surface of the wood and paint over it.

Dismantle to reassemble

Sometimes it is possible to dismantle a door or window if the joints are very loose. Carefully tap the uprights (called stiles) off the horizontals (called rails). If they don't come apart easily, look for nails or dowels pinning them together; drill out dowels and drive nails right through with a fine nail punch. Wear gloves, goggles and stout footwear if you are dealing with a window, because it is almost inevitable that the glass will break and drop out.

Test for squareness

Measure the frame diagonals (left) when cramping a repaired frame back together. The two measurements should be identical. Confirm that the frame is square by laying a try square on the corners; the two sides of the frame should match it exactly. If the frame is not square, slacken the sash cramps, angle them slightly, retighten and test again for squareness.

Pin the joint with a dowel

Wooden dowels can be used to reinforce loose corner joints. Drill holes for them through the faces of the stiles, so that they pass right through the joint. Make sure the drill doesn't cause splintering when it breaks through (see page 342). Dowels with fluted sides provide a stronger bond for the glue than plain ones do.

Pile on the paint

The bottom edge of an outside door should be painted to keep moisture out and prevent swelling. A strip of carpet is useful for doing the job without taking the door off its hinges. Slip a sheet of newspaper under the door. Then apply some paint to the pile side of the carpet, slide it under the door and rub it back and forth to coat the bare wood.

Hinges with lift

Don't plane the bottom edge of a door that scrapes on the floor the wider it is opened. Otherwise, you'll end up with a wide, draughty gap when it is closed. Change the hinges for rising butts. The spiral on the knuckle of the hinge lifts the door as it opens. You will need to know how the door is 'handed' (see page 95) when you buy them.

hardware
Solutions to problems with hinges

Left hand or right hand?
Some items of door furniture, such as rising butt hinges, are 'handed'. In other words, they are made in left-handed and right-handed versions that are mirror images of each other. In order to buy the correct version for the job, imagine yourself standing inside the room, looking at the door. If it is hinged on the left and opens inward, you need a left-handed hinge. If it is hinged on the right, you need a right-handed one.

Aligning bolt and plate
If work on your door hinges means that a lock or latch bolt no longer engages cleanly in its striking plate, use shoe polish to reveal the distance by which it is overlapping the plate (right). Smear a little polish on the end of the bolt, then close the door and operate the lock to leave a mark on the plate. Use a file to enlarge the cut-out if the discrepancy is small (above); if it is more than about 1 mm, reposition the plate instead.

Stop doors binding
If a door binds in its frame as you close it, and the rebate into which it fits is formed by a planted stop (a strip of wood nailed to the frame), prise this off and refit it. Trap some card between door and stop to provide the necessary clearance. If the rebate is machined into the frame, reposition the door hinges with their knuckles projecting a little farther beyond the edge of the frame.

Avoid the joints
Solid panelled doors are assembled with either mortise-and-tenon or dowelled joints. You can avoid cutting into these when fitting door hinges by positioning the upper hinge about 150 mm (6 in) below the top edge of the door and the lower one 225 mm (9 in) up from the bottom. Follow the same principle when positioning hinges on a casement window.

hardware Solutions to problems with hinges

Fit a third hinge

Heavyweight hardwood front doors may need a third hinge, fitted midway between the top and bottom ones, to carry the extra weight and spread the load on the existing hinge screws.
Make sure that all three hinges are fitted with their knuckles precisely in line, otherwise the door won't open and close smoothly and the hinge screws will be forced out.

How to centre the screws

Use a countersink bit in a hand drill or power drill to mark the positions of the hinge screw holes. Then use these as a guide when drilling holes for the screws.

Add some packing

Use material of appropriate thickness–card or hardboard, for example–to pack out hinges which have been recessed too deeply. You can spot the problem by looking at the hinged edge from the opening side: there will be no space between the edge of the door (or window) and the edge of the frame.

Clear the frame

Fit parliament hinges if you want a door to open right back against the wall behind it. The T-shaped leaves ensure that the door clears the architrave or the sides of the reveal in which it is set. The hinges are sold with different depths of projection, or 'throw', so you need to measure the depth of the recess to calculate the size of hinge required.

When screws cause trouble

Providing a better grip

Try replacing loose hinge screws with longer ones of the same gauge. If you are working on a window, make sure the screws are not so long that their points can strike the edge of the glass and crack it as you drive them in.
Alternatively, remove the hinge and drill out the troublesome screw holes to accommodate lengths of dowel. Dip the dowels in woodworking adhesive, tap them into place, then cut off the excess with a chisel when the adhesive has dried. Drill pilot holes in the dowels for the new screws and refit the hinge.

Removing seized screws

Scrape paint from the slots in screw heads so the screwdriver can get a grip. If the screw won't budge, tighten it slightly if you can to free the threads. Next, try striking the screwdriver handle head-on with a hammer, heating the screw head with a soldering iron, or using an impact driver. This turns the screw slightly when hit with a hammer. As a last resort, drill out the screw.

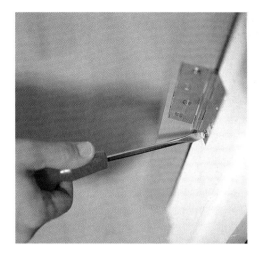

Steel before brass

When fitting brass screws, drive holes with steel screws of the same length and gauge first. You will then be able to drive the softer brass screws without burring their heads. Rub some candle wax on the brass screw threads first.

Mend a split frame

A frame can split along the line of the hinge screws if the door or window it encloses blows open violently. Mend the split by squeezing woodworking adhesive into it, then forcing it shut with a G-cramp until the adhesive dries. Alternatively, drive screws through the face of the frame and through the split, countersinking the heads so that they can be concealed with filler.

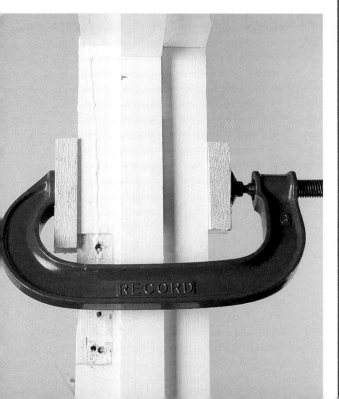

1 Open hinge to 90°. Hold knuckle against edge of door at hinge position and mark around the leaf of the hinge with a sharp trimming knife

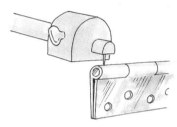

2 Set marking gauge to half total thickness of hinge and mark face of door with gauge

3 Use sharp chisel and mallet to chop out marked recess for hinge to gauged depth

4 Screw hinges to door. Then wedge door in open position and mark and cut recesses for hinges on frame

hardware

hardware Upgrading locks on external doors

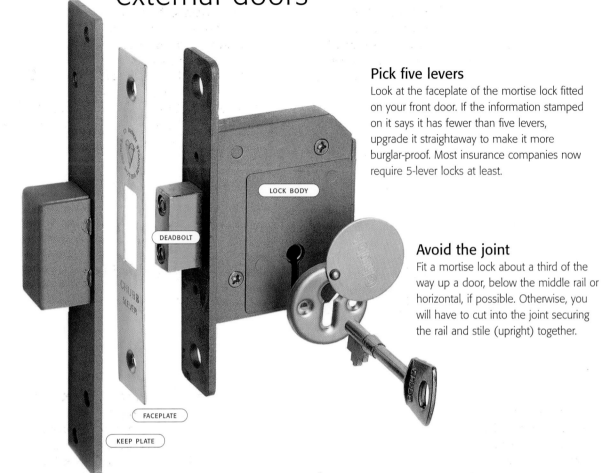

LOCK BODY

DEADBOLT

FACEPLATE

KEEP PLATE

Pick five levers

Look at the faceplate of the mortise lock fitted on your front door. If the information stamped on it says it has fewer than five levers, upgrade it straightaway to make it more burglar-proof. Most insurance companies now require 5-lever locks at least.

Avoid the joint

Fit a mortise lock about a third of the way up a door, below the middle rail or horizontal, if possible. Otherwise, you will have to cut into the joint securing the rail and stile (upright) together.

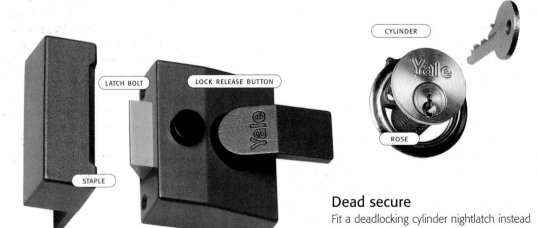

CYLINDER

LATCH BOLT

LOCK RELEASE BUTTON

ROSE

STAPLE

Dead secure

Fit a deadlocking cylinder nightlatch instead of a standard type if your front door is glazed. When locked from the outside, the indoor handle cannot be operated, so a burglar cannot get in by breaking the glass, reaching through and turning it as he can with a non-deadlocking type.

Better safe than sorry

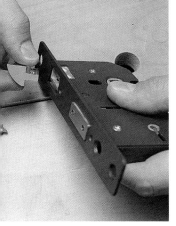

Who's there?
A door viewer, or peephole, is a valuable security device, but is of little use after darkness unless your doorstep is well lit. Keep the porch or hallway light switched on after dusk, or fit a sensor-activated light that will come on whenever someone approaches the door.

The strongest chain
The strongest door chains have a right-angled plate which fixes into the side of the rebate and turns round the frame edge. These are highly resistant to forcing. You can strengthen an existing fitting by exchanging the screws supplied with the chain for longer ones.

Making front doors more resistant to forcing

Matching the latch
A sashlock is a mortise lock plus a latch. When the door is unlocked, it allows you to open and close the door by operating the latch with a handle. The body of the lock is always fitted into the door edge with the handle at the top, and is made in both left-handed and right-handed versions (see page 95). If you can't obtain a correctly handed one, look for the type with a small cutaway in the casing. This allows you to reverse the latch by simply removing two screws (above). The alternatives are to take the body of the lock apart and reverse it yourself, to ask a locksmith to do it for you, or to buy one with a roller latch, which will work in a left-handed or right-handed situation.

Reinforcement for a cylinder latch
One way to give your front door extra security at relatively low cost and with very little DIY work is to fit reinforcements to the door, the frame, or both. Doors secured with a rim lock or cylinder nightlatch are quite easily forced: a heavy blow drives the latch against the staple, which is held in place by just a couple of screws, shearing it away from the inside face of the frame and allowing an intruder to get in. The reinforcement (above) is designed to prevent this; it consists of a long steel bar shaped to fit tightly over the staple and is fixed all the way down the inside face of the frame with screws. (See also page 102.)

Sandwiched for strength
You can strengthen doors and frames around locks and hinges with so-called partnered reinforcements. These consist of two metal strips, joined together by bolts which pass right through the door or frame. For example, a mortise lock can be protected with a pair of strips bolted through the frame on either side of the keep plate, and by a further pair on the door, sandwiching the lock.

hardware Seven tips for fitting mortise locks

When to stop drilling

Drilling too deeply into the door stile can weaken the door and, if it's glazed, you could also crack the glass. To avoid this, wrap some tape round your drill bit so you can see when you've drilled holes to just the right depth—a fraction more than the length of the lock body. If your drill has a depth stop attachment, you can use that instead.

Avoiding an eyeful of dust

Resist the temptation to blow into the mortise to clear out loose shavings: you can easily end up with an eye full of splinters and wood dust. Pull out the waste with the drill bit or scrape it out with a narrow chisel.

Measure to fit

Look at the width of the door stile and the thickness of the door before buying a mortise lock for it. Lock bodies come in several different thicknesses and lengths. This is particularly important if you are buying a lock for a glazed door, which may have very narrow stiles.

Don't split your sides

Choose a drill that's just a fraction wider than the thickness of the lock body. If you create a wider mortise, you will weaken the door so much that it could split around the lock if forced.

Getting a firm grip

Turn the key to extend the bolt of the lock before you insert it in the mortise to test the fit. If it jams you can then grip the bolt with pliers and pull the lock body out again.

Measure up for a perfect fit

With the lock fitted, measure the distance between the bolt and the closing face of the door. Use this measurement to position the keep plate on the door frame so that the bolt just engages in the recess when the door is locked.

Mark the keyhole

When you have cut the mortise and the faceplate recess, hold the lock body against the face of the door so you can mark the position of the keyhole on it with a bradawl or pencil.

Improving window and door security

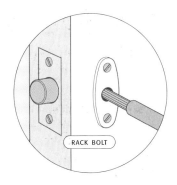

RACK BOLT

Awayday precautions

If you have sash windows without locks which you fear might be forced while you're away from home, drill two clearance holes through the top rail of the inner sash and drive long screws through them into the bottom rail of the outer sash. This will lock the two sashes securely together.

Open invitation

An intruder could quietly remove the panes of louvred windows by bending the metal clips that hold them in place. Prevent this by gluing the glass to the clips with an epoxy-resin adhesive.

Use longer fixings

Most window locks come with screws so short that they won't withstand forcing. Replace them with longer screws that will penetrate the wood as far as possible at the fixing point.

Replace worn parts

If the mechanism of a door lock is worn but the body is in good condition, you can replace just the worn component—a new cylinder in the case of a cylinder nightlatch, or new levers for a mortise lock. Take the lock to a locksmith to make sure that the new components will fit. You will also need new keys.

Fit concealed bolts

Fit rack bolts in pairs to external doors and to casement windows—one near the top corner and the other near the bottom. The bolt engages in a hole in the frame. They are more secure than surface-mounted locks, and are also much less obtrusive.

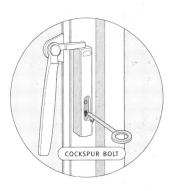

COCKSPUR BOLT

Block the handles

Screw a cockspur bolt to a metal-framed window to stop an intruder operating the handle after breaking the glass. The key locks the bolt in the up position for security, and lets it drop when you want to open the window. Avoid cracking the glass by drilling no deeper than necessary when making holes for the bolt's self-tapping screws.

Make external glazing beads secure

The best locks will not keep out a thief if all he has to do is prise away external glazing beads and then lift out the glass. You can secure wooden glazing beads to their frames with clutch-head security screws, which cannot be unscrewed. If you have double-glazed windows with external plastic glazing beads, ask your local glass merchant for advice. The usual method of securing these is to remove the beads and stick them back in place with special adhesive sealant.

hardware

hardware Improving window and door security

Push the button

Make sure wooden windows are always secure by fitting locks that don't need a key to lock them. With some types, you simply push a button in to secure the two parts of the lock together after closing the window. Other types lock together automatically as the parts meet. Both need a key to undo them.

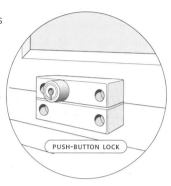

PUSH-BUTTON LOCK

Lock the window stay

If you want security plus the option of leaving a window ajar for ventilation, and the window has a stay pierced with holes, replace the plain peg on which the stay normally fits with a casement stay lock. You can then secure the window in any position by attaching the screw-on lock to the threaded peg with the key, which is also used to unlock it.

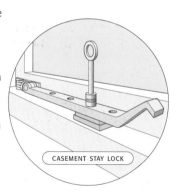

CASEMENT STAY LOCK

Bolt sliding sashes together

Fit dual screws—one at each side of the meeting rails—to secure sash windows. These consist of an internally threaded barrel that passes through the inner rail, and a bolt that passes through the barrel and screws into the outer rail.

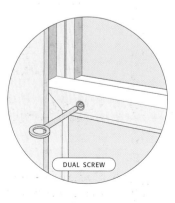

DUAL SCREW

Drill doors from both sides

If you have to drill through a door—to fit a cylinder nightlatch, a door viewer, a handle or a door knocker—take care not to burst through the wood and splinter its opposite face. Whether you are using a power drill and flat bit, or a hand brace and auger bit (above), drill until the tip of the bit just emerges through the opposite face of the door. Then withdraw the bit, insert the tip in the hole on the opposite face and finish drilling the hole from there.

Cramp on a scrap block

If you're drilling a hole close to the door edge—for a cylinder nightlatch, for example—you can use a G-cramp to hold a block of scrap wood tightly against the opposite face of the door as an alternative to drilling from both sides. Then you can drill right through the door and into the block without stopping and without causing any splintering. Use packing to protect the door face from the exposed cramp jaw.

Add locking bolts

Double up security on old aluminium-framed patio doors. If the only lock is part of the handle on the sliding door, fit surface-mounted patio door locks at the top and bottom of the door frame. These will stop intruders lifting the door off its track from outside the house. As you drill the holes in the doors to accept the bolts, make sure that they don't come too close to the edges of the sealed double glazing units.

More strength for hinges

Security hinges are an alternative to hinge bolts for outward-opening doors. When the door is closed, punched-out tabs on the hinge leaves interlock, preventing the door being lifted away from the frame even if the hinge pins are removed.

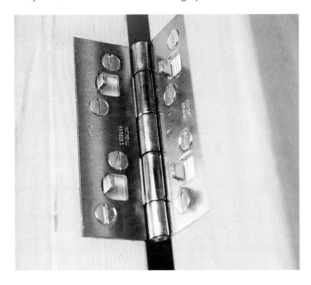

Secure the hinged edge too

Fit hinge bolts to prevent a front or back door from being forced, and to stop outward-opening french doors from being lifted out if their hinge pins have been removed. Two bolts are usually fitted, one near to each hinge. Insert the fixed bolt in the door edge and drill a hole in the frame to receive it. Make sure that the bolt is set centrally in the edge of the door, or it won't fit cleanly into the hole in the frame as the door closes.

1 Use power drill and flat wood bit, or brace and auger, to drill hole for bolt barrel

2 Insert bolt in its hole, then draw round faceplate and chisel out a shallow recess for it

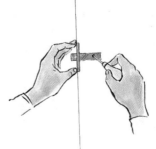

3 Hold bolt against face of frame and mark position of keyhole. Drill hole, fit bolt in place and test key operation

4 Fit keyhole cover plate. Operate bolt to mark position of receiver on frame, drill hole and fit receiver plate

hardware

glazing Fix a broken window

Emergency cover
Seal a cracked pane temporarily with transparent waterproof glazing tape, applied to the outside. If the pane is smashed, cover the whole window with heavy-gauge polythene secured by timber battens nailed round the frame.
If good security is vital, nail a sheet of plywood across the window frame until you can replace the glass.

Protection from cuts
Always wear thick leather shoes when removing a broken pane or cutting glass, in case a jagged piece falls on your foot. Protect your hands and eyes by wearing heavy gloves and safety spectacles or goggles.

Tape a cracked pane
If glass is cracked but intact, crisscross the pane with masking tape to lessen the risk of flying shards when you break it, then use a hacking knife to remove the putty. Break the pane from inside with a hammer and a block of wood. Lift out large shards first, then chip out and remove the smaller pieces.

The best glass for the job

Light and privacy
Choose patterned (obscured) glass where you need to let light in but at the same time retain your privacy–in bathroom windows and glazed front doors, for example.

Safe and secure
Use safety glass in doors and for any fixed panes prone to impact damage.
Toughened glass shatters into harmless granules if broken. It must be ordered to size because it can't be cut or drilled once it has been made.
Laminated glass, which can be cut in the usual way, is made of two layers of glass sandwiching a plastic interlayer. It cracks but doesn't fragment because the interlayer holds the pieces together. It also makes good security glazing.
Safety wired glass is often used in fire doors to reduce the rate of spread of fire. It should not be confused with ordinary wired glass, which has little security value.

TOUGHENED GLASS

LAMINATED GLASS

WIRED GLASS

Reduce glare and fading

Prevent soft furnishings, rugs and paintings in sunlit rooms from fading by installing laminated glass. The plastic interlayer filters out most of the sun's damaging ultraviolet rays.
Cut the heat build-up in a south-facing conservatory by using tinted or coated solar control glass (below).

Safety glass is essential

If you are carrying out improvements or alterations to your home that involve the installation of new glazed doors and windows, you must use safety glass in areas that are prone to impact damage to comply with Building Regulations. For full details of where it must be fitted, contact your local authority Building Control office or ask a glass merchant.

Allow for escape from fire

Include an opening casement big enough to act as a fire escape when choosing new windows, especially for upstairs rooms. Fixed double-glazed panes are very difficult to break in an emergency. Keep the keys to window locks to hand in each room and make sure everyone knows where they are.

Cover with safety film

You can make conventional glass in high-risk areas safer by covering it on the inside with a special strong self-adhesive plastic film which holds it together if broken.

glazing Keeping heat in and noise out

Choose extra efficiency

Fitting sealed double-glazed units in any window will reduce heat losses.
Cut these even more by specifying the use of low-emissivity glass in any new units you are ordering. Its thin metallic surface coating helps to reflect heat back into the room. It also reflects away heat from the sun, reducing unwanted heat gain in the room without cutting the level of light it receives.

Watch the weight

Replacing existing glass with double glazing means doubling the weight of any opening casements. You may have to fit stronger hinges to carry the extra load if the casements sag and bind.
If you have sash windows, the sashes will be carefully counterbalanced by matching weights. Putting in double-glazing units will make the sashes difficult to open—and to keep open—unless you replace the weights with heavier ones.

Secondary choice

Fit secondary glazing for thermal insulation inside windows that are an irreplaceable part of the building's architecture, such as leaded lights or Thirties-style curved steel windows. It can be set close to the glass to leave a narrow internal sill.

Step into the frame

If existing window frames are sound but their glazing rebates are too shallow to accept standard square-edges units, you can overcome the problem by fitting so-called stepped units instead. With these, the outer layer of glass sits in the glazing rebate as a single pane does, while the body of the unit fits within the casement frame. Order them made to measure from a glass merchant.

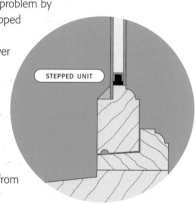

STEPPED UNIT

Roofing with plastic

Pick polycarbonate sheeting for roofing conservatories. It is light but strong, and current types neither discolour in sunlight nor become brittle with age. The triple-wall version has two layers of enclosed cells for insulation, so it keeps in heat more effectively than the original twin-walled product with its single layer of cells. It is even stronger and more rigid too.

Measure and cut with confidence

Measuring for new glass

When sizing old windows for new glass, measure the height and width of the openings at several points in case they're not exactly square. Then size the glass according to the smallest dimensions. Deduct a fitting and expansion allowance of 3 mm from the exact width and height of openings when you are cutting the glass yourself, but if you're ordering it, give the glass merchants the tight measurements and let them make the allowance.

Soaking up the sound

Double-glazed units keep out traffic and aeroplane noise better than single glazing—but not much better. For effective sound insulation you need secondary glazing—an additional glass layer inside the existing glazing and up to 200 mm (8 in) away from it. Since the inner panes must be openable for ventilation, and as a means of escape, they are usually fitted into a sliding track mounted within the window opening.
For optimum performance, the secondary glazing should use glass of a different thickness from the existing glazing, and acoustic tiles should be stuck to the top, bottom and sides of the window opening between the two layers of glazing.

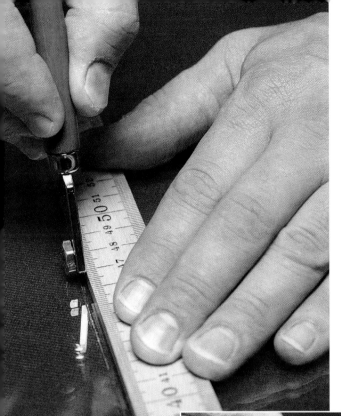

Protect your hands

Glass can break under its own weight, so always carry it on edge–but not tucked under your arm, which is dangerous. Wear leather work gloves, and to cushion your palms even more slit two short lengths of garden hose and slip them over the edge of the glass where you are going to grip it.

Making a paper template

If an opening is an unusual shape, taking accurate measurements can be difficult. To get round this problem, remove the old glass and tape a piece of paper over the outside of the frame. Then trace the edges of the rebate (or mark them onto the back of the paper from the inside). Remove the paper and cut along the marked lines to make an exact template for the replacement.

Listen for the sizzle

Before cutting glass, lay a blanket on a bench or table surface. Position the ruler to allow for the width of the cutter's shoulder, then score the glass with one smooth movement (top). Listen to the sound: if the cutter sizzles, you are applying the correct pressure. White flakes of glass mean you're pressing too hard, and a dull scraping sound shows that the cutter is blunt. **Fracture the glass** by lifting it and tapping the underside of the scored line with the cutter (centre). Then slip a pencil lengthways under the scored line at each end and press down gently on either side to snap the glass.

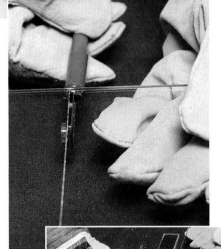

Nibble edges away

Glazier's pliers break off thin slivers of glass better than the notch on a glass cutter. Whichever tool you use, press down along the scored line, not up.

Taking a rubbing

To size a replacement piece of glass for a leaded window, carefully lever up the lead strips until they are sticking out at 90°. Then hold a piece of paper across the opening and take a rubbing of the lead strips. Flatten the lead strips with a small strip of hardwood, once the new piece of glass is sealed.

Clean with meths

Wipe a piece of glass with a clean rag dampened with methylated spirits just before you're ready to cut it. The meths gets rid of any greasy fingerprints and dust, and encourages the cutter to glide smoothly across the glass surface. Mark the cutting measurements onto the glass with a felt-tip pen, and wipe away any splinters of glass after cutting.

glazing Get the hang of using putty

Is the putty compatible?

Use linseed-oil putty on wooden frames and acrylic or universal putty for metal ones. Putty can cause laminated glass to discolour and the seals of double-glazed units to break down, so seek advice if you're fitting either of these.

Prime the rebate first

On wooden frames, apply wood primer to any bare wood in the rebate before fitting the glass. Otherwise the oil in the putty will be absorbed, causing it to dry too quickly and crack.

Seal against condensation

Press a bed of putty around the rebate before putting the glass in place. Push the pane firmly against the putty until it squeezes up and makes a continuous seal against condensation behind the glass. Then tap a couple of glazing sprigs into each of the four sides to hold the glass in place before puttying the outside.

Get a workable consistency

Dust your hands with talc to stop the putty sticking to them, then knead it on a sheet of absorbent paper to remove excess oil and get a smooth, even consistency. Don't work the putty on newspaper; the printer's ink will stain it black.

Be a smooth operator

Keep the blade of your putty knife clean and shiny to stop more putty sticking to it as you work. Dipping it in a container of clean water from time to time will also help.

Hold the glass securely

Tap in glazing sprigs (small headless nails) to hold the glass while the putty hardens, by sliding the head of your pin hammer flat against the glass. Fix sprigs every 200 mm (8 in) or so, and knock them well in so they won't catch your putty knife as you apply the putty.
Spring clips secure the glass in metal windows. If you need any replacements, take an existing clip along to your glass merchant for matching.

Finish with beads

You don't have to use putty. A simple alternative is to secure the glass with hardwood beads. Cut and mitre the beads individually, and number them so you know which goes where. Apply putty or glazing sealant to the inner faces of the beads before pressing them into place and securing them with nails or brass screws.

Practice makes perfect

Once you have pressed the putty into place, tilt the putty knife so its straight edge rests on the glass and the side of the blade is against the edge of the rebate. Press down firmly, then draw the knife along one edge in a continuous movement, not stopping until you reach a corner. The result will be a neatly bevelled bead of putty.

REPLACING A PANE OF GLASS

1 Remove broken pane and putty using hammer and old chisel or hacking knife

2 Press thin bed of putty all around rebate to seal back of glass to frame

3 Place new pane in rebate and press around edges to bed it firmly on putty

4 Tap in sprigs, apply putty and smooth off all round with putty knife

glazing

WEIGHT BOX

PARTING BEAD

PULLEY

OUTER SASH

SASH CORD

WEIGHT

INNER SASH

STAFF BEAD

sliding sashes
Restore to working order

Prise out the staff bead

You have to take the sashes out of the frame to replace broken cords. Start by prising out the staff bead at each side to release the inner sash. Use a wide chisel and begin at the centre of the bead to avoid damaging the corner mitres. If the beads split as you prise them out, keep the pieces. You can then use them as a pattern for cutting replacements.
Number the pieces and the corresponding frame edges if the old beads are intact and you intend to reuse them.

Don't drop the weights

If you cut an old sash cord, the weight will crash down inside its box at the side of the frame, taking the end of the cord with it. To avoid this, pull each sash down as far as it will go, and tie a length of string to each cord (below left). Then cut the cords (right) and lower the weights to the bottom of their boxes, letting the strings run over the pulleys. Lift the sash away from the frame. Leave the strings in position over the pulleys, so they can be used later to draw the new sash cords up inside the weight boxes and out over the pulleys.

Replace the parting beads

To release the outer sash, you have to remove the parting beads–narrow strips of wood at each side of the frame, which hold the two sashes apart. They are usually covered in paint and may have been nailed in place, so you will probably have to split them to get them out and then fit new parting beads. Use a narrow wood chisel or an old screwdriver to clean out the grooves in the frame into which they fit.

New cords all round

If one sash cord is broken, replace all four. The others will be worn, and this will save you having to repeat the repair in the near future. Look at the pulleys too. If they are old and caked with paint, unscrew them and prise them out so they can be replaced at the same time.

Finding the pockets

To get at the weights, locate the pocket covers–small removable panels in the sides of the frame near the bottom of each weight box. If layers of paint hide them, look for the saw lines which mark the edges of the pockets. Some covers are held in place with a screw, others with a nail that has to be prised out.

Label your weights

Although all sash weights look similar, the ones operating the outer sash may be a slightly different weight from those working the inner one. When you are replacing the cords, label the weights as you remove them so you know which ones belong to which sash.

STAGES IN
FITTING SASH CORDS

1 Prise off staff bead, lift out inner sash and cut through cords. Remove parting bead and free outer sash too

2 Measure and cut new cords, tie on string and weight, pass over pulleys and drop down to bottom of weight boxes

3 Tie each cord to its weight with a figure-of-eight knot and tuck into hole in weight. Melt cut ends of synthetic cord in flame of lighted match to prevent fraying

4 Nail sash cords into grooves. Replace outer sash in frame first, then inner one

sliding sashes

sliding sashes
Restore to working order

Stretch fibre cord

Polypropylene sash cord is the best type to use, because it doesn't rot or stretch. If you have to use traditional fibre sash cord, always stretch it before fitting it. If you don't, the weights will slowly stretch it until they touch the bottom of their boxes, and this will prevent the sashes from opening and closing properly.

Tie one end of the cord to a fixed object (a tree, for example), then pay out about 4 m (13 ft) of cord and pull on it with all your weight. When it won't stretch any more, untie the stretched length and cut it off. Repeat the process to stretch further lengths.

Guiding new cord into the box frame

If the old cords have dropped back into the weight boxes, tie some string to the end of the new cord. Then tie a screw, small enough to pass over the pulley, to the other end of the string. Push the screw over the pulley so it drops inside the weight box, pulling the string behind it. Reach into the pocket for the string and pull it to draw the cord over the pulley. Tie a loose knot in the other end of the cord so it can't pass the pulley while you are tying on the weights.

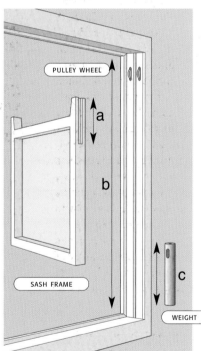

How much cord?

Measure the length of the groove which holds the cord in the side of the sash (a) and add 200 mm (8 in). Measure from the pulley wheel to the top of the sill (b) and subtract the length of the weight (c). Calculate a + 200 + b − c to find the cord length you need.

Remedies for rattles

Sashes rattle when they are a loose fit in the frame. If the inner sash is at fault, reposition the staff bead so it's closer to the face of the sash. Part-drive the fixing nails and test whether the rattle is cured by sliding the sash up and down a few times. Then drive them fully home.

Fit a fitch catch (right) if the outer sash is rattling. Its cam-shaped design draws the two sashes tightly together when they are closed. Another type–the Brighton catch–has a knurled knob on a threaded bolt and acts in a similar way.

Dual screws–a security device for sash windows–will also hold sashes firm and help to prevent rattles (see page 102).

Don't nail too high

If you nail the cord too close to the top of the sashes, it will bind on the pulleys and the sashes won't slide all the way up. Measure from the underside of the top of the frame to a point 38 mm (1½ in) below the pulley wheel. Position the top cord nails the same distance down the grooves in the sash sides.

Let a wedge take the strain

After tying the weights on, pull each one up until it stops against the back of its pulley. Then let it down by about 25 mm (1 in) and jam each cord in its pulley with a small wedge, while you nail the cords to the sashes. When you have finished, remove the wedges and let the sash close.

repairs Treating rotten woodwork

Checking the danger areas

Wet rot develops wherever rainwater gets trapped. Two of the commonest danger areas are the undersides of windowsills and the bottoms of exterior door frames. Joints open up as the wet wood swells, allowing water to soak into the vulnerable end grain. Then paint and varnish fail and rot soon takes hold.

Identifying dry rot

Dry rot rarely affects doors and windows; it needs poorly ventilated damp conditions, such as those found under a wooden ground floor. However, dry rot can spread into the hollow box frames on traditional sash windows if they are not well maintained. Many Victorian houses also still have vertically sliding shutters which extend into the underfloor space when they are not in use, and dry rot can get into these from the underfloor void.

Prospect for rotten wood

Poke suspect woodwork with a screwdriver to assess the extent of the rot. Remove blistered paint from sound wood so trapped moisture can escape and the wood can start to dry.

Let the wood dry out

After removing all the rotten timber, allow the newly-exposed surfaces to dry out thoroughly before splicing in a new piece of wood or using a filler. This process can take a week or two if the wood has absorbed a lot of moisture. However, you can speed it up with frequent short blasts from a hot-air gun. **Tape a piece of plastic sheet** over the wood to keep the rain off while it dries out, but don't make this airtight. Air needs to circulate freely underneath it.

Finding a replacement sill

Cutting out and replacing a wooden windowsill, or a section of one, is not a difficult job. Take a section of the original sill to your timber merchant, who will use it as a guide to help you select a matching replacement.

Preservation treatment

Always read the label on the tin before using any wood preservative, because some types can corrode metal fittings and affect glued joints in door and window frames, while others can kill nearby plants if splashed onto them. When applying preservative, rubber gloves, goggles and a face mask are the minimum essential safety wear. For complete protection, especially when you're putting preservative on with a spray gun rather than a brush, wear a disposable coverall with an elasticated hood and use a battery-powered respirator, both available from plant hire shops.

repairs Treating rotten woodwork

Using filler or adding new wood

The easiest way to replace small areas of timber destroyed by wet rot is with a proprietary wood repair system (see below). But when the damage is extensive, or the wood is varnished or stained and a repair with filler cannot easily be disguised, cut out the rot and patch in a new piece of wood.

Seal the gaps

To prevent rain getting in between a new door or window frame and the surrounding masonry, fill the gap between the two with a flexible frame sealant (see page 353). This is available in white or brown to match painted and stained woodwork, and can be overpainted in another colour once it has formed a surface skin.

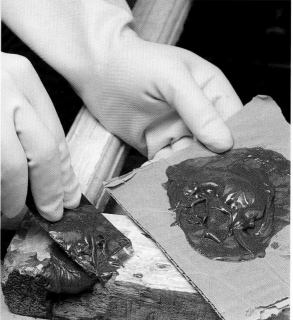

Two-stage repair

Patch small areas of rotten wood using a proprietary repair system consisting of liquid wood hardener and a specially formulated exterior wood filler.

After cutting away all the rot, put on rubber gloves and brush a generous coat of hardener onto the area to be filled, using an old paintbrush (left).

Spread the wood filler with the plastic spatula provided (right), overfilling the repair slightly so you can sand down the dried filler flush with the surrounding surface. Work quickly: the filler begins to harden after about 5 minutes at normal temperatures and even more quickly in warm weather.

Repairing door frames

The bottoms of exterior door frames often start to rot because moisture gets into the end grain of the uprights. Cut out the rotten wood, sawing upwards at an angle of 45°; this makes the repair stronger. If the bottom of the post is anchored to the door sill or the ground by a metal dowel, you will have to split the rotten wood away with a wood chisel. Then cut off the dowel flush with the sill or the ground with a hacksaw, and glue and screw the new piece of wood in place, having primed and painted it first.

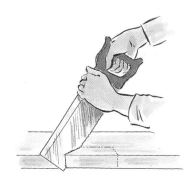

Keep rot at bay

You can help prevent rot from attacking repaired woodwork by drilling holes at roughly 50 mm (2 in) intervals in the surrounding wood, inserting preservative pellets and filling the holes. These pellets slowly release preservative into the wood, destroying any remaining rot spores and preventing future attacks.

Protective coating

Before fitting new doors and windows, paint those surfaces you won't be able to get at once the item is in place—the bottom edge of a door, for example.

1 Cut wedge-shaped piece out of sill, extending at least 50 mm (2 in) beyond rot

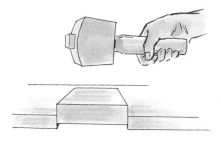

2 Mark outline of cut-out on replacement wood, then saw insert to shape and test for fit

3 Spread adhesive on mating surfaces and tap patch into place. Plane or sand patch flush with sill, then fill joints, prime and paint over it

repairs

plumbing

systems Controlling the flow

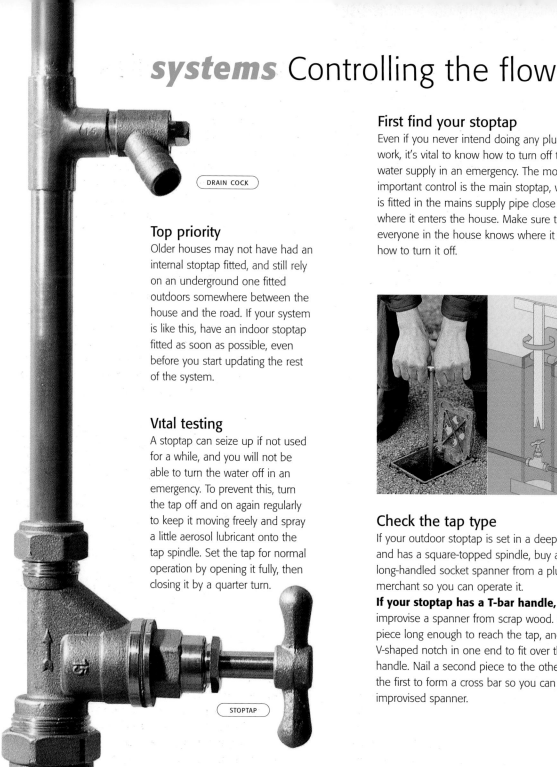

DRAIN COCK

Top priority

Older houses may not have had an internal stoptap fitted, and still rely on an underground one fitted outdoors somewhere between the house and the road. If your system is like this, have an indoor stoptap fitted as soon as possible, even before you start updating the rest of the system.

Vital testing

A stoptap can seize up if not used for a while, and you will not be able to turn the water off in an emergency. To prevent this, turn the tap off and on again regularly to keep it moving freely and spray a little aerosol lubricant onto the tap spindle. Set the tap for normal operation by opening it fully, then closing it by a quarter turn.

STOPTAP

First find your stoptap

Even if you never intend doing any plumbing work, it's vital to know how to turn off the water supply in an emergency. The most important control is the main stoptap, which is fitted in the mains supply pipe close to where it enters the house. Make sure that everyone in the house knows where it is and how to turn it off.

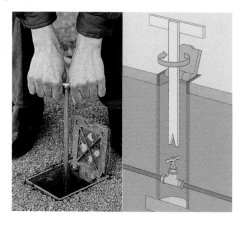

Check the tap type

If your outdoor stoptap is set in a deep hole and has a square-topped spindle, buy a special long-handled socket spanner from a plumbers' merchant so you can operate it.

If your stoptap has a T-bar handle, you can improvise a spanner from scrap wood. Cut a piece long enough to reach the tap, and saw a V-shaped notch in one end to fit over the tap handle. Nail a second piece to the other end of the first to form a cross bar so you can turn the improvised spanner.

Trace the pipe runs

If you have a cold-water storage tank, look for on-off valves (called gatevalves) on the outlet pipes. One allows you to cut off the supply to the cold taps; the other controls the supply to the hot-water cylinder. Identify which is which by tracing the pipe runs if you can. If you can't, lean into the tank and insert a proprietary plastic bung in one of the outlet holes. Then check which taps run dry, and label the valves accordingly.

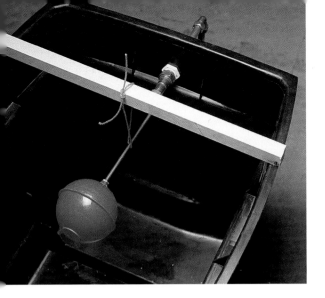

Coping without valves

If there are no gatevalves on the outlets from your cold-water storage tank, or if the existing valves are jammed in the open position, lay a batten across the tank and tie the arm of the float-operated valve to it. This will keep the valve closed while you empty the tank by opening all the taps supplied from it. Once the tank is empty, no water will flow from either your cold or hot taps.

If you need to drain a pipe in a hurry–because it's sprung a leak, for example–you may not have time to wait for the tank to empty. In this case, bung a carrot into the relevant outlet pipe and open the taps to drain the affected pipe.

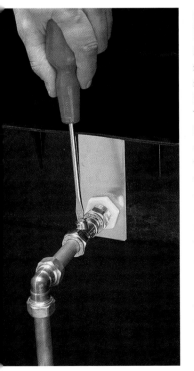

Look for local valves

Modern plumbing systems have small shut-off valves on individual supply pipes. These allow you to isolate a tap, a float-operated valve or a water-using appliance without having to turn off the mains supply or drain down tanks and cisterns. You operate them by inserting a screwdriver blade or a slim coin in the slot and rotating it by a quarter turn. The valve is open when the slot is in line with the pipe direction.

Water supplies

Safe to drink?

Unless the cold-water tank is fairly new and well sealed, you should not drink water from taps supplied by the tank. Always take drinking water from the kitchen cold tap (or any other tap which you know is connected to the mains supply). If you have old lead pipes and live in a soft-water area, run the tap for a while in the morning to drain off water that has been standing in the pipes overnight, before filling a glass or kettle.

Replace a rusty tank

Once the galvanising breaks down on an old galvanised water tank, it will start to rust. If this happens to yours, have it replaced with a new plastic tank. Flexible round polythene tanks can be crushed for transit so they will fit through even a small loft hatch. The old tank can be disconnected, moved to a corner of the loft and left there if you don't want the job of cutting it up and removing it from the roof space.

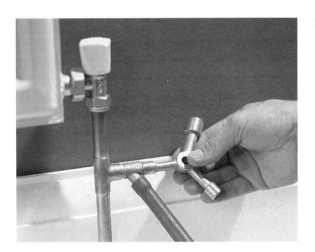

Locate the drain cocks

To carry out certain plumbing jobs, you do not just have to turn off the water supply; you also have to empty the pipework of water. The plumbing and heating system will have several special fittings called drain cocks, where you can attach a hose and open the fitting to allow the water to flow out.

On the plumbing system, one should be fitted immediately on the house side of the rising main stoptap, and another near the base of the hot-water cylinder.

On the central-heating system there may be several drain cocks, fitted at the low points of the system (usually next to radiators and the boiler). Make sure that you know where all yours are.

systems

119

systems Home heating

Hot-water options

If you have an old-fashioned heating system relying on gravity circulation, it is not economical to use the boiler to heat your hot water in summer, when the central heating is not needed. It is better to use the electric immersion heater in the cylinder. Connecting it to a time clock will ensure that you always have hot water when you need it.

Obey safety rules

Call a qualified fitter

It's dangerous and illegal to work on any gas appliance or pipework unless you are competent to do so. Have all gas installation and servicing work in your home carried out by a qualified fitter who is a member of CORGI (Council for Registered Gas Installers). You'll find local firms with CORGI registration listed in the telephone directory.

Detect deadly gas

Gas boilers and other gas appliances should be serviced every year. Never block up air vents, because an air supply is essential for complete combustion. When appliances are not working properly, they can emit deadly carbon monoxide gas. Carbon monoxide alarms are inexpensive and can be fitted near boilers, wall-mounted water heaters or gas fires. Choose one that complies with British Standard BS7860.

Avoid the risk of scalding

If your heating system is fully pumped, there will be zone valves on the circuit pipework to divert water to the hot cylinder or the radiators, depending on which needs heat the most. Keep the cylinder thermostat set at no higher than 60°C to avoid scalding water coming from the taps, and adjust the room temperature as required using the room thermostat.

Earth all metalwork

All the metal plumbing and heating fixtures and appliances in your house—the circuit pipework, the radiators and any metal sinks and baths—must for safety be cross-bonded to earth with special screw-on earth clamps. If you are in doubt about whether your system is properly bonded in this way, have it checked by a qualified electrician.

pipes Working with copper and plastic

Identifying the old

Houses built before the late 1940s may still have lead or steel pipework. Identify which is which by scraping the surface with a knife (lead is soft) and by examining the joints. Joints in lead pipe are smooth and bulbous; those in steel pipes have raised collars. Lead pipes should be replaced, especially if you live in a soft-water area. Ask your local water company for advice.

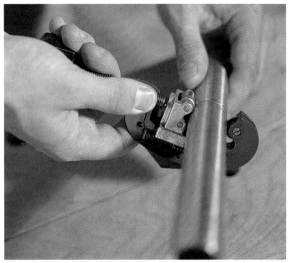

Using a pipe cutter

If you are tackling a large plumbing job, a pipe cutter will cut through both copper and plastic supply pipe with minimum effort. Fit the cutter on the pipe, tighten the clamp until the wheel just scores the surface, then rotate the cutter around the pipe. Tighten the clamp after each rotation until the cut is complete. Then use the V-shaped reamer on the end of the tool to remove the internal burr.

With plastic supply pipes, you may need to finish the cut with a trimming knife after scoring the pipe with the cutter. Alternatively, you can use special secateurs for plastic pipe.

Cutting with a jigsaw

You can cut through pipes with an electric jigsaw. Choose a fine-toothed blade for metal or plastic pipes, and clamp the pipe in a vice or in the jaws of a portable workbench.

Cut waste pipe square

It's easier to cut plastic waste pipes squarely if you hold them in a mitre box. Use a full-size hacksaw—the frame of a junior one will foul on the box—and be sure to keep the blade vertical.

Coping with a hacksaw

Hold copper pipe in a vice and cut it with a junior hacksaw. Wrap a strip of paper or masking tape around the pipe at the cutting position as a guide to help you to get a square cut. Use a file to remove rough burrs from the pipe end.

pipes Making joints

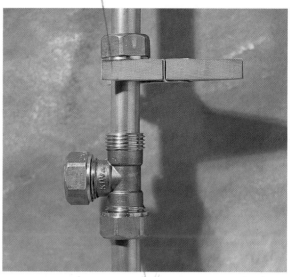

Springing into shape

When bending a pipe with a spring, overbend it slightly, then bend it back to the angle you want; this makes the spring easier to withdraw from the bent pipe. Tie a piece of string to the spring before bending a long pipe, so you can pull it out again when you have finished; with short pipes the spring will protrude from the end. Bending springs for pipes 12 mm or less in diameter are slid over the pipe, not inside it.

Stop the drop

When you are inserting a compression tee into an existing vertical pipe run, cut the pipe at the connection point. Then thread the cap nuts and olives onto the pipe and use clothes pegs to stop them sliding down while you fit the cut pipe ends into the tee. Do up the lower cap nut first, then let the upper nut and olive drop down and tighten them too.

Imperial to metric

Copper pipe went metric in the 1970s, but older houses still have pipework in imperial sizes. If you plan to connect into old pipe with soldered capillary fittings, you will need special adaptors for all pipes, whatever the size. **Metric compression fittings** connect 15 mm and 28 mm pipes directly to ½ in and 1 in pipes. However, to connect new 22 mm pipe to old ¾ in, you will have to replace one of the metric olives with a metric/imperial conversion olive.

Pushing together

Copper and plastic supply and heating pipes can be joined with plastic fittings into which you simply push the pipe ends. The pipes are locked in place by steel-toothed rings inside the fitting, and can be freed by releasing a ring round the pipe opening. These fittings are not suitable for stainless-steel or chrome-plated pipes as these are too shiny for the toothed ring to grip.

Bending large pipes

Bending 22 mm or 28 mm pipe by hand is hard work. Consider hiring a pipe bending tool if you have a lot of bends to make in large-diameter copper pipe. Alternatively, you can make the pipe more flexible by heating the area of the bend with a blowlamp until the metal glows red. Allow the pipe to cool, then use a bending spring.

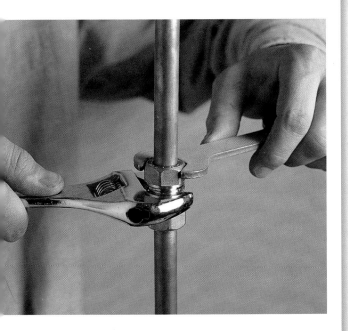

Compression fittings for solder-free joints

For most DIY pipework, compression fittings assembled with a spanner are easier to use than soldered capillary fittings. Before assembling the fitting, wrap a couple of turns of plumber's PTFE tape over the thread to reduce the risk of a leak. It is a good idea to use PTFE tape on any plumbing fittings that screw together, to ensure that the interlocking threads form a watertight join.

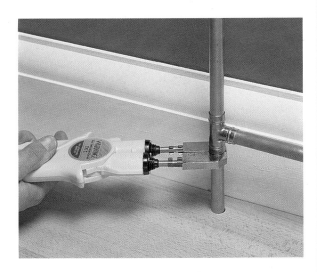

Clamping capillary fittings

You can make pipe joints with soldered capillary fittings in seconds using these cunning electric tongs. They work like a pair of soldering irons, clamping round the fitting and heating it up quickly and evenly. You change the clamp heads to suit the size of pipe you're soldering.

STAGES IN JOINING COPPER PIPES

1 Dismantle old fitting, noting which way olives face. Slip nuts and olives over pipe ends

2 Push pipe into fitting until it meets internal-stop. Push up olive and then hand-tighten first nut

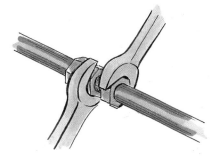

3 Repeat for other olive and nut. Then use a spanner to tighten each nut one full turn while holding fitting with a second spanner

pipes

123

pipes Connecting up

Bridge plastic fittings

If you use any plastic fittings on metal pipe runs, these will break the earth continuity (see page 120). It is vitally important to bridge every plastic fitting. Attach earth clamps to the pipes on either side of the fitting and link them with a short length of 4 mm² earth cable: unless all metal supply pipework is bonded to earth, there is a risk of severe electric shock if an electrical fault occurs and makes the pipe live.

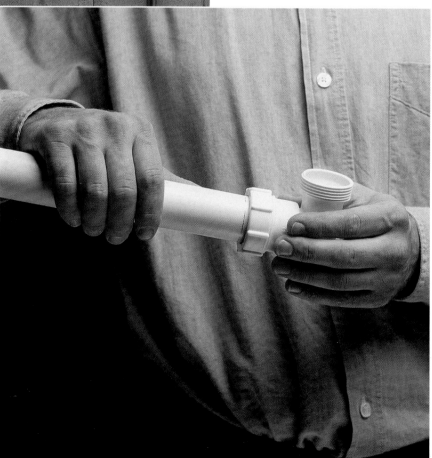

Allow space for expansion

Plastic waste pipes expand as hot water runs through them, so you need to make an allowance for this. If you are using compression or push-fit fittings, make up each joint and then pull each pipe out of the fitting by about 3 mm (⅛ in). With rigid solvent-weld fittings, fit a flexible expansion coupling in the pipe run about every 2.4 m (8 ft).

Line up the joints

When making up a run of pipework with solvent-weld joints, assemble the run dry first of all and make sure the joints line up, especially elbows and tees. Make small pencil marks on both pipe and fitting at every joint to help you to align them correctly as you weld them together.

Easy assembly

Make compression and push-fit joints on waste pipe runs easier to assemble by chamfering the cut end of each pipe slightly, so it slips into the O-ring inside the fitting without snagging on it. Smear a little silicone grease on the end of the pipe so it slides into the fitting more easily.

Choosing plastic

Some plastic pipes can be used for domestic hot and cold-water supplies. Look for polybutylene (Hep$_2$O) pipe and cross-linked polyethylene (PEX pipe). These pipes are flexible, and because they are available in relatively long lengths (Hep$_2$O comes in coils too), you do not need many joints. Connections can be made with standard brass compression fittings or with special plastic push-fit ones.

STAGES IN SOLVENT WELDING JOINTS

1 Assemble joint dry, and make register mark on both pipe and fitting if precise joint alignment is essential

2 Roughen end of pipe and inside of fitting with medium-grade abrasive paper

3 Brush solvent-weld cement into fitting, taking care not to get any on outside

4 Push pipe into fitting, give it a slight twist and align register marks. Then hold joint still for 10 seconds

pipes

pipes Fixing leaks

Quick fix for a leaking fitting
If you need to stop a leak without dismantling the fitting, use an external leak sealer. Epoxy resin repair putty sets quickly but is very difficult to remove later. Silicone paste sealant is better if the fitting is a compression type. Turn off the water, undo the fitting and warm the pipe slightly to dry it out. Smear on the sealant and reassemble the joint.

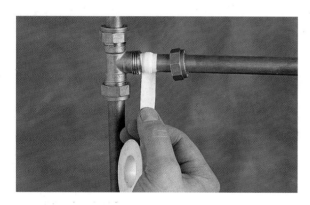

Wrap around
If a compression fitting still drips after you've tried tightening the nuts, dismantle it and start again. Turn off the water and drain the pipe. Then undo the nuts and slip the pipes out of the fitting. Wrap the brass olives with two turns of PTFE tape. Then reassemble the fitting and tighten the nuts.

Flux for flow
If you get a leak from a soldered joint, drain the pipe and use heat from your blowlamp or hot-air gun to dry it out thoroughly. Feed a little self-cleaning flux into the warmed joint. Then reheat the joint to melt the existing solder. The flux will help it to flow into the gaps and seal the joint properly.

Stop leaks with tape
Small leaks in pipes can be contained with self-amalgamating tape. Turn off the water, then wrap the tape tightly around the pipe like a bandage. It will knit together to form an effective seal.

Leave the nail in place
If you accidentally put a nail through a pipe while fixing floorboards, leave the nail where it is. It will form an almost perfect seal while you turn off the water and drain the pipework ready for repair.

Emergency clamp
Keep a proprietary pipe clamp (above) in your tool kit for emergencies. It can be fitted to a burst pipe in seconds with just a screwdriver. For a temporary solution use a piece of garden hose and some hose clips or strong wire. First turn off the water. Split the hose, fit it over the pipe and secure with the hose clips or loops of wire, twisted tight with pliers.

Freeze a burst pipe
A pipe-freezing kit lets you repair a burst pipe without having to turn the water off and drain down the system. Flatten the pipe upstream of the damage to stop the flow, then freeze the pipe a little farther upstream. Make sure you have replacement pipe and fittings to hand. Cut out the damaged section downstream from the frozen zone and make the repair as quickly as you can.

Turn the nuts
When a compression fitting starts to leak, try tightening each nut very slightly. Don't tighten it by more than a quarter turn, because you might squash the olive inside and make the leak worse.

INDICATOR DISC

RETAINING SCREW

HANDLE

SHROUD

SPINDLE

HEADGEAR

TAP WASHER

taps Getting at the works

Plug in first

Before starting to dismantle a tap, turn off its water supply and put the plug in the plughole. This will prevent any small parts you might drop from disappearing into the trap beneath the appliance.

Washers or discs?

Traditional taps have a mechanism that moves a rubber washer against or away from the water inlet to stop or start the flow. Many modern taps contain a pair of ceramic discs with holes through them, one of which rotates to control the flow. Turn the tap on fully to find out which type you have. A ceramic disc tap needs just a quarter turn, a traditional tap at least two turns.

Removing the handle

Some tap handles can be pulled off, but most have a small screw to retain them. Look for it on the side of a traditional (cross-top) tap handle. On a modern shrouded-head tap, it is usually beneath the hot/cold indicator disc. Gently prise this off to reveal the screw, which may also retain a small washer.

Reverse the washer

If you don't have a suitable replacement tap washer, remove the old one, turn it over and refit it. It will last a little longer, until you have a chance to get a new one of the correct size.

taps

Turn on the heat

Play a hot-air gun over a stuck tap shroud to warm it up. This should make the metal expand and break the grip of the threads. If it doesn't, squirt a little silicone lubricating fluid into the thread. You might need to repeat the heating and lubricating once or twice before the thread is freed. Don't try this on taps fitted to a plastic basin or bath, however, as the heat could damage it.

TAP TAIL

SPACER WASHER

HEADGEAR

TAP WASHER

Soften the bite

When dismantling chrome or gold-plated taps, it's a good idea to wrap the jaws of your adjustable spanner with a few turns of PVC insulating tape to stop them damaging the plating.

TAP TAIL

taps Getting at the works

When the handle is stuck

If the cross-top handle won't come off an old fashioned shrouded tap, you might be able to remove it by using its shroud to push it off. Remove the screw securing the handle to the spindle and turn the tap on fully. Loosen the shroud and insert a thin spanner round the headgear nut. Then turn the tap handle to off; this action should jack the handle off the spindle.

Keep some spares
Tap washers are very cheap, so you can afford to keep a supply in your tool kit. They are still made in just two imperial sizes—½ in and ¾ in. The larger size fits bath taps, the smaller size everything else.

Fitting a new washer

Try a domed washer

If the seating (the water inlet inside the tap against which the washer closes) is worn, a standard washer may not make a watertight seal against it. Try fitting a domed washer instead. This sits inside the seating and effectively changes the sealing point. The only drawback is that it takes several more turns than usual to open the tap fully for a fast flow rate.

Dissolve scale

The most common cause of jammed headgear nuts in hard-water areas is limescale. Once you have removed the headgear, soak the threaded parts in vinegar, lemon juice or a proprietary scale remover to dissolve the scale. Smear some silicone grease on them to lubricate and protect them before you reassemble the tap.

Bed in an insert

If a domed washer doesn't do the trick, the seating is probably badly corroded. Buy a nylon insert to push into the tap seating and give the washer a new surface to seal against. If you cannot

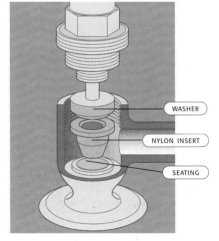

bed the insert all the way into the seating by hand, replace the headgear and turn the tap on and off a few times (before turning the water back on). This will push the insert evenly into place.

Stop weeping

When water oozes up from round the spindle of a tap, the packing gland round it is faulty. You don't have to turn the water off to fix this. Tighten the small hexagonal gland nut on the top of the headgear by half a turn. If the leak persists, remove the gland nut and pack in some PTFE tape pulled into a string. Replace the nut and test the tap.

Protect the pipework and ceramic ware

Remove the brass headgear from the tap body by turning it anticlockwise with a spanner. As you do so, brace the tap with a piece of wood so that it cannot rotate, otherwise the connection between the tap and the pipework may be damaged. Allowing the tap to rotate could also result in a cracked ceramic fitting.

Replacing O-rings

Take it with you

The diverter on a shower mixer tap will drip if the O-rings and washers inside are worn. To replace them, you will have to remove the diverter by turning off both taps then raising the diverter knob and undoing the headgear nut with a spanner. Take the complete unit with you to a plumbers' merchant so you can be sure of obtaining the correct replacement O-rings and washers.

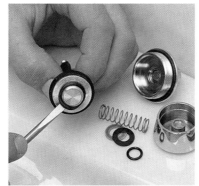

Ringing the changes

Modern taps have O-rings instead of a packing gland. Remove the headgear, hold it securely in one hand and turn the spindle clockwise to unscrew and remove the washer unit. Prise off the old O-ring with a small screwdriver and fit a new one after smearing it with a little silicone grease.

Spouting off

Swivel-spout mixers use one or two O-rings to seal the join between spout and tap body. If they are worn, water will ooze out between the two. To remove the spout, locate and remove the grub screw behind it if there is one. Otherwise turn the spout so it's parallel with the tap body and pull it sharply upwards. Remove the worn O-ring(s) and fit same-size replacement(s), applying a little silicone grease first.

Swapping supplies

Baths, basins and sinks usually have the hot tap on the left and the cold tap on the right. If yours are the other way round and you find this confusing, undo the tap connectors and cut back the supply pipes by 150 mm (6 in) or so. Attach a flexible pipe and tap connector to each pipe, then link each connector to the correct tap. Swap over the hot and cold indicators on the tap handles.

Measure the two tails

Look at the two inlet pipes on a monobloc basin or sink mixer tap before fitting it. If they're 10 mm or 12 mm in diameter, you'll need reducing adaptors to connect them to the hot and cold supplies. But if the pipes are expanded to 15 mm, then standard 15 mm straight coupling will do the job.

HOT TAP

COLD TAP

Check the spacing

When replacing a two-hole mixer tap on an old sink, you may find that the distance between the holes doesn't match the standard separation to which modern mixer taps are made. If this is the case, ask your plumbers' merchant for mixer taps with cranked swivel tails which can cope with a range of non-standard hole separations.

Made for mains

Most imported taps are designed to operate at mains pressure, so do not fit them on appliances supplied by low-pressure water from a cold-water tank or a hot-water cylinder. Water will merely trickle from them.

COLD SUPPLY PIPE

HOT SUPPLY PIPE

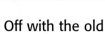

Off with the old

Replacing old taps means disconnecting the supply pipework from the tap tails, which can be difficult (see page 140). For a start, you have to work in a confined space, and the tap connector may be corroded. Apply some penetrating oil to the tap connector nuts, leave it for a while to soak into the threads, then use a crow's-foot spanner (also called a basin wrench) to undo the nuts.

Pick a longer spout

If you are choosing a sink mixer tap to serve a sink with two bowls, pick one with a spout that projects by 230 mm rather than the standard 180 mm to make it easier to fill a kettle or pan.

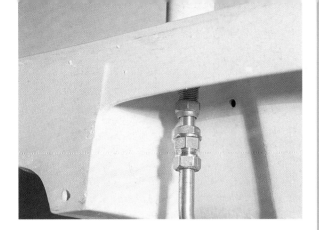

Bridging the gap

Check the length of the tap tails on any new taps you buy. Modern taps have tails around 10 mm (⅜ in) shorter than older types, so you will need adaptors called tap extenders to bridge the gap between them and the existing pipes.

Match the taps to the pressure

British bath and shower mixer taps and valves are designed to use hot and cold water at low pressure. If your bathroom has mains-fed cold water, ask your supplier for taps that can cope with the pressure difference.

Plan for the future

Turning the water off so you can fit new taps often involves finding gatevalves in the loft or draining down the cold-water tank. Take this opportunity to install an in-line isolating or shut-off valve on each supply pipe. Thereafter replacing the washers and any other work on the taps will only involve closing these valves.

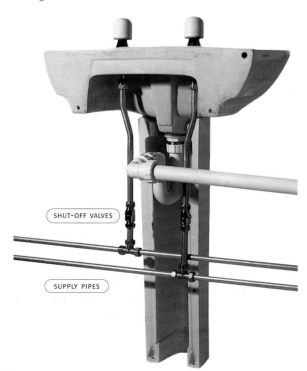

SHUT-OFF VALVES

SUPPLY PIPES

1 Turn off water supply to tap. Then undo nut on tap connector that links supply pipe to tap tail

2 Use a basin wrench to undo backnut on the tap tail

3 Lift out tap and clean away any sealant round the hole. Then offer up the new tap, complete with its gasket

4 Secure the new tap with its backnut and reconnect supply pipe. Use a tap extender if the new tap tail is too short

taps

taps Fixing ceramic disc taps

Dripping discs

Ceramic disc taps were designed to end the need for tap washers, but they can still drip and they cost a lot more to put right. Before buying a new cartridge, remove the existing one–a job that's similar to taking the headgear out of a conventional tap–and fit a thicker O-ring on the base of the cartridge. This pushes the discs together and may stop the drip.

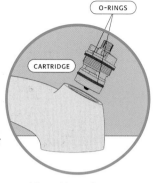

O-RINGS

CARTRIDGE

Changing cartridges

If fitting a thicker O-ring doesn't stop the drip, you have no alternative but to replace the entire cartridge. To get the right spare you need to know the make of tap, which may be stamped on the indicator disc. If it isn't and you have no other way of identifying the manufacturer, remove the cartridge, and take it with you to a plumbers' merchant in the hope of finding a matching spare. Note that cartridges are either left-handed or right-handed, so make sure that your replacement turns on in the same direction as the original.

Water in the garden

Ensure one-way flow

By law, a tap serving a hosepipe must be fitted with a double-check valve to stop back-siphonage (caused by loss of mains pressure) contaminating the mains water supply. You can either fit a tap with an integral check valve (below), or fit a separate valve in the pipework after the indoor stoptap.

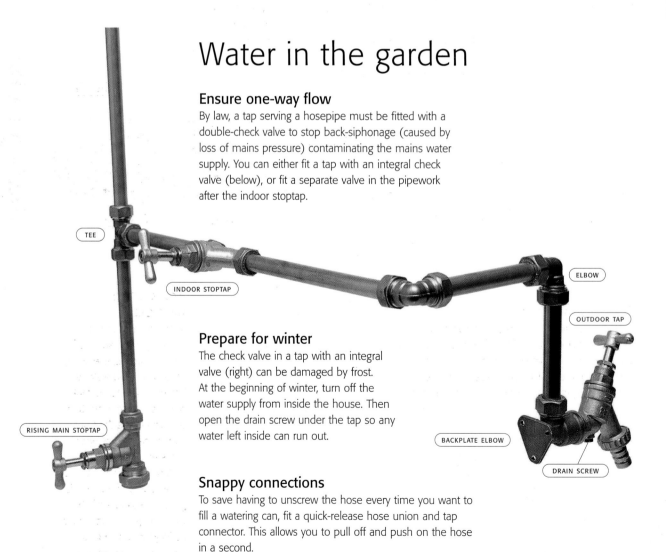

TEE

INDOOR STOPTAP

ELBOW

OUTDOOR TAP

RISING MAIN STOPTAP

BACKPLATE ELBOW

DRAIN SCREW

Prepare for winter

The check valve in a tap with an integral valve (right) can be damaged by frost. At the beginning of winter, turn off the water supply from inside the house. Then open the drain screw under the tap so any water left inside can run out.

Snappy connections

To save having to unscrew the hose every time you want to fill a watering can, fit a quick-release hose union and tap connector. This allows you to pull off and push on the hose in a second.

overflows Trouble with valves

SCREW ADJUSTER

END CAP

PISTON

DIAPHRAGM SEAT

WASHER

WATER OUTLET

DIAPHRAGM

VALVE SEAT

BACK NUTS

FLOAT ARM

Diaphragms or pistons?

It's well worth examining the valves in your loft tanks before anything goes wrong with them, so you know which type you have. Newer homes will have diaphragm valves (above), while older homes will probably still have piston-operated ones (below). Diaphragm valves are usually made of plastic, while piston-operated ones are brass.

END CAP

PISTON

VALVE BODY

WASHER

BACK NUTS

VALVE SEAT

UNION NUT

WATER OUTLET

SPLIT PIN

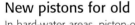

FLOAT ARM

New pistons for old

In hard-water areas, piston-operated valves can grind to a halt because of a build-up of scale inside them. You can dismantle them and clean them out, but it's better to replace an old-style valve with a new diaphragm type, which is more reliable and less likely to scale up and seize.

Beware the big freeze

In cold weather, water escaping down an overflow pipe can freeze, eventually blocking it. If no water is being drawn off, the tank or storage cistern can then overflow inside the house and cause a major flood. If this happens, adjust or replace the ballvalve to stop the water overflowing. It is a good idea to turn off the water supply before winter holidays in case a fault occurs while you're away.

overflows
Problems with appliances

A regular press

The valve in a feed-and-expansion tank operates only if the heating system needs topping up. Because this occurs so rarely, the valve has a tendency to jam in the closed position–a fault that can lead to the heating system running low on water eventually. Check regularly that the valve is operating freely by pressing the float arm down. The tank should be about a third full when the heating system is turned on.

Don't make a splash

The valve in the cold-water storage tank opens and shuts many times a day. If it's a piston-operated type, this heavy wear can cause the washer to perish. Fitting a replacement is easy, but don't try to do the job while leaning over the tank; you are bound to drop and lose a vital component. Unscrew the union nut so you can remove the complete body of the valve and take it to a work surface to replace the washer.

Curing cistern drips

A damp patch on the floor below a toilet cistern fitted with a bottom-entry overflow pipe is probably due to a failed sealing washer where the pipe passes through the base of the cistern. To cure the problem, empty the cistern and disconnect the overflow pipe. Fit a new sealing washer between the inner back nut and the cistern and re-make the connection.

Early warning

Go outside and check the toilet cistern overflow pipe from time to time. If the cistern is persistently overflowing, even very slightly, the water dripping from the pipe can trickle down the house wall and cause unsightly stains. At worst, it can lead to damp penetrating the wall to the inside.

It's in the bag

A metal float can corrode and develop pinhole leaks. As the float fills with water, it sinks lower and lower and no longer closes the valve properly, so the tank overflows. Until you can fit a new float, unscrew the old one and empty out the water (by drilling a larger hole in it if necessary), then tie a plastic freezer bag tightly over it to stop the leak temporarily.

Pressure counts

Before fitting a new valve in a toilet cistern to cure an overflow, check where the cold-water supply comes from so you can fit the correct valve seat inside the new valve. You need a narrow seat for a high-pressure mains supply, and a wider one for a low-pressure supply run from a storage tank.

Free to move

Because space is limited inside the toilet cistern, the float arm may catch on the siphon mechanism, resulting in a jammed valve and overflow. If this happens, bend the arm of a metal valve so it is free to move, or rotate a plastic valve slightly so it clears an obstruction.

Clean the tubes

Baths and sinks often have flexible plastic pipes that link the overflow to the trap below the plughole. These must be clear of any obstructions to work properly. Check yours from time to time to see if they can cope with the flow when both taps are left running and the plug is in. If they can't, dismantle them and flush them through with hot soapy water.

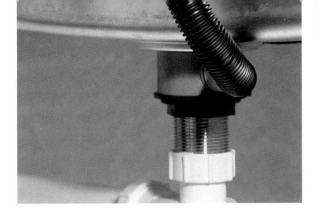

Line up the banjo

When reassembling bath and sink waste and overflow connections, make sure that the hole inside the plastic collar (known as the banjo) at the bottom end of the flexible overflow hose is lined up with the slot in the waste outlet.

Storage tank tips

Beating the bugs

Insects can crawl up an overflow pipe, drop into the tank and enter the water supply. You can stop them getting in by replacing the existing overflow pipe connector with one that incorporates an insect screen (above).

Draught stopper

In very cold weather, draughts blowing up the overflow pipe can cause the cold water storage tank's inlet valve to freeze up. Prevent this by fitting an elbow and a short vertical length of same-size pipe to the inner end of the overflow pipe so it dips below the water level inside the tank.

1 Turn off water supply to valve and unscrew large end cap on body of valve

2 If nut is on end of valve, remove end cap and piston. If nut is between water inlet and outlet, remove valve body

3 Use slim screwdriver blade to prise old diaphragm out of valve body

4 Clean any dirt from valve. Fit new diaphragm the right way round, reassemble valve and restore water supply

overflows

135

blockages Clearing a waste pipe

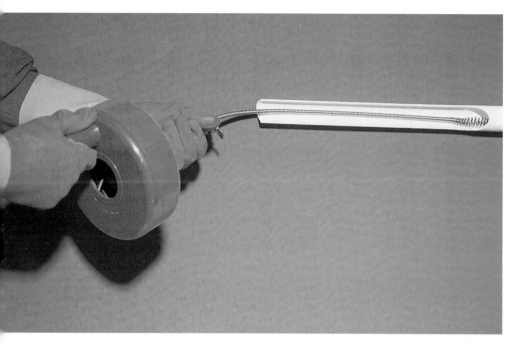

Try a plumber's snake

For blockages which cannot be cleared with a plunger, it is worth trying a device called a spiral cleaner or plumber's snake. You can buy one or hire one. Disconnect the blocked pipe from its trap and feed the end of the wire into it. Then turn the handle to rotate the spiral. This drives the cutting head into the blockage and breaks it up.

Take the plunger

For clearing blocked waste pipes, a simple plunger is hard to beat. As you plunge it up and down it pushes and pulls the blockage apart, rather than compacting it. **For a plunger to work,** its cup must be covered with water, and the appliance's overflow inlet must be sealed. Holding a wet cloth over it is the best method.

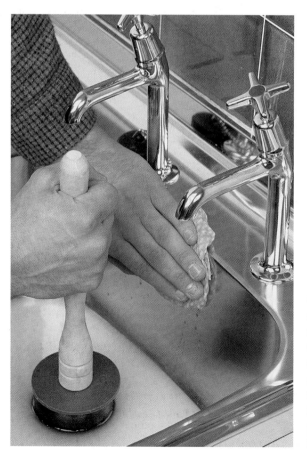

Start from the outlet

Waste pipes joined with push-fit connectors are easily taken apart when there is a blockage. Start dismantling the pipe at the outlet end and work your way back. When you reach the blocked section, put a bucket under the end of the pipe and dislodge the obstruction with a length of stiff wire.

Reassemble with care

Once you have cleared a blockage, you have to reconnect the various components you dismantled. Check that all the sealing rings are correctly positioned inside screw-up fittings, or the joints will leak. Replace any rings that are worn or have been stretched out of shape, and apply a little silicone lubricating grease to the sealing rings inside push-fit connectors.

Chemical soup

Avoid using strong chemicals—especially caustic soda—when you are trying to clear sink blockages. If they don't work, you'll still have the blockage, plus a sink and trap full of unpleasant and possibly dangerous liquid to deal with.

Warmth and water

If you have poured hot fat down the kitchen sink and it has blocked the trap, try warming the bend of the trap gently with a hair dryer. This should soften the fat plug enough for you to disperse it. Once the waste is on the move, run the hot tap for a minute or two to make sure that all traces of fat are flushed well out of the system.

Hose it out

If a blockage can't be shifted from the sink end, and the waste pipe discharges into an outside gully, push a garden hose up the pipe from outside. This might do the trick by itself, but if you need to turn on the tap, use only enough pressure to move the blockage. Otherwise, the contents of the pipe could be sprayed out of the plughole and all over the kitchen.

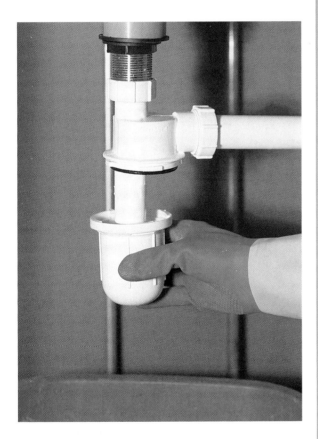

Open the bottle trap

If you cannot clear a blocked waste pipe from either end, the next step is to take the trap apart. Modern plastic traps are easy to dismantle without tools.

Put the plug in the plughole and a bowl or bucket beneath the trap first. Then unscrew the base of a round bottle trap or undo the coupling nuts on a pipe trap. Remove any blockage from the trap, rinse it out and reassemble it.

1 Screw two or three lengths of drain rod together and fit plunger disc to one end

2 Feed rods into drain, adding more as needed. Rotate rods clockwise or they will unscrew and be lost in the drain

3 If plunger will not shift the blockage, withdraw rods and fit corkscrew head to pull the obstruction out

4 Once blockage is cleared, fill bath with cold water. Then pull out plug so water gushes out and sluices drain clean

blockages

137

blockages Unblocking a toilet

Make do and mend

If you don't have a proper toilet plunger to deal with a blockage, improvise by wrapping a plastic bag round a mop head. Tie the bag to the handle of the mop so it can't work free.

If you have a set of drain rods and a rubber plunger disc, fit this to one of the rods to make a toilet plunger.

Snake with a hook

You will need a plumber's snake with a hook attachment to clear the blockage caused by an item such as a disposable nappy. Feed the snake into the trap until you feel it has reached the blockage, then rotate it and push it forward gently so it grabs the object. Withdraw it slowly from the trap.

Heat treatment

Try clearing a partly blocked toilet by pouring a bucket of hot water down it. If it seems to be draining more quickly after one bucket, follow up immediately with two or three more.

Problems outdoors

Clearing debris from a gully

Water spilling out of a garden gully usually indicates a blocked trap below ground level. Remove the gully grating and scoop out the debris by hand, wearing heavy-duty PVC gloves. Then flush the gully through with water to clear any remaining debris and discourage another blockage from forming.

Rodding out a soil pipe

You will need a set of drain rods to clear a blockage in a soil stack. Climb a ladder so you can reach the top of the stack safely, and remove the cowl if there is one. Fit the rubber plunger disc to the end of a rod and lower it into the stack. Keep adding rods until you can reach and dislodge the blockage. Haul the rods out again, dismantle them and flush the stack through with water from a bucket or garden hose.

Removing a drain cover

Often the hardest part of unblocking a drain is getting the metal cover off the inspection chamber (manhole). Lever the edge up with a spade or brick bolster. If it won't budge, tap around the edges with a hammer to break the rust seal. If the grab bars are intact, tie a loop of rope through each one. Pass a length of wood through the loops and lever off the cover.

Beef up your wrench

Undoing old tap connectors from tap tails can be hard work, as corrosion often locks the nuts on their threads. To get more leverage on the nuts, clamp an adjustable spanner onto your basin wrench. It's also a good idea to spray some penetrating oil onto the locked nut first.

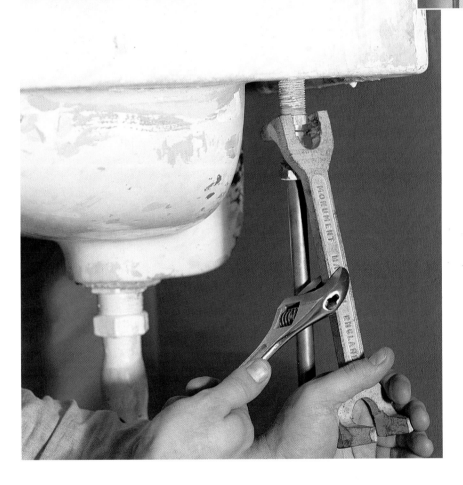

Strap gives more grip

Disconnect the waste pipe by unscrewing the connector linking the trap to the waste outlet. You should be able to undo this by hand, but if it will not move try loosening it with a Boa Constrictor strap wrench. This works in the same way as the smaller versions designed for opening screw-top jars.

Seal sink slots

If you are fitting an inset sink or basin in a worktop, seal the cut edge of the chipboard with diluted PVA sealer first. Otherwise moisture may be able to seep in, causing the chipboard to swell and lift the laminated surface.

new fittings

Watch the earth

Look out for earth bonding wires as you plan the removal of old plumbing fittings. They are covered in green-and-yellow PVC insulation and connected to special metal clamps or tags on the pipes. Undo these and set them aside for reconnection later. If there are no earth wires, call in a qualified electrician to check your whole plumbing system for electrical safety.

Prepare to mop up

Before starting to remove an old plumbing fitting, double-check that you have turned off its hot and cold water supplies. Even so, the pipes will still contain some water, so have old towels or other absorbent material handy to mop up the spills as you disconnect or cut through them.

new fittings
Out with the old...

...and in with the new

Remove an untidy collar

Old pipe collars behind toilet pans are unsightly, and are no longer necessary thanks to modern push-fit connectors. Cut off a cast-iron collar with a hacksaw or chain cutter where it passes through the wall, and break off an earthenware one where it goes into the floor. Provided you strike from the inside outwards, the collar will break off cleanly at floor level. The new push-fit connector will fit inside the pipe and should cover the exposed end neatly.

The right adaptor

If you are replacing a toilet pan, choose the correct type of adaptor to match the existing soil pipe. You need a straight connector if the pipe passes through the wall immediately behind the pan, and a right-angled one otherwise.

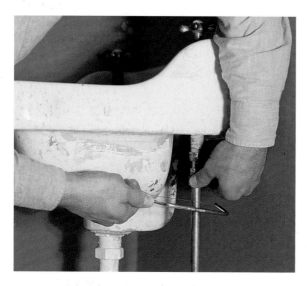

Cut the connection

If tap connectors refuse to budge when you're trying to remove an old fitting, just cut through the pipes with a hacksaw. You can replace the pipework when you install the new fitting. This also gives you the chance to fit a new tap connector and an in-line isolating valve to each pipe, which will make future tap repairs a simple job.

Demolition job

If you need to remove an old cast-iron bath, and it isn't a valuable Victorian roll-top type worth saving and selling, break it with a sledgehammer to make it easier to move. Wear safety goggles, ear defenders and strong gloves, and drape the bath with an old blanket to contain flying debris. Smash holes through the inside corners of the bath first, then punch more holes across the base and up the sides until you have pieces you can lift away easily.

Skip the mortar

Don't bed a new toilet pan on mortar, which can shrink and crack the pan. Instead, secure it to the floor with woodscrews, fitted with rubber washers to protect the china. Alternatively screw nylon pan fixings to the floor, place the pan over them, trim the threads to length and fit and tighten the nuts.

Slowing down the flush

Modern toilet pans are made for use with low-level cisterns. You can use a high-level cistern if you particularly want one, but you might need to fit a flow restrictor in the pan inlet to reduce the speed of the flush. Without it, the water can splash over the edge of the pan.

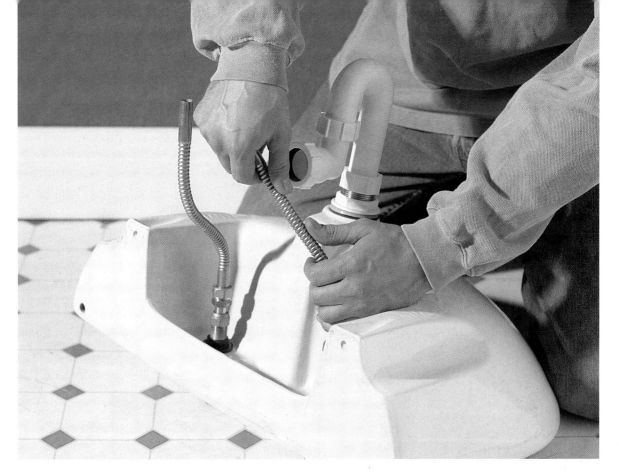

Pedestal planning

When installing a new pedestal washbasin, first turn the basin upside down on the floor. Fit the trap and the tap connectors, then bend the two flexible supply pipes so they will fit neatly out of sight behind the pedestal once the basin is installed.

Before you begin

Attach everything you can to a new plumbing fitting before you start work to install it–space will be limited once it is in place. Tighten the back nuts of taps well so that the bodies of the taps do not rotate when they are turned on and off, and bed waste outlets in non-setting mastic for a waterproof joint. Check that flexible overflow pipes are correctly linked to their waste outlets.

Slide a sink into place

To save having to make connections in awkward positions, fit a new sink to its base unit and make all the plumbing connections to the taps and waste outlet before you push the unit up against the wall. Then slide it into place and connect up the existing supply and waste pipes with compression fittings.

Metric sizes

It is now virtually impossible to find new lay-on sinks to fit old imperial-size base units. New metric size sinks are smaller, but you can make up the shortfall if you fit an in-fill piece of worktop at one end of the unit. An alternative is to install a new inset sink in a section of worktop cut to fit the base unit.

Knocking out tap holes

Some washbasins come with a choice of tap holes that have to be broken out with a hammer and a centre punch. If you work in good light, you should be able to see the outline of the knock-out on the glazed surface. Work from the top, otherwise you risk flaking or chipping the surface of the china.

Improve access to tap connectors

Whether you're working on a sink, a basin or a bath, tap connectors are always difficult to get at. To make life easier next time around, replace the old tap connectors with new push-fit ones which screw onto the tap tails by hand, rather than needing a basin wrench. They contain an integral rubber sealing washer to ensure a watertight joint.

141

baths Attaching the fittings

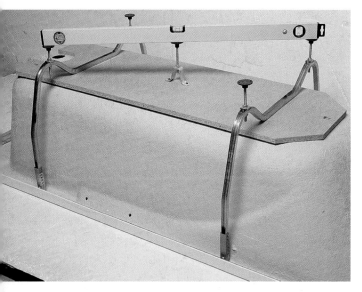

A level footing
A plastic bath usually comes with a supporting frame. Turn the bath upside down to fit it and use a spirit level to get the adjustable feet approximately level, so that you have only fine levelling adjustments to make once the bath is in position.

Choose thick plastic
Don't choose a plastic bath on style and colour alone. Check the thickness of the material from which it is moulded; it must be 4 mm at least, and preferably nearer to 6 mm. A bath thinner than 4 mm will distort in use.

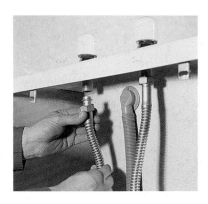

No leak, no strain
Bath mixer taps come with a rubber or plastic gasket. Fit this between the tap body and the bath to stop water seeping beneath the tap.
On a plastic bath, fit a metal reinforcing plate between the back nuts and the underside of the bath rim to prevent any strain on the plastic.

Line up the overflow
Baths come with an all-in-one hose and connector for the overflow. One end is fitted to the overflow opening near the rim of the bath. The other, called the banjo because of its shape, fits round the waste outlet. Align the hose inlet with the waste outlet slot carefully.

Tails you win
Once a bath is in place against the wall, it is almost impossible to reach up and attach the tap connectors to the tap tails. Overcome the problem by fitting a length of flexible pipe to each tap tail (above) and by cutting down the existing supply pipes to nearer floor level. Then there's plenty of room to reconnect the pipes using compression fittings. These will be easier to undo than soldered fittings when the bath is next replaced.

Applying a waterproof seal

Mind the gap
Fill a plastic bath with water before applying any seal to the join between bath and wall. This will widen the gap between the edge of the bath and the splashback to its maximum, and help to prevent the seal from pulling away with use at a later date.

Silicone is best
You can use any type of nonsetting sealant to waterproof the join between bath and wall, but silicone is best. It comes in clear, white and several popular sanitaryware colours. Look for one containing a fungicide that will stop black mould growing on its surface.

A neat finish
As an alternative to masking tape (page 143, top), you could use a handy scoop called a Sealright tool, available from DIY stores. Just run it along the join after applying the sealant. It will lift out the excess and form a neat concave joint.

Getting it taped

To get a neat bead of sealant around a bath, stick parallel strips of masking tape to the base of the wall and to the bath rim. Then fill the gap with sealant and smooth its surface with a moistened finger or the back of a small plastic teaspoon. Pull the tape off once the sealant has formed a skin.

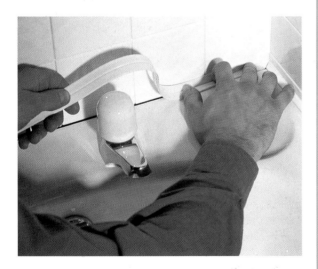

Stick on plastic strips

Use self-adhesive plastic sealing strips around the bath if the gap is wider than about 6 mm (¼ in), or varies in width from place to place. Silicone sealant will simply keep disappearing into the void. Clean the wall and bath surfaces scrupulously, first with strong household detergent and then with methylated spirits. Then cut the seals to length, peel off the release paper and bed them in place with firm hand pressure.

1 Screw two 50 x 25 mm sawn timber battens to floor directly beneath bath rim

2 Clamp matching battens beneath bath rim. Then fit 50 x 50 mm posts about every 400 mm, and at corners

3 Cut front and end panels to size. Hardboard is lightweight, but use 9 mm plywood if you want to apply tiles

4 Attach all the panels with decorative mirror screws or pairs of magnetic catches so you can remove them easily for access to the plumbing

baths

baths Remedies for surface damage

Read the label

If you plan to use a branded limescale remover to get rid of a build-up of hard limescale around the bath taps or the plughole, read the manufacturer's instructions carefully before you buy. Many of these chemicals are unsuitable for plastic baths, and some may also damage enamel.

Disguise scratches and chips

If a plastic bath has become scratched, rub the surface lightly with metal polish wadding. The colour goes right through the plastic, so you will not mark it. Deeper chips in the plastic can be filled with a special two-part acrylic paste, available from plumbers' merchants and DIY stores.

Restore the shine

Treat an old metal bath that's lost its shine with a car body restorer. Then put a shine on the surface with a high-glaze liquid car body polish. A lambswool polishing bonnet fitted to a mains electric drill does the best job; cordless drills don't spin fast enough to polish the surface properly.

Renew old sealant

To replace existing silicone sealant, cut away the bulk of the strip with a sharp trimming knife and then use special silicone sealant remover to take off the last traces. Wipe the cleaned surface with a cloth soaked in methylated spirits before you apply new sealant.

Rust buster

If a chipped steel bath has developed rust spots, remove them with a car body rust remover. Then paint the bare metal surface with a rust inhibitor and fill in the chips with fine car body filler. Smooth the repair with very fine wet-and-dry abrasive paper (used wet) before disguising it with enamel paint.

Enamel restorer

Remove stains from the enamel surface of a cast-iron or pressed-steel bath by rubbing the surface hard with a device called a bath rubber, which is available direct from bath manufacturers or from plumbers' merchants. Use enamel paint touch-up kits to conceal minor scratches, but be sure to clean the bath thoroughly before applying the paint.

toilets Curing flush problems

A straightforward job to handle

If you have to pump the handle to make the toilet flush, and the water level in the cistern is up to the 'full' mark on its inside wall, the plastic flap valve inside the siphon unit needs renewing. The replacement part is inexpensive and the job requires no skill, although it can take time—so do it yourself rather than calling out a plumber.

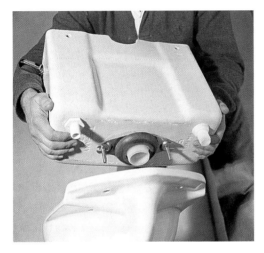

Siphon sequence

Unless your close-coupled toilet is fairly new and contains a three-part siphon unit (right), you will have to take the cistern off its pan to replace the flap valve. Cut off the water supply, flush the cistern and bale it out. Then disconnect the supply and overflow pipes. Next, undo the screws holding the cistern to the wall, and remove the wing nuts below the rear edge of the pan. Now lift off the cistern, remove the doughnut seal round the siphon outlet and undo the back nut to release the siphon unit.

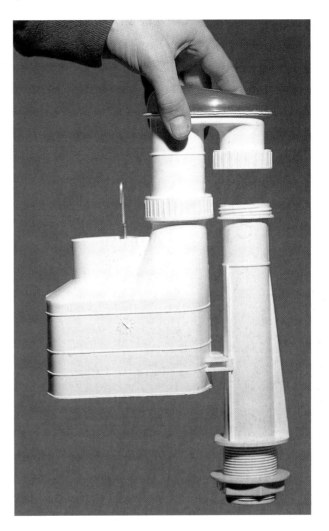

Time to improvise

You probably won't have a wrench big enough to grip the siphon back nut. If this is the case, use your forefinger and thumb to measure its diameter. Then use this rough measurement to make a matching cut-out in a plywood offcut and use it as a makeshift spanner.

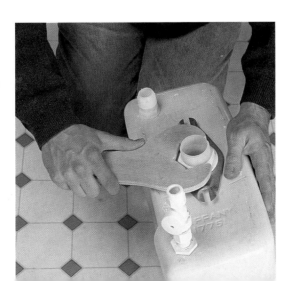

Easier next time

The flap valve in the siphon unit can last years or may fail in months. To make future replacement easier, fit a three-part siphon unit in place of the existing one. You will then be able to change the flap valve in future without having to go to the trouble of removing the cistern or even turning off the water. You just undo the coupling nuts and slide the siphon unit up so you can get at the flap valve from below.

145

toilets Curing flush problems

Raise the water level

When a toilet won't flush, check that the water level in the cistern is up to the 'full' mark. If it is too low, adjust the angle of the float arm. How you do this depends on the type of valve you have.

With a plastic valve (below), you alter the angle of the arm by turning its adjustment screw with a screwdriver.

With a brass valve, you may have to bend the float arm up a little, or loosen the securing nut on a movable float and slide the fixing up the arm slightly.

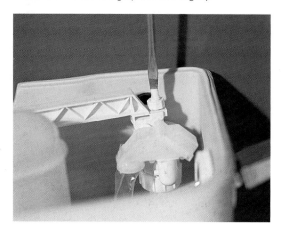

A broken arm

The flush lever arm in a cistern links the end of the flushing lever with the wire link that lifts the siphon lift rod. If the arm is plastic, it can snap. However, a universal replacement is available from plumbers' merchants. It fits most makes of cistern, although you may have to shorten it with a junior hacksaw to stop it catching on the siphon unit.

Perpetual running water

Toilets with cisterns that are supplied by mains-pressure water can suffer from continuous flushing. It happens because water enters the cistern through the inlet valve at the same speed as it leaves through the siphon, so preventing air from entering the siphon and breaking the flow. The problem can be cured either by replacing the low-pressure seating inside the inlet valve with a high-pressure one, or installing an in-line isolating valve on the supply pipework and using it to reduce the water pressure.

Reconnect the link

If you cannot flush the toilet because the handle is hanging limply, check the connection inside the cistern between the flush lever arm and the siphon lift rod. This S-shaped or C-shaped wire link may have become unhooked. Simply reconnect it to restore the flush action. To do this you may have to slip a finger beneath the siphon unit and push the plate inside up so that the top of the lift rod is exposed.

A smoother action

The flush action of a toilet cistern should be smooth. If it starts to feel stiff, check whether the flush lever arm has worked loose on its spindle—it should be held in place by a small grub screw. If the arm has moved along the spindle, it will no longer raise the siphon lift rod vertically. Reposition the arm on the spindle and tighten the screw to ensure a straight lift.

Remedies for leaks

Replacing the doughnut

Leaks from beneath a close-coupled cistern are a
sure sign that the sealing washer between the
cistern and the pan (called a doughnut) has
perished. To replace it, start by removing the cistern,
following the same sequence of operations as if you
were replacing the flap valve (see right). Then pull
the old washer off and fit a new one, seating it
evenly over the siphon retaining nut. If the leak has
rusted the mild-steel plate that retains the two
cistern fixing bolts, remove the rust with wire wool
before reassembling everything.

Tighten the nut

Water running down the outside of the flush pipe
when a separate cistern is flushed is due to a
leaking seal. Try gently tightening the nut that joins
the flush pipe and cistern.
If this doesn't work, turn off the water supply to
the cistern and bale out the water. Then undo the
nut and slide it down the pipe to reveal the
damaged rubber washer inside it. Remove this and
wrap at least ten turns of PTFE tape around the top
of the pipe. Replace and tighten the nut.

Fit a flexible cone

The flush pipe from a separate cistern is connected
to the back of the pan with a rubber connector. If
this perishes and starts to leak, replace it with a
universal flush cone. You can turn the cone inside
out like a sock to fit either 32 mm (1¼ in) high-
level pipes or 38 mm (1½ in) low-level ones. The
cone won't work with metal flush pipes.

STAGES IN REPLACING A FLAP VALVE

1 Turn off water to a separate cistern, flush it
and bale out. Disconnect flush pipe and undo
siphon back nut

2 Disconnect supply and overflow to close-
coupled cistern and undo pan fixings. Lift pan
off and undo siphon back nut

3 Undo wire hook from top of siphon lift rod
and lift siphon unit out of cistern. Slide out
lifting plate and rod

4 Pull off worn flap valve and fit replacement,
cut to same size first if necessary. Then
reassemble everything

toilets

147

showers Picking the right hardware

Minimal plumbing

If you want a shower that needs the bare minimum of installation work, fit a bath/shower mixer tap in place of your existing bath taps and take your shower standing in the bath. Thermostatic types are more expensive than conventional mixers, but they do prevent unexpected water temperature fluctuations. You will get a reasonably powerful shower so long as your cold-water storage tank is at least 1 m above the level of the shower rose. If not, add a pump to the system to boost flow rates.

A safe temperature

To guard against the danger of scalding, fit an antiscald device to manual showers. This tiny wax-filled cylinder screws onto the mixer and stops the flow almost immediately if the water rises above a safe temperature. Simply undo the hose, screw on the device and then re-attach the hose to it.

Worth the raise?

Lifting the cold-water tank in the loft will increase the flow rate to a shower, but the job is worth considering only if you have to replace an old tank anyway or are carrying out a loft conversion. Otherwise fit a shower pump.

Check the seals

When an over-bath shower is fitted, make sure the seal between the bath and any wall tiles is completely watertight. Much more water will splash onto the tiles when you shower than when you bathe, and this will quickly find any gaps. A neglected leak could rot the floor beneath the bath, or bring down the ceiling in the room below.

An electrical alternative

Install an electric shower (above left) if you have no storage tank. This takes cold water via a single supply pipe direct from the incoming mains. The most powerful units are now rated at more than 10 kW, so you should call in a qualified electrician to provide the new power circuit and controls, unless you are fully competent at doing your own wiring work. You can install the shower unit over a bath, but it is more commonly fitted in a separate shower cubicle.

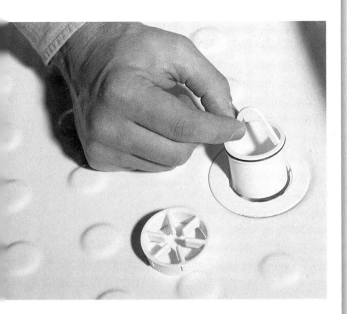

Allow for access

Once a shower tray is installed, the trap and waste pipe will probably be fairly inaccessible. Unfortunately, blockages are common, caused mainly by people washing their hair in the shower. Make sure the waste pipe run includes a rodding eye so you can clear it easily if it blocks. Better still, fit a top-access trap. This can be unblocked simply by removing the grid.

Pressure booster

Fit an integral low-voltage pump and mixing valve to boost the flow rate of a sluggish shower that is fed from the cold tank and hot cylinder. The pump can be installed on the wall of the shower cubicle or over the bath.

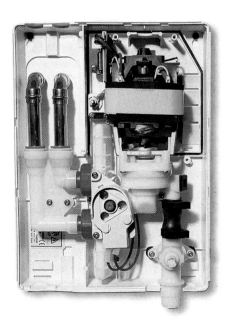

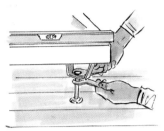

1 Set shower tray in place and level it, adjusting feet if these are fitted. Secure tray to floor with brackets

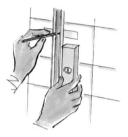

2 Mark positions of all fixings that secure cubicle uprights to walls. Then drill holes and screw them into place

3 Connect top frame rails with corner block and add cubicle wall panels, following maker's instructions carefully

4 When assembly is complete, seal joints between cubicle, bathroom walls and shower tray with silicone sealant

showers

149

showers Picking the right hardware

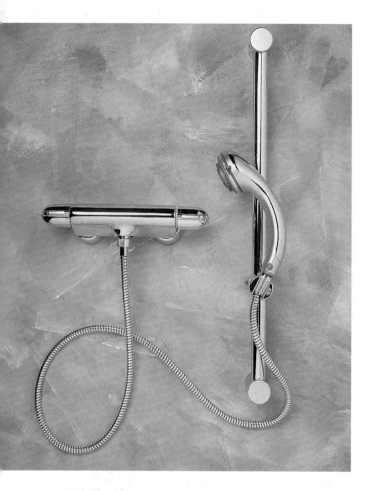

T is for thermostat
The most popular shower arrangement is a wall-mounted shower mixer valve fitted in a separate shower cubicle. Pick a thermostatically controlled mixer, and you can 'tee' its water supplies directly off the existing hot and cold pipes in the bathroom. The thermostat will prevent fluctuations from occurring in the shower water temperature if hot or cold water is drawn off anywhere else in the house.

The long way round
A manual mixer is cheaper to buy than one with a thermostat, but its cold supply must be taken directly from the cold-water storage tank. This ensures that the flow rate to the shower can't be reduced by cold water being drawn off elsewhere in the house. If that happened, the shower temperature could suddenly reach scalding point.

Keeping the water flowing freely

Have a clear head
To descale a clogged up shower head, unscrew it from its hose and immerse it in a container of lemon juice, vinegar or proprietary descaler. This will soften the limescale and, when you replace the head and turn the shower on, it will wash away. Keep the descaler and re-use it every few weeks. When it no longer makes the limescale fizz, the acidity has been neutralised and you need fresh descaler.

Clean the filters
If the flow rate of your shower starts to slow down noticeably and you have already descaled the shower head, clean the shower pump filters—located within the hot and cold pump inlet connections. Accumulated debris will restrict the flow unless it is cleaned out every year or so.

Scale problem-solver
If you live in a hard-water area, fit an electromagnetic or a chemical-dosing water conditioner on the supply pipe to an electric shower. Without one, the heat exchanger inside the shower unit will clog up very quickly as scale is deposited inside it. Both types of conditioner are very easy to fit.

Prime position

The easiest place to fit a washing machine is in the kitchen, close to the supply and waste pipes which serve the sink, but if space is limited, try to accommodate it in a cloakroom or utility room. It's seldom possible to install a washing machine in a bathroom because of wiring safety restrictions.

Preventing back-siphonage

If you have an old washing machine that doesn't have British or European Standard approval, consider fitting a device called a check valve on the cold-water supply pipe. This will prevent back-siphonage—dirty water from the machine being drawn into the mains supply if the water pressure drops. Ask the manufacturer of the machine for advice. All modern approved washing machines incorporate internal check valves.

A longer reach

When you have to site a washing machine or dishwasher farther from its supply pipes than the existing hoses can reach, use longer hoses, available from plumbers' merchants. Check the machine handbook for the maximum permitted length you can fit.

Connect to cold only

There's no need to plumb in a hot water supply to a washing machine. Unless it is sited close to the hot-water storage cylinder, most of the 'hot' water it draws will probably be cold and the machine will have to heat it again. For washes below 60°C (140°F), the machine will only fill with cold water anyway. The one advantage of having both hot and cold inlets is that the machine will fill more quickly and will complete a hot-wash cycle faster.

Choose connectors carefully

Before using self-cutting supply connectors, check the appliance manual to make sure they are suitable. Since they cut only a small hole in the main supply pipe, the flow rate to the machine may be insufficient, especially with supplies that are not at mains pressure. If so, use a tee fitting instead to provide a larger bore. Fit a tee with a stoptap (right), and you can attach the machine hose directly to the outlet.

Clamp and go

Self-cutting supply connectors provide a quick and easy way to link your washing machine or dishwasher to existing hot and cold supply pipes but they are not suitable for all appliances, so check the user manual first. Clamp the two-part base around the existing pipe, then screw in the tap to pierce it and make the connection. Screw the hose directly onto the threaded outlet of the tap.

appliances Providing a water supply

Soap solution

If the plastic connector nuts bind on the threaded plastic spigots at the back of the washing machine as you tighten them, smear a little soap on the threads before making the connection. This will make the hoses easier to undo later.

Fit a slip-tee connector

You may not have enough play on the pipes to be able to spring the cut ends into a standard compression tee fitting, so fit a slip-tee connector, which has no internal stops and can slide freely onto one end of the pipe and then back over the other. Mark the position of the ends of the tee on the pipe, without the cap nuts attached, before fitting so you know when it is centred on the cut.

Washer backup

Don't tighten a leaking supply hose connector with a wrench: you'll crack the plastic. Instead, turn off the washing machine tap, disconnect the hose and add a second sealing washer. Reattach the hose, which shouldn't leak even when the nut is just hand tight.

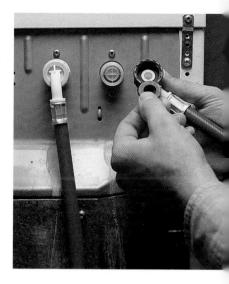

Getting rid of waste water

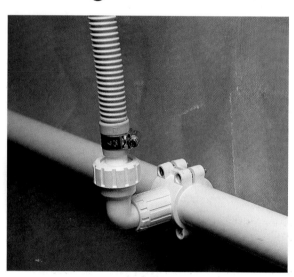

Easy link from waste to hose

If there's an existing 38 mm diameter waste pipe behind or close to the position of your washing machine or dishwasher, you may be able to use a self-cutting plastic waste connector to link into its outlet hose; check with your machine's instructions. The connector works in the same way as a self-cutting supply connector, and incorporates a non-return valve. Attach the hose to the connector outlet with a hose clip so it cannot be pulled off.

Soil-pipe connections

You can connect a new waste pipe into a soil pipe if it is near the machine. First cut a hole in the soil pipe with a hole saw. Then stick a boss connector in the hole with solvent-weld cement and fit the strap around the soil pipe. Finally, push the waste pipe into the boss. Connect the machine outlet hose to a standpipe fitted with a 75 mm deep trap.

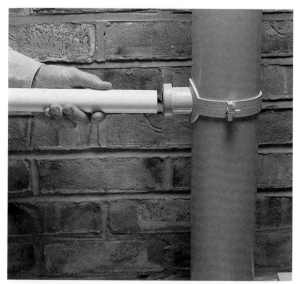

SUPPLY HOSES TO MACHINE

SUPPLY STOPTAPS

SINK OVERFLOW

OUTLET SPIGOT

ANTI-FLOOD LOOP

WASHING MACHINE TRAP

OUTLET HOSE FROM MACHINE

Prevent back-flow

When connecting a machine's outlet hose direct to a washing machine trap, create an anti-flood loop in the hose to prevent water from the sink flowing down the hose and into the machine. Hook up the loop behind the sink unit so its highest point is above the sink overflow outlet (the picture shows it lower than this for clarity only).

Add more hose

If the machine's outlet hose won't reach a convenient connection point on the waste pipe, you can usually add more hose using a hose connector. Check the machine handbook to see if there is a recommended maximum length for the outlet hose. Secure the hose to the connector spigots with hose clips.

Capping open standpipes

Washing machines and dishwashers can cause a flood if the open standpipe that their outlet hoses are hooked into becomes blocked. Eliminate the risk by fitting an elbow to the top of the standpipe, attaching a sealed air admittance valve and then fitting a screw-on spigot to which the outlet hose is connected. Secure the hose with a hose clip.

boilers
Problems you can tackle yourself

Traditional reliability

For a gas-fired boiler that is reliable and inexpensive, choose a traditional boiler with a cast-iron heat exchanger. It may be free-standing, or a back boiler that is built into a chimney breast and linked to a room heater. Though cheap, it uses fuel less efficiently than other types.

Hot water on demand

If you can manage without stored hot water, choose a combination boiler. This provides water for the heating system in the same way as a traditional boiler, but heats up water for washing on demand. It can be expensive to repair, however, and suits a small home better than a large one with high water consumption.

For greatest efficiency

If you want the best possible fuel efficiency, select a condensing boiler, which extracts heat from the flue gases. It can heat water for instant use or for storage and is less complicated and more reliable than a combination boiler.

Check out the flue

A boiler with a balanced (room-sealed) flue must meet the requirements of the current Building Regulations. These govern how close the flue outlet can be to the corners of the building, to walls opposite the flue outlet, to any opening windows and to overhanging eaves.

Oil-fired boilers

Consider an oil-fired boiler if you don't have mains gas. Made in traditional, combination and condensing versions, they are connected to open or room-sealed flues. They are cheaper to run than gas boilers but servicing costs are higher, and you have to provide safe, approved storage facilities for the fuel.

Check the light

If a boiler stops lighting, check that the pilot light is on, or comes on when the ignition sparks at the start of the lighting sequence. Open the front panel to get at the spark generator button if you can. Following the instructions on the inside of the panel, press in the control knob on the gas valve and try to light the gas by pushing the button. You should see the spark through the observation glass.

Sleeve the lead

If pressing the spark generator button doesn't create a spark, check that the lead from the spark generator to the electrode is not shorting out. The tiniest spark shorting across from the lead to the body or casing of the boiler will impair the ignition. Rearrange the lead so it is away from the casing, or cover it with a piece of heat-resistant sleeving, sold in electrical shops for insulating cable cores in enclosed light fittings.

Reduce scale in the system

In hard-water areas, scale gradually builds up on the heat exchanger inside a boiler and this will eventually reduce its efficiency. You can prevent it by fitting a self-dosing phosphate scale inhibitor on the supply pipe from the feed-and-expansion tank to the boiler circuit pipework. The cartridge needs replacing about once a year.

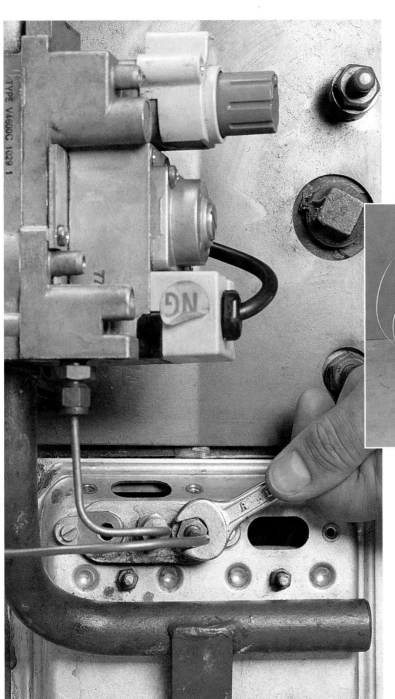

Universal thermocouple

If the pilot light goes out when you release the spark generator button, you need to replace the thermocouple. Spares are widely available, and a universal model fits most boilers. Fitting one is usually straightforward. Undo the nuts holding the old thermocouple (left), remove it from its tube and slide in the replacement (below).

Stuck switch

A complex electronic management system controls the ignition sequence on fan-assisted boilers. If the fan starts but the boiler doesn't ignite, the air pressure switch may have stuck and failed to detect the fan running. The switch will need to be replaced, but as an interim measure try switching the boiler off and on a few times to put it through the ignition sequence.

Thermostat tactics

If a boiler switches on and off constantly and there is a room thermostat and a cylinder thermostat on the system, turn the boiler thermostat up to full and control the room and hot water temperatures with the other two thermostats. If this doesn't stop the on/off cycling, ask a heating engineer for advice on having an energy management system installed.

Adjust the flame

Some boilers have a clearly marked and easy-to-operate adjusting screw which can be turned to change the size of the pilot flame. Adjust it so the flame just covers the tip of the thermocouple probe. Do not have the pilot light set so high that the flame appears to be detached from the gas jet.

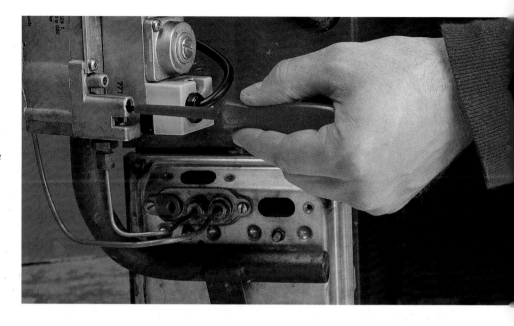

Leave jets alone

If you have a spark but the pilot light won't ignite, you may have a blocked gas jet. The boiler will need expert servicing. Don't try to clean the jet with a pin, because this will over-enlarge the hole and cause the flame to soot up. **If the flame lights** but will not stay lit, suspect a faulty thermocouple–the safety device that shuts off the gas flow to the burners if the pilot light goes out.

Safety first

The Gas Safety Regulations state that it is illegal for anyone to carry out any work in relation to a gas fitting who is not 'competent' to do so. This means that in practice you should leave all but the most simple boiler servicing jobs to a qualified gas fitter who is on the register of CORGI (Council for Registered Gas Installers).

Sealed for total safety

Pump in some air

If you notice a dribble of water coming from the safety valve outlet on a sealed system, pump some more air into the expansion vessel. This is spherical and usually painted red and is located at the back of the boiler. **Find its air inlet valve** (which looks similar to the ones on car tyres), and pump some air in with a bicycle pump or a car foot pump. Measure the pressure with a tyre pressure gauge, or the gauge on the foot pump if it has one. The pressure needs to be slightly above the cold pressure level on the boiler pressure gauge but below the hot pressure level. This allows water to enter the vessel when the system heats up and its contents expand.

Keep up the pressure

If you have a sealed hot water or heating system, check regularly that the water pressure in the system matches the recommendations given by the maker. Typically the pressure gauge will show about 1 bar when the system is cold, and a maximum of 3 bar (marked with a red line) when it is hot. To raise low water pressure to the correct level, let in water by turning the taps on at either side of the system filling loop.

Reset the cut-out

Many boilers have a cut-out that turns the boiler off if it overheats–a fault that can occur if the pressure drops on a sealed system, or the pump stops working on a vented one. Put the fault right if you can (by topping up the system water, for example) and press the manual reset button to restart the boiler. This is usually clearly marked; look for a red button with a cross on it. If you can't fix the fault, call a plumber.

radiators Cures for valves with problems

Dry repair for a faulty Belmont valve

You can repair leaking valves with the name Belmont on them without having to drain the system. Remove the valve handle and then undo the gland nut by turning it clockwise; it has a left-hand thread. Remove the nut quickly so the spring-loaded plunger inside the valve snaps up and cuts off the water flow. Remove the spindle (right) and the O-rings; they will be either red or green, depending on how old the valve model is, and should be replaced with new ones of the same colour. Finally reassemble the valve.

Clear the jam

Thermostatic radiator valves (TRVs) can jam in the closed position, especially if they are not used regularly. To free the internal mechanism, try tapping the valve body (not the top sensor head) gently with a mallet or hammer. If this fails to free it, pull off the sensor head (left). Then grip the exposed end of the valve activator pin with pliers and move it up and down gently. Don't wiggle the pin from side to side; it may bend or even break.

No need to dismantle the leaking joint

Leaks can occur between the valve tail (the short pipe to which the valve is connected) and the threaded inlet to the radiator itself. This can often be cured with a smear of silicone leak sealant. Run the radiator hot to dry out the leak, then apply the sealant. The leaking water will start it setting immediately, but you should leave the heat on for at least 2 hours to get a total seal.

Check the obvious

A single cold radiator may simply have been turned off at the hand-operated valve (called the handwheel valve and fitted with a fluted handle). Check that the valve is open fully. If a TRV has been fitted instead, turn it to a higher temperature setting so the valve opens.

radiators Cures for valves with problems

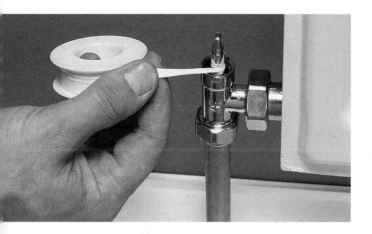

Repack the gland

Radiator valves, especially cheaper ones, often weep round the spindles. Before replacing the valve, it is worth trying to repack the gland to cure the problem. Turn the valve off, remove the plastic handle and undo the small gland nut at the base of the spindle. Wrap some PTFE tape around the spindle and then push it down into the gap between spindle and valve with a small screwdriver. Add a little silicone grease round the spindle, then replace the nut and handle.

Isolate first

Before you can clear a blocked air vent or carry out any other repair work on a radiator, you need to isolate it from the rest of the central heating system to stop water pouring out of it. First turn the handwheel valve off in a clockwise direction. Then remove the plastic cover from the lockshield valve and use pliers or a small spanner to turn the spindle clockwise as far as it will go. Note how many turns this takes, so that when the repair work is done you can reopen it by the same number of turns and leave the system properly balanced.

Different solutions for cold radiators

Brass vent keys are best

Radiators that feel cold at the top and warm at the bottom need bleeding to remove air from the system. Because air rises, upstairs radiators are more often affected than ground floor ones. Keep a radiator bleed key in your tool box—brass keys are stronger than aluminium ones—to open the air vent found at one top corner of every radiator. You may need a screwdriver instead of a key to bleed some modern radiators.

Only some radiators are cold

If radiators are cold upstairs but hot downstairs, check the water level in the feed-and-expansion tank—it should be a third full when the system is hot. If either the upstairs or downstairs radiators are cold and the system has zoned heating, suspect a faulty motorised valve (see page 163).

Blocked with sludge

A radiator with a cool patch at the bottom and a warm top and ends is probably full of black sludge. This is produced by corrosion within the system, a problem that needs curing by the addition of a corrosion inhibitor (see page 160). To clear the blockage, remove the radiator, take it outdoors and flush it through with water from a garden hose (see panel).

Suspect a broken pump

Cold radiators downstairs, lukewarm ones upstairs, but plenty of hot water in the taps, are a sign of pump failure. If the hot taps are running cold as well, check the timer settings on the programmer and then make sure the boiler pilot light is on.

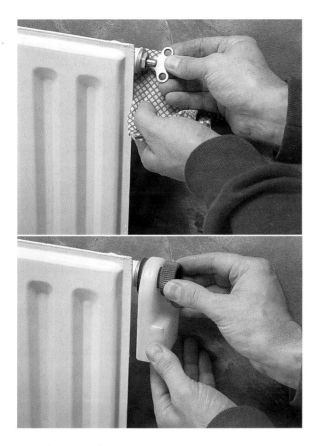

Gently does it

Open a radiator air vent by at most half a turn anticlockwise. Undo it further, and you might drop and lose the tiny needle that seals the vent. Hold a cloth under the vent (top) or use a combined bleed screw and container (above) to catch the water. Close the vent when water starts to run out.

Water shortage

If no water emerges from a radiator when you open the air vent, then the hole may be blocked, or the system may be short of water. Try bleeding another radiator on the same floor. If this has water in it, you can return to the original radiator and set about unblocking the hole. If no water comes out of the second radiator, then check that there is water in the feed-and-expansion tank. Refill it if it has run dry by pressing down the arm of the float valve.

Clean as a new pin

To unblock an air vent, turn off the radiator valves. Then open the vent with the key; remove the small needle and put it in a safe place. Use a thin piece of stiff wire to clear the hole in the body of the vent by pushing any obstruction back into the radiator. Replace the needle and reopen the radiator valves. Water should now flow out through the vent.

1 Close valves at each end. Lift or protect flooring and put a container under one of the coupling nuts to catch water

2 Brace valve body so you don't bend supply pipe. Undo coupling nut and let water run out of radiator

3 Open air vent to speed up flow of water. When it stops, undo coupling nuts fully on both valves

4 Lift radiator off wall brackets and empty out any remaining water. Stuff tissue paper or cloth into the outlets to stop drips before taking it aside

radiators

159

radiators Draining the system

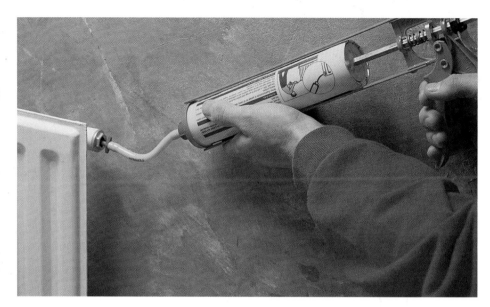

Keep it healthy

Keep a sealed heating system healthy by adding a chemical corrosion and scale inhibitor to the water. As there is no feed-and-expansion tank, you have to pump it in from a special cartridge through a radiator air vent.

Flush out the pipes

You can add special flushing agents to your heating system to loosen debris from the circuit pipework and radiators. Turn off the water supply to the feed-and-expansion tank. Then drain about 20 litres of water from it through a hose attached to the drain cock at the lowest point on the system. Pour in the cleansing agent (normally a whole bottle) and turn the water back on so the tank refills to the original level. Run the heating with the cleanser in for about a week. Then drain the system completely and refill it with clean water.

Allowing the water out

Letting air into the system helps water to run out of it. Locate the drain cock at the bottom of the system, and run a hose from it to an outside gully. Open the drain cock and then open the air vents on each of the radiators in turn, working from the top of the system downwards (see page 119).

Shut off the water

Before repairing your radiators and central-heating pipework, you will need to drain the heating system. If it is an open system (see page 119), first turn off the boiler. Then shut off the water supply to the heating circuit by turning off the stoptap on the supply pipe to the feed-and-expansion tank. If there is no stoptap, tie up the arm of the float valve to a length of wood laid across the tank so the valve can't let in water.

Fill from the bottom up

To re-fill the system, close the drain cock and all the air vents. Then allow water back into the feed-and-expansion tank so the system fills up again from there. Bleed the system, opening the lowest air vents first until water flows out, and working back until you reach the top of the system.

Clean the heating system pipework thoroughly by emptying and filling the system two or three times. After the final refill, turn the boiler back on and let the pump circulate the heated water around the system. Bleed the radiators for a few days to release air driven out of the water by heat.

Fitting a replacement

An exact match

The most common reason for replacing a steel panel radiator is because it has sprung a leak caused by corrosion eating it away from inside. If possible, buy a replacement that is the same model and size as the one it's replacing, so it will fit on the existing brackets and will connect up to the existing pipework without the need for time-consuming adjustments. Measure the old radiator, paying special attention to the position and separation of the bracket hooks, and use this information to track down a suitable replacement.

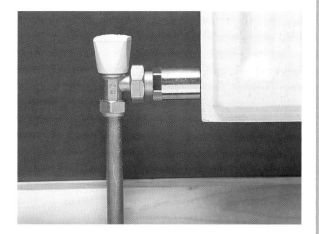

Imperial to metric

Metric radiators are often a little shorter than their imperial-sized equivalents, so the valve connections will not meet. Fit valve tail extenders to one or both ends of the new radiator to make up the gap and avoid having to modify the circuit pipework.

Double the output

Choose a new convector radiator with fins on the back to replace a standard panel radiator of the same size, and you will virtually double the heat output. However, the fins attract dust and fluff and can be difficult to keep clean. Make a simple dust buster by fixing a wad of washing-up sponge or any old rag to a straightened-out wire coat hanger.

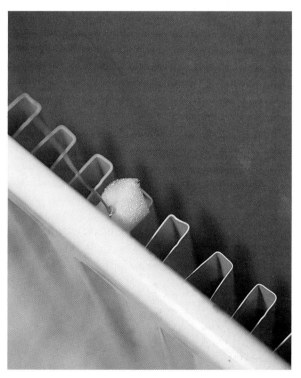

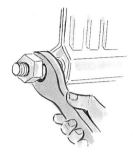

1 Wind PTFE tape around valve tail. Screw in until hand tight, then a further 1½ turns

2 Fit new olive on circuit pipe and sit valve body on top. Connect coupling nut on valve tail to valve body by hand

3 Tighten nut fully. Brace valve with second spanner to stop it bending circuit pipe

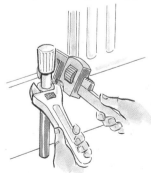

4 Push up new olive on circuit pipe to meet valve inlet. Slide cap nut up inlet and tighten with spanner

radiators

radiators
A new valve

Check out the parts

A new valve should come with a new valve tail, an olive (compression ring) and a coupling nut. You will need a special hexagonal radiator valve key for removing the old valve tail and screwing the new one into the radiator.

VALVE COVER

VALVE BODY

COUPLING NUT

VALVE TAIL

OLIVE

CAP NUT

Shop with care

If a faulty handwheel or lockshield valve resists all attempts at repair, you will have to replace it (see panel on page 161). Remove the old valve and take it with you when you shop for a replacement, so you can choose one of the same style that will align with both the circuit pipework and the radiator connection.

Removing an olive

You may be able to remove the olive left squashed onto the circuit pipe when you take off the old valve by sawing carefully through it with a junior hacksaw. Work slowly; if you nick the pipe beneath, the connection to the new valve will leak and you'll then have to cut off and replace the damaged section of pipe to cure the problem.

Hidden connection

An alternative approach to dealing with the old olive is to cut off the existing circuit pipe just above floorboard level, and then to join on a new section of pipe to reach up to the new valve inlet. Use a capillary fitting so the join to the existing pipework is inconspicuous. Dry the existing pipe first by playing the flame of your blowlamp over it.

Spotting the flow

Fit a new thermostatic radiator valve (TRV) on the flow (inlet) side of a radiator. Before draining the system to fit the new valve, switch the heating on and feel the two circuit pipes that supply the radiator; the one that gets hot first is the flow pipe.

Automatic balance

Fit the body of a new TRV as you would a standard handwheel or lockshield valve (see page 161). Then fit the sensor onto the valve body. The new valve will balance the flow rate into the radiator automatically, so the existing manual valve on the other end of the radiator becomes redundant, whether it is a handwheel or lockshield type. Leave it fully open.

Taking off the old valve

To remove an old radiator valve, you must first drain the heating system (see page 119). Then place some absorbent material such as an old towel beneath the valve to catch any drips. Undo the coupling nut linking the valve to the radiator, then the cap nut connecting it to the circuit pipework, and lift off the valve body. Before you can fit the new valve, remove the old valve tail from the radiator with a hexagonal radiator valve key (below) or a spanner on some types of radiator. You will also have to remove the old olive from the pipe.

Flushing through

If a motorised valve appears to be jamming, turn off the power and remove the actuator. Then try turning the spindle with a pair of pliers. If the spindle feels stiff, the valve either needs cleaning or replacing. Drain the heating system, undo the connections to the circuit pipework and remove the valve. Take it to the sink, flush it through with water to remove any debris from the mechanism, then reconnect it. If it still jams, fit a replacement valve body.

Replace the actuator

You do not normally have to replace a motorised valve if the motor has burnt out. On some models you replace the actuator–the top part of the valve. On others you remove this and replace just the motor unit within it. Turn off the electricity supply to the control system. Then undo the screws attaching the actuator. Disconnect the wires, reconnect them to the terminals on the replacement actuator or motor and reattach it to the valve.

Avoid a flat battery

Most modern programmers have a battery that ensures you will not lose all the settings if the electricity supply is turned off or is interrupted by a power failure. Replace this every year so you are never caught out with a flat battery.

Match up the sizes

Motorised valves come in 22 mm and 28 mm sizes; ensure you buy one to match your pipe diameter. Note the length of the valve too, and try to buy a replacement the same size so you do not have to modify the pipework in order to install it.

Manual operation

Many motorised valves have a manual lever you can operate to open the valve if it has jammed or the motor has burnt out. Slide the lever as far as it will go and then engage it in the J-shaped 'parking space' to keep the valve open. The heating and hot-water temperatures will now be controlled by just the boiler thermostat, so turn this down to a setting of 2 or 3 to avoid overheating.

radiators

Many heating systems now have permanent live supplies which bypass the programmer, so it is not safe just to turn that off. Isolate the controls by switching off the power at the fused connection unit or socket outlet that supplies the junction box—to which all the controls are connected.

New for old
If the programmer doesn't work even after you have checked that it has a power supply, try fitting a new one (see far right). So long as the unit is a relatively recent one with a so-called 'industry-standard' backplate, you will be able to remove the old faceplate and fit the new one to it without having to do any complicated rewiring.

Check the fuse first
If the system stops working, check the electricity supply to its controls. The fuse may have blown, leaving you with no display on a digital programmer and no response when thermostats are reset.
Turn off the socket outlet or fused connection unit (FCU) supplying the wiring junction box, and fit a new 3-amp fuse in the plug or fuseholder.

Take the bypass
A faulty programmer need not bring the heating system to a halt as it is possible to do without it, temporarily. Turn off the power supply, remove the faceplate and fit a live link wire between the 'hot water on' and 'central heating on' terminals. The system should now function continuously. However, do not attempt to tackle this modification unless you're confident you can do it correctly. Call in an electrician otherwise.

Checking thermostats

Ignore the thermometer
Don't expect the temperature setting on the room thermostat and the temperature recorded by a thermometer sited elsewhere in the room to agree precisely. The thermostat can only sense the air temperature close to it. Adjust it until you get the room temperature you want, and make a note of the thermostat setting required to achieve it.

Change the range
A typical room thermostat is calibrated to operate between about 10°C (50°F) and 30°C (86°F), but you can change the operating temperature range if you wish. On the model right, you pull off the control knob and reposition the two wire pointers in the numbered notches on its reverse; one represents the 'off' temperature setting, the other the 'on' one.

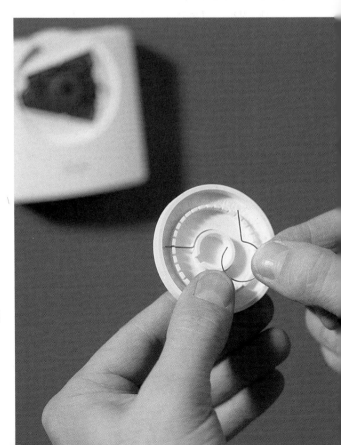

Make sure it's working

Check that the room thermostat is reacting to temperature changes by holding a switched-on table lamp underneath it for a few seconds. If all is well, the thermostat should turn the heating off as it is warmed by the heat from the lamp, and then back on after a few minutes as it cools down.

Continuity counts

If the water overheats or doesn't heat up at all, check whether the cylinder thermostat has failed. Turn off the electricity supply to the controls and remove the thermostat cover. Use a circuit tester to make sure there is continuity between the common terminal marked C and the terminal marked 1. Then turn the knob to the maximum setting and see if there is continuity between C and 2. If there isn't, fit a new thermostat.

The optimum position

The cylinder thermostat should be securely strapped to the cylinder about a third of the way up the side, and must be in contact with the bare copper if it is to work properly. If it is too high, cut away part of the foam insulation on the cylinder and move it. Fit the cylinder jacket so that the thermostat is exposed between the sections.

Swapping the valves

For more precise control of individual room temperatures than can be provided by a room thermostat, fit thermostatic radiator valves (TRVs) in place of standard on/off valves. To ensure that water can circulate freely through the heating circuit even if all the TRVs are closed, retain manual valves on at least one radiator.

STAGES IN
UPDATING A PROGRAMMER

1 Turn power off. Then undo screws securing programmer faceplate and remove it from its wallplate

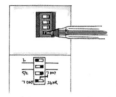

2 Set microswitches on back of new programmer to give required functions and on/off times (as per its instructions)

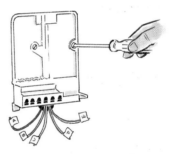

3 If new programmer will not fit on old wallplate, label and then disconnect cable cores. Remove and discard old plate

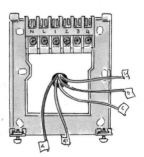

4 Fit new wallplate and wire it up following your labels and maker's instructions. Push on new faceplate. Restore power

165

noisy plumbing
Problems arising with pipework

Knock out water hammer

Turn down the water pressure slightly at the rising main stoptap to reduce banging noises in supply pipes to cold taps and washing machine inlet valves. Turning off the tap or valve stops the water flow suddenly and sets up shock waves in the pipework, which are the cause of the hammering noise.

Stop vibration

Pipes running parallel with the joists under suspended timber floors need firm support to stop them vibrating. Copper pipe 15 mm in diameter should rest on a support batten or be clipped to the joists every 1.2 m on horizontal runs and every 1.8 m on vertical ones. For 22 mm pipe, increase the spacings to 1.8 m and 2.4 m respectively.

Cushions for creaks

Hot-water and central-heating pipes are often run in notches cut in the floor joists. If they are a tight fit, they will creak as they expand and the noise will be amplified in the underfloor void.

Lift boards to expose suspect pipes, and widen tight notches by cutting out a little more wood with a sharp wood chisel. Then cushion the pipes in the notches by resting them on slim pads of loft insulation blanket.

Under arrest

Fit a water-hammer arrester on the supply pipework if reducing the mains pressure fails to cure banging noises in the pipes. This device contains a small air-filled bellows or piston which absorbs the shock waves causing the noise.

Cough remedy

A spluttering kitchen sink hot tap is caused by a partial airlock in the pipe run from the hot cylinder. To cure the problem, attach a short length of garden hose between the hot and cold taps. Then turn on first the hot tap, then the cold one. The higher pressure in the cold tap, which is supplied directly from the rising main, will blow the airlock back up the hot pipe so it can escape into the cylinder.

Gurgling away

A sink, bath or basin that empties with a gurgle has a problem waste pipe. It's either too long or it doesn't have sufficient fall. In each case the waste pipe runs full until the appliance is empty, when air is drawn into the pipe and causes the noise. The only solution to an over-long pipe is to replace it with pipe of a larger diameter. You may be able to increase the fall on the waste pipe by fitting a shallower trap so the pipe starts at a higher level.

Plastic fantastic

You can cut down on the amount of noise transmitted along copper pipework by cutting out a section and inserting one or two plastic push-fit fittings into the run. You can even replace troublesome sections of copper pipework with semi-flexible plastic pipe if the noise persists.

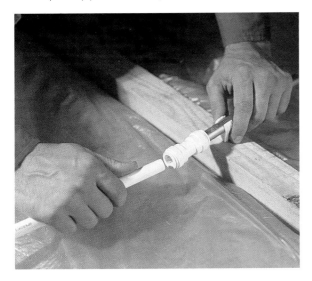

Trouble at the tank

Fit a bigger float

Drawing water from the cold-water storage tank can set the arm of the ballvalve bouncing up and down as water rushes into the tank. This in turn causes the valve to open and close rapidly, sending a tell-tale chugging sound through the supply pipework. Try curing the problem by replacing the existing float with a bigger one.

Silence noisy valves

Worn components inside old brass ballvalves can cause a variety of high-pitched sounds in the supply pipework. If you have a noisy old valve controlling your storage tank, replace it with a modern plastic one. Ask for one with a spray inlet, which helps to reduce the sound of water splashing into the tank as it refills.

Hush-hush opportunity

Replace a noisy old-fashioned brass ballvalve in a toilet cistern with an almost-silent plastic one, such as a Torbeck or Hushflo valve. At the same time, fit an in-line isolating valve on the supply pipe to the cistern. Then you can shut off the water easily when any maintenance work is needed on the ballvalve or siphon unit in the future.

Dampen the bounce

Another way to stop ballvalve bounce is to fit a float damper. This can be a small plastic flower pot hung from the arm on a length of stiff wire, or a proprietary clip-on damper disc. The extra drag created by the submerged pot or disc stops the float bobbing up and down.

Brace the tank wall

Fit a tank bracing plate between the tank wall and the backnut on the threaded tail of the ballvalve. This plate is designed to stop the wall of the tank flexing and causing vibration in the supply pipe as the valve operates. A plate should be fitted on every plastic tank, but it is often omitted. You can buy one from any plumbers' merchant.

noisy plumbing
Noises in heating systems

Check the thermostat
Banging noises in the pipes may be due to overheating. To find the cause of the fault, start by checking if the boiler thermostat is working. Turn the boiler off but leave the pump running to help to cool the system down. Then turn the boiler on and turn up the thermostat. If you do not hear a click, turn everything off again and call a heating engineer.

Cure a water shortage
A common cause of overheating and pipe noise in the heating system is a shortage of water. This is usually caused by losses from evaporation not being replaced by the feed-and-expansion tank. Check your tank, and operate the ballvalve to refill the tank to about a third full if it has run dry. Service or replace the ballvalve if it is stiff to operate, to ensure that in future it tops the tank up when necessary.

Stop pipes humming
A humming sound in the heating system pipework usually comes from the pump, and is often caused by the pump speed being set too high. Try turning down the speed control knob on the pump body by one setting. If this fails to cut the noise and also makes the radiators take longer to heat up, call in a heating engineer for some expert advice. He may suggest relocating the pump.

Banish boiler scale
Noises from the boiler like a kettle boiling indicate a build-up of scale, caused by hard water, inside its heat exchanger. Remove this by adding a chemical descaler to the system at the feed-and-expansion tank. Turn on the heating to pump the descaler around for a while, then flush the system with clean water. Empty it once more, then refill it and add a corrosion inhibitor.

Air in the system
Vent the radiators if a sound like rushing water travelling around the heating system pipework occurs whenever the pump switches itself on. This is a sure sign that air or gas has got into the system. Air is most commonly sucked in via the system's open vent pipe because of poor system design, and you will need expert advice to cure the problem. Hydrogen gas is created by corrosion which can be prevented by adding a chemical corrosion inhibitor at the feed-and-expansion tank.

insulation Keeping the pipes warm

Spiral wrapping

Where you can't easily fit split-sleeve foam insulation, such as around a gatevalve, wrap the pipe and fitting in hessian-based hair felt—available in rolls from plumbers' merchants. Overlap each turn by 50 per cent so the insulation is doubled in thickness, but don't pull it too tightly or you will squeeze all the air out and reduce its insulating value. Use wire or string to secure the cut ends and any other parts of the wrapping which could possibly work loose.

A thicker coat
Replace old insulation on vulnerable pipes with new split-sleeve insulation. Following a spate of harsh winters, the manufacturers have increased its wall thickness so it can cope with lower temperatures for longer.

Tailored to fit

Shape a length of insulation to encase a pipe with a gentler bend, such as a vent pipe, by making a series of wedge-shaped nicks in it. The insulation will then fit snugly round the curve. Again tape the joints to keep them closed.

Foam alone

Polyurethane foam filler, which comes in aerosol form, is ideal for insulating pipes in inaccessible places such as where they pass through walls. Squirt the foam into the gap, leave it to expand and set hard, then trim off any excess with a sharp knife. **It is also good for insulating** outside pipes and garden taps, since it sticks well to the metal. This stops rainwater penetrating the insulation and freezing the pipe inside. Make a weatherproof box to fit round the tap and pipework from exterior-grade plywood, then fill the box with foam. Trim excess foam away from the tap handle with a knife and fit a wooden cover to the box.

Cut neat joints

Make 45° cuts in split-sleeve pipe insulation with scissors or a sharp bread knife so you can form neat joins at elbows and tees. Use PVC insulating tape to keep the joints tightly closed and avoid a freeze-up.

insulation How to keep the heat in

Add an extra layer

Where plumbing pipes run across the loft floor, double up their protection against frost by insulating them in the usual way (see page 169) and then placing the loft insulation over them. Keep electricity cables above the insulation wherever possible, so they can't overheat.

Remember the hatch

Tape a piece of insulation blanket to the upper side of the loft hatch and fit self-adhesive foam draught-proofing around the edges of the hatch opening, to prevent valuable heat from the room below escaping into the roof space.

Meet the standard

Add another layer of insulation blanket in your loft if what you have is less than 100 mm thick. The current Building Regulations require a minimum of 200 mm of loft insulation in new houses, so adding an extra 100 mm or 150 mm blanket on top of what is already there will bring your property up to present-day standards. **Because glass fibre can irritate the skin,** buy insulation blanket that's wrapped in a thin layer of plastic to make it more pleasant to handle (above).

Allow breathing space

Keep loft insulation blanket away from the eaves by fitting proprietary plastic ventilator trays between the joists. If the eaves ventilation is blocked, warm moist air rising from the house will condense within the cold loft space and settle as moisture on the roof timbers. This condensation can cause the wood to rot, saturate the insulation and spoil the plaster and decoration on the ceilings in upstairs rooms.

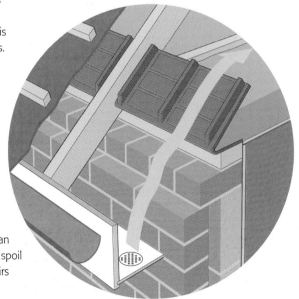

Keep the tank warm

Don't insulate the loft floor under the cold-water storage tank; a little warm air from the room below should be allowed to rise around the base of the tank, helping to prevent it from freezing in very cold weather. Instead, make as tight a seal as possible between the loft floor insulation and the insulation around the tank itself, so that heat is trapped below the tank rather than being lost into the roof space.

Fast and loose

If the space between your joists varies, as it may in older homes, or if your loft is an awkward shape, insulation blanket may not fit very well. Get round the problem by laying loose-fill material instead. You can use vermiculite granules (above) or loose mineral wool, both of which can be pushed into hard-to-reach parts of the roof space with a broom. Plastic ventilator trays will stop the granules being lost down a cavity wall if it is open at the top.

Blowing in the wind

Vermiculite granules laid as insulation in a well-ventilated loft will almost certainly be blown into heaps by draughts. You can prevent this by laying the granules level with the tops of the joists and then covering them with sheets of building paper, stapled over the joists. Don't use polythene; it will trap water vapour and cause condensation.

Warming the loft

Insulate the underside of the roof slope if you want a warm loft (to use as a playroom, for example). You need to maintain a ventilation gap immediately below the roof covering to prevent any risk of condensation, so use insulation 50 mm thick and don't push it against the underside of the slates or tiles. Slabs of mineral wool are stiff enough to wedge between the rafters and stay in place without support, but strips of 50 mm-thick insulation blanket will need to be held up by string wound between nails driven into the rafter sides.

Line the roof slope with hardboard or plasterboard if you want to conceal the insulation and achieve a neater look.

electrics

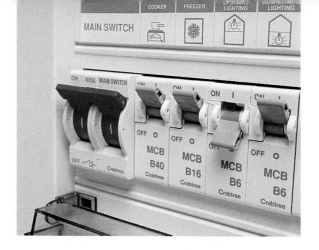

systems
Investigating your power supply

Be a detective

Before you can fix faults or make any changes to the wiring system, you need to know where the main fuse board is, what circuits it supplies, which lights and appliances are on which circuits, what sort of electrical protection the system offers and how everything is wired up. In short, you have to be an electrical detective. What you discover will be invaluable when you come to work on your wiring, and is crucial for your safety. The first thing to do is to find out where to turn the house's power supply on and off.

Switching off

Before doing any work on the wiring, make sure the power is off. If the system has MCBs, and you intend to work on a single circuit, just switch off the relevant MCB (above). If the dead circuit is a lighting one and you need light, plug a lamp into a socket. Run an extension lead to a separately supplied socket if you've switched off a power circuit and need to use power tools.

Out with the old

The fuse board may be located in an entrance hall, understairs cupboard, or even in a basement if the property has one. In older homes, if the wiring has not been modernised, the board will contain a main on/off switch and a series of separate fuse boxes, each controlling an individual circuit. Such a system is obsolete and is probably highly unsafe to use. If this sounds like the system in your home, have it replaced immediately by a qualified electrician and, until then, do not attempt to do any wiring work.

Upgrade from a fuse box to a consumer unit

In homes built or rewired since the 1960s, there will be a one-piece fuse box containing the system's on/off switch and all the individual circuit fuses side by side. It may be housed in a cupboard or in an attached or integral garage, or may be openly displayed on a wall surface. The most modern type of fuse box is known as a consumer unit, and contains a series of switches called miniature circuit breakers (MCBs) rather than circuit fuses. These are safer and more convenient than fuses, so if you still have the latter it is well worth considering getting them replaced with a consumer unit containing MCBs.

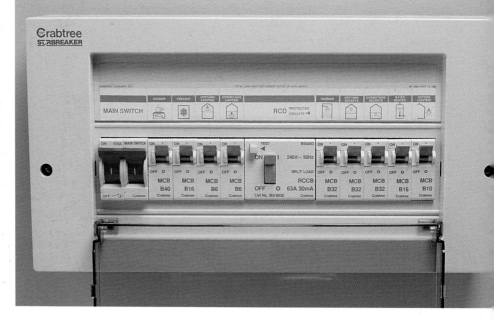

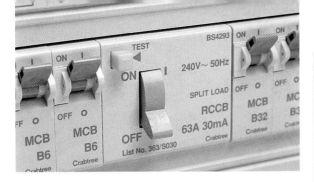

Preventing shocks and fires

As well as MCBs, modern consumer units also contain a separate circuit breaker called a residual current device (RCD). This is a safety feature that detects the current imbalance caused if you touch something that's live and current starts to flow to earth through your body. It cuts off the current in a fraction of a second–fast enough to prevent the shock from stopping your heart beating. It also detects current leaks resulting from problems such as faulty insulation, which can cause electrical fires to start, and again shuts off the power. If you have an RCD, check from time to time that it is working properly by pressing its test button to trip it off.

Pocket for safety's sake

If you have circuit fuses, turn off the power at the main on/off switch before starting work. Then remove the fuse for the circuit you will be working on. Keep it in your pocket so no one else can replace it until you have finished.

Counting circuits

A typical modern home may have two or three lighting circuits, a similar number supplying socket outlets into which portable appliances are plugged, plus circuits to individual appliances that use a lot of current–a cooker, an immersion heater or an electric shower, for example. Each circuit will have its own circuit fuse or MCB in the consumer unit. Check your unit so you know how many different circuits you have, and stick a label inside the lid so you can see at a glance which fuse or MCB controls which circuit.

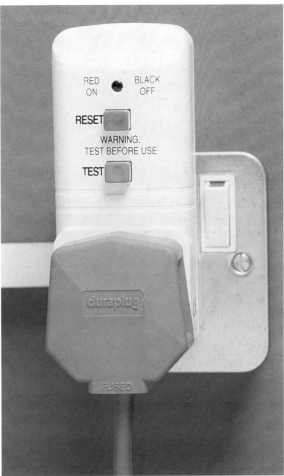

Stay safe outside

Even if your wiring system has an RCD to protect it, always plug garden power tools, such as lawnmowers and hedge trimmers, into a special socket outlet or adaptor containing a high-sensitivity RCD (above). This will give you even greater protection against the risk of shock if you cut through an extension lead and touch a live conductor.

Don't blow a fuse

Fuses exist to protect circuits from overloading. If you try to draw more current from a circuit than it's intended to supply, the cable may overheat and cause a fire. The fuse is a weak link, designed to melt and cut off the current if overloading occurs. Take care when plugging in a number of appliances containing heating elements all at once: they are the big current consumers.

In modern installations the fuse's job is done by an MCB. This switches the current off if it detects an overload, and cannot be switched back on until all of the offending appliances have been turned off or disconnected.

systems Investigating your power supply

Which light, which circuit?
A 5-amp or 6-amp circuit fuse rating means that the circuit is supplying fixed lights. If you have more than one such circuit, it is helpful to know which one supplies which rooms. The way to find out depends on whether you have fuses or MCBs. Either turn off the main switch and remove one of the fuses, or simply switch off one of the MCBs. Then turn on all the fixed ceiling and wall lights in the house, and make a note of which ones are lit and which are not. That will tell you which lights are on which circuit.

Check socket allocation
To find out which socket outlets are on which power circuit, follow the same procedure as for the light circuits, but with the 30-amp circuit fuses or 32-amp MCBs. Don't expect all the sockets in a room to be on the same circuit; electricians often wire up outlets that are physically remote from one circuit—at the end of a long room, for example—as spurs from adjacent circuits. It is important to know this, as you might otherwise go to work on an outlet you think is isolated but which is live.

Keeping spares
If your system is fitted with rewirable fuses, buy a couple of spare wired-up fuseholders—one rated at 5 amps and one at 30 amps—and keep them next to the consumer unit. You will then be able to replace a blown fuse as soon as the fault has been rectified, and rewire the fuse later at your leisure.

Health checks for plugs
Your plugs should look like the one on the left, not the one on the right. Once a year, set aside a couple of hours to give the plugs on all your appliances a quick health check.

Open each one up and check that all the terminal screws are tight and are gripping their flex cores securely, with no stray wires visible. Hold the plug and tug the flex to see that the cord grip is working. Replace any plug that has a cracked casing. Finally, check that the plug contains the correct fuse for the appliance—a 3-amp one (colour-coded red) if the wattage is below 700 watts, a 5-amp fuse if it's under 1200 watts, and a 13-amp one (brown) otherwise.

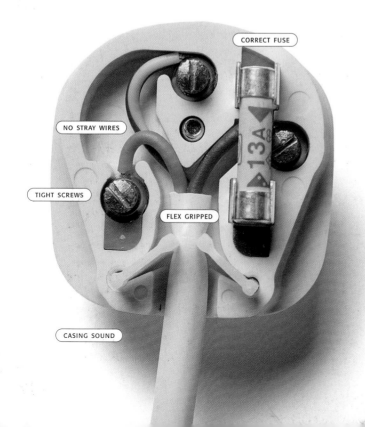

NO STRAY WIRES

TIGHT SCREWS

CORRECT FUSE

FLEX GRIPPED

CASING SOUND

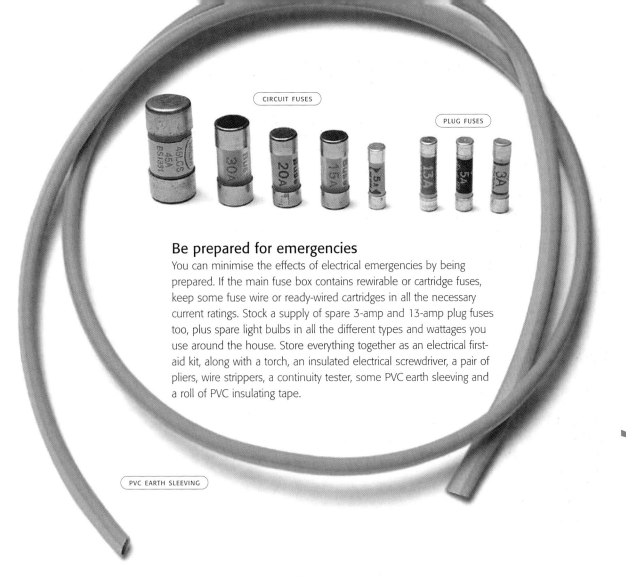

CIRCUIT FUSES

PLUG FUSES

PVC EARTH SLEEVING

Be prepared for emergencies

You can minimise the effects of electrical emergencies by being prepared. If the main fuse box contains rewirable or cartridge fuses, keep some fuse wire or ready-wired cartridges in all the necessary current ratings. Stock a supply of spare 3-amp and 13-amp plug fuses too, plus spare light bulbs in all the different types and wattages you use around the house. Store everything together as an electrical first-aid kit, along with a torch, an insulated electrical screwdriver, a pair of pliers, wire strippers, a continuity tester, some PVC earth sleeving and a roll of PVC insulating tape.

faultfinding Tracing problems

No lights?

Suspect a blown light bulb first, and fit a replacement of the correct type and wattage. If mains lights still don't work, inspect the consumer unit to see if the lighting circuit fuse has blown or its miniature circuit breaker (MCB) has switched itself off.

If plug-in lights do not work, check first whether the plug fuse has blown or whether there is a loose flex connection inside the plug or the light. Then check whether the power circuit fuse has blown or whether the circuit MCB has cut off the supply.

No power?

Unplug the appliance and plug in another. If this works, the first appliance is at fault. If it does not, then there is probably a fault in the circuit. If the faulty appliance feels hot or is smoking, take it to a service engineer for repairs. Otherwise check the plug and flex for loose or broken connections.

Circuit down?

When nothing on a circuit works, turn off the lights and unplug the appliances that run from it. Then check the main fuse box to see if the circuit fuse has blown or the MCB has switched off. Replace the fuse or switch the MCB back on. If it blows or trips immediately, there is a fault on the circuit wiring and you need to call an electrician to find it. If it does not, switch on lights or plug in appliances one by one to identify which is causing the problem. Check, too, that you are not overloading the circuit.

faultfinding Tracing problems

Watch the watts

When replacing a bulb in a light fitting, check inside the lampshade for a label indicating the maximum bulb wattage the manufacturer recommends. Do not exceed this, or you risk damaging the shade or the fitting.

Look for the fuse rating

Make sure that every appliance has the correct fuse in its plug, by checking its wattage (power consumption). For light fittings this is on the bulb; appliances have it printed somewhere on their outer casing. Fit a 3-amp fuse if the wattage is less than 700 watts, a 5-amp fuse if it's under 1200 watts (1.2 kw), and a 13-amp fuse for higher wattages.

A safe grip

If a light bulb is smashed, turn the power to its circuit off at the mains. Then use pliers to grip the stump of the bulb and remove it from its lampholder. Wear safety goggles in case any of the broken glass falls out.

Reducing sensitivity

Some lighting circuit MCBs can trip off whenever a light bulb fails. The problem is caused by pieces of rupturing element wire causing a short circuit inside the bulb. The solution is either to get an electrician to fit less sensitive MCBs on your lighting circuits, or to buy top-quality light bulbs which have a fuse in the base designed to blow when the lamp fails.

Total power failure

If the whole house has no power, check first whether there is a local power cut. If there is, report it to your electricity supply company. If yours is the only house without power and there is a residual current device (RCD) in the consumer unit, this may have tripped off. Try resetting it; if you cannot, the fault is still present. In this case run through the appliance and circuit checks, or call an electrician. Lastly, your main service fuse may have blown. If it has, call your supply company and ask for an engineer to come and replace it.

Using testers

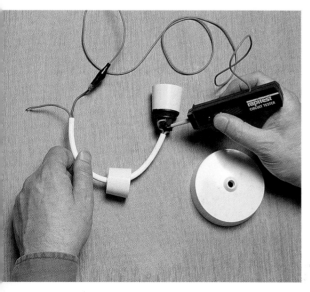

Look for the light

One useful job for a continuity tester is checking whether flex and cable cores are unbroken, since you cannot inspect them visually. Just touch the probe to one end of each core and attach the clip to the other; if the core is sound the indicator light comes on.
If you have a multimeter, use it as an ohmmeter to measure the resistance of the circuit or core (a low reading shows there is a continuous current path).

Plug in and test

A socket-outlet tester will show whether outlets have been wired up correctly. Plug it into the outlet you want to test, switch the power supply on and see which combination of the three indicator lights is lit.

Indispensable item

There is one piece of equipment every DIY electrician needs—a continuity tester. It allows you to identify breaks in any electrical circuit, and to test components such as switches and fuses.

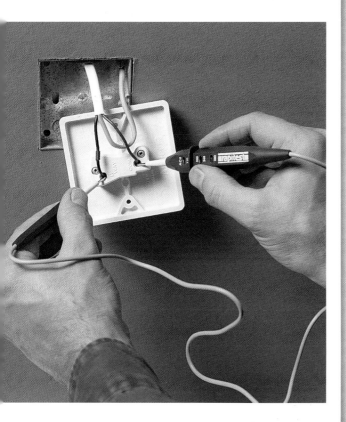

Checking for live parts

A voltage tester tells you whether a cable or a wiring accessory such as a light switch or socket outlet is live. Touch its probes to the end of a bare conductor or across live terminals. It will light up or bleep if mains voltage is present.

1 Turn mains switch off and remove fuse-holder for blown circuit from its socket

2 With rewirable fuses, loosen terminal screws and remove remains of burnt-out wire

3 Feed new wire through tube or across bridge of fuse-holder and connect it to the terminals. Trim off excess wire

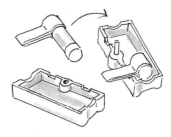

4 With cartridge fuses, take out old fuse and fit new one. Some fit into clips; others are held by the fuseholder pins

faultfinding

flex Make safe and secure connections

Getting inside appliances

To fit a new flex to an appliance, you need to be able to get inside it so that you can reach the terminals to which the flex is connected. If you cannot see immediately how to open the appliance casing, or if screws with unfamiliar head types have been used to fix it together, don't try to go any further. Have the flex replaced by an electrical repair shop.

Dispose of plugs safely

Discard a moulded-on plug if you have to replace the flex to which it is connected; you can't re-use it because the plug casing is designed not to be opened. Hammer one of the plug pins to bend it out of line, so the plug cannot be inserted in a socket outlet by an inquisitive child; the cut ends of the flex would be live in this situation.

Yearly inspection

Flex–short for flexible cord–links appliances and portable light fittings to the mains supply. If the outer sheath gets damaged, you could get a shock. So inspect all your flexes once a year for wear and tear. When you find flex that's been damaged, make it safe temporarily with PVC insulating tape, and replace the whole flex as soon as possible.

Use the right size

Flex is sized by the cross-sectional area of the conductors. Use 0.75 mm^2 flex for lights and small appliances, the 1 mm^2 size for appliances rated up to 2.3 kW and 1.5 mm^2 flex for more powerful appliances. If you are buying flex for a pendant light with a heavy lampshade, use 1 mm^2 flex; it's stronger than the 0.75 mm^2 size.

Earthed or not

Most appliances are fitted with flex containing three cores–live and neutral to carry the current in and out, plus an earth core that takes current away safely in the event of a fault. Use two-core flex with no earth core on light fittings with no metallic parts, and also on double-insulated appliances such as power tools. The latter have a double-square symbol on the outer casing to show that they are double-insulated.

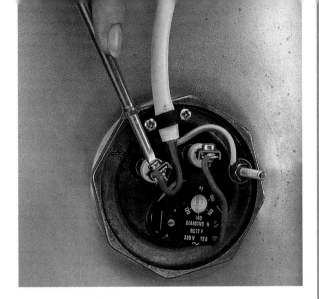

Resistant to heat

PVC-sheathed flex can withstand heat well enough for everyday use. However, you should use special heat-resistant flex of the appropriate current rating—usually the 1.5 mm² size—to wire up immersion heaters (above), water heaters and night storage heaters.

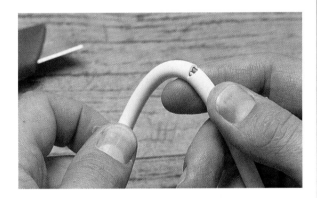

Nick and split

Before connecting new flex to a plug or appliance, you need to remove some of the PVC outer sheath and also the insulation on the individual cores to expose the conductors inside. Fold the flex at the point where you want to cut the sheath, and nick it with a sharp knife. The tension will open up a split. Fold the flex the other way and repeat the process to extend the cut all round the sheath. This method avoids any risk of your knife cutting into the core insulation.

Tidy up loose ends

Fabric-covered non-kink flex, used mainly on irons, has an outer layer of braided fabric over a flexible rubber sheath. After nicking and cutting these away as for PVC flex, wrap the end of the flex in PVC tape to stop the cut fabric from unravelling in use.

1 Strip outer sheath from flex, lay flex over open plug and lead each core to its terminal. Cut each core to length

2 Remove the insulation from each core with wire strippers, then twist strands of wire together neatly

3 With pillar terminals, loosen screw, insert core in hole and tighten down screw again. Check that core is secure

4 With stud terminals, remove nut and its captive washer. Wind core clockwise round stud and screw down nut

flex

flex Make safe and secure connections

Leave the earth long

After removing the outer sheath, you need to cut the individual flex cores to length so they can comfortably reach their terminals inside a plug, or at an appliance terminal block. Always cut the earth core a little overlong, so that if the flex is tugged and the cord grip fails to work, this core will be the last to be pulled away from its terminal.

Eliminate guesswork

Use wire strippers to remove the core insulation. Depending on the type of tool you have, either set the separation of its jaws to match the core diameter, or select the right aperture in the tool's body. Then grip the core to cut through just the insulation, and slide the severed portion off the conductors. If you cut through any of the conductors as you do this, cut off the rest and start again.

Connect and extend

If an appliance needs a longer flex, you can add an extra section using a one-piece flex connector. Connect like cores to like within the connector, and ensure that the sheath on each section of flex is securely held in its cord grip.

Use a two-piece connector if you need to disconnect the extension for storage or use with another appliance. The part with the pins must always be fitted on the flex to the appliance.

Heat softens insulation

You can remove the insulation from flex cores without any risk of cutting the conductors by using heat to soften the plastic. Simply light a match or use a cigarette lighter and heat the core at the point where you want to remove the insulation. Then strip the insulation with pliers before it can harden again.

Remember remember

To remind you of which flex core goes where inside a plug, use this simple reminder. Looking down on the open plug with the flex inlet at the bottom, the core with the BRown insulation goes to the Bottom Right terminal and the core with the BLue insulation goes to the Bottom Left terminal. If the flex also contains an earth core, this goes to the top terminal.

Using extension leads

Extension leads are long lengths of flex with a plug at one end and a socket outlet at the other. Always unwind them fully before using them, even though you may not need all the length. This prevents the coiled-up flex from overheating. Check the flex rating if you intend to use it with a fire or heater; many leads are rated at only 5 amps and will overheat if used to supply the higher current these appliances take.

Taking the strain with a cord grip

The flex sheath should extend inside a plug or appliance and should be held by a cord grip so that a tug on the flex does not put any strain on the flex cores or pull them away from their terminals. If any flex cores are visible outside the plug or appliance, unplug it. Remake the connections after shortening the cores a little, and ensure that the flex sheath is securely held in the cord grip. Press the sheath between pairs of nylon jaws (left) or screw down the crossbar onto it (right).

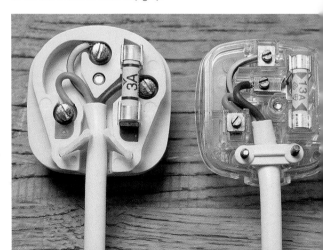

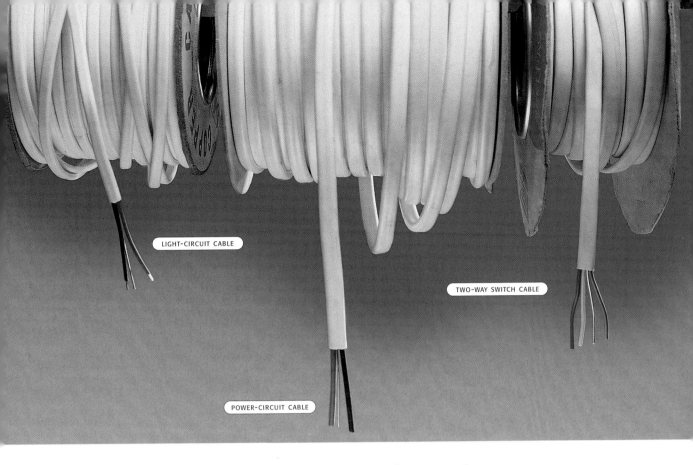

LIGHT-CIRCUIT CABLE

TWO-WAY SWITCH CABLE

POWER-CIRCUIT CABLE

cable The right type for the job

Sizing things up
All the concealed wiring in the home is made up of cable. Like flex, cable is sized by the cross-sectional area of its conductors. The 1 mm^2 is used for lighting circuits and the 2.5 mm^2 for circuits supplying socket outlets. Heavy current users such as electric cookers and showers are usually supplied by 6 mm^2 or 10 mm^2 cables.

Identifying the cores
Cable contains live and neutral cores (insulated in red and black PVC respectively) to carry the current, and a third core (the earth), which provides a continuous path throughout the wiring system along which current can flow to earth in the event of an electrical fault. Never disconnect it or cut it away.

For two-way switches
One special cable has three insulated cores, plus an earth core. Use it solely for wiring up two-way switches. The cores are colour-coded red, yellow and blue for identification purposes only; all may be live at one time or another, depending on which switch is on.

Buying in bulk
If you have a lot of wiring to do, buy 1 mm^2 and 2.5 mm^2 cable by the reel. Each reel contains 50 m or 100 m of cable, giving you a unit price far lower than buying by the metre.

Avoid kinks
If you are using cable off a reel, mount it on a makeshift axle. Then you can rotate it and pull off lengths of cable without it curling into an awkward spiral, as it will if you lay the reel flat.

Safety sleeve for the earth
The earth core in cable is a bare copper conductor. Whenever it is exposed inside a mounting box, to make a connection to a wiring accessory, it must be covered with a piece of slip-on green-and-yellow PVC sleeving. Cut this to length to leave about 10 mm (3⁄8 in) of earth core exposed. Fold the end of the bare core over the sleeving to retain it until you are ready to connect it to an earth terminal.

183

cable
Routes to take

Avoiding disruption

When a house is built, circuit cables are concealed under timber floors, above ceilings, beneath wall plaster and inside stud walls. Hiding new cables once a house is complete means disturbing wall and floor decorations, so run them on the surface as a temporary measure, either secured with clips or in stick-on plastic mini-trunking. You can conceal them properly next time you decorate.

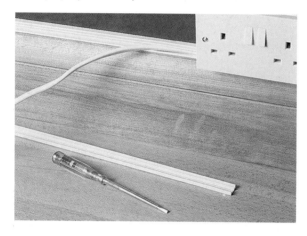

Beware of insulation

In lofts, make sure cables are kept above any insulation that's laid on the loft floor, especially if you have loose polystyrene granules. These contain a chemical that can damage PVC cable sheath, making it brittle and unsafe.

Keep tiles intact

If you need to run cable to a new wiring accessory that will be mounted on a wall that is already tiled, you can avoid disrupting the tiling by cutting a chase for the cable in the plaster on the other side of the wall. Drill a hole through the wall from the tiled side first so you know where the chase is to terminate.

Slide over the bumps

In older homes, original ceilings may be made of lath and plaster, and you will not be able to push a length of new cable through an upstairs underfloor void, because its end will keep snagging on the ridged plaster. Tape the cable end to a paper picnic plate or a plastic Frisbee. This will slide over the ridges as you push the cable through.

Out of harm's way

Clip surface-mounted cables next to mouldings such as skirting boards and door architraves. These will give them some protection from accidental knocks. The clips are easy to remove if you later decide to cut a chase in the wall and conceal the cable permanently.

Inside the box

Sockets and switches are installed on metal or plastic mounting boxes, either fixed on the surface or recessed in the wall. Strip enough sheath from the incoming cable to allow each core to reach its terminal easily, but make sure that the sheath itself terminates just inside the box, not outside it.

Installing in new stud walls

The horizontal braces, or noggings, inside stud walls (see page 74) prevent cable from being dropped down the full height of the wall once it has been covered with plasterboard (see page 76).

To keep disruption to a minimum, feed cables up the wall from below to supply new socket outlets (see right). Because light switches are fixed above standard nogging level, you will have to drop lighting cable down between the studs from above.

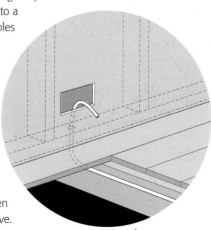

Under the floor

If you have timber floors, it is possible to extend circuits by running new cables beneath them. This is easiest to do in upstairs rooms with a plasterboard ceiling below, and where the new cable is to run parallel to the joists. Lift a section of floorboard at each side of the room and slide the cable through the 'tunnel'. On ground floors, lift boards at intervals across the room so you can pass the cable along from one opening to the next, and clip it to the sides of the joists as you do so.

Crossing the joists

When a new cable runs at 90° to the line of the floor joists, lift a couple of adjacent floorboards—or maybe just one—across the room. Then you can drill a hole through the centre of each joist and feed the cable through. When you replace the floorboards, fix them with screws rather than nails to make them easier to lift if you need access to the cable. Write 'cable under' on the boards if they are covered by carpet, to remind you of what lies underneath.

STAGES IN
PREPARING CABLE

1 Mark cable sheath at point where you want to cut. Then split sheath lengthways with a sharp trimming knife

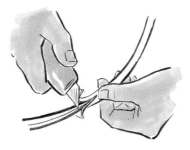

2 Peel back split sheath and cut off excess neatly to expose required length of cores

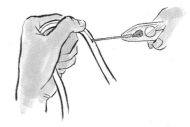

3 Alternatively, grip bare earth core with a pair of pliers and pull backwards along cable to split sheath

4 Remove about 10 mm (³⁄₈ in) of insulation from live and neutral cores with wire strippers, set to suit core size

fittings Replacing switches and socket outlets

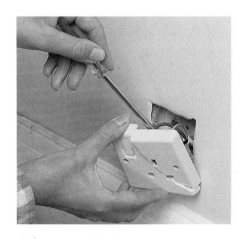

Off with the old

New wiring accessories in place of dirty, damaged or simply old-fashioned ones add a finishing touch to a redecorated room. It is best to remove the old fittings before you start to paint or hang wallpaper. Turn the power off at the fusebox or consumer unit first. Then undo the screws holding old faceplates to their mounting boxes and ease them away from the wall. Loosen the terminal screws so you can disconnect the cables and free the faceplates.

Make a sketch

It is generally obvious which cable cores go to which terminal. However, if you are in any doubt, make a sketch of the existing wiring arrangement before you disconnect anything. Then you can mimic this as you connect up the new faceplate. If you are confused by what you reveal, ask an electrician to make the changeover for you.

Danger signals from old rubber

What you find when you turn off the power and open up old-fashioned wiring accessories tells you a lot about your wiring system. The circuit cables should be insulated and sheathed in plastic. If you find old rubber insulation, do not disturb it. The cables are highly dangerous and the system needs rewiring without delay by a professional electrician.

Save the screws

Keep the old faceplate fixing screws; the ones supplied with the new wiring accessory may have metric threads, and these won't mesh properly with the old imperial threads inside the lugs in the existing mounting box. If the new faceplate is thicker than the old one, you may need longer screws to fit it.

Spray to unlock

If you want to replace a ceiling rose or a pendant lampholder, you may not be able to undo the covers because heat has locked the threads. To free them, turn the power off and spray some aerosol lubricant such as WD-40 onto them. Leave it to penetrate for a few minutes before trying to undo them. If this doesn't work, use a hammer to crack the cover in two.

Sleeve all the earths

You may find one or more bare earth cores within the mounting box when you open up an existing faceplate. If you do, disconnect them from the earth terminal and slip a length of green-and-yellow PVC earth sleeving over each core, then reconnect them to the terminal. You must also use earth sleeving on the earth cores of any new cables you add to your wiring system.

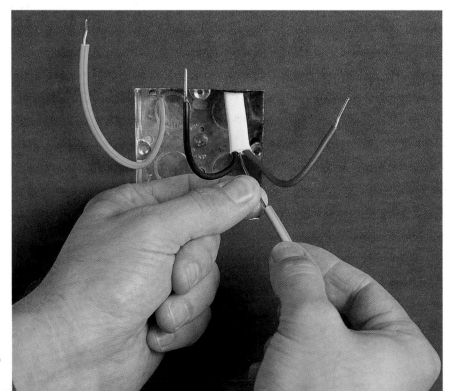

Name each switch

Many kitchens have switches above the worktop that control appliances fitted underneath. To make it clear which switch controls which appliance, replace existing plain switches with new ones that have the appliance name printed on them.

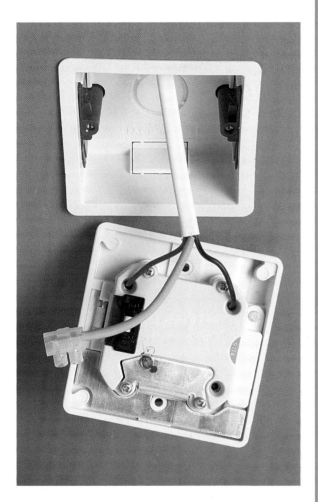

Controlling brightness

Consider replacing existing light switches with dimmer switches, which allow you to control the light level in the room. When choosing one, make sure its stated wattage range matches the wattage of the light(s) it will be controlling. Check too that it will fit on the existing switch mounting box; some dimmers need a deeper box.

Safety insulation

If a plastic faceplate is broken and the live parts are exposed, make it safe at once by covering the hole with PVC insulating tape. Tape over the switch in the off position, too, so that you can't use it until you replace the faceplate.

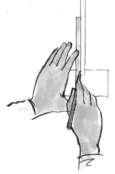

1 Mark out cable route and, if necessary, position of new flush mounting box to which it will run

2 Use a sharp bolster chisel and club hammer to chop out chase and recess for box. Cut plaster back to solid masonry

3 Drill down behind skirting board with long masonry drill bit, to clear cable route down to floor level

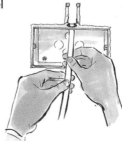

4 Fit mounting box in recess. Fix oval PVC conduit in chase with galvanised nails and feed in new cable

fittings

fittings Replacing switches and socket outlets

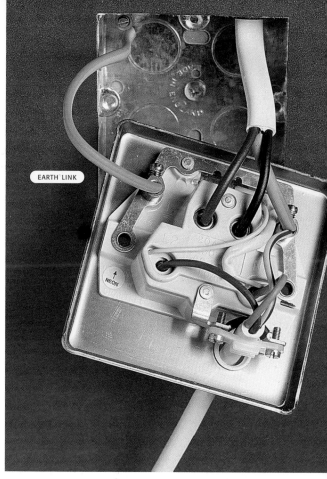

EARTH LINK

NEON

Cut the seal
An old faceplate may be stuck to the wall with paint or wallpaper. Turn off the power and run a trimming knife around the line where the two meet to break the seal. Then the decorations won't be damaged as the faceplate is removed.

Brand new cord
The pull cord on a ceiling-mounted switch can become dirty and frayed in use. To fit a new cord, undo the two-part 'acorn' fitting just beneath the switch. Then push the knotted end of the cord out and cut it. Fit a new length of cord, knotting it to retain the toggle and acorn, and re-attach it to the switch.

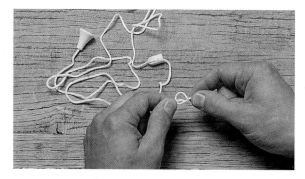

Earth metal faceplates
If you are replacing a plastic faceplate with a metallic one on a metal mounting box, fit an earth link to connect the earth terminal in the box to the one on the faceplate. This prevents the fixing screws from becoming live if a cable core gets loose and touches the box. Use earth core from a bit of spare cable, and cover it in green-and-yellow PVC sleeving.

Extending existing power circuits

Floor area limit

NEW OUTLETS

NEW CABLE

NEW CABLE

DISCARDED CABLE

You can extend an existing ring circuit to provide extra socket outlets—in a new home extension, for example—so long as the total floor area of the rooms to be supplied by the extended circuit does not exceed 100 m². Disconnect the circuit wiring at two socket outlets next to each other on the ring, and discard the cable that connected them. Then run 2.5 mm² cable from the first existing outlet on to the new outlets in turn. Finally run cable back to the second existing outlet to complete the extended ring.

Convert a radial
You can achieve the same effect if you have a radial power circuit. Convert it into a ring circuit by running 2.5 mm² cable from the last socket outlet on the existing circuit back to the consumer unit via a number of new socket outlets. At the consumer unit, connect the live core of the new cable to the existing radial circuit fuse or MCB, and the neutral and earth cores to their terminal blocks inside the unit. If the circuit fuse or MCB was rated at 20 amps, replace it with one rated at 30 amps.

extra sockets More places to plug in

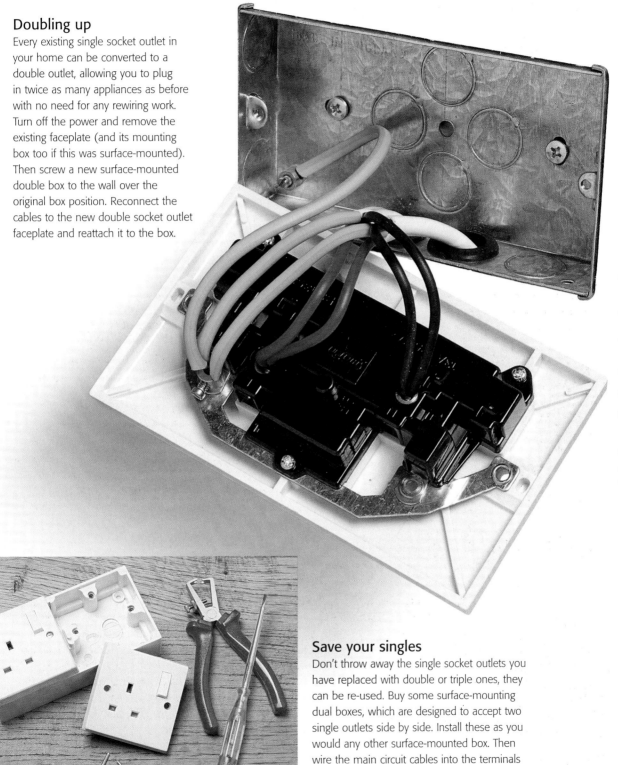

Doubling up

Every existing single socket outlet in your home can be converted to a double outlet, allowing you to plug in twice as many appliances as before with no need for any rewiring work. Turn off the power and remove the existing faceplate (and its mounting box too if this was surface-mounted). Then screw a new surface-mounted double box to the wall over the original box position. Reconnect the cables to the new double socket outlet faceplate and reattach it to the box.

Save your singles

Don't throw away the single socket outlets you have replaced with double or triple ones, they can be re-used. Buy some surface-mounting dual boxes, which are designed to accept two single outlets side by side. Install these as you would any other surface-mounted box. Then wire the main circuit cables into the terminals of one of the outlets, and wire the second outlet as a spur from the first.

extra sockets More places to plug in

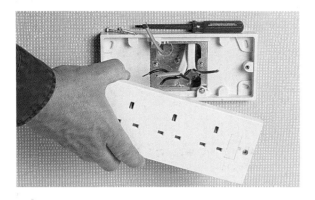

Clever conversion
There is a clever alternative to the standard mounting box which you can use if you are converting flush single outlets to surface-mounted doubles (or triples). It is called a pattress, and is designed to be screwed to the lugs of the existing box rather than to the wall. Save the old faceplate fixing screws for use in attaching the pattress.

Multiple outlets
You need more socket outlets for home entertainment and computer equipment than for any other type of appliance. The individual components take relatively little power, so you can safely plug them into multi-way adaptors. Each adaptor needs only one single socket outlet for its power supply.

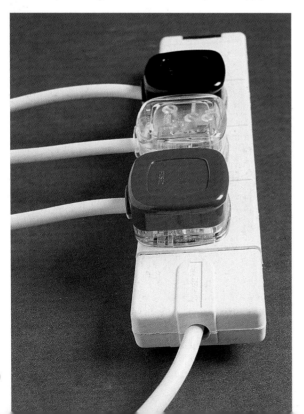

Adjust until level
Always try to fix socket outlets so they are level. Metal flush-mounting boxes have one adjustable fixing lug, which can be moved up or down as the faceplate fixing screws are tightened, allowing you to get the faceplate level even if the box is not. Plastic surface-mounting boxes have slotted fixing holes, allowing you to get the box level on the wall.

Check the cables
If you open an existing socket outlet and find circuit cables insulated with hard rubber, rather than soft PVC, do not attempt to carry out any wiring work. Call in a professional electrician to check whether the system is safe to use and, if it is not, have it fully rewired at the earliest opportunity.

Firm, safe contacts
Plug pins may become a loose fit in the slots of an old socket outlet. This indicates that the metal contacts inside are worn, and this can lead to sparking, overheating and the risk of an electrical fire. Replace the old socket with a new one.

Clip in a box
Use a clip-in cavity wall box if you are fitting a new socket outlet on a timber-framed partition wall. Hold the box in place and draw round it. Then cut out the plasterboard with a padsaw and push the box into the recess. Its spring-loaded lugs will grip the inner face of the board securely. Feed in the cable and connect it to the faceplate.

Use a drilling jig
If you want to flush-mount a socket outlet in a masonry wall, you will have to chop out a recess to a depth of at least 25 mm (1 in) for the mounting box. A special drilling jig, available from DIY stores and electrical suppliers, makes the job easy. Once fixed over the new socket position, you can drill out a honeycomb of closely spaced holes and then knock out the remaining waste.

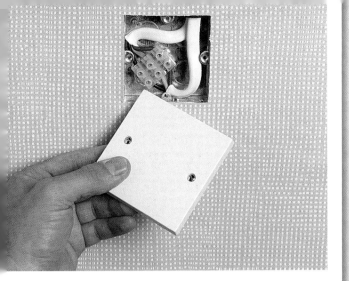

Reposition an awkward socket

A socket outlet on a spur in an inaccessible position—behind heavy furniture, for example—can be used as a junction box, allowing you to resite the outlet somewhere more convenient. Disconnect the existing faceplate, connect the circuit cable cores to strip connectors and wire in the spur cable which is to run to the new socket position. Fit a blanking-off plate to the junction box and use the old faceplate for the new socket.

Playing by the rules

Follow the regulations

The Wiring Regulations define best working practice, so follow them when you do any wiring work. In Scotland they're mandatory, which means if you don't follow them and an accident occurs, you could be held responsible.

Adding sockets on spurs

You can add as many spurs to a ring circuit (see right) as there are socket outlets or fused connection units on the main circuit. Each spur can supply one single or one double socket outlet, or one fused connection unit.

Down to earth

Any socket outlet faceplate that is installed over a flush metal-mounting box must be connected to it by a so-called flying earth link. This is a short length of sleeved earth conductor, fitted between the earth terminal on the rear of the faceplate and the small brass earth terminal fitted in the base of the mounting box. Its purpose is to earth the exposed heads of the faceplate fixing screws, which could become live if a cable core inside the mounting box became detached from its terminal and touched the box.

1 With power off, locate an outlet with two cables and connect in new cable. Run spur to new outlet position

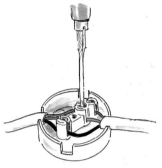

2 Alternatively, find circuit cable under floor, turn power off and cut it. Reconnect ends in three-terminal junction box

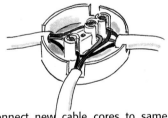

3 Connect new cable cores to same three terminals, linking cores like to like, and run cable to new outlet position

4 At new outlet position, fit mounting box, feed in spur cable and connect it up. Add flying earth link to metal box

extra sockets

lighting Extending existing circuits

Count the cables before extending a circuit

If you want to add extra light fittings to existing circuits, you first need to find out how the system is wired up so you can decide how to extend it. Switch off the power to the circuit you are likely to be working on, then unscrew the cover of one of the ceiling roses. If just one cable is present, this tells you that your system has been wired using junction boxes. If you find two or three cables, as pictured, you have loop-in wiring–the commonest system in modern homes.

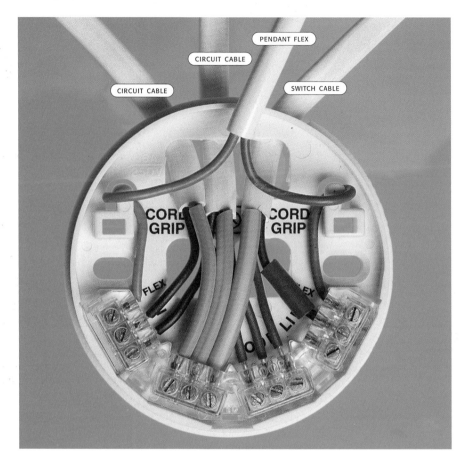

PENDANT FLEX
CIRCUIT CABLE
CIRCUIT CABLE
SWITCH CABLE
CORD GRIP
CORD GRIP
FLEX

How many light points?

When planning to extend a circuit, first count up how many separate lighting points it supplies. Lighting designers rate each point at a nominal 100 watts, so a circuit that is protected by a 5-amp fuse or MCB (miniature circuit breaker) can in theory supply up to 1200 watts (5 amps x 240 volts), or 12 lighting points. In practice this is usually restricted to eight, to allow for the use of higher-wattage lamps or multi-lamp fittings at each individual lighting point. If an extra light fitting will overload an existing circuit, you need an extra circuit–a job for a qualified electrician.

Dealing with stuck roses

You may find that you can't undo the cover of a ceiling rose because it has become encrusted with paint. Turn the power off first, then try to free it by running a knife blade around the edge. If this fails, you have no option but to crack the cover with a sharp hammer blow to get it off. Disconnect and discard the old baseplate and fit a complete new rose.

Black cores are live in switches

Most light switches are wired up with ordinary two-core-and-earth cable, so the black core (properly called the switch return core) is in fact live whenever the switch is on. Every exposed black core in a switch cable should be wrapped in some red PVC tape or covered with a slip-on length of red PVC sleeving to warn of this.

Spur from a junction box

If you are adding a light and you have junction-box wiring, locate the box that's nearest to where you want to install the new light fitting. With the power off, unscrew the box cover and identify which terminal is which.

If you want the existing switch to control the new light, wire in the spur cable using the switch return, neutral and earth terminals in the box. Fit the cable sheath into one of the cut-outs in the side of the box base, and replace the cover. Run the spur cable from the box to the new light position.

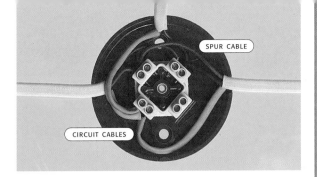

SPUR CABLE

CIRCUIT CABLES

Cut into the circuit

To add a spur to an independent light and switch, locate the circuit cable. With the power off, cut it and reconnect the ends in a three-terminal junction box. Then wire in the spur cable (above) and run it on to the new light position, where its new switch can be wired in.

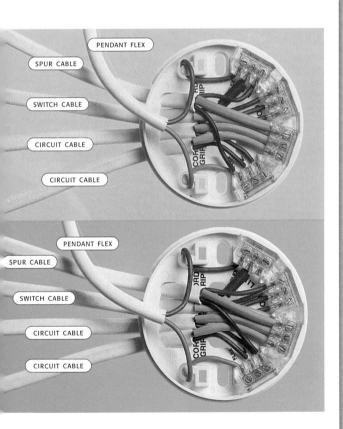

PENDANT FLEX

SPUR CABLE

SWITCH CABLE

CIRCUIT CABLE

CIRCUIT CABLE

PENDANT FLEX

SPUR CABLE

SWITCH CABLE

CIRCUIT CABLE

CIRCUIT CABLE

Take a spur from a rose

If you have loop-in roses rather than junction boxes, you can connect your spur at one of them. With the power off, unscrew the rose cover and feed the spur cable in from above, through the rose baseplate. Break out an extra central section of the baseplate if necessary, using a screwdriver blade. To add another light that will be controlled by the existing switch, connect the new cable cores to the 'pendant' terminals (top) and replace the rose cover. For an independent light, wire it to the through terminals instead (above).

1 Mark box outline on ceiling, drill a hole within waste area to admit padsaw blade and cut out the hole

2 Cut batten to fit between joists, then drill a hole in it to accept conduit box spigot and screw box to batten

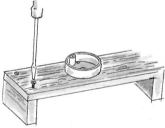

3 Screw scrap blocks to each end of batten, then position it between joists so lip of box is flush with ceiling below

4 Screw scrap blocks to joists to secure batten in place, ready for cables to be run in

lighting

193

lighting Installing new lights

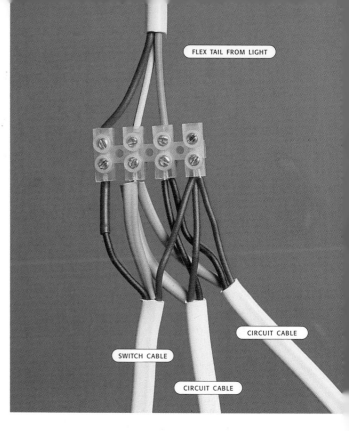

FLEX TAIL FROM LIGHT

CIRCUIT CABLE

SWITCH CABLE

CIRCUIT CABLE

Plug-in pendants

If you are installing new pendant lights, consider fitting the plug-in versions, called luminaire support couplers (LSCs), instead of conventional roses. These allow the pendant flex and the lampholder to be unplugged and removed in seconds for cleaning or maintenance, or when decorating.

Knock out a knockout

Modern ceiling roses are designed so they can be screwed to the underside of a ceiling joist with the cable entry point offset to one side. This means that the cables can be run down the side of the joist, through a hole in the ceiling and straight into the rose. Break out the thin plastic sections (called knockouts) from the centre of the rose baseplate before fixing it in place.

How many strip connectors are needed?

If you are installing a new light fitting over a conduit box, use small insulated strip connectors to link the flex tail from the light fitting to the circuit cables. You need three to link the flex to a single cable run to the conduit box from a junction box, and four if the switch cable is looped in at the lighting point (above).

All-in-one refit

Old ceiling roses, lampholders and pendant flexes eventually become discoloured. Replace them quickly and easily using pre-wired pendant sets. All you have to do is to disconnect and discard the old rose and then fit the new one, complete with a new pendant flex and lampholder, in its place.

Space for connections

Many light fittings fit flush with the ceiling surface, and unless they have a terminal block within a hollow baseplate, you have to make an enclosure above the ceiling to contain the wiring connections. This is usually a round conduit box. To install it you need to cut a hole in the ceiling and fix a supporting batten between the adjacent joists, to which the box can then be screwed (see page 193).

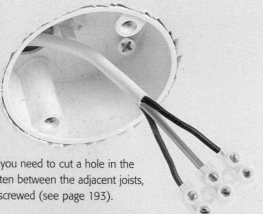

Mounting the fitting

Ceiling light fittings have holes in their baseplates so you can screw them in place. If the holes are at the same 51 mm centres as the screwed lugs on the conduit box, you can screw the baseplate to them using 3.5 mm diameter (M 3.5) machine screws. Otherwise, use ordinary woodscrews long enough to pass through the ceiling and into the batten above.

lighting Fitting wall lights

Useful when decorating

Most wall lights are designed to be installed in a similar way to close-mounted ceiling lights. Their baseplates also fit over (and conceal) an enclosure, but in this case it's recessed into the wall surface. Some modern wall lights have a special plug within their baseplates, which engages in a matching socket in the wall. This device, called a luminaire support coupler (or LSC for short), allows you to remove and replace the fittings in seconds without having to do any wiring work–a bonus when you want to clean the fittings or redecorate the room.

Convenient connections

When fitting new wall lights, think about the most convenient source of power. As far as those in upstairs rooms are concerned, it is generally easiest to connect into the upstairs lighting circuit, which is accessible in the loft. Downstairs, it may be easier to extend via the upstairs or downstairs power circuit. This will avoid the need to lift carpets and move built-in furniture in upstairs rooms to gain access to the downstairs lighting circuit under the upstairs floorboards.

Cable prospecting

Once you have decided where you want your wall lights to be fitted, use a battery-powered cable detector to check whether there are any existing cables buried in the wall, so that you can avoid them when laying the new cables.

Hiding the cables

If you are installing wall lights on a timber-framed partition wall, conceal the supply cable by running it up or down between the studs to the light position.

On solid walls, you'll have to run the cable on the surface until you redecorate the room; then you can bury it into a vertical chase. To disguise it for now, paint it to match the existing wall.

New lights, old switch

If you want new wall lights to come on with the existing room light, wire a spur cable into that lighting point with its cores connected to the switch and neutral terminals. Take it on to a junction box in the ceiling void, then run a cable from this box down to each new light position.

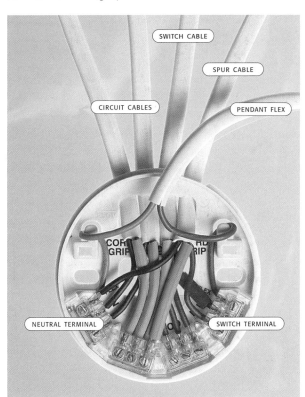

SWITCH CABLE

SPUR CABLE

CIRCUIT CABLES

PENDANT FLEX

NEUTRAL TERMINAL

SWITCH TERMINAL

Check for overload

If you plan to power your wall lights from an existing lighting circuit, check whether the additional lights will overload the circuit. The circuit should not supply more than 12 lighting points in all, and ideally no more than eight. If an overload is likely, plan to supply the new lights through a fused spur taken from a power circuit instead (see page 197).

lighting Fitting wall lights

The perfect height

Wall lights are best sited about 1.5 m (5 ft) above floor level. However, if they're used as reading lights in bedrooms, fix them a little lower–at about 1.2 m (4 ft)–to minimise glare.

Protection for brassware

Brass light switches can be corroded by the alkalis in plaster, if they are in direct contact with the wall surface. Avoid this by buying switches that come with a protective plastic mount; this fits between the switch faceplate and the wall.

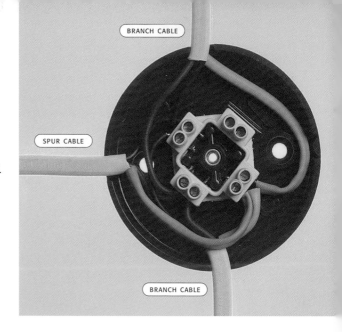

BRANCH CABLE

SPUR CABLE

BRANCH CABLE

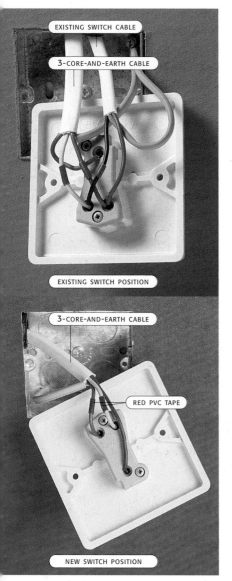

EXISTING SWITCH CABLE

3-CORE-AND-EARTH CABLE

EXISTING SWITCH POSITION

3-CORE-AND-EARTH CABLE

RED PVC TAPE

NEW SWITCH POSITION

Dual control for lights

It is often useful to be able to switch a light–especially a wall light–from more than one position. Replace the existing one-way switch with a two-way switch and wire in the existing red and black switch cable cores to it (top left). Then fit another two-way switch at the new switch position, and run three-core-and-earth cable between the two switches (bottom left). The red cable core links the terminals marked C or COM, the yellow core links those marked L1 and the blue core those marked L2. The blue and yellow cores in the cable must be identified as live with red PVC tape.

Branching out

You can use a junction box to supply two or more wall lights from the same spur cable. Connect its cores to three terminals within the box, then connect in the branch cables as shown, with all like cores going to the same terminal in the box. Remember to sleeve each cable's bare earth core.

Replacing a light

If you want wall lights instead of an existing ceiling light, you can make use of its power supply. Disconnect and remove the existing rose or fitting, and draw the circuit and switch cables supplying it into the ceiling void. Reconnect them to a four-terminal junction box, copying the original wiring arrangement in the rose. Then wire in the spur cable and take it to a junction box as above to supply the new lights. They'll all still be controlled by the existing ceiling light switch.

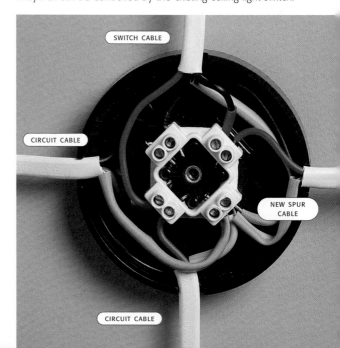

SWITCH CABLE

CIRCUIT CABLE

NEW SPUR CABLE

CIRCUIT CABLE

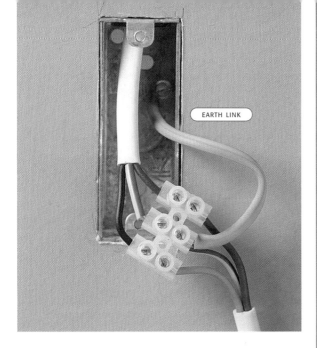

EARTH LINK

Slim-line connections

Some wall lights have baseplates too small to conceal a circular conduit box. Use a flush metal architrave switch box instead to house the wiring connections. Wall lights with metal baseplates have three flex tails—live, neutral and earth. Fit an earth link between the strip connector and the box (above).

Use a fused spur

Sometimes taking a power supply for new wall lights from a power circuit involves the least upheaval and the shortest cable runs. This is especially true if there are socket outlets on the wall where you want the new lights. With the power off, open a nearby socket outlet and connect in a 2.5 mm² spur cable. Run it to a switched fused connection unit (below) fitted with a 3 amp fuse. This can act as the light's on/off switch. Then run 1 mm² cable on to the wall light.

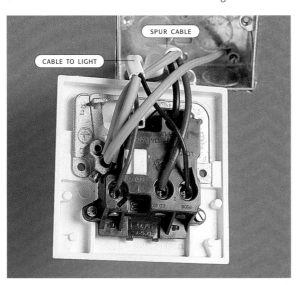

SPUR CABLE

CABLE TO LIGHT

1 Mark position of conduit box and cable run on wall, cut recesses with a cold chisel and club hammer

2 Fix box and conduit in place, then feed in cable to new light. Prepare cable cores for connection to the light

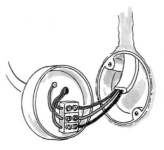

3 Connect flex tails from wall light to new cable using strip connectors. Sleeve the earth core and mount light over box

lighting

197

lighting Stay on track

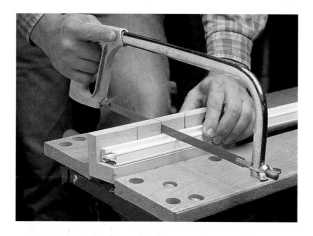

Made to measure

With some track systems you can connect lengths together with push-in couplers. If you need to shorten a standard length of track to fit your plans, use a sharp hacksaw, taking care to cut cleanly through the slim copper conductor strips inside the body of the track.

Beware of an overload

Each lighting track can supply several individual light fittings. So if you are installing one in place of a single light fitting, count up the total wattage of all the new fittings and add this to the wattage of the other fittings the circuit is already supplying. The total for the circuit must not exceed 1200 watts. If it does, you'll have to supply power to the track from an alternative source.

Earth when required

Separate transformers supplying low-voltage lights don't need an earth connection, but a combined metal track and transformer housing will. Connect the live and neutral cores of the supply cable to the transformer input terminals, and the sleeved earth core to the earth terminal provided.

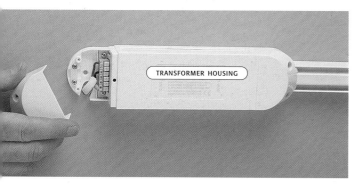

TRANSFORMER HOUSING

More lights, less fuss

Track lighting allows you to install several light fittings with little change to the existing wiring. The fittings may clip into surface-mounted track or may hang from track wires (left).

Mains-powered types get their power supply from an existing ceiling or wall lighting point, while low-voltage types run off a transformer. Once you have fixed the track or wires in position and made the power connection, you can position the lights as required to create the lighting effects you want.

Start at floor level

Lay out track sections on the floor first. Not only does this help you to plan the track arrangement accurately, it also identifies where you will need to reduce the length of the track sections.

Using the rose

You can use an existing ceiling rose to power mains-voltage track. Just replace the existing two-core pendant flex with a length of two-core-and-earth cable, so the track will be safely earthed.

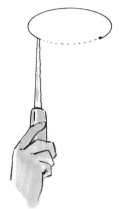

1 Mark hole for fitting, drill a hole to admit padsaw blade, and saw round. Feed in cable and prepare for connection

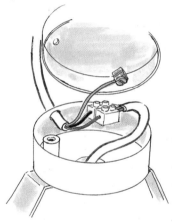

2 Connect cores to terminal block, linking like cores and covering the bare cable earth core with green-and-yellow PVC sleeving

3 Push light fitting up into hole in ceiling until its spring-loaded jaws grip perimeter of hole and lock it in place

lighting

lighting Spots and tubes

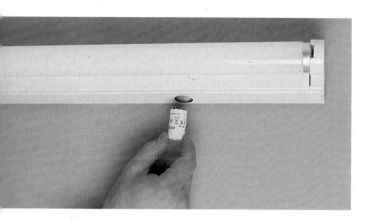

Guard against grease

Some low-voltage lighting tracks use tiny pea-shaped quartz halogen bulbs that fit into small parabolic reflectors. Always handle these with paper tissue or a handkerchief; otherwise grease from your skin can cause hot spots that will make the bulb fail prematurely. Avoid turning them on and off repeatedly too–this also shortens their life.

Get a better grip

Many spotlight bulbs are quite a tight fit in their reflector lampholders. If you have trouble undoing and removing a failed bulb, wind a couple of rubber bands around your finger and thumb to enable you to get a better grip on the smooth end of the bulb.

Curing a false start

If a fluorescent tube is reluctant to start, suspect a faulty starter. Locate it on the base of the fitting, push it in and twist it anticlockwise to release it from its socket. Take it to the shop so you can identify the correct replacement.

Recessed fittings

Use joists for planning

Plan the wiring to a row of recessed light fittings according to which way the ceiling joists run. If the row is parallel to the joists, cut the holes for the fittings and then feed the supply cables between the joists from one hole to the next, working from below. If the row is at right angles, lift a single floorboard in the room above and drill holes through the joists, so the cables can be run through them from light to light.

Templates make fitting simple

Use the template provided with the light fitting to mark the positions of the fixing screws. Wherever possible position the fitting directly below a joist and align its baseplate so at least two fixing screws go into the joist.

A batten between joists

If you cannot attach the light fitting to a joist, it is possible to fix it to the ceiling (providing it is lightweight) using cavity fixings such as spring toggles. Large fittings with heavy glass diffusers need screwing to timber battens secured between the joists, so you will need access to the ceiling void to fit these.

Protection in the loft

Make sure that loft insulation is pulled clear of recessed light fittings, so they cannot overheat and create a fire risk. If the fittings project above the tops of the joists, make open-sided protective boxes from offcuts of plywood or chipboard to fit over them. Then the fitting will not be damaged accidentally by anyone moving about within the roof space.

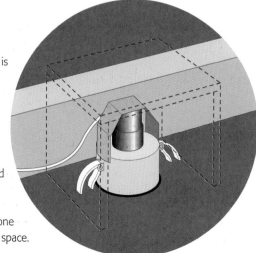

Protect cores from heat

The temperature inside enclosed light fittings can be surprisingly high when the light is on. Fit heat-resistant sleeving over any exposed flex and cable cores within these fittings, to protect them from overheating.

outdoors
Effective lights

Find the best locations
Work out where to put outside lights by wiring up the fitting to an extension cable. Then, after dark, get a helper to hold the switched-on fitting against the house wall in a variety of positions, so you can see exactly what is lit up. Use steps or a ladder if necessary. Remember that a little light goes a long way in the dark, and over-bright lights merely dazzle. Carry out the same exercise to position lights beside paths and steps in the garden (right).

Watch the glare
Floodlights suit football stadia more than back gardens, but if you decide you must install them, think about your neighbours and angle the fittings so the light is directed down and onto your property only. Carelessly aligned floodlights can also be a hazard if they're fitted at the front of the house, where they could dazzle drivers.

Corner positions
Cut the number of outside lights you need by positioning them on the corners of the house. Each light will then shine along two adjacent walls.

Automatic control
Your outside lights can be controlled by a simple on/off switch situated inside the house. Alternatively, they can be turned on automatically whenever anyone approaches the house, if they are wired up to a passive infra-red (PIR) detector (left), which senses body heat. Some outside lights have the detector built in. If you already have a number of outside lights, installing a separate PIR detector to control them is a relatively straightforward wiring job.

Tilt the drill bit
Drill a hole through the house wall with a large-diameter masonry drill bit for the cable to an outside light. Check that the hole will emerge somewhere accessible indoors, and angle the drill bit so the hole runs slightly uphill from the outside, to discourage rainwater from getting in. Feed a length of round PVC conduit through the hole to protect the cable from chafing, and waterproof the exit point with exterior sealant.

outdoors
Effective lights

Choose a pick-up point
A light on the outside wall can be wired as a spur from an indoor circuit—a lighting circuit if the extra light won't overload it, a power circuit otherwise. Pick whichever is the more convenient to access. Wire a spur from a power circuit via a fused connection unit (FCU) fitted with a 5 amp fuse. The FCU can also act as the light switch.

Low voltage, low cost
Mains-voltage lights in the garden must have their own circuit, with the protection of a residual current device (RCD). Installing this circuit is a job for a professional electrician. You can save the expense of this by choosing a low-voltage lighting set powered from a transformer instead. The cable can safely be left lying on the surface of flowerbeds as it runs from light to light.

Easy wiring
Choose light fittings with a terminal block inside to make the wiring as easy as possible. Then all you have to do is feed the supply cable through the house wall into the back of the fitting, and connect its cores to the block. Some fittings have a waterproof rubber sleeve through which the incoming cable passes. With others you need to seal the join between the fitting's baseplate and the wall with a generous bead of exterior sealant (below).

Power in the garden

Burying cable
Ordinary PVC-sheathed cable can be run underground so long as it is first threaded through impact-resistant PVC conduit, assembled with solvent-welded joints. Bury it at least 450 mm (18 in) deep where paving will be laid. Increase this to 750 mm (2 ft 6 in) beneath lawns or flowerbeds. Wrap black-and-yellow plastic warning tape (available from electrical wholesalers) over the conduit before backfilling the trench, to warn anyone digging the ground in the future that a cable is buried underneath it.

Overhead power
It is always best to take cable runs to outbuildings underground. But if there is an existing patio or drive in the way that you don't want to dig up, the cable will have to run overhead. It must be at least 3.7 m (12 ft) above ground over a path or patio and 5 m (17 ft) high if it crosses a driveway, so bring it out of the house at eaves level to get maximum clearance. Take the cable to a tall post bolted to the outbuilding, and suspend it from an overhead support wire if the span is more than 3.5 m. Link this wire to earth with a 4 mm² earth cable.

Safety shutdown
Any socket outlet powering an electrical appliance that is being used outside, must be protected by a high-sensitivity residual current device (RCD). This trips to off more quickly than the type of RCD usually fitted to protect circuits in the house, so offering even better protection against electric shock.

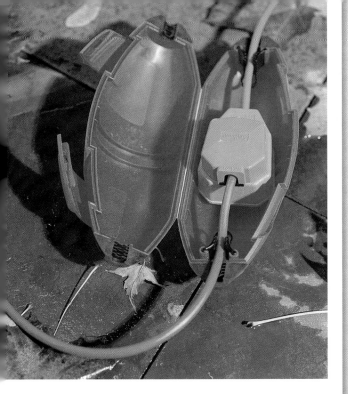

Waterproof connections

An extension lead is vital if you want to use power tools outdoors, but the plug-and-socket connection isn't waterproof and this is dangerous if conditions are damp. Make it waterproof by placing it in a snap-together enclosure (above).

Extension rules

If you are using garden power tools with blades, such as lawnmowers and hedgetrimmers, always use brightly coloured leads–they are easy to see and to avoid. If you need to extend a flex with a two-piece flex connector, fit the part with the pins to the flex leading to the appliance, and the part with the sockets to the flex leading to the power supply.

Tough customers

In outbuildings, fit metal-clad switches and socket outlets, set on matching surface-mounted metal boxes. These will withstand knocks and general wear and tear far better than plastic ones. Run cables in mini-trunking or conduit.

1 Drill through house wall where you want the light, and line hole with PVC conduit. Then feed in cable

2 If light fitting has a hollow baseplate, link cable to flex with strip connectors. Then screw baseplate to wall

3 If baseplate is solid, chop out recess in wall to house conduit box for connections and mount light fitting over it

4 If fitting has an internal terminal block, feed cable in through waterproof seal and make connections to it

outdoors

Phone overload

You can have a telephone socket in every room, although it is best not to have one in the bathroom because of moisture. However, you should not plug a phone into every socket; if you do, you will overload the system and none will ring. All phones, answering machines, faxes and modems have a power rating called a Ring Equivalence Number (REN). This is 1 for a phone and 2 or 3 for other equipment. The REN total on any one line should not exceed 4.

Use cable economically

You can wire up extra phone sockets in series, with the cable running from socket to socket, or in parallel, with up to three cables radiating from a junction box. Pick whichever wiring arrangement makes the more economical use of cable.

Keep it short

Phone circuits operate at low voltage, and voltage drop is a problem if the house circuits exceed about 50 m (165 ft) in length. To check that you haven't exceeded this limit when extending your system, buy a 50 m drum of cable and make sure you have some left over when you have finished the job.

Designed to make connections easy

There is no need to strip the insulation from the individual cores in telephone cables when you are connecting them to the sockets. As you push each core into its terminal with the special connector tool, metal jaws inside the terminal block strip a small amount of insulation and make good electrical contact with the wire inside. Snip off the excess length from the cores with side cutters.

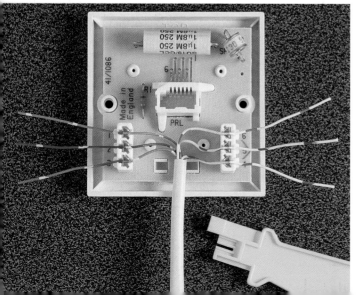

Pull the drawstring

It is extremely difficult to strip the outer sheath from phone cable using a knife, without nicking the insulation on the thin cores inside. The secret is to make use of the tough drawstring that the cable manufacturer inserts alongside the bundle of cores. **Split the sheath at one end** with a sharp trimming knife (this is unlikely to damage the insulation on the individual cores, but you can cut them off if it does). Grip the drawstring and pull it steadily along the cable to split the sheath and expose the cores. Snip off the excess sheathing.

Take out the kinks

If phone cable has been coiled up for a long time, it can be difficult to make it lie flat between cable clips. You can stretch out the kinks by pulling the cable steadily under tension through a dry cloth held in a clenched fist.

Call check

When you have wired up all your extension sockets, call a friend from each one and ask for a call back so you can check that the phone is sending and receiving calls successfully.

Running cable

Phone cable is slim enough to be run almost unnoticed along the top of skirting boards and around door architraves. Tap in a clip every 300 mm (12 in) or so. Fix clips either side of corners rather than in the angle. Pass the cable from room to room through holes drilled next to door frames, and from floor to floor along the same route taken by plumbing pipework. Keep it

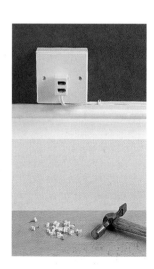

at least 50 mm (2 in) away from mains cables and wiring accessories, which can cause interference on the line.

The last connection

Complete all the wiring before making the connection to the linebox, especially if you are connecting cable directly into its terminals rather than using a plug-in converter. Otherwise you might get a mild shock if someone rings you while you are handling bare phone wires.

Television aerial points

Split the signal

Many people now want televisions in more rooms than just the living room, which is usually the only one with an aerial socket connected to a roof-top or loft aerial. The simplest way of providing one extra socket is to insert a device called a splitter into the existing aerial downlead. The original lead continues on to the existing socket, and you connect a new lead into the splitter to supply the second socket.

Matching accessories

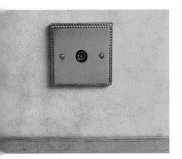

Surface-mounted aerial sockets are quick and easy to install, but flush ones are much neater and you can match their style to the light switches and power points. They fit over a standard 25 mm deep metal mounting box.

Boosting the signal

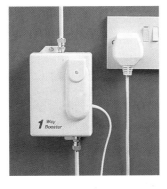

You can't split the aerial downlead more than once to supply extra sockets, because the signal strength drops off rapidly. Wire the aerial to a mains-powered signal amplifier instead. This sends a boosted signal on to each new aerial socket.

Two in one

If you need an FM radio aerial as well as one for your television, you can connect both TV and FM aerial leads into a double aerial outlet in the roof space. This contains a device called a diplexer, which allows two signals to travel along a single coaxial downlead. The lead runs to a matching double outlet in your living room. The TV and radio are then connected to the relevant outlet with a short coaxial lead.

1 Make slit down outer plastic sheath, peel back and trim off about 25 mm (1 in)

2 Roll screening braid back over end of sheath and cut about 12 mm (½ in) of plastic insulation off core wire

3 Fit cap and braid grip over cable end and crimp grip onto braid with pliers

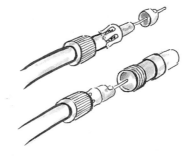

4 Slide on protective pin moulding and plug body, snip off projecting core wire and screw cap onto plug

services

decorating

Wash with sugar soap

Clean dirt and grease off old paintwork by washing it thoroughly with sugar soap and water. The solution also takes the shine off gloss-painted surfaces, providing a good key for the new coat of paint. Rinse off the sugar soap with clean water and allow the paintwork to dry before repainting.

Dress for the job

Protect your eyes and skin from sugar soap by wearing safety spectacles and a long-sleeved top, with the cuffs tucked securely inside a pair of rubber gloves. The eye protection is especially vital when washing a ceiling.

Score and soak

Wallpaper is easier to strip if you soften it first. Score it with a wallpaper perforator or stripping knife, then soak the surface with hot soapy water. Adding a small quantity of wallpaper paste to the water thickens it slightly, so that it doesn't run down the wall quite so quickly.

Use a steam stripper

Make the task of removing old wallpaper easier and quicker by using a steam stripper. A lot of hot water is generated by the equipment, so wear rubber gloves over long sleeves and protect the floor well. If you intend to hire a steam stripper, it is probably worth reserving it–they're always in demand.

Dust-free woodwork

After rubbing down woodwork with an abrasive paper to provide a key for new paint, wipe it with a clean rag dipped in white spirit to remove the dust.

Thin the first coat

Newly plastered walls must be allowed to dry out completely before painting. They will be very absorbent, so thin the first coat of emulsion by adding an extra 20 per cent of water.

Protect light fittings

Use plastic bags to guard ceiling lights and fans against paint drips. First, switch of MCB or remove fuse at the consumer unit, then unscrew the ceiling rose cover and slide it down the flex. Enclose the fitting in a bag, securing the neck of it around the flex with a freezer bag tie. Make tubes from stiff paper to slip over wall lights, removing shades and bulbs first.

Painting over wallpaper

You can save time by painting over wallpaper that is well stuck down, although doing so will make it much more difficult to remove at some future date. Test paint a small area first; if the paper bubbles, over-painting is not an option.

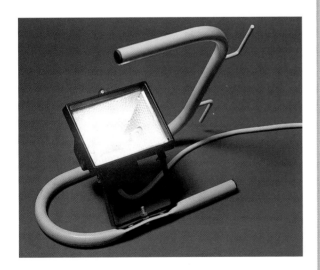

Bright idea for seeing clearly

If you are painting a poorly lit room, or have disconnected the lighting circuit for safety, consider hiring a portable work light. Plug it into a socket and angle the light so that it bounces off the ceiling—then your shadow won't be cast on the wall you're decorating. The powerful bulb will show up imperfections.

1 Remove rugs and lift fitted carpets if possible. Move the furniture to middle of room and cover with dustsheets

2 Remove curtains and blinds and prepare all surfaces

3 Use masking tape to protect glass and internal woodwork from paint splashes

4 Turn off electricity, then loosen faceplates of fittings so edges of old wallpaper can be stripped from behind them

preparation

preparation
Stripping the woodwork

Beware of melted paint
Wear long-sleeved clothing and cotton or leather gloves to protect your skin from melted paint burnt off with a hot-air gun or blowlamp. Newspaper or dustsheets laid on the floor can catch fire, so place a container of water–an old baking tray or grill pan is ideal–on the floor instead.

Dangerous lead
Any pre-1960s paintwork is likely to contain lead; DIY stores sell inexpensive kits for testing paintwork. If yours contains lead, it should be stripped with great caution. Keep children out of the way. Never use a blowlamp, hot-air gun, or abrasive paper, all of which will create lead-rich fumes and dust. Instead, wear gloves and a dust mask and use a chemical paint stripper. Seal the waste in a bag and put it in the dustbin–don't burn it.

Resisting the force of gravity
Use a gel-type paint stripper on vertical surfaces. Because it doesn't run off quickly, the chemical has more time to get to work. Alternatively, thicken the standard stripper by mixing a little wallpaper paste into it (see page 269).

Stay on the move
The golden rule when stripping paint with a blowlamp or hot-air gun is to keep the tool moving. Playing too much heat on one spot will burn and char the paint rather than softening it. You also risk scorching the wood itself.

Seal the knots
Use knotting fluid to seal knots in bare wood, or apply aluminium wood primer to the whole surface, otherwise resin in the knots can show through new paint.

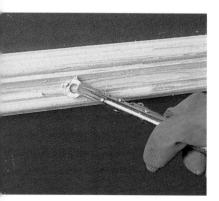

Follow the contours
Preserve the definition of wooden mouldings by rubbing them down as little as possible. Remove as much old paint as possible with scrapers and homemade tools–for example, a small metal washer held with mole grips for concave areas (left). Then finish with fine abrasive paper wrapped around a suitable base–for example, a piece of wooden dowel (right). Alternatively, use an abrasive sponge block.

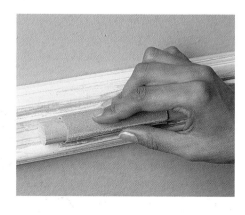

sanding floors
Stripping back to bare boards

Remove furnishings and fixtures

Sanding floorboards creates a great deal of fine dust, despite the collection bag on the machine, so take down curtains, lampshades, pictures and other removable wall and ceiling fixtures before you start. Polythene sheets pinned over door frames will help to keep the rest of the house dust free.

Protect ears, nose and throat

Drum sanders are noisy and stripping the floorboards of an average-sized room takes several hours, so wear ear protectors—and tell your neighbours what you're doing.

Avoid inhaling dust by wearing a respirator with a good filter, not just a disposable dust mask, and open the windows.

Empty the dust bag frequently because the dust—a mix of wood and old finish—is hot and can catch fire spontaneously.

Heavy work gloves help to cushion your hands against the vibration created by the sander, while those worn by mountain bikers have even more effective padding. Even so, take frequent breaks—don't wait until your hands start tingling.

Spare the belts

Carpet tacks, staples and projecting floorboard nails will shred the expensive abrasive sheets a floor sander uses. Before starting sanding, inspect the floorboards carefully. Pull out any tacks you find, and punch nail heads well below the surface of the boards.

Disguising old nail holes

Stop up all the old nail holes with a suitably coloured wood filler once the top layers of dirt have been sanded off. Then wait for the filler to dry and carry on sanding the boards.

sanding floors
Stripping back to bare boards

Reaching the edges

An edging sander is indispensable for getting right up to the face of skirting boards. In small rooms where a drum sander is heavy and unwieldy to manoeuvre, it may be the only machine you need. Hire kneepads at the same time as the sander, because you'll be working on your knees all the time.

Bottoms up

If the top surface of a floorboard is too damaged to be worth sanding, try lifting it and inspecting the underside; you might be able to re-use it if you nail it down bottom side up.

Start and stop routine

Press down on the handle or operate a special lever to raise the drum off the boards before starting or stopping. If you allow it to be in contact with the boards while building up to full speed or slowing down, they will be scarred.

Old for old

If possible, replace badly damaged floorboards with secondhand ones of the same width and thickness, obtained from a salvage yard. Take a short length of the old board along with you for comparison. Secondhand replacements will blend in with the original boards far better than new ones.

Diagonally across hollows

Old floorboards may be cupped—hollow along their centres and curled up at the edges. As long as the cupping is not too marked, you can get rid of it by running the drum sander diagonally across the boards before you begin working along the grain (above). Use coarse abrasive.

When the dust settles

A floor sander creates a lot of dust. Once it has settled, and immediately before varnishing the floor, clean the entire room with a vacuum cleaner. Then get rid of any remaining dust by wiping the floor with a lint-free cloth dipped in white spirit.

Getting into the corners

You will need a sander with a pointed base (see page 336) to get right into corners (left). An alternative is to use a wide chisel or a plane blade to scrape the old finish off the boards. Hold the blade with bevel away from you and scrape in the direction of the grain (right).

A protective coating for the new-look boards

Three sorts of sealer

Polyurethane varnish is the usual choice, but it is solvent-based and takes a long time to dry. It also tends to yellow with age. Water-based varnishes and two-part catalysed lacquers provide a clearer finish, with less tendency to discolour. They dry fast, so you can apply several coats in a day, although that does mean you have to work quickly to keep a wet edge. Mix only as much of a two-part lacquer as you can use before it starts to set–usually in around an hour.

Read the instructions, because varnishes come in various grades and you need to choose one that is suitable for floors. Flooring-grade varnish may itself be graded for use according to the amount of wear and tear the floor is likely to receive.

Rub on the first coat

Thin the first coat of varnish with a little white spirit and apply it with a clean rag, rubbing it into the boards. Then use a brush for subsequent coats. Never shake the tin; the bubbles formed will appear as tiny blemishes in the dried varnish.

Buy a new brush

Don't risk getting specks of old paint or bristles in the varnish by using an old or cheap brush. Invest in a new, good-quality brush before you start. Synthetic fibre brushes are less prone to hair loss than natural bristle types.

Use a narrow brush to varnish the edge trims and the perimeter boards, then switch to a wider brush for fast coverage of the rest of the floor.

Be alert to fire risk

Open the windows, ensure gas flames–including pilot lights on a boiler or cooker–are extinguished, and don't smoke nearby when varnishing a floor. Rags used to apply varnish or oil are highly flammable and should be left outside to dry before being thrown in the bin.

Alternative to varnish

An oil polish will provide a hard-wearing alternative to varnish, and is well worth the effort if you have a beautiful old timber floor. Use a product such as Danish oil, or mix your own using 1 part of raw linseed oil to 8 parts of turpentine. You can colour the oil by mixing a stain into it (see page 281).

Warm the oil to make it more fluid and to help absorption. It could be 24 hours or more before the floor is dry enough for a second, more sparing coat. Keep applying coats until buffing raises a silky sheen, and water forms beads on the surface.

painting
Working outdoors

Stabilise surfaces
Test the stability of existing paint on an outside wall by rubbing it down with a dry, dark-coloured rag. If the rag collects a chalky deposit, scrub the wall with a stiff dry brush to remove loose material, then apply a stabilising solution.

Protect from splashes
Cover porch and bay window roofs, to prevent them from getting splashed as you paint. To protect paths and other hard surfaces, lay some old dustsheets or plastic sheeting along the base of walls, but don't stand a ladder on plastic sheeting in case the ladder slips.

Handiest for the job
Use a long-nap roller with a tough nylon pile or a large, synthetic-fibre brush to apply masonry paint. A medium-bristle dustpan brush with a comfortable handle is also good for the job. Apply the paint to the wall in vertical zigzags and fill in the gaps with vertical strokes.

Clearly a better choice
Painting ornamental brick surrounds of doors, windows and chimney stacks is an irreversible decision–you won't be able to get the paint off if you want to at some later date. If ornamental brickwork has deteriorated, you can protect it with a clear water-repellent silicone sealer.

Weather eye

Don't decorate outside on windy days; dust and grit is bound to get blown onto the wet paint. Cold weather can make gloss paint dry without a shine.

Stay ahead of the sun

On sunny days, try and paint walls while they are in shadow, otherwise they will dry too quickly. If you are caught in the sun's glare, protect the back of your neck, and if you're using white paint, wear sunglasses.

Exterior woodwork

Seal against rain

Position masking tape 2–3 mm (⅛ in) away from the edge of the putty when masking window glass. Paint across this gap; it seals the junction between putty and glass against rain. Remove the tape before the paint has hardened.

Let paint spots set

Use a rag dampened in white spirit or water to wipe wet paint off glass. Scrape off any spots you miss after the paint has set, but before it goes really hard.

Let the wood breathe

Microporous paints and varnishes are the best choice for exterior woodwork. They are formulated to allow any moisture trapped in the wood to escape, while at the same time preventing rain from getting through. The finish is also flexible, so it won't crack under the stress of thermal movement.

Right brush for the job

Painting windows with many small panes is a fiddly job. As an alternative to sticking masking tape around the wood to stop paint getting on the glass, use a cutting-in brush to paint glazing bars.

STAGES IN
PAINTING EXTERIOR OF A SASH WINDOW

1 Lower top sash and raise bottom one to its full extent. Then paint exposed surfaces

2 Reverse both sashes to gain access to rest of bottom sash and complete painting it

3 With both sashes closed, paint lower half of jambs and parting beads. Allow to dry

4 Lower top sash to complete painting of jambs and parting beads. Then close sashes and paint face of frame

painting
Exterior woodwork

Prevent windows and doors sticking
Paint windows and exterior doors early in the day, so that by evening the paint is dry enough for them to be closed. Paint surfaces where openings and frames meet first. Wedge doors open, so they can't blow shut or be closed by mistake. To ensure the joinery doesn't stick when you open it next day, smear a little petroleum jelly onto the frame rebates before shutting up for the night; it will wipe off easily in the morning.

Keep clear of grit
Pour small quantities of paint into a paint kettle when you're painting masonry and rendered walls. It prevents bits of grit from the wall being transferred to the tin (see page 225).

End on a complete board
If you cannot paint the whole of a timber-clad wall at one go, call a temporary stop when you reach the bottom edge of one complete board. Always 'feather' or blend areas of wet paint into one another with light brush strokes and little paint, otherwise you will end up with lap marks, especially if you are using gloss paint.

Gutters and downpipes

Camouflage or contrast?
Choose a colour that camouflages or highlights gutters and downpipes. Modern plastic gutters and pipes are probably best painted to blend into their background, but decorative cast-iron fittings may be worth highlighting by painting them a different colour.

Getting behind a downpipe
You can buy a special brush with an angled head for painting behind downpipes, but if you don't have one position a piece of card behind the pipe to mask the masonry.

While it's on the ground
When you take down metal guttering in order to replace a fascia board, take the opportunity to remove any rust with a wire brush and repaint the gutter before putting it back up. Make sure you use a suitable primer on aluminium.

Neighbourhood watch
Look at what your neighbours have done before choosing an exterior colour scheme for your home, espcially if you live in a terrace. Apparently simple choices, such as the colour of a front door, can have a large impact on the street scene. Do you want to stand out or blend in?

Painting plastic pipes
Plastic gutters and pipes can be left unpainted; just wash them down with water containing a little bleach. If you do want to paint them, there's no need to use an undercoat. Key the surface of new plastic with fine abrasive paper to make the paint adhere better, or wait a year before painting, by which time the weather will have taken the shine off the surface.

Primer, undercoat and finish

Pick healthier paints
Water-based paints and varnishes have a lower volatile organic compound (VOC) content than solvent-based ones. This means they do less environmental damage and pose less of a health risk to people using them regularly. Use products with a low VOC rating if solvent-based paints give you nausea or headaches. Information about VOCs is now often given on the container.

Stick to separate coats
Primers are designed to seal surfaces, undercoats to obliterate underlying colour and provide a strong key for the protective top coat. Using a combined primer/ undercoat may save time and money, but you will generally not get results as good as those achieved with separate coats.

Primer choice
A primer specially formulated for a particular surface–plaster, wood or metal–will last longer and produce a better finish than a universal primer. **Copper pipe needs no primer,** but an undercoat may be necessary to hide the colour of the metal.

Obliterate stains
Wax crayon and felt-tip pen marks, tar from cigarettes and water stains from plumbing leaks will all eventually show through layers of conventional paint. Smother them permanently with an aluminium primer-sealer or with a proprietary stain-block. The latter is sold in aerosol form, ideal for small areas.

White won't yellow
White paint on radiators and central-heating and hot-water pipes won't yellow if you use a proprietary radiator enamel. This gives off strong fumes as it dries, so open the windows wide.

Hide the imperfections
Gloss paint shows up every blemish in a surface. If your woodwork isn't perfect or you don't want to spend long hours on preparation, use a more forgiving matt or eggshell finish instead.

Keep mould at bay
Steamy kitchens and bathrooms can be ideal breeding grounds for mould, because of the condensation that forms on wall and ceiling surfaces. Decorate them with special kitchen and bathroom paint containing a fungicide.

Volatile combination
Polystyrene ceiling tiles and solvent-based paints make a highly combustible combination. Always paint these tiles with a water-based paint.

painting

painting Brush, roller, pad or spray gun?

Invest in a flexible frame

It's worth buying a good-quality paint roller, with a cage that spins freely and springs back into position when you squeeze it. Look for a comfortable handle, with a threaded insert to take an extension pole. The pole will save you bending if you want to paint a floor, or climbing a stepladder to reach ceilings. A telescopic pole is the most versatile type.

Choose your sleeve carefully

Use a cheap foam roller sleeve for general painting work where the standard of the finish is not important. For a good finish on a very smooth surface, a mohair sleeve with a short pile is best. A sleeve with a long lambswool or synthetic fibre pile forces paint into every crevice on a highly textured surface. Use a long-nap sleeve with a tough nylon pile on rough exterior surfaces such as pebbledash.

Create a textured finish

A sculptured roller sleeve will add a textured finish to a flat surface. Hessian, bark, swirl, patchwork and stipple effects are among those available. Some can be used to create a repeating pattern with successive parallel passes of the roller.

Reaching behind a radiator

Use a radiator roller or brush to paint behind a radiator. Both tools have long handles, so the new paint colour can be taken right out of sight. Be sure to remove dust and cobwebs before you start. Mask the newly painted wall with plastic sheeting or hardboard when you come to painting the radiator itself.

Natural versus synthetic

Modern synthetic fibre brushes will perform as well as all but the finest hog bristle brushes, and suffer far less from 'hair loss' in use. They are also easier to clean than bristle brushes, and keep their shape better too.

What size brush?

The general rule is to use the widest brush that you can handle comfortably, and which is appropriate for the surface being painted. A 100 mm brush is ideal for applying emulsion paint to walls, while a 75 mm one is better for gloss-painting flat woodwork. The wider the brush, the quicker you can paint, making it easier to keep a wet edge as you work.

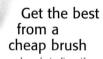

Get the best from a cheap brush

A cheap brush is fine if a good finish isn't important—when brightening up an understairs cupboard, for example. Try to use the brush for priming and undercoating first, so that when it's time to apply the top coat it has stopped shedding bristles.

Power through the job

Consider hiring a power roller if you have a large area to cover. Because paint is continuously fed along the hollow extension pole, you can finish the job much more quickly. You need to keep the roller moving to avoid drips and runs.

When a pad is best

A paint pad is the best choice for applying thin coats of paint to smooth surfaces easily and without drips. In the past, pads used to fall apart when used with solvent-based paint, but these days they last well, whether you need to clean them in white spirit or just wash off water-based paint.

Airless is best

Use an airless spray gun (right), with an electric pump that forces paint through the nozzle. It is easier to use and causes less overspray than a spray gun powered by compressed air.

Allow time for masking

Applying paint with a spray gun is faster than putting it on with a brush or roller, but remember that the time you gain from faster application has to be offset against the time it takes to mask off adjacent surfaces that won't be painted.

219

Protect your hands

Wear a pair of fabric gloves while painting, especially when using solvent-based paints. They save having to remove paint from your hands with white spirit, which can irritate the skin. A barrier cream will help to stop paint sticking to your skin if you prefer to work without gloves.

Ceiling before walls

Emulsion the ceiling first, so that any splashes on the walls are covered later. Start to paint a wall at the top right-hand corner if you are right-handed, from the opposite corner if left-handed.

Brush the margins

If you are going to paint the ceiling or adjoining walls different colours, use a brush for the edges first, then a roller to infill the rest of the surface.

Danger overhead

Wear safety spectacles when painting a ceiling. They will protect your eyes from paint splashes when you look upwards. Avoid making splashes with a roller by pushing it slowly; don't snatch it away at the end of each pass. **Try not to overload the brush** when painting a ceiling. Dip just the bottom quarter of the bristles into the paint; then it won't seep into the ferrule and run down the handle—a common problem when painting ceilings.

Bands and strips

Apply paint in horizontal or vertical bands, then blend the parallel bands together. Paint walls and ceilings in strips about 600 mm (2 ft) wide, working quickly so that the edge of the paint doesn't get a chance to dry. Finish off around door and window frames after the rest of the wall is covered. Turning the heating off and closing windows will extend the drying time—worth doing if you have a large room to paint.

Frames before paper

Paint door and window frames before hanging wallpaper, so there's no chance of getting paint on the paper. Extend the paint beyond the edge of frames and onto the walls by about 6 mm (¼ in), then any gaps you leave between the edges of the wallpaper and the frames won't show up.

Don't shoot yourself!

Keep your spare hand out of the way of the nozzle when spray-painting: the paint is forced out at high pressure and can become embedded in the skin. Wear gloves and long sleeves as a precaution. Safety goggles and a face mask or, preferably, a respirator are vital protection against fine paint droplets.

Every other tread

Paint or varnish every other tread when decorating an uncarpeted staircase, and identify which can be walked on by taping sheets of newspaper over them. Adapt the same method when painting or varnishing a floor you need to use all the time, doing half of it one day and the rest the next.

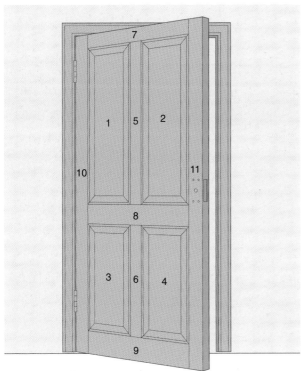

Keep a spray gun on the move

Practise on a test surface with a spray gun. Always keep the gun parallel to the surface; do not swing it in an arc. Begin moving your arm before you press the trigger, and continue the movement for a moment or two after releasing it.

Check that the hose on the spray gun is long enough before you start to use it; a sudden jolt will ruin the job.

Start at the centre

Paint outwards from the centre of a door towards the edges: do the panels and the vertical surfaces separating them first, then the horizontal sections (called rails), next, the verticals (stiles) and edges. Leave the frame until last.

Connecting colours

If a door is a different colour on each side, paint the latch or lock edge the same colour as the face that opens into the room. Match the hinge edge to the other side of the door.

Remove the grit

Don't forget to wipe surfaces with a clean damp cloth or a tack rag (see page 279) after rubbing down between coats of paint or varnish. Otherwise, specks of grit and dust deposited by the abrasive will show in the next coat, spoiling it, and you'll have to sand it back again once it has dried.

painting Dealing with flaws and spills

Avoid overloads

Sags and runs are difficult to remove from paintwork. Sometimes you have to sand the surface back to the bare wood to get rid of them. Try to prevent them by not overloading the paintbrush. If any do form, don't try to remove them while the paint is still tacky.

Hard attack

Attack dried emulsion paint on carpets by repeatedly dampening the stain and teasing lumps of paint out of the pile with an old toothbrush.

A water-based paint stripper may remove solvent-based paint from carpets and hard floor surfaces. Test on an inconspicuous corner first. Neutralise stripper residue with water immediately afterwards.

Dab hand with spills

Act fast if you spill paint. Scrape up as much as you can with a flat-bladed tool. Then dab off what's left with dry absorbent cloths and paper before lifting the last traces with clean cloths dampened with cold water (for spilt emulsion) or white spirit (for solvent-based paint). Use washing-up liquid on a damp cloth to remove traces of white spirit from fabric.

Scrape paint off glass

The best tool for removing paint from a window pane is a plastic scraper fitted with a trimming knife blade. The blade should be inset very slightly so it cannot mark the frame.

Rub insects off dry paint

Don't try to remove small insects that become trapped on gloss paint when it is still tacky. Wait until the paint is dry, then rub them off with a rag dampened with white spirit.

Surgical removal

Unless you spot a stray bristle as soon as it appears and can lift it off the paint before it gets stuck, wait until the surface is thoroughly dry before attempting to remove it. Then use a scalpel or sharp craft knife to carefully cut it away from the new paintwork.

Keep equipment as good as new

Overnight break

When you take a break during painting, wrap your paintbrush tightly in either kitchen foil or cling film so air cannot get to it. The brush will then be ready for use later–or even the next day. **Keep a loaded roller** without it drying out by sliding a plastic bag over the sleeve; exclude as much air as possible before securing the neck with a wire tie.

Cleaning a spray gun

Flush a spray gun out with water or solvent as soon as you have finished using it, squirting the waste into a container (left). When the flushing liquid comes through clear, remove the nozzle from the gun and leave it to soak in clean water or solvent to get rid of any remaining paint.

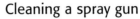

In suspension

Don't leave brushes soaking in white spirit unless you intend to use them again within a day or so. The way to prevent the bristles becoming bent and out of shape in the jar is to suspend the brush from a length of stiff wire or thin dowel, passed through a hole drilled just above the brush ferrule.

Keep bristles shapely

Wrap polythene around the bristles of cleaned brushes, secured with rubber bands, and hang them from hooks or nails. Next time you need to use them, your brushes will be clean and, most importantly, the bristles won't be misshapen.

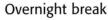

painting

223

painting Best ways to store and dispose of paint

Wrap up a roller
Make sure a roller sleeve is completely dry before storing it. Then wrap it in paper or polythene and tie up the ends to keep it clean.

Never down the drain
When you finish using a water-based paint, wipe as much of it as possible off brushes and rollers before rinsing them in the sink, so that as little as possible is washed down the drain. Never pour used white spirit or solvent-based paint down the sink or into a drain. Unwanted water-based paint can be sealed in its tin and put out for the refuse collectors. It's best to consult your local authority about getting rid of any solvent-based product; it may have special disposal facilities.

Foil the formation of a skin
Use a piece of kitchen foil to prevent a skin forming on the top of an opened tin of paint. Using the lid as a guide, cut a circle of foil just large enough to cover the surface of the paint. Press it down gently to exclude air trapped beneath it.

Decant a little at a time
Pouring paint into a paint kettle is a good idea for several reasons. For a start, large full paint tins are heavy to hold for long periods. If you pour just a little paint into the kettle at a time, you won't waste much if you upset it. And, if your brush picks up some dirt, it will contaminate only what's in the kettle, rather than the paint in the tin. Use kitchen foil to line the kettle; it cuts cleaning-up time and delays the build-up of dry paint in the container.

Give an old brush new life
Before reusing a poorly stored brush, flick the bristles against your hand to remove any dust or hardened bits of paint. Try removing any remaining paint with an old comb. Then restore life to the bristles by soaking the brush in a solution of water and hair conditioner, or a proprietary brush restorer.

Quick way to filter out grit

If there's grit in the paint, stop it getting onto your brush by tying a piece of material cut from a pair of old tights over the rim of the tin (left). Use the tip of the brush to push the material down into the paint, so that clean paint rises up through it. The same trick allows you to filter contaminated paint back into a clean container before storing it.

Recycle white spirit

Save money by recycling white spirit after using it to clean brushes and rollers. Let the paint residue settle in the spirit container, then strain the clear solvent off into a clean container with a tamper-proof lid and label it clearly. Wrap up the hardened paint residue and the dirty container in newspaper before putting them in the dustbin.

Seal the lid

Tipping a tin of paint upside down for a few seconds before storing it helps to stop a skin from forming. The paint flows around the underside of the lid to form an airtight seal when the tin is turned the right way up. Don't store the tin upside down—a skin will simply form below the paint instead of on top of it.

Dilute the waste

When you've finished painting, use newspaper to remove as much water-based paint as possible from brush bristles and roller sleeves. Then wash them out in running water to dilute the paint before it enters the drains.

Store leftovers in jars

A small amount of paint will keep better if you decant it from the tin into a jar with a screw-top lid. Make sure you have enough paint to fill the jar, or a jar small enough to just take the paint, so there's little room for air. Rub some petroleum jelly around the neck of the jar before pouring in the paint; then any that spills down the outside won't make the lid stick fast. Remember to label the jar for future reference.

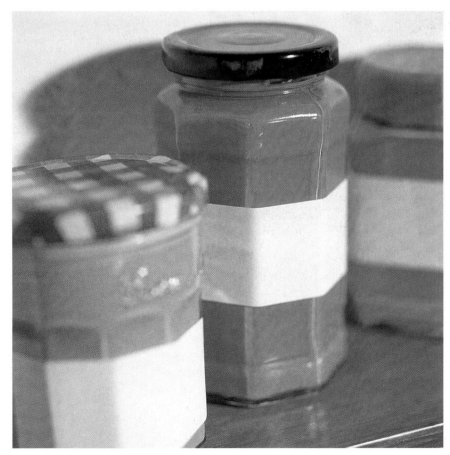

tiling Keys to a strong bond

Get rough with worktops

Before tiling a laminated worktop, score it with a metal abrasive disc fitted to a power drill. Coarse abrasive paper or a file will also do the job, but will take longer.

Strip a papered wall

Don't be tempted to stick tiles over wallpaper: the paste bond will fail and the tiles will fall off. Strip the paper, then wash off any remaining paste so the tile adhesive can bond well to the plaster.

Plywood is perfect

Use 12 mm exterior grade plywood for the walls of a tiled shower cubicle. Mount it on a firm timber framework and seal it with a wood primer. Unlike plasterboard, chipboard and MDF, the plywood won't distort if it gets wet, and because it is very stable, tiles stuck to it are unlikely to crack.

Primed plaster

Tiles can be stuck straight onto bare plaster or plasterboard, but seal the surface with a plaster primer first. This makes it less absorbent, so that the adhesive does not dry too quickly.

Test the paintwork

Stick test strips of adhesive tape onto a painted wall before tiling it. Leave the tape overnight; if the paint pulls away with the tape, you'll need to strip the wall before tiling. If the paint bond is strong, with no paint coming away with the tape, sand the wall surface with a coarse abrasive paper to provide a good key for the tile adhesive.

Preparing to lay the tiles

Visual effect

Large tiles are quicker to lay than small ones. However, they make a small space look even smaller, especially if a lot of cut tiles are required to cope with corners and features.

Read the pack

Check whether the number of square metres a pack of tiles will cover is printed on the box. This will save time when calculating how many packs you need to buy. Allow an extra 10 per cent for cutting and breakages. Keep any left-over tiles in case you ever have to replace any cracked or broken ones.

Match the batch

Try to buy boxes of tiles with the same batch number to reduce the possibility of colour variation. Then shuffle the tiles to disperse and hide any slight differences in colour. If there is a marked variation, try grading the tiles by shade, so that the differences in colour are 'lost' across the wall.

Edging options

The edge of a tiled area can be finished off with a coloured plastic edging trim, tiles with glazed edges (sometimes the box contains a quantity of these), slim border tiles or a hardwood moulding.

Design preview

To envisage what a tiling pattern will look like once it is on the wall, set out the tiles on the floor or a table first (below). This will give you the opportunity to work out exactly how many of each tile are needed, as well as to make changes to the design.

1 Cut batten and fix to wall with masonry nails. Use tile and spirit level to set batten one tile above skirting board

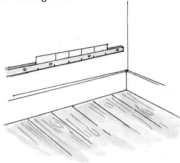

2 Use tiling gauge to work out tile joint positions, transferring marks from gauge to batten

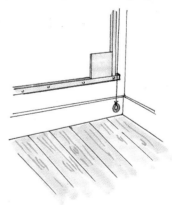

3 Position a vertical batten on start batten so its edge coincides with first whole tile in row. Spread adhesive and start placing tiles

tiling

227

tiling
Preparing to lay the tiles

Make yourself a gauge
Use a straight batten to make a tiling gauge for positioning the first row of tiles. Draw evenly spaced marks on the batten–each one representing the combined width of a tile and one joint.

Tiling over tiles
As long as old tiles are firmly fixed, new ones can be stuck on top of them. This is easier than removing the old tiles, which normally results in damage to the plaster that has to be made good. Wash the old tiles with sugar soap, then use double-sided adhesive pads to fix a starting batten to them. **Arrange the new tiles** so that the joints are not directly above those of the old ones. Then if the old grouting cracks, the new grouting won't.

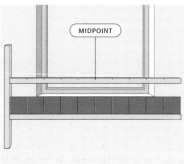

MIDPOINT

Ensuring symmetry
Using a tiling gauge to lay out tiles from the midpoint of a wall ensures equal-size cut tiles in the room corners. If the wall has a major feature such as a window, tile out from its midpoint, using the gauge to equalise the size of the cut tiles on each side of the window.

Fix a starting batten
Don't align the bottom edge of the first row of tiles with the skirting board, especially if you are tiling all round the room; it is unlikely to be perfectly level. Instead use a spirit level to position a batten horizontally so that the top edge is one tile height above the skirting board. Nail it temporarily to the wall.

Clean cuts every time

Effective nibbler

A platform tile cutter is not the best tool for cutting narrow slivers off tiles. Use it to score the line, then nibble the waste off with pliers or pincers. Be sure to protect your eyes against flying bits. Smooth the edge with a tile file.

Experiment first

The cutting wheel of a pliers-type tile cutter should make a clear whispering noise when run across the glazed surface of a tile. If it makes a dull sound instead, and the tiles won't snap cleanly in the jaws of the tool, they are too hard for this type of cutter. Buy or hire a heavy-duty platform tile cutter instead.

Saw and snap

To take a notch out of the edge of a tile—so that it fits around a pipe or bracket, for example—use a tile saw. Make the two parallel cuts at 90° to the edge, score between these, then snap out the waste with pliers. Remember to make an allowance for the grout when cutting a tile to fit around an obstacle.

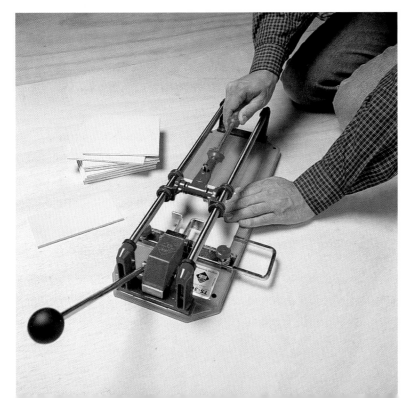

Hard and harder

The platform tile cutter sold in DIY stores will cut tiles up to 6 mm thick. For thicker ones, especially quarry tiles for floors, hire a professional version (left). There will be less wastage because you'll get a clean cut every time, so the cost of hiring the tool will soon be recouped, especially if you are working with expensive tiles.

File alternative

Coarse silicon carbide abrasive paper wrapped around a sanding block is a good alternative to a proper tile file when you want to rub down cut edges.

tiling Clean cuts every time

Reduce vibration when cutting

Anchor the tile to the workbench with a G-cramp when using a tile saw (right). Use a wooden packing piece between the cramp and the tile so you don't crack the tile as you tighten the cramp. The packing piece also reduces the vibration caused by sawing. To minimise the risk of cracking the tile, position it so that it overhangs the edge of the bench as little as possible.

Mind the marker

Use a chinagraph pencil to mark tiles before cutting them. Felt-tip pens should never be used on tiles; they leave a stubborn smudge on the surface of the glaze, and if you use one to mark the edge of a tile where you want to make a cut, the colour can migrate into the grout and stain it.

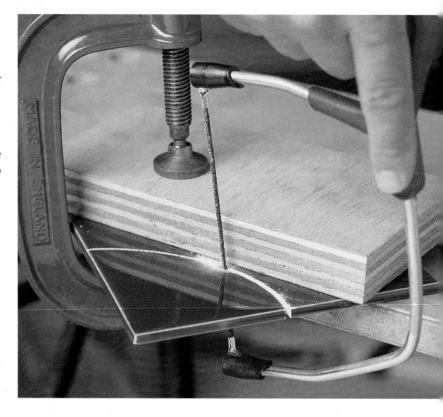

Sticking tiles in place

Sliding into trouble

Place tiles straight down in their final position. If you slide them into place, you will create a ridge of adhesive on the edge of the tile, which will be forced up between the tile joints. Wipe adhesive off the face of tiles before it can harden.

Roll over mosaics

A paint roller is the ideal tool for bedding sheets of mosaic tiles into the adhesive. It ensures even pressure and the avoidance of high and low spots across the wall or work surface. A rolling pin makes a good alternative if you don't have a paint roller handy.

Look for daylight

Lay a straightedge, such as a spirit level, across the surface of tiles before the adhesive dries to test for hollows and high spots. Prise off the affected tiles and add or remove adhesive.

Better to butter

The general rule is to put the adhesive on the surface you are covering, not the tile. But when it comes to fixing narrow cuts and edge tiles, it's better to butter the back of the tile with adhesive, then press it into place.

Waterproof worktops

Use special angled tiles to make the edge of a homemade chipboard worktop waterproof. Stick cut tiles along the edge of the worktop first, then position the angled tiles (right) so that they overlap the face tile. Finish off by tiling the worktop from front to back, with cut tiles fitted against the wall.

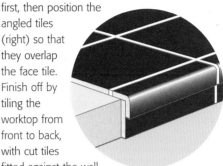

Drilling holes in tiles

Stop drill bits from skating

Make fixings in tiled walls by drilling into the grout lines wherever possible. If you have to drill through the face of the tile, use a sharp spear-point or masonry drill bit so the glaze doesn't chip. Stop the bit from skating on the glaze by sticking masking tape on the tile where you want to drill (left); this will give the bit an initial 'bite'. Make sure the drill isn't set on hammer action and start slowly if it has variable speed control.

Neat holes for pipes

A hole-boring attachment can be fitted to a platform tile cutter to cut holes for plumbing and central-heating pipes. Bore from the back of the tile, but stop before you go right through and tap out the hole from the glazed side.

Sealed against moisture

Apply waterproof silicone sealant to the tips of screws when mounting fixtures on tiled walls that get wet. As the screw tightens in the wall plug, the sealant is forced up the threads, helping to stop water getting down the fixing and behind the tiles.

Sink the plug

If you're inserting a wall plug into a tiled wall, drill the hole at least 3 mm (⅛ in) deeper than the length of the plug so it can be pushed into the wall past the tile. Otherwise, when a screw is driven into the plug, the sideways pressure it exerts can crack the tile.

tiling Grouting the joints

Switch to a squeegee
If you've never grouted tiles, a small piece of natural sponge is the best tool to start with. Once you've gained confidence, however, a rubber squeegee (above) does a quicker job, followed by a wipe with the sponge.

External corners
Coloured plastic trims will protect tiles on external corners from damage and give the edge a neat finish. Use the trims along the edges of tiled door and window openings as well.

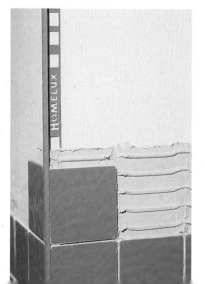

Internal corners
Lay the tiles on each side of an internal corner in pairs to achieve an even horizontal joint. In bathrooms run a bead of waterproof sealant down the corner to waterproof it, and to accommodate any slight movement.

Wipe off quickly

A combined adhesive and grout is much harder to clean off a tiled surface than ordinary grout once it has set. Mix small quantities at a time and clean up as you go. Use a kitchen scouring pad to remove the grout if it's starting to harden on the face of the tiles.

Strategy with spacers

If you're laying thin tiles and there's a risk that plastic spacers will show through the grouting, remove them before applying the grout.

Finishing touch

A ball-point pen cap makes an excellent tool for recessing grouting joints (above). A lollipop stick will also do the trick. Work while the grout is soft, carefully wiping away the surplus with a damp sponge. Don't be tempted to use your fingertip, though, grout is surprisingly abrasive and will soon rub your skin raw.

Hygienic surfaces

When you are tiling a kitchen worktop, finish the grout so that it is flush with the surface of the tiles. If you recess the joints, as you would on a wall, crumbs and grease will collect in them.

Repel mould

In rooms with a high moisture level mould thrives, causing brown or black stains on grout that won't wash off. To keep mould at bay, wipe a fungicidal wash over newly placed tiles in kitchens and bathrooms before grouting between them. Use an epoxy-based waterproof grout on tiled worktops and in bathrooms. It won't harbour mould and is easier to clean.

STAGES IN REPLACING A DAMAGED TILE

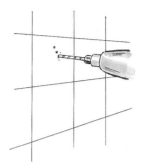

1 Make holes in centre of tile with power drill and masonry bit, then insert cold chisel into space made

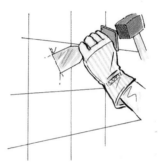

2 Wear eye protection while chipping out damaged tile. Spread adhesive on new tile and press into place

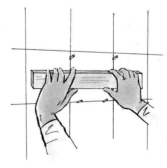

3 Lay a straightedge across repair to check that wall is flat, adding or removing adhesive as necessary

tiling

tiling Keep tiled surfaces looking good

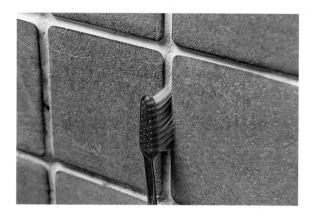

Clean between the tiles

A toothbrush is the ideal tool for cleaning grout. Remove dirt and grease with a solution of liquid detergent in warm water or a non-abrasive cream cleaner. Don't use abrasive cleaners on tiled surfaces; they may dull the glaze and 'pit' the grout.

Getting into the groove

A trimming knife is good for scraping old grouting out of narrow joints, if you don't have a proper grout removing tool. Start at the top of the wall and take care not to chip the edges of the tiles. Use a small, stiff-bristled brush or a vacuum cleaner with a narrow nozzle attachment to remove all the debris from joints before regrouting.

Mould solution

Treat spots of mould on grout with a solution of 1 part bleach in 6 parts of clean water. Wear safety spectacles to protect your eyes from splashes. Proprietary grout cleaners containing a mould inhibitor are also available.

Back to white

Revive discoloured grout by painting it with a proprietary grout whitener, applied with an artist's brush. But be warned: it's a slow tedious job.

Keep tiles sparkling

A solution of borax or liquid household ammonia in hot water will revive tiled surfaces discoloured by dirt and grease. Rinse the tiles with clean water then dry them off with a chamois leather.

Remove soap splashes with a mix of 1 part white vinegar to 4 parts water. Rinse the surface with clean water and then wipe it dry.

Disguise or display?

Choose a colour to match your tiles if you want to disguise the grout, but you can make a feature of it; for example, black grout with white tiles. Check that the tile surfaces are flat before using a contrasting grout, because it will accentuate any unevenness.

Scrape away

Dried-on grout can be removed from tiles with a glass scraper. If you squeeze a little washing-up liquid along the edge of the blade, it will glide over the tile without scratching the glaze.

Paper polishes

Once grouting has dried, use a ball of screwed-up newspaper to remove smears of dried grout and to give the tiles a final polish (above).

Estimating grout

About 1 kg (2¼ lb) of grout is needed for every 3.5 m² (40 sq ft) of tiling; for small mosaic tiles you will need at least twice the quantity.

wallpaper Choose carefully for success

Consider all the options
Think about the sort of wear wallpaper will get before you buy. Uncoated papers are fine for bedrooms and living rooms, but a washable or vinyl type will resist steam and stains better in kitchens, bathrooms and children's rooms.

Easy-to-hang paper
The heavier the wallpaper, the easier it should be to hang. Thin, cheap wallpapers tear and crease easily, making them hard to handle. Vinyls are the strongest wall coverings of all. They consist of a tough printed plastic film bonded to a paper backing so you can hang them like ordinary wallpaper.

Covering an uneven wall
A textured or embossed wallpaper will help to disguise minor imperfections in a wall that is sound but slightly uneven. Smooth wallpaper tends to highlight every surface defect.

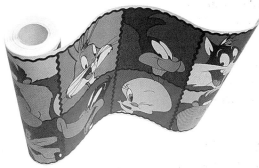

Quick change
Borders can be used on painted or papered walls. Pick a self-adhesive type or use ready-mixed border adhesive if you plan to hang one over a washable or vinyl wall covering. Ordinary powder wallpaper paste will not stick to them.

Best for beginners
For your first attempt at paperhanging, choose a paper with no pattern match (or with a random pattern) so you have one less thing to worry about as you hang each length.

Stagger the joins
Lining paper is a plain wallpaper used to hide minor surface defects before hanging smooth wall coverings. Start with a half-width strip, so the joins between the lining paper and the wallpaper don't coincide.

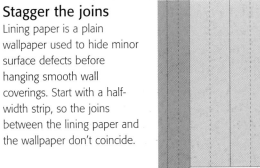

235

wallpaper How much paper to buy?

Count the widths

Use a standard 530 mm-wide wallpaper roll as a measuring stick to estimate how many strips will be needed to paper all the way round a room. Count doors and average-size windows as wall–the extra paper will be used up in trimming and pattern matching–but ignore large windows and patio doors.

Multiply the metric height of the room by the number of strips to get the total length of paper required. Divide this figure by the length of a standard roll (10 m) to find out how many rolls you'll need for the room.

Buy an extra roll

Check that all the rolls you buy have the same batch number; colours can vary from batch to batch. Buy an extra roll to be on the safe side in case your estimating is inaccurate; getting an extra roll with the same batch number at a later date may be difficult. You can usually return unused rolls for a refund.

Read the packaging first

If you are hanging wallpaper with no pattern match in a room with a typical ceiling height of around 2.3 m (7 ft 8 in), you will get four lengths from each roll. However, you may get only three (plus a lot of wastage) if the paper you have chosen has a large pattern repeat. Read the wallpaper packaging to find out what the vertical distance is between repeats.

Measuring and marking out

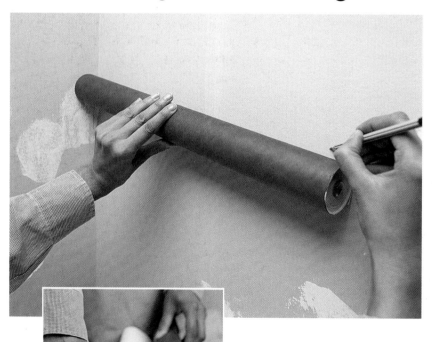

Start with a plumbed line

Mark a vertical guide on the wall before you start hanging wallpaper. Hold one end of a roll of paper into the corner, then make a mark for the line on the wall about 25 mm (1 in) from the other end, so that when you hang the paper you can turn a narrow strip round the corner and onto the adjacent wall.

Pin the top of your plumb line to the wall at ceiling level, so it hangs down over the mark. Then make pencil marks down the wall immediately behind the line and join them up with a pencil and ruler. Draw a new plumbed line when you start papering the next wall, in case the corner is not vertical.

Just fold and cut

Don't bother with a pencil and ruler to draw a cutting line through the length mark across the wallpaper. Just fold the paper at the mark with its side edges carefully aligned, and cut along the creased line. This guarantees a line at right angles to the paper's edge.

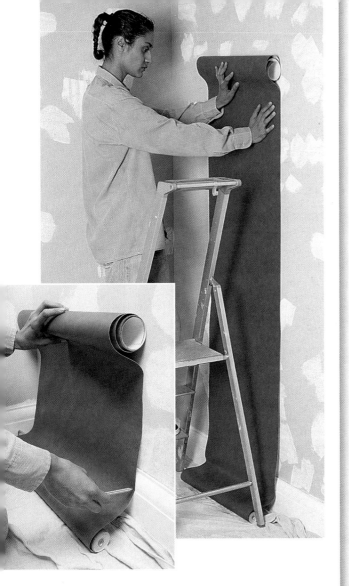

The right length every time

Don't use a metal tape to measure the length of pieces of wallpaper. Instead, unwind the roll–the pattern will be the right way up–and hold the top of it against the edge of the ceiling, allowing an overlap for trimming. Then walk your hands down the wall, letting the paper roll up above them as you descend (above). When you reach skirting board level, mark the paper for cutting, again allowing a margin for trimming (above left).

Keep track of wall plugs

Use matches or cocktail sticks to mark the positions of the wall plugs once you have unscrewed and taken down wall lights, shelves and wall-mounted display cabinets. If using matches, break off the heads so they can't stain the wallpaper. As you brush the length into place, the projecting stick will pierce the paper, giving you a clear indication of the whereabouts of every wall plug.

1 Use a plumb line to mark a vertical guide on wall for first length of paper

2 Press top of paper to wall so 50 mm (2 in) overlaps onto ceiling. Then slide it to guideline and brush into place

3 Press back of scissors into angles at ceiling and skirting board to make creases to cut to. Peel back paper, cut along creases and brush into place

4 Repeat procedure to hang subsequent lengths of paper. Butt adjoining edges and use seam roller to press down

wallpaper

wallpaper
Clever ideas with scissors, string and paste

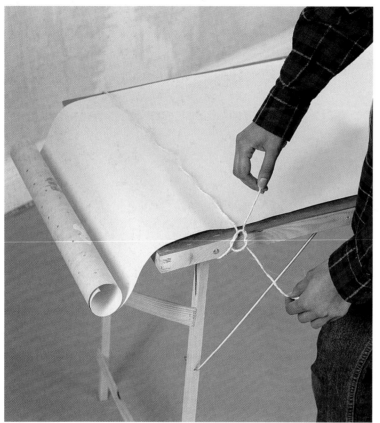

Two tricks with string

Stop the unpasted part of the paper rolling up onto the area you've pasted by trapping it under a string loop.

Wipe excess paste off the brush onto a piece of string tied across the paste bucket. Lay the brush across the string with its handle resting on the edge of the bucket when you're not using it.

Table-top tip

Before using a new purpose-made pasting table, tap down any pins or staples sticking out of the hardboard or plywood top; they can snag and tear the wallpaper. Next, seal the table top with a couple of coats of varnish to stop it absorbing paste. The table will then be much easier to keep clean.

Use a batch at a time

You can store left-over paste in a cool place overnight. Next day, use up what's left; don't add extra water and powder to an old mix—it will go lumpy.

Guarantee a clean cut

A build-up of paste on the blades stops wallpaper scissors from cutting cleanly. Keep a bowl of water nearby and get into the habit of dipping the blades into it every time you trim the waste from a length of pasted paper. Dry the scissors before using them again.

Pick the right paste

Choose the paste type recommended by the manufacturer of the wallpaper you're hanging. The strength of some pastes can be varied to suit the weight of the paper by increasing or decreasing the volume of water used in the mix; follow the instructions on this point. Nearly all pastes contain a fungicide to prevent mould growth; make sure you use one if you're hanging a vinyl or washable paper.

Paste up on a door

If you don't have a pasting table, take a hardboard-faced flush door off its hinges, remove one of the handles and rest the door across two trestles.

Size new plaster

Brush a coat of size or diluted wallpaper paste over new or unpainted plaster to seal its surface. Otherwise it will absorb water from the paste too quickly, and you will not be able to slide the paper into position easily as you hang it.

On painted walls, excess paste may ooze out along the edge of each length as you brush it into place. Wipe this away with a damp cloth, and make sure that no residue is left on the face of the wallpaper as it will dry in shiny smears.

Keep paste off the table

Avoid getting paste onto the pasting table—and from there onto the face of the paper, where it can cause stains—by following a simple routine. Align one edge of the paper with the far edge of the pasting table. Apply a generous daub of paste down the centre of the paper and brush it outwards to the far edge. Then slide the paper across to the near edge of the table and brush paste out to that edge too.

1 Stand water trough on newspaper next to wall where first length will be hung, and fill with cold water

2 Roll length loosely, pattern side in and top end at outside of roll. Leave immersed for recommended time, then pull top end of length upwards so water drains back into trough

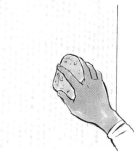

3 Position top of length on wall as for ordinary pasted wallpaper and brush length into place. Use sponge to wipe off excess water. Have some mixed paste ready for sticking any dried-out edges

wallpaper

239

wallpaper Clever ideas with scissors, string and paste

Support from table to wall

When you've pasted a length, fold each end in on itself, paste side to paste side (below). This makes sure no paste can get onto the face of the paper. Drape the folded length over one arm and take it to the wall. Then use your free hand to draw the top edge clear, ready to be hung at the top of the wall (right).

Avoid trouble with bubbles

Allow paste to soak in

Before pasting wallpaper, read the hanging instructions to see how much time you should allow for the paste to soak in. Wallpaper expands when it gets wet, and if you hang a length while this expansion is still going on, the paper will form bubbles as it stretches and lifts away from the wall surface. The thicker and heavier the paper is, the more time will be needed for this expansion to stop—as much as 15 minutes in the case of some heavy embossed papers. Each length you paste should be left to soak for precisely the same time.

New paper over old
Don't risk trying to paper over existing wallpaper. The new paste will soak into the old paper, softening its paste, and both layers will then bubble up on the wall. Always strip old paper first.

An invisible repair

A bubble that doesn't flatten out as the paste dries is usually caused by careless pasting leaving a dry spot on the back of the paper. Make two cuts across the bubble at 90° with a sharp trimming knife or razor blade (above). Peel back the flaps and apply a little paste with a small paintbrush (above right), then press the flaps back into place with your paperhanging brush.

Wash off grease spots

Greasy marks on the walls will cause bubbles because the wallpaper can't stick properly. Wash the surfaces down thoroughly with household detergent or sugar soap before you start papering.

Turning an internal corner

Don't try to hang a full-width strip of wallpaper round an internal corner. The corner will probably not be truly square, so the edge of the turned section of paper won't be vertical and that will misalign every length on the next wall.

Measure the distance from the edge of the last full length to the corner, and cut a length of paper to that dimension, plus about 15 mm (⅝ in) for turning around the corner onto the next wall.

Measure the width of the remainder of the cut length and mark a plumbed line this distance from the corner on the next wall. Hang the length to this line so its other edge overlaps the turned strip.

Turning an external corner

Use a technique similar to that for internal corners (left) to paper round external ones. Cut the strip of paper that reaches the corner so that about 25 mm (1 in) will turn onto the next wall, and hang it. Then hang the offcut on the next wall. You'll be able to butt it to the turned edge if the corner is true. If it is not, hang it to a plumbed line so it just overlaps the turned edge, then cut through both layers, using a straightedge and a sharp trimming knife. Peel away the offcuts and finish the two edges with a seam roller.

Papering behind radiators

If you are unable (or unwilling) to remove the radiators before papering a room, cut the paper to length so you can tuck about 200 mm (8 in) down behind them. Use a radiator paint roller if you have one to press the paper into place. Otherwise improvise by taping some sponge to a slim batten.

Invisible seams

It can be difficult to get a neat butt joint between lengths of fabric wall coverings such as hessian. Overlap adjacent lengths by about 6 mm (¼ in), then cut through both layers using a sharp trimming knife and a straightedge. Peel away the waste strips and press the cut edges together for a perfect seam.

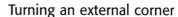

wallpaper Tackling the tricky bits

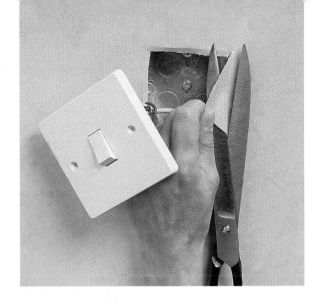

Masking a crease

Wallpaper may crease as you turn it round an out-of-square corner. If it does, tear the paper along the crease line while it's still wet, then smooth it back into place with the 'white' of the tear on the underside. The repair will be almost invisible.

Don't tear vinyl: cut the creases instead. You'll need to use overlap adhesive to stick the cut edges down.

Special treatment for vinyls

Vinyl will not stick over vinyl, whether it's ready-pasted or not, so when you overlap edges at a corner, either cut through both thicknesses to make a butt joint or stick the two together with special vinyl overlap adhesive.

Switches and sockets

Hang wallpaper straight over a light switch or wall socket so that the fitting marks the surface of the paper. Pierce the paper over the centre of the fitting and make diagonal cuts out to the four corners. With the power off, unscrew the faceplate and pull it away from the wall. Then trim off all but about 6 mm (¼ in) of the paper triangles and trap the rest behind the faceplate.

Papering a ceiling

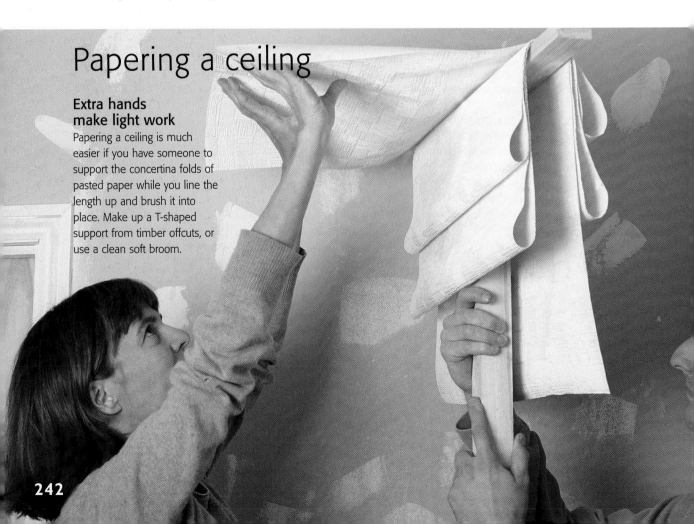

Extra hands make light work

Papering a ceiling is much easier if you have someone to support the concertina folds of pasted paper while you line the length up and brush it into place. Make up a T-shaped support from timber offcuts, or use a clean soft broom.

Work in comfort

Make up a work platform with scaffold boards supported on two pairs of steps, so you can reach the ceiling easily. It should span the room and leave about 75 mm (3 in) of space above your head.

Take down the lights

Turn the power off, then take down any ceiling light fittings and insulate the bare cable cores. If you have a ceiling rose, just disconnect the pendant flex from it.

Where to start

Snap a chalked string line on the ceiling to show where to position the edge of the first length of paper. Place it about 25 mm (1 in) less than the paper's width from the side wall. Then you can trim the edge of the paper to match the wall profile, which may not be straight.

Dealing with blemishes

Pencil marks

Rub away marks with an artist's soft putty rubber, which is less likely to damage the surface of the paper than a hard one. It will remove dirty finger marks too, unless they're greasy.

Water marks

To stop stains from past plumbing leaks showing through new ceiling paper, use an aerosol stain blocker to seal the surface. This product will also conceal stains left by tar from cigarette smoke.

Grease marks

You may be able to remove grease marks on printed wallpaper by dabbing them with a pad of kitchen paper dipped in white spirit. Try this on an out-of-the-way area first to check that the printing inks used are colourfast.

Invisible patches

If you have to patch badly marked or damaged wallpaper, tear rather than cut the patch so the 'feathered' edges will blend in with the surrounding paper. Then stick the patch over the damage with a little wallpaper paste. **Cut the patch** if you're repairing vinyl wallpaper. Hold an offcut over the damaged area, align the pattern and cut through both layers with a sharp trimming knife (above). Peel off the vinyl top layer, remove the backing paper with a sharp wallpaper scraper, then align the patch and stick it on.

Rust spots

Plasterboard nails are galvanised, but their coating is often damaged as they are driven in. If a ceiling or partition wall gets damp, the nail heads can rust and mark the decorations. Seal them with a dab of solvent-based paint or primer.

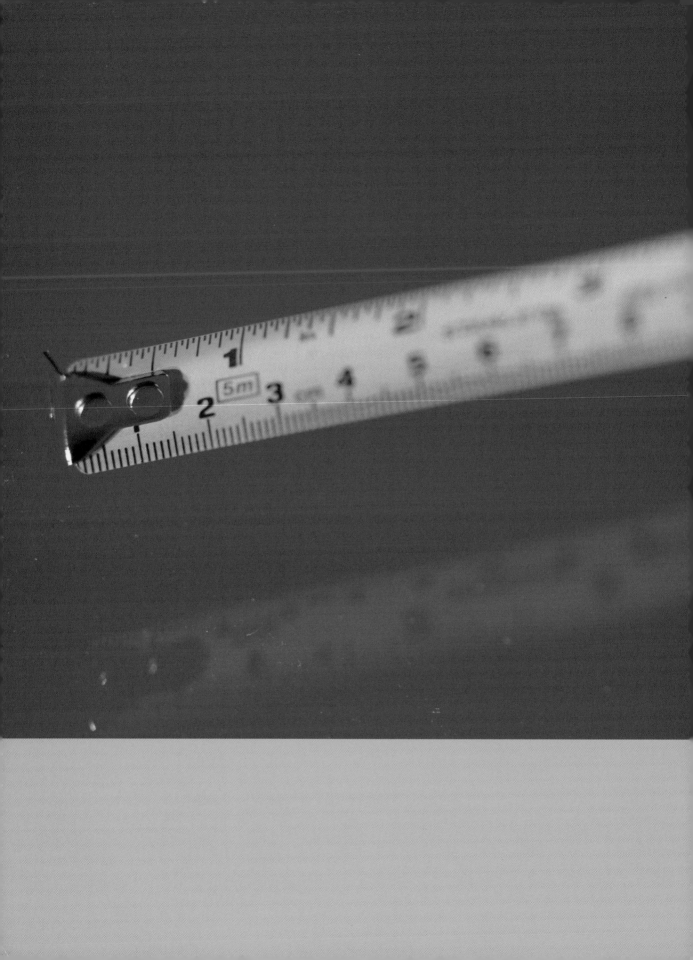

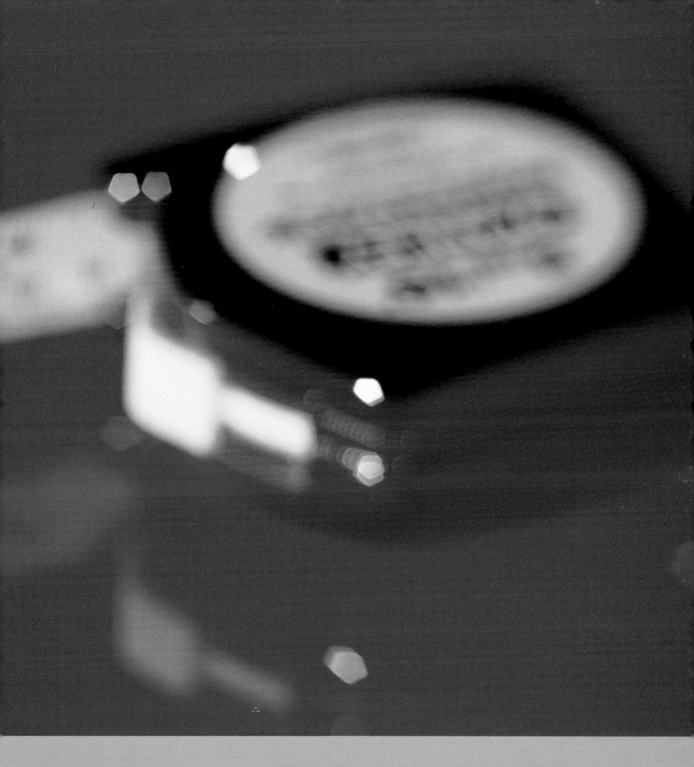

fittings

shelving
Taking the weight

Long enough to grip

Whatever type of shelving you are putting up, always provide good fixings. For masonry walls, this means using screws that will penetrate the wall by a minimum of 50 mm (2 in), driven into plastic wall plugs that match the screw gauge. On timber-framed walls, where the screws pass directly into the framing, 38 mm penetration will be adequate unless a heavy load will be placed on the shelves, when screws should go in by 50 mm.

Prospecting for cables

Use a battery-powered cable detector and common sense to locate cables buried in walls on which you plan to fix shelves. Cables normally run vertically (and sometimes horizontally) to socket outlets and wall lights, so avoid fixing shelving supports in these areas.

Watch the shelf spacing

Individual shelf brackets are fitted with the longer arm against the wall surface and the shorter one supporting the shelf. The length of the longer arm will define how close together shelves can be fitted one above the other. Don't forget to take this into account when planning a stack of shelving.

Improved rigidity

You can make a thin shelf more rigid by gluing and screwing a batten under its front edge, but bear in mind that the batten will slightly restrict the height of items you can store on the shelf below.

Match shelf and load

Space brackets according to the shelf material, its thickness and the load the shelf will be supporting. MDF and plain or veneered chipboard are the weakest shelving materials, so space brackets no more than 450 mm (18 in) apart for heavy loads such as books. Increase the spacing to about 750 mm (2 ft 6 in) for 19 mm plywood. Planed 19 mm softwood boards should be supported every 600 mm (2 ft).

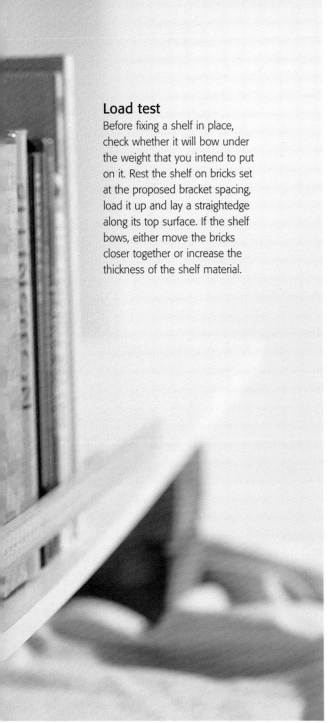

Load test

Before fixing a shelf in place, check whether it will bow under the weight that you intend to put on it. Rest the shelf on bricks set at the proposed bracket spacing, load it up and lay a straightedge along its top surface. If the shelf bows, either move the bricks closer together or increase the thickness of the shelf material.

Choosing glass

Glass shelves should be made from toughened glass at least 6 mm thick, and should be set on brackets spaced no more than 400 mm (16 in) apart. If the thickness of the glass is increased to 9mm, the spacing can increase to 700 mm (2 ft 4 in), unless the shelf is carrying heavy items, when it should be no more than 500 mm (20 in).

For light loads only

Shelves can be fixed to plasterboard rather than to the timber frame behind them (see pages 354–355), but they should be used to carry very light loads only—small ornaments, for example. Fix the brackets using spring toggles or other cavity fixings that spread the load against the inner face of the plasterboard.

Cupboard shelves

There are two easy ways to support shelves in cupboards. You can attach two lengths of slotted bookcase strip to each side of the cupboard and slot in slim metal tongues at the required shelf spacing. Alternatively, drill exactly corresponding rows of holes in the cupboard sides for plastic shelf-support pegs.

Fix the brackets to the wall

If a single shelf is more than 1 m long, it's best to put the brackets up first. Fix an end bracket in position on the wall. Then support one end of the shelf on it and use a spirit level to determine the position of the other end bracket. Fix this in place. Then position and fix intermediate brackets as required, lay the shelf in place and screw the brackets to it.

Fix the brackets to the shelf

When putting up a single shelf less than 1 m long, attach the brackets to the shelf first (above). Then offer the assembly up to the wall. Use a spirit level to position the shelf and mark the bracket screw-hole positions on the wall. Drill the holes, insert the wall plugs and fix the shelf in place.

shelving Level, secure and fitting perfectly

Ensuring vertical supports

Get the tracks of adjustable shelving systems truly vertical by hanging each one loosely from its topmost screw hole. Then hold a plumb bob and line—more accurate for verticals than a spirit level—alongside it. When it is truly vertical, mark the other screw positions through the holes in the track. Then swing the track aside while you drill and plug the holes. Reposition the track and drive in all the screws.

Matching the side walls of an alcove

An alcove beside a chimney breast is an ideal site for shelves, which can rest on battens fixed to the side walls. Few alcoves are square or have perfectly flat walls, however, so square-cut shelves will leave gaps. Get a perfect fit at the shelf ends by using an adjustable bevel. Measure the precise width of the back wall of the alcove, then mark the same measurement on the back of the shelf. Set the adjustable bevel to one internal corner of the alcove and use it to mark a cutting line across one end of the shelf. Repeat for the other corner. **Use two sheets of card** if you don't have an adjustable bevel. Butt the edge of one sheet against the back wall of the alcove and lay the other piece on top so that it butts against the side wall (top). Tape the sheets together and mark one shelf end (bottom). Repeat the process for the other corner.

Hiding the gaps

Gaps around shelves in an alcove can be hidden by pinning strips of quadrant beading over them. You can also conceal brackets and gaps at the ends of shelves by gluing and pinning a narrow strip of wood along the front edges, although this will slightly reduce the height of the space below.

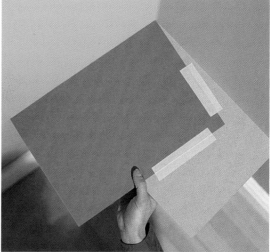

It can't fall down

Make sure a shelf cannot get knocked off by choosing brackets that can be screwed to the underside of the shelf. Check that the screws are not so long that they will burst through the top of the shelf—they only need to grip it.

Flush to the wall

The tracks used in adjustable shelving systems hold the rear edges of the shelves away from the wall. If you want them to fit flush, place each shelf on its brackets and mark the track positions on its rear edge. Then mark the depth of the track at each set of marks, and cut out notches with a saw and chisel so the shelf will fit round the track.

storage Ideas for every room in the house

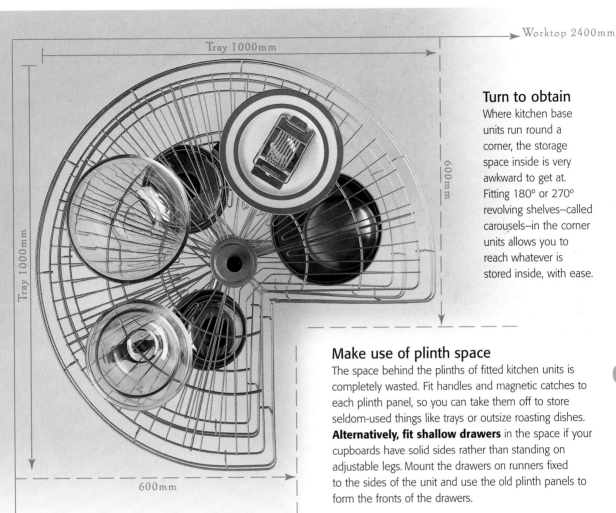

Tray 1000mm

Tray 1000mm

600mm

Worktop 2400mm

Worktop 2400mm

600mm

Turn to obtain

Where kitchen base units run round a corner, the storage space inside is very awkward to get at. Fitting 180° or 270° revolving shelves—called carousels—in the corner units allows you to reach whatever is stored inside, with ease.

Make use of plinth space

The space behind the plinths of fitted kitchen units is completely wasted. Fit handles and magnetic catches to each plinth panel, so you can take them off to store seldom-used things like trays or outsize roasting dishes. **Alternatively, fit shallow drawers** in the space if your cupboards have solid sides rather than standing on adjustable legs. Mount the drawers on runners fixed to the sides of the unit and use the old plinth panels to form the fronts of the drawers.

Double your hanging space

Since few items of everyday clothing are ankle length, full-height hanging space in wardrobes is a waste. Convert most of the space you have available to twin-level hanging, with a low-level rail midway between the top rail and the floor.

No hiding place with baskets

Replace full-depth shelves in kitchen base units with sliding wire baskets of various sizes, which can be pulled out for easier loading and retrieving. They are ideal for storing dry goods, tins, jars, fruit and vegetables, and miscellaneous kitchen utensils. You can store more things in a basket than on a fixed shelf. What's more, with this type of storage nothing is ever pushed to the back of the shelf and lost for years.

storage Ideas for every room in the house

Corner space

If bathrooms have any spare space, it is often in the corners of the room. See if you have space for a floor-standing corner unit that could house both family toiletries and cleaning materials.

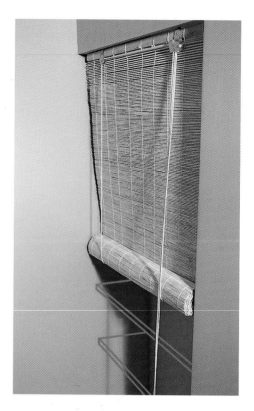

Use a concealed corner

Create inexpensive bedroom storage by filling an alcove beside a chimney breast with an array of sliding wire baskets, or a set of shelves supported on battens or adjustable track. Then you can hang a roller blind at ceiling level to conceal what's stored behind it.

Out of sight in the bathroom

If you have a homemade bath panel rather than a proprietary moulded plastic one, turn a section of it into a drop-down flap or a removable panel, and store things like bathroom cleaning materials and spare toilet rolls behind it.

Open with care

Always open flatpack furniture with care. Never use a knife to slit open the packaging, or you could damage the panels inside. Lay the pack flat and release the staples, tape or other fixings one by one, instead of relying on brute force. Then you can lift out the panels individually, stack them up neatly and retrieve any small bags of fixing devices that may be concealed within the packaging.

Preserving floor space

Sliding door wardrobes are one of the best bedroom storage solutions, since their doors need no floor clearance in front of them. In rooms with high ceilings, choose a door system with height reducers—adjustable brackets that suspend the track at standard ceiling height and are hidden by clip-on fascias.

Access from both sides

A double-sided room divider in a large living room can give you twice as much storage space as a unit of the same size standing against a wall, because each shelf and cupboard is used to its full depth. The same principle applies to breakfast bars and peninsula units in kitchens.

In place of fire

Turn a disused fireplace into storage or display space. Have the flue capped to keep rain out, then close it off above the fireplace opening with a panel containing a ventilator.

Put the ball in the net

In children's rooms, use homemade fabric sacks with drawstring tops or big net bags for storing soft toys, footballs and similar awkwardly shaped things that never seem to stay on shelves or in cupboards. You can hang the bags out of the way on wall hooks or on the backs of room or wardrobe doors.

Raised beds

Beds take up a vast amount of valuable floor space. Slide shallow drawers—fitted with castors so they're easy to move—underneath beds on legs. Build a raised platform for divan beds to create useful storage space beneath, accessible via sliding doors in the platform sides. Alternatively, replace existing beds with drawer divans, which have large storage drawers in the bed base.

In a child's room, the bed could be raised to the level of a top bunk, with clothes and toy storage space or a desk built underneath it.

Beneath your seat

Build a seat in a bay window to create some valuable long-term storage space. You can access it either by lifting the seat, or through hinged or sliding doors fitted along the front.

pictures A professional display

The weakest link

How secure a picture is, hanging on a wall, depends on the strength of the weakest link involved—often the small eyes or rings screwed into the frame. These seldom penetrate far into the wood, and on all but the lightest picture frames it is best to replace them with more substantial pinned-on D-rings.

Get it taped

Use special linen tape available from picture framers to tape pictures to their mounts. Avoid ordinary household sticky tapes; the adhesive can soak into the paper and damage the picture.

Down the wire

Twisted brass wire is used to hang most pictures. The wire can be attached to the small fixing eyes by twisting it round itself. However, twisted wire can unravel in time, and you'll get a much more secure fixing if you crimp special brass ferrules onto the wires with pliers.

Form a group

Sets of small pictures look best hung as a group, especially if they share a common theme or are framed in a similar style. Lay the pictures on the floor first, moving them around to experiment with different arrangements. Then measure the overall dimensions of the group and transfer the whole arrangement to the wall.

SINGLE-PIN HOOK

DOUBLE-PIN HOOK

The best hook

Always use appropriate picture hooks to hang your pictures. Single-pin hooks will support a glazed frame up to a size of about 900 x 600 mm (3 x 2 ft), and a double-pin hook can hang a picture half as big again. Consider using two hooks for larger pictures and mirrors.

Hung from the rails

If your room has picture rails, hang your decorations from them using S-shaped picture rail hooks, and avoid the holes in the walls picture hook pins make. Nylon cord or even fishing line is less obtrusive than picture wire. You can use fine decorative chain if you prefer to make a feature of the hanging method.

Leave room for fixing

The rebate in a typical picture frame has to accept the glass, the picture itself, its mount and a backing board. Once all this is in you'll need 2–3 mm (⅛ in) of rebate still visible to take the fixing pins that will hold everything in place. Use a thinner mount and board if you do not have this much clearance.

Special framer's triangles–sharpened steel fixings–can be used instead of pins and are less likely to split the frame. They can be hammered in or stapled with a special tool.

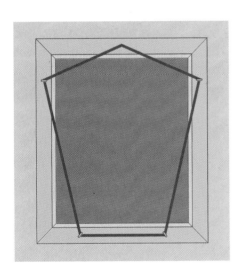

Spreading the strain

Heavy frames can open up at the corners under their own weight. • To prevent this, rig the wire so that it supports the frame at the bottom by passing it through two extra screw eyes driven into the bottom frame section.

Handling heavyweights

The safest way to hang large and very heavy pictures is to use interlocking wall battens. Make a 45° cut down the centre line of a 75 x 25 mm softwood batten and screw one piece across the back of the picture frame and the other to the wall. To hang the picture, hook its batten over the one on the wall.

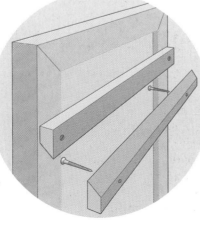

Seal cord ends

Many picture framers use special braided nylon cord, guaranteed to be rot and insect-proof. Always check that the knots are really tight before hanging a corded picture. To stop the ends fraying or the knots unravelling, seal the cut ends of the cord by holding them in a lighter or match flame for a moment.

pictures Looking into mirrors

Washers take the strain

If you are putting up a pre-drilled mirror with screws, fit a rubber tap washer on each screw between mirror and wall. These stop the mirror cracking as you tighten the screws. In steamy bathrooms they also hold the mirror away from the wall and allow air to circulate behind it, stopping condensation from forming and damaging the silvering.

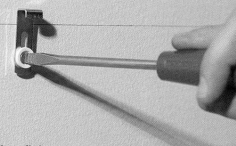

Perfect reflections

Do not stick mirror tiles directly to a plastered wall. It is unlikely to be truly flat, and you'll end up with a distorted reflection. Instead, stick them to a piece of 6 mm thick plywood, cut a fraction smaller than the complete mirror tile panel you want. Stick four double-sided adhesive pads on each tile, then stick the tiles to the board.

Don't butt mirror tiles tightly. Put strips of paper between the tiles as you fix them, to act as spacers and leave a tiny expansion gap. Remove them when you've finished fixing the tiles.

Sliding fixings

Use proprietary mirror clips to fix mirrors without screw holes. The lower clips are fixed, while the upper clips (shown) drop down over the mirror's top edge after its bottom edge has been positioned on the lower clips.

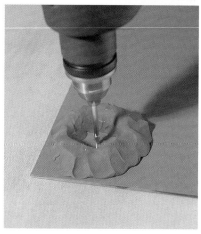

Lubricate the drill

To drill holes in a mirror, use a spear-point glass drill bit at a slow drill speed. Mark the hole position on the back of the mirror with a felt-tip pen, and drill a small starter hole. Then stick a ring of putty or modelling clay round it and pour in some white spirit or light oil to lubricate the bit. Locate the drill tip in the starter hole and drill until the point just breaks through the surface of the glass. Then remove the putty and finish drilling the hole from the front side.

window dressing Hanging curtains

How heavy are they?

Weigh your curtains before you buy the track. First, get on the scales yourself and record your weight, then get back on them carrying the curtains. The difference is their weight. Choose an appropriate track by reading the manufacturer's load rating printed on the packaging.

Fitting and cutting track

Put up all the brackets before taking exact measurements for the track and cutting it to length. A junior hacksaw is ideal for cutting plastic or metal track. Remove burrs from the track ends with fine abrasive paper to protect your hands from scratches and the curtain material from snags.

Pulling power

Fit extra-long screws and heavy-duty wall plugs to support track brackets next to cord pulls. It is surprising how much downforce is exerted on these brackets, especially when you are drawing full-length curtains.

window dressing
Hanging curtains

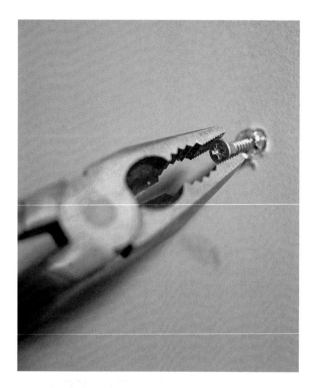

Bending plastic track
Use a hair dryer to warm plastic track where you want to bend it; once warm, it will be more flexible. The tighter the track can be bent to the angles or curves of a bay window, the less room the curtains will take up, although very heavy curtains may tend to 'bunch' if the bend is too tight.

Fixing to a concrete lintel
Putting up track can be difficult if there is a concrete lintel above the window opening. A solution involving fewer wall fixings and less awkward drilling is to mount a wooden batten on the wall. Drill holes in the lintel with a masonry bit in a hammer drill, then put up the batten with screws and wall plugs and fix the track brackets to this.

Out with the old
If you are putting back the existing curtain track, check that the old wall fixings are up to the job. Replace frayed or split wall plugs by inserting a screw just far enough to engage in the plug, and then pull the screw and plug out with pliers.

Gluing track to the wall
To put up lightweight curtains or a blind without the need for wall fixings, use panel adhesive to stick a timber batten to the plaster above the window, and attach the track to that.
Tap the plaster first to make sure it is firmly bonded to the masonry; if it sounds hollow, it may pull away under the combined weight of the batten and curtains.

Automatic closing
Motorised curtain closers offer the ultimate in home security if your house is usually empty at dusk. By putting the unit under the control of a photoelectric sensor or a time switch, you can set it to close your curtains (and to switch on some lights) automatically as dusk arrives.

Make your own brackets
Brass brackets to support a curtain rod above a window or doorway are a decorative feature, but if the rod runs inside the reveal, the brackets are an incidental item and you can save money by making simple and unobtrusive wooden end brackets yourself. Hardwood is the best material, but you can use softwood instead if you are going to paint the brackets to blend in with the wall colour. Make the shaped cut-outs with a coping saw. Once the brackets and rod are in place, screw a small removable metal plate across the top of one bracket to prevent the rod being dislodged.

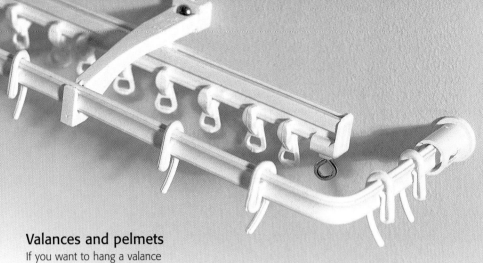

Valances and pelmets

If you want to hang a valance or pelmet, choose a brand of curtain track designed to take a complementary clip-on valance track. The returns at each end carry the valance and hide the track.

Hang from the ceiling

In some bay windows there isn't enough space above the window frame to secure the track to the wall. To provide a fixing, screw a softwood batten to ceiling joists above the bay and then suspend the track from that.

Curtains in a bay

In bay windows, fit the track so that it runs out of the bay and onto the wall at each side. Then the open curtains won't hang over the windows. In a large bay, consider dividing the curtain run into four and letting the two centre sections hang in tiebacks over the main window uprights.

Clear the frame

Some sash windows have an architrave moulding round them which can catch curtains hung from track mounted on the wall above. Fit a batten the same thickness as the architrave above the window and mount the track on that.

Installing blinds

Stiffen the fabric

If you are making up a roller blind using your own fabric, spray aerosol blind-stiffening fluid onto both sides of the material. Not only does this increase the stiffness, it also prevents the fabric edges from curling up or fraying.

Putting the roll back into roller

To increase the tension in the spring of a roller blind so it rolls up on its own, pull it down fully and then lift the roller off its brackets. Roll it up about half way, replace it on the brackets and test the tension. Repeat the process, rolling up a bit more of the blind each time, until you get the tension right.

Avoid drilling the wall

Dispense with drilled wall fixings when fitting top-hung Roman and festoon blinds by bonding a length of touch-and-close fastening strip to the wall above the window with panel adhesive. Stick the other part of the strip to the back of the blind's top batten. Then press the batten onto the wall strip.

Stick screws to the screwdriver

Mounting roller blinds at the top of window frames can be tricky because the brackets have to be fitted tight into the corners of the window reveals. The solution is to hold each bracket in place and make the screw holes with a bradawl. Then stick a Pozidriv screw to the blade of your screwdriver with a little Blu-Tack, hold the bracket in place with one hand and drive the screw into its hole with the other.

furniture

blemishes First identify the finish

How to tell wax from oil

Try the white spirit test to distinguish between a waxed and an oiled surface. Dampen a cloth with a little of the solvent and wipe a hidden corner of the item of furniture. If the surface finish dissolves and leaves a smear on the cloth, it has been waxed; if it turns slippery but does not smear, an oil finish has been applied to it.

Look at the colour

Cellulose lacquer and acrylic varnish are almost completely clear when dry, while polyurethane varnish yellows with time. You can therefore often distinguish something coated with varnish just by the discoloration. As an extra test, rub a little cellulose thinners on a hidden spot. A lacquered finish or one created with acrylic varnish will rapidly dissolve; one coated with polyurethane varnish will be unaffected.

Fast face-lifts and disguises

Cut through grime

Clean away layers of dust-ingrained wax with a homemade furniture cleaner, made up of equal quantities of vinegar, white spirit and water. Add a squirt of washing-up liquid to the mixture, then apply with a house-plant spray. Wipe off the liquefied residue before it hardens.

Try the meths test

You can find out if a piece of furniture is finished with french polish by rubbing an inconspicuous part of it with a cloth dipped in methylated spirits. If the surface softens in seconds and leaves smears on the cloth, you know that you're dealing with french polish.

Removing white rings

Car rubbing compound and metal polish are good for getting rid of white ring stains on french-polished surfaces. Both are abrasive so apply them gently with a soft damp cloth.

Baby oil for scorches

Heat makes french polish craze. Restore the finish by flicking some baby oil onto the surface, then rub it over gently with a cloth dampened in methylated spirits.

Beware of health hazards

Many of the materials used to refinish furniture are flammable and give off noxious fumes. Work in well-ventilated spaces and don't smoke. Wear a respirator if you're using a two-pack lacquer or rubbing down glass-fibre filler.

When a solvent won't work

Polyurethane and cold-cure or two-pack lacquers don't readily react to solvents. You can usually identify polyurethane varnish because it yellows over time, but to confirm the finish, try scraping a hidden area with a trimming knife. Polyurethane varnish lifts in flakes and dust, a cold-cure lacquer as dust only.

Erase ink blots

Oxalic acid is often recommended for bleaching ink stains out of furniture, but it is a drastic remedy and dangerous to use. Salt and lemon juice rubbed over the stain often works on bare wood. On a finished surface, ink blots are best ignored, especially if the piece of furniture is an old desk or bureau.

1 Use an artist's paintbrush to apply hot water to dent. As water is absorbed, add more so that wood fibres swell

2 Alternatively, lay a 'poultice' of wet cotton wool over dent and leave overnight

3 To speed things up, apply tip of a hot iron to the damp cotton wool to create steam

4 If surface is french polished, use car rubbing compound or metal polish to remove white marks caused by treatment

blemishes

blemishes First identify the finish

Cosmetic treatment

Use clear nail polish as a filler for chips and scratches in varnish. Overfill the damage and leave the nail polish to harden thoroughly before carefully rubbing it down with a fine grade wet-and-dry abrasive paper.

Professional remedy

You can disguise superficial scratches on french-polished surfaces with a concoction used by antique restorers. Pour equal volumes of white spirit, methylated spirits and linseed oil into a container, then shake the mixture thoroughly before using it. Use a clean soft cloth to apply it to the scratched area, rubbing with a circular motion.

Scorch repair

Most burns in wooden furniture are caused by cigarettes or cigars. There is no quick fix or chemical cure for a burn; the black mark must be scraped out with a trimming knife or chisel. You'll then need to fill and camouflage the resulting depression. Depending on the depth of the gouge and the finish of the surface you are repairing, use either a wax stick (see opposite) or matching wood stopping (see page 265).

Make scratches vanish

Use Danish oil to disguise scratches on polyurethane-varnished surfaces. Once the oil has dried—after about 4 hours—wipe the surface with clear wax.

Match the colour

A felt-tip pen that matches the colour of the finish is good for camouflaging scratches, but if you want to fill the blemish, thicken up the right shade of artist's oil paint with clear furniture wax and apply it with an artist's brush.

repairs Holes, cracks and gouges

Hot wax treatment

Children's wax crayons make a fast-setting stopper if you cannot get hold of any wax filling sticks. Melt the crayon in a spoon over a candle, blending hot wax from different coloured crayons to match the piece of furniture. Trickle the molten wax into small gouges, deep scratches and woodworm holes, smoothing it with a knife dipped in hot water. Use a plastic scraper to remove the excess wax once it hardens.

Detecting woodworm

Check for active woodworm by looking out for tiny tell-tale piles of sawdust, called frass, at the bottom of cupboards and drawers, and particularly around the parts of a piece of furniture that haven't been painted or varnished: the beetle prefers to eat its way out through bare wood.

Keeping track with wax

Disguise woodworm holes with wax or a wood filler. As well as making the damage less conspicuous, a fresh attack will be easier to spot.

Liquid filler

Shellac sticks are sold for repairing damage and stopping up holes in furniture finished with french polish, but you can use liquid shellac (normal french polish). Pour it into a saucer and leave it for 30 minutes or so to thicken. Pick up some of the viscous shellac on the end of a matchstick and trickle it into the damage. Build up the repair layer by layer if necessary, then carefully scrape off the excess with a sharp blade before rubbing down with fine-grade wet-and-dry abrasive paper.

repairs

263

Dye your own filler

Instead of building up a stock of several differently coloured wood fillers, buy a single tin of light-coloured stopper. Then stain a little of it a different colour whenever you want to match a different wood. Make sure, however, that all the stains you buy are compatible with your single tin of filler.

Death or deterrent

Dark woodworm holes are the sign of an old infestation, but treat the piece of furniture with a woodworm killer anyway: if there are larvae in the wood, they will be killed, while adult beetles won't lay eggs in treated wood.

Wear safety spectacles or goggles when injecting fluid into flight holes; it can shoot out of other holes into your eyes.

Resin reinforcement

You can use glass-fibre resin, available from car accessory shops, to reinforce furniture that has been badly weakened by woodworm. Drill small holes about 6 mm (¼ in) or less in diameter around the damaged area and force the resin into them. It will set solid. Damaged cupboard hinge areas on chipboard units can be reinforced in the same way.

An alternative use for car body filler

Car body filler is an economical material for repairing damaged furniture. You can use it with solid wood and manufactured materials such as chipboard and MDF. Small screws driven into the damaged area first will help to bond the filler and to prevent it cracking away.

You can make a mould to contain the filler (and minimise the amount which has to be sanded off) with small blocks of wood tacked into place around the repair (right). Line the blocks with a clear cellulose tape such as Sellotape to prevent the filler sticking to them. Shape the final layer of filler with a trimming knife while it is soap-hard. Then smooth the repair with fine abrasive paper once it has hardened.

Hiding damage with wood patches

Put a plug in it

Plug cutters and matching drill sets enable you to drill out a flaw in a piece of furniture and replace it with a plug of wood that fits snugly into the hole. Select a piece of wood with matching grain and colour to the surface being repaired from which to cut a plug, then the repair will be virtually invisible.

Diamonds are inconspicuous

If you don't have a plug cutter, make a diamond-shaped insert. Plane a slight bevel on the edges of the insert before using it as a template to mark out a recess around the damage. As the insert is tapped into the recess, the bevel will ensure a really tight, invisible fit.

265

repairs
Take components apart without breaking them

Injection booster
Try injecting glue into a loose joint before you resort to taking it apart. Drill a small hole into the joint, where it cannot be easily seen, then use a plastic syringe to force new glue into the gap. PVA or urea-formaldehyde glue is the best choice.
Plug the drilled hole with a blob of Plasticine or putty until the glue has set.

Protect your skin
Some woodworking glues can cause skin irritation. Wear latex gloves when using urea-formaldehyde glues, such as Cascamite, and also epoxy resin glues. If any glue does get on your skin, wipe it off immediately.

Bracing sloppy corners
Loose corner joints in inconspicuous places—at the back of a bookcase, for example—can be reinforced and kept square with small triangular braces made from plywood. Glue and screw the braces, sometimes called ply webs, into place across each corner.

Dissolve scotch glue
Knocking joints apart risks damaging the components. If the piece is old, however, it will have been assembled with scotch glue, which is soluble in methylated spirits. Try swabbing joints with meths before using more forceful methods.
Drill a small hole to improve access to the joint if necessary, and use a plastic syringe to flood the hole with meths.

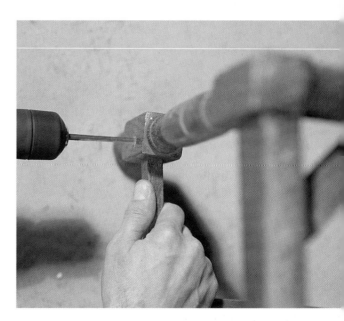

Drill out nails and dowels
If a nail or dowel has been used to reinforce a mortise-and-tenon joint in a piece of furniture, you'll have to drill it out with a twist drill before you can dismantle the joint.
When removing a nail, punch the head in first, so that the drill is less likely to jump off it and damage the surface of the wood as you drill out the shank.
To remove a dowel, use a drill bit that matches the diameter of the dowel you will be fitting as a replacement.

Clean up old joints

A strong glued joint depends on some absorption into the wood. This won't happen if there's old glue sealing the grain, so get rid of it first. Traditional scotch glue can be softened and dissolved with meths (opposite), but synthetic glue has to be carefully pared and scraped away with a chisel (left). Try to avoid removing any wood with the glue or the new joint will be a loose fit and will be weak.

Extract a loose dowel

Loose 'dry' dowels in mortise-and-tenon joints can be removed by driving a screw into the end of the dowel, then gripping the head of the screw with a pair of pincers and pulling it out of its hole.

Putting pieces back together

Mind the gap

Examine the drawer fronts on an old chest of drawers. There should be an even gap at the top and bottom when they are shut, but wear on the drawer runners often means the fronts 'drop' and clash on the frame ledge below, leaving all the gap at the top. Even things up by gluing and pinning slips of thin plywood to the ledge of the frame—two for each drawer. Set the pieces of ply back from the edge slightly so they don't show. Then, when the drawers are shut, their fronts will be supported on the ply slips and the gap will be evened out.

Room to move

A solid wooden table top can split if it is simply screwed to its supporting frame. Replace the screws with slotted shrinkage plates, which are designed to allow the top to expand and contract independently of the frame.

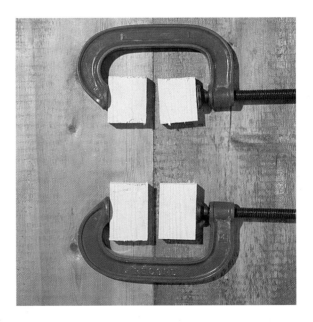

Mending split panels

If the wood is thin, glue blocks of scrap wood onto the underside or back of the panel, at either side of the split. When the blocks are firm, squeeze glue into the split, then tighten G-cramps on the blocks to force the split closed. When the glue has set, knock the blocks off with a mallet and chisel.
For thick panels, use screws to fix the blocks, but make sure they don't penetrate the face of the panel.

repairs Putting pieces back together

Test the fit first
Make sure that all the pieces fit together perfectly before gluing any furniture back together. This serves as a check that you've assembled joints with the right pieces of wood in the right places. It's better to discover a problem at this stage than have to undo cramps and remake the joints.

Don't let the jaws bite
Note where cramps are best positioned during the dry run. Then tape offcuts of wood, corrugated card or pieces of hard rubber in place, to spread the pressure of the cramp jaws and stop them biting into the wood. Don't overtighten cramps–it risks forcing the joints out of square.

Apply a tourniquet
If you have to re-glue the stretchers between the legs of a wooden chair, make a tourniquet to hold them while the glue sets. Loop a length of cord around the legs–protecting the wood with corrugated card–then put a stick or screwdriver through the loop and twist it to tighten the arrangement.

stripping Take great care with chemicals

Don't strip an asset
Removing the patina–the surface sheen produced by age–from a valuable antique lowers its worth dramatically, so don't strip a piece of furniture if you suspect it may be valuable.

Chemical stripper is best
The best way of taking off old paint and varnish is with a chemical stripper. Sanding surfaces removes some of the wood, which can easily spoil delicate, well-defined mouldings. With a hot-air gun or blowlamp, you run the risk of charring the surface. Using abrasives and heat also poses a health risk if you are dealing with old lead-based paint; always strip this with a chemical.

Beware of caustic dips
A hot caustic soda bath provides the cheapest form of commercial stripping, but also poses the greatest risk to furniture. Items are subjected to a sudden increase in temperature when they go into the dip; then they are hosed with water to remove the chemical from the wood. These sudden stresses cause cracked panels, weakened joints and raised grain. Hardwoods may also become discoloured.

Gel or liquid?
Use a gel stripper on vertical surfaces. It won't run towards the floor, is easier to control and more effective. You can use it on other surfaces too, although a liquid is better for getting into intricate carvings and mouldings. If you don't have a proprietary gel stripper, mix a little wallpaper paste into a water-based liquid one (above).

Vinegar solution
Salty white stains on the wood are a sign that an item has been left in a caustic dip for too long. Remove them with a strong solution of white vinegar. You'll probably need to repeat this several times, over a period of weeks, before all the chemical has leached out.

Scourer for stubborn bits
Use the scouring pad side of a washing-up sponge, dipped in paint stripper, to remove any vestiges of paint and varnish stuck in the grain of the wood. Rub in the direction of the grain.

269

stripping
Be organised and start with small items

Don't be too ambitious
Making a good job of stripping a piece of furniture demands great patience, so start with something small. A good rule of thumb for beginners is: don't tackle a piece that you cannot lift easily. Leave wardrobes, dining tables and four-poster beds until you've gained some experience.

Plenty of fresh air
The safest place to work with chemical stripper is outside in the open air. If you do have to work indoors, open the windows because these products can give off strong fumes.

Make yourself comfortable
Stripping a piece of furniture is a long job. Make yourself comfortable and avoid an aching back by standing the item on a support. Working without having to bend also means you'll be less likely to miss any parts.
Keep some water handy in case you splash any stripper onto your skin.

A section at a time
If you're stripping a large piece of furniture, tackle it a section at a time—the top of the table before the legs, for example. By completely stripping one area at a time back to the bare wood, you will feel encouraged to persevere.

Turn over a new leaf
An old magazine printed on glossy paper is useful for removing the gunge from your scraper. Fold a page round the blade and wipe it clean, then use a fresh page for the next wipe. Afterwards, put the magazine in the dustbin; the chemicals contained in the stripper will have made it unsuitable for recycling.

A job for old brushes
Don't throw away old paintbrushes; they are ideal for applying paint stripper. Leave the brush soaking in a jar of the stripper for a short time before you need it. Dried-on paint will soon soften and separate from the bristles.

Protect the floor
If stripper drips on the floor, it can damage linoleum, vinyl, cork and varnished boards. Spread plenty of old newspapers or dustsheets. Stand the feet of chairs and tables in old aluminium baking trays or foil pie cases to catch any runs; don't use plastic tubs because the stripper may dissolve them.

Rinse off the residue
Most chemical strippers have to be rinsed off with water before you apply a new finish, but this tends to raise the grain and make the wood feel fuzzy, so use as little of it as possible. Water can also cause veneers to lift, so use a solvent-based stripper if you are working on veneered furniture.

Newspaper poultice
If you are trying to strip a piece of furniture that's caked with many layers of old paint, brush on a thick layer of gel or paste stripper and top it with a layer of newspaper. Then fill a garden spray gun with soapy water and use this to keep the paper and stripper wet.

Leave the stripper for an hour to do its job. Then lift a corner of the paper to check if the finish has softened. When you can scrape a test area back to bare wood, lift off the paper carefully; you should be able to remove the stripped paint in one go. If the paper breaks up, simply scrape off the layer of stripped paint bit by bit.

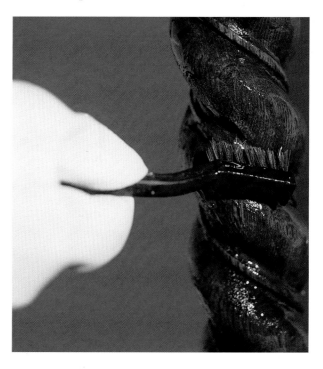

Scrub up the details
A wire suede shoe brush is the ideal tool for removing softened paint and varnish from turnings and mouldings, and for scrubbing it out of open-grained hardwoods such as mahogany and oak.

metalware
Putting a shine on old brass

Pin it down
Secure small intricate brass fittings to a scrap of wood. You will find cleaning them much easier this way than if you hold them in your hand.

Ketchup marinade
Badly tarnished pieces of brassware can be restored by leaving them to soak overnight in tomato ketchup. Scrub them with an old toothbrush and rinse in water to restore the lustre.
Substitute paint stripper for the ketchup if the item has been coated in paint, then scrub with the type of small brass wire brush used for cleaning suede shoes.

Base metal showing
Make sure brassware is solid before you start rubbing at it too enthusiastically. Look for dull grey patches in the finish—a sure sign that brass plating has worn away to reveal the base metal underneath. If the worn patches are not too obvious, clean the remaining brass, but if the plating is badly worn, use car rubbing compound to strip away the remaining brass to give a uniform, steely finish.

Protection for wood
When restoring a piece of furniture, try to remove any metal fittings first. This will prevent the wood from being dulled by metal polish and wadding, and the fittings from being tarnished by the wood finish, if both are treated in place.

Protect brass with wax
If you cannot remove metal fittings easily from a piece of furniture before giving it a new finish, carefully brush a layer of melted candle wax or beeswax onto them. The wax will resist stains and oils, but you will still need to be careful that the methylated spirits in french polish does not dissolve the wax.

Finding the key

Old cabinet locks are usually simple mechanisms, often just screwed to the back of a cupboard door or drawer front. So if you don't have a key, try removing the lock and taking it to a secondhand furniture dealer. Most keep a selection of old keys, and the chances are that one of them will fit your lock.

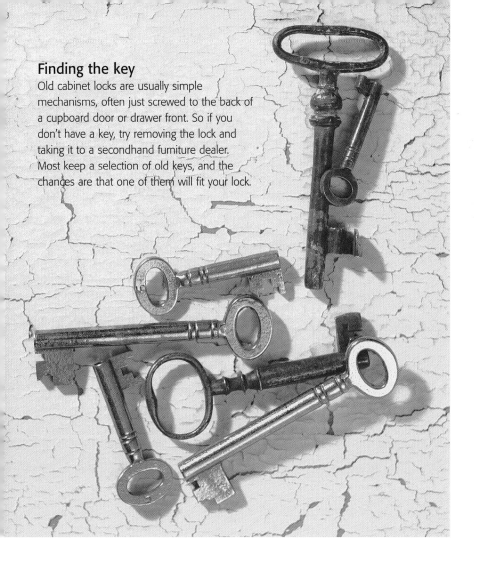

Lost lacquer

New brass is often lacquered to stop it tarnishing. Eventually the lacquer begins to peel, so that the exposed metal tarnishes but the areas which are still lacquered don't. The only course of action is to take off the remaining lacquer with a chemical paint stripper. Then rub the whole item with fine wire wool dipped in metal polish or car rubbing compound. Finally, buff the brassware with a soft duster.

Short cut to an antique look

To soften the bright, garish look of new brassware on old furniture, it can be artificially aged. Put the fittings into an airtight box containing an open pot of liquid ammonia (available from pharmacists) for a few hours. Don't let the brass touch the ammonia and try to avoid breathing the fumes. Rinse the items after you remove them from the box to wash away traces of ammonia. Then gently polish them. The 'brand new' look will have disappeared.

metalware
Solutions to problems with catches, hinges and locks

Matchstick plug

If the doors on an old cabinet don't shut, look at the hinges. Loose screws are often the cause of the problem. The remedy is to remove them and plug the hole by pushing in a matchstick or a sliver of wood dipped in woodworking adhesive. Trim the end of this plug flush with the surface and replace the screw once the adhesive has set.

Card tricks

A pair of cupboard doors can swing open if the lock securing them together cannot engage. Move the meeting edges of the doors closer together by packing out the hinges. Unscrew the leaves of the hinges—one at a time—and line the recesses cut for them with one or more pieces of thin card. On old furniture a single deep recess is often cut in either the door or the carcass for both leaves of the hinge, so it may only be necessary to unscrew one hinge leaf to insert the packing. Pack out just the upper hinge if the door is jamming along its top edge, and treat the lower hinge if it is the bottom edge that binds.

Is it level?

When cupboard doors bind, or won't stay shut or open, make sure the piece of furniture is standing level before you do anything else. If a spirit level reveals that the floor is sloping slightly, pack pieces of card under the base to cure the problem.

Spring adjustment

Double ball catches are useful for securing cupboard doors that are slightly bowed or twisted. Small adjusting screws allow the compression on each spring-loaded ball to be altered. Fix the ball catch to the carcass first, then secure the striker plate—with its small fixing screws in place—in the catch. Push the door lightly against the protruding screws so that their points mark where to fix the striker plate on the back of the door. Once the striker plate is fixed, operate the door while adjusting the tension of the catch.

Magnetic attraction

Small magnetic catches are an efficient, unobtrusive way of securing cupboard doors. But they only work if the doors are not bowed or warped, so make sure the door closes flat against the carcass before fitting them. Fit the magnet catch to the carcass first. Then place the striking plate on the magnet and dust the back of it with chalk. Push the door shut against the plate. The chalk will mark exactly where you need to position the striking plate on the door.

Positioning handles

Narrow drawers often require only one handle or knob. Make sure you fix it exactly half way across the width of the drawer front and central to its depth, otherwise the drawer will jam when you open and close it. Wider drawers usually need two handles. As a rule, cabinet-makers measure the width of the drawer front and fix them a quarter of the way in from each end—but be guided by the position of the knobs on any other drawers in the item.

Lubricate with pencil lead

Don't try to ease an old stiff lock with oil; it will seep out for months to come and probably stain the wood. Instead, use a sharp trimming knife to shave fine scrapings of graphite from a soft lead pencil and brush these into the keyhole.

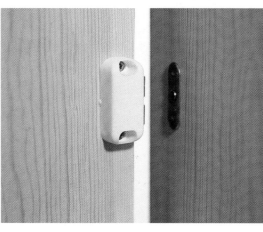

veneers Patching and matching

A perfect patch

Repair damage, such as a dead knot in a veneered surface, by preparing a patch of new veneer that covers the damage and matches the surrounding grain. Hold the patch over the damage and cut round it carefully, using it as a template (right). Prise out the damaged veneer, pare old glue from the wood beneath and stick the patch in place.

Polish on the stopper

Seal wood stopper with two thin coats of french polish before using a spirit-based wood stain to colour-match it to the surrounding veneer. Experiment on a hidden part of the furniture first, and keep some meths handy for wiping off poorly matching stain while it is still wet.

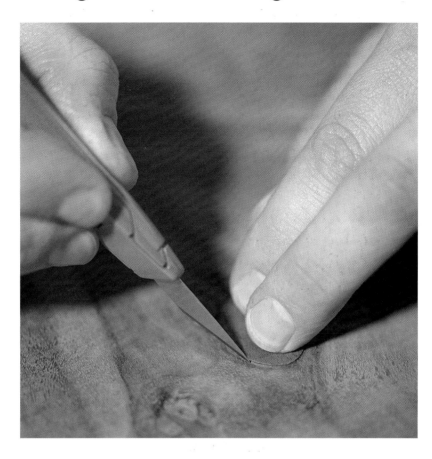

Choose a lighter shade

If you cannot find a wood stopper to match a veneer, choose a lighter shade and mix in a little liquid wood stain with a compatible base to darken it. Test the colour match of the dried stopper before using it on the veneer.

Stop the gap

Repair very small holes in veneer with wood stopper. Fill the hole slightly proud of the surrounding surface then, when it is hard, rub it down with fine wet-and-dry abrasive paper.

veneers Smoothing over the bumps and blisters

Use a little force

A tear repairs less visibly than a cut, so if a blister is already split, slide a wide, flat blade into the split and lever the lifted veneer until it tears away, shielding the area with your hand to catch the fragments. Thoroughly clean off old wax and glue with a toothbrush dipped in methylated spirits. Then piece the bits back together, glue them in place, and put a weight on the repair while the glue dries.

When to call in an expert

Don't try to repair veneered furniture unless you are sure that the piece is a modern reproduction made with thin veneers. If the veneer is more than 3 mm (⅛ in) thick, it is probably hand-sawn and it is likely that the piece is old–and possibly valuable. Get items like this valued, and seek advice about having them repaired by an expert.

Don't dally with the iron

Very slightly dampen the veneer blister, then iron it through a sheet of clean kitchen foil (below). Use the tip of the iron and keep it moving. After a few passes, try pressing the blister down; if the veneer sticks, quickly dry off any moisture on the surface and cover it with a weight for an hour or so.

Putting the squeeze on

Cramps can save the trouble of putting a weight on a veneer repair, as long as there is an edge to secure the cramp to. A single G-cramp can reach a repair just less than the depth of its throat from the edge. With a pair and a bridging batten, you can cramp repairs anywhere on the surface while the glue sets.

Test before ironing

If traditional scotch glue has been used to bond the veneer, blisters can sometimes be re-stuck with an iron; the heat re-dissolves the fast-setting glue. Do not set the iron too hot, or the veneer will stretch. Test the temperature by holding the iron about 50 mm (2 in) away from your hand; it should feel hot but not uncomfortably so.

Resort to the knife

If ironing down bubbled veneer doesn't work, cut it open with a trimming knife fitted with a new sharp blade. Cut along the grain of the veneer, guiding the knife with a straightedge, then insert a little PVA glue into the cut–an artist's palette knife or a spark-plug feeler gauge blade (below) is ideal for this job.

Rub a hammer lightly back and forth across the cut (bottom) to expel any excess glue, and wipe it away with a damp rag. Then seal the cut with masking tape and put a weight on top of the repair until the glue has dried.

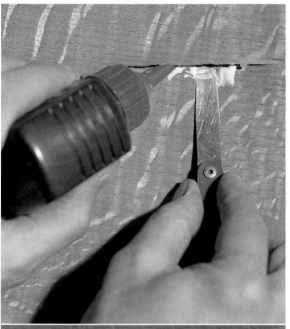

1 Tape new veneer over area to be patched and cut through both new and existing veneers, using a sharp trimming knife

2 Prise out old veneer with a sharp chisel and clean off all traces of old glue from wood surface underneath

3 Stick patch in recess and tape down. Cover with brown paper or kitchen foil and iron

4 Place weight on patch until glue has set

veneers

277

finishes A transparent choice

Quick and clear

Two-part or cold-cure lacquers and water-based varnishes have two big advantages over polyurethane varnish: they dry more quickly, so the risk of dust settling on the wet surface is reduced, and the finish stays clear, without any tendency to yellow with age.
Cellulose lacquer also dries clear, but it is not as tough as polyurethane and water-based varnishes, or two-part lacquers.

Isolate from dust

To stop the brush picking up dust from the floor or work surface, stand the legs of a piece of furniture on foil dishes or plastic lids before applying the finish.

Mix in a glass jar

A two-part lacquer won't cure if it reacts with the container it is mixed in, so play safe and use a glass jar rather than anything made of metal or plastic.

Stirred but never shaken

Avoid shaking a tin of varnish. This creates air bubbles which spoil the finish. Instead, use a clean flat stick to stir the liquid slowly and gently.

Raising the grain

Water-based varnish will swell the grain of the wood, making it slightly rough and fuzzy to the touch. There are two ways of dealing with this. You can either dampen the bare wood with water to raise the grain and smooth the surface with abrasive paper, then varnish it, or you can apply the first coat of varnish and then rub down the raised grain.

Wipe with a tack rag

Varnish and lacquer accentuate every speck of dust left on a surface. Get rid of dust by wiping the piece of furniture with a tack rag before you begin, and also between coats. To make one, dip a clean lint-free cloth into a thin mixture of polyurethane varnish and white spirit (do not use a water-based varnish for this). Alternatively, use boiled linseed oil. Keep the rag slightly sticky, not wet.

Turn the tin upside-down

Invert a tin of varnish for about half an hour after resealing it, then store it the right way up. This will create a better seal and help to stop a skin forming.

Minimise bristle loss

Use a good-quality paintbrush or a special varnishing brush to apply varnish and lacquer. Cheap brushes tend to lose bristles, which stick to the wet surface and are difficult or impossible to remove once the varnish dries.

Before using a new brush, dip it in a mix of solvent and varnish, and brush it vigorously on a piece of scrap board or paper to get rid of any loose bristles.

Deter woodworm
Don't overlook the backs of cupboards and the bottoms of drawers when painting or varnishing a piece of furniture. Traditionally, cabinetmakers left them unfinished, but the bare wood is an open invitation to woodworm.

Exclude air bubbles

Pour varnish from the tin into a new paint kettle or one kept just for varnish. Load your brush, then press it against the side of the kettle. This removes any air trapped in the bristles, which can otherwise appear as tiny bubbles on the newly varnished surface.

Storing lacquers

It is possible to extend the usable life of some two-part lacquers after mixing. Pour the mixture into a clean jar. Seal the top with cling film and an elastic band. Then store in a cool place..

Rub in the first coat

Use a clean, lint-free cloth to apply a thinned first coat of varnish or lacquer to the wood surface. Use firm hand pressure to force the sealing coat into the wood—an effect that you can't achieve with a brush.

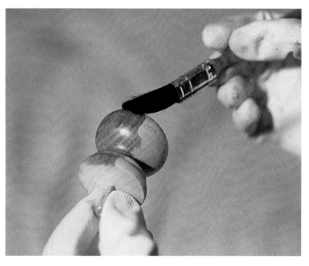

Finish before fitting

Remove wooden knobs and handles before you varnish or lacquer furniture. Then apply the finish to the knobs and handles separately before refitting them.

finishes Techniques for a smooth, durable finish

Conceal imperfections

It is easier to get a good finish with matt or satin varnish than it is with gloss. The latter highlights any surface imperfections, whereas the others hide them. If you want a more glossy finish, you can always apply wax polish over satin varnish.

Seal stained wood

The solvent in polyurethane varnish can partly dissolve wood stain when applied over it. Stop this problem by sealing the stained surface with a coat of sanding sealer first. Let the sealer dry thoroughly before applying the varnish.

Create coloured varnish

Customise varnish by adding a small quantity of a compatible wood stain: use a spirit-based stain in polyurethane varnish and a water-based one in water-based varnish. Add the stain a little at a time—an eyedropper is an ideal dispenser—then mix well and test the colour. Remember that because stains contain pigments, the more coats of stained varnish you apply, the more the grain of the wood will be obscured.

Don't hang about

Two-part and cellulose lacquers allow you little brushing time. Apply them quickly, holding the brush at a shallow angle. Blend in wet edges but don't overbrush, or you risk leaving marks which will remain as the coating dries.

Clean brushes in the appropriate thinners or solvent straight after use. Once the finish hardens on the bristles, the brush won't be usable again.

Guaranteed to dry

Add a dash of paint dryers (terebene) to varnish that has been stored for a long time, to speed drying. Terebene replaces the original drying additives in varnish, which evaporate over time. It is sold by trade decorating suppliers.

Make up a keeping solution

Don't clean the brush between coats of polyurethane varnish. Instead, suspend it in a 'keep mix' consisting of 2 parts of varnish to 1 part of white spirit. When you want to use it again, brush it out first on some clean absorbent paper.

Introducing colour

For a coloured finish, mix a little spirit-based wood stain (see page 284) into the oil before applying it. For a brighter tint, stir in artists' oil colours diluted with a little white spirit.

Beware of fire risks

Rags soaked in oil can burst into flames spontaneously as they dry. Drop them into a bucket of water or hang them outside to dry thoroughly before throwing them in the bin.

Ensure the surface is bare

Oil is the most penetrative of the finishes used for furniture. Because it depends on absorption by the wood, oil cannot be applied over a previously varnished or waxed surface. You will have to strip the old finish first.

finishes Oil gives deep protection

Wipe away excess

Leave a coating of oil to soak into wood for about 30 minutes, then wipe off any excess before it turns thick and sticky. If you do leave it too long, apply some more oil, thinned with white spirit to wet the sticky patches, then wipe off.

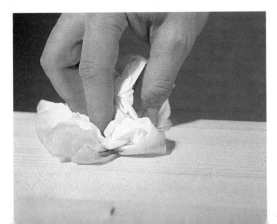

Choose boiled linseed oil

Linseed oil is the cheapest of the furniture oils. However, it is not the easiest to apply, takes longer to dry and doesn't give as hard a finish as other oils. If you do use linseed oil, pick the boiled sort, which dries more quickly than the raw product. Thin initial coats with white spirit to speed absorption and shorten the drying time still further.

Protect the end grain

Oiled hardwood is a popular choice for kitchen worktops, because the finish resists moisture and heat well. Make sure that all end grain is well sealed before installation, especially within the cut-out needed for an inset sink. If it is not, water will penetrate it and make the wood swell.

Protect timber garden furniture too by treating it with oil, rather than applying paint or varnish. Immerse the feet of chair and table legs in shallow containers of the oil, so that the end grain can absorb it.

finishes Enhance with wax

Knowing when to stop

Test a waxed surface by drawing your finger across it. If you can see a mark, carry on buffing the surface; if you can't, it's time to stop and admire the shine.

Warming to the job

You can encourage initial coats of wax to penetrate the wood by warming the surface with a hair dryer, immediately after you apply the wax, then rubbing the surface with terry towelling.

Seal before polishing

Traditional waxing involves applying many coats of beeswax and turpentine to the base wood. You can create a waxed finish more quickly by treating the wood with a shellac or cellulose sanding sealer and then using a modern wax polish.

Traditional recipe

You can make your own wax polish by melting about 500 g (1 lb) of beeswax. Use the double-pan method: heat some water in a saucepan, then put a smaller metal container for the wax into the hot water. Make sure your kitchen is well ventilated to disperse the inevitable build-up of fumes as you heat the wax.

When the wax has melted, turn off the heat, remove the small pan from the water and slowly add about 300 ml (½ pint) of white spirit to the hot wax, stirring all the time.

Use the molten polish as an initial hot wax treatment for bare wood. Work quickly, using a brush to force the hot wax into the grain.

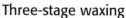

Nature's way
Pick a beeswax polish to which some carnauba wax has been added. This makes the polished surface a little harder than pure beeswax, and also produces a deeper sheen.

Three-stage waxing

You need three cotton cloths to apply a wax finish. Apply the wax with the first cloth, begin polishing with a second, and keep the third for the final polishing. You'll need to replace the third cloth frequently. Discard it as soon as it starts to gather a waxy deposit and leaves a smeary finish.

Imitation limed effect

True liming involves using slaked lime, which is caustic, but you can imitate it with this safe method. Colour the bare wood with a dark brown stain, then seal the surface with clear french polish or a sanding sealer. Work across the grain and wipe off any excess at once. Next day, apply a thick coat of liming wax. Work it in well, finishing by rubbing across the grain with a clean cloth.

Colouring wax polish

To alter the colour of wax polish, mix a little spirit-based wood stain into it, drop by drop, stirring vigorously, until you have created the colour you require.

Instant ageing

To make new furniture look older, try making an 'antiquing' wax. Stir a few teaspoons of fine dust from a vacuum cleaner bag into a proprietary wax. Alternatively, add a little black french polish or dark-coloured spirit-based wood stain to the wax.

For mouldings or carved areas, warm your antique wax up using the double-pan method (see opposite page), then apply it with a paintbrush and polish it with towelling.

To make a cream wax, add a little water and a dash of washing-up liquid to the wax and shake well. This mixture is suitable for cleaning and restoring waxed and french-polished furniture.

finishes

283

finishes Stains and dyes to enhance and disguise

What's the difference?

Stains protect wood and are suitable for outside and inside use. They come in a range of natural tones which imitate different types of timber—from palest pine to darkest mahogany. Dyes are purely decorative and are for indoor use only; even then they must be covered with varnish, lacquer, french polish or wax. They're transparent; they tint the wood and emphasise the grain.

Protective dress code

Wood stains and dyes are very difficult to clean off your hands and are almost impossible to remove from clothing. Always wear rubber gloves and old clothes when you are using them.

Mix and test

Shake a container of wood stain before opening it. This disperses the pigment in the liquid, and the deposit left on the underside of the lid gives you some indication of the colour and intensity of the stain—although not an accurate one. Test the stain on an inconspicuous part of the furniture you're working on. Once it has been applied, it will be impossible to remove totally, except by sanding the stained wood down to reveal clean wood underneath. However, rubbing with wire wool and white spirit will get rid of some of it.

For bare wood only

Dyes are formulated to be absorbed by the wood. They should be used on new, unfinished furniture or thoroughly stripped pieces. If any old finish is left in the pores of the wood, it will prevent uniform absorption. Excess dye will stay on the surface and will be redissolved if a coat of lacquer or varnish is applied over the top. Dried adhesive around joints also prevents dye absorption.

ONE COAT

TWO COATS

FOUR COATS

How many coats?

You can emphasise the stain colour by applying more coats of it to a piece of furniture. However, the pigments in the stain will gradually obliterate the grain patterning, or 'figure', of the wood, as well as its natural colour.

Are they compatible?

Make sure that stains and dyes are compatible before mixing one with another. Most dyes are water-based, but stains may be water or solvent-based. Different types can't be mixed, so always read the labels first.

Customising colours

Keep the effect even

End grain, found at the ends of tables or the edges of wooden chair seats, for example, is very absorbent and so will appear much darker than the rest of the piece if it absorbs too much dye. Stop this from happening by staining the long grain first. Then, when the cloth pad is almost dry, rub the residue on the pad into the end grain until you achieve an accurate colour match.

Be suspicious of samples

Don't trust the colour of stain samples displayed in shops to be a true likeness, especially if they have been left on show in a sunny window. The stain is often applied to pieces of inexpensive pine (above right), with no indication of how many coats have been used. On more expensive hardwoods such as oak (above left) or mahogany, the same stain will create a quite different colour.

Creating a palette

Artists' oil paints can be mixed with solvent-based stains, and watercolours with water-based ones. Use small amounts of colour to avoid obscuring the transparency of the finish.

Mix oil paint with a little linseed oil, then dilute it with white spirit before adding it to a compatible dye.

Mixing colours in a jar will give you some idea of the end result, although you'll still need to test the mixture on a hidden corner of the piece of furniture.

finishes

SIX COATS

285

finishes
Customising colours

Layered effects

A variety of interesting effects can be obtained with aniline dyes by layering them. Apply a coat of one colour to the bare wood; then, once it has dried, add a second coat of another colour, and so on. Experiment first on a scrap of wood to get the effect you want.

Easier for the amateur

Aniline dyes provide the brightest range of wood colourings, and you can buy them ready-mixed or in powder form from good decorating shops. It's best to buy the water-based type. Some aniline dyes are soluble in methylated spirits, but these dry quickly and are hard for the amateur to use without creating ugly overlapping tide marks.

Keep dyed furniture out of bright sunlight, which can make the colour (especially reds and browns) fade.

Mixed for a perfect match

The type of aniline dyes that are soluble in methylated spirits are excellent for disguising repairs to surfaces finished with french polish.

Mix some powder dye in meths (or use a ready-mixed dye), then add it to a little clear french polish. Then use a fine artist's brush to apply the dyed mixture to the damaged area.

Retard drying time

If you are using a spirit-based aniline dye, apply a generous wipe of meths to the wood surface first. This reduces the speed at which the finish dries, giving you valuable extra time to achieve an even coverage. Do not saturate the surface with meths, however, because it can raise the grain.

Versatile threesome

Three aniline dyes—yellow, red and black—can be used to simulate a wide range of hardwoods. The mixtures can be thinned down to give the required intensity of colour.

Mix a dark oak colour using 6 parts of black dye, 1½ parts of yellow dye and 1 part of red dye.

Brown walnut is closely imitated by combining 3 parts of black with 2 parts of yellow and 2 parts of red.

For mahogany, mix 14 parts of red, 3 parts of black and 2 parts of yellow.

Simulate rosewood by combining 2 parts of red dye with 1 part of black.

Seal the grain

Open-grained wood will require several coats of french polish to seal it. Save yourself time by using a proprietary grain filler instead, or take the traditional course and rub a slurry of plaster of paris into the grain. When the filler has dried, colour it with linseed oil.

Using traditional french polish

Colour choice

Proprietary french polish is sold in several different formulations. Standard french polish is the usual choice for dark hardwoods, and white polish for very pale woods. Transparent polish enhances the grain but leaves the natural colour of the timber unaltered. Button and garnet polish produce tones of orange and red-brown, while adding aniline dyes (see opposite page) to french polish creates a range of bright, non-traditional polish finishes.

Satin or gloss?

For a high gloss, give the polish seven days to dry hard, then buff with a clean rag dipped in a mixture of meths and baby oil. Alternatively, use metal polish or a proprietary burnishing cream.

For a satin finish, rub down with fine-grade wire wool dipped in wax, working in the direction of the grain. When the entire surface is evenly matt, burnish it with a duster.

finishes Using traditional french polish

Carvings and mouldings
Use an artist's brush to apply french polish to carvings and mouldings, diluting the polish first with a little meths to reduce the likelihood of leaving brush marks. Once the finish has hardened, burnish the high points.

Acclimatise the workpiece
Do not bring a piece of furniture in from a cold or damp storeroom and start work straightaway. The wood will need several hours to acclimatise otherwise tiny bubbles, caused by air expanding in the wood fibres, will appear in the finish.

Keep warm and dry
Apply french polish in a warm dry atmosphere–about 20°C (68°F)–so that successive coats dry quickly. If the air is damp, moisture gets trapped in the polish, making it turn cloudy.
Never smoke while using french polish, or work near an open flame, as the solvent in the polish is highly flammable.

Practise your skills
French polishing is a skill, so don't imagine you'll get perfect results first time. Before beginning work on a favourite piece of furniture, visit a timber merchant specialising in hardwoods and pick up some offcuts of solid timber, or some scraps of plywood faced with hardwood veneers, to practise on.

The rubber method

Press out the polish
Always get rid of excess french polish in a rubber–the homemade, cotton-covered piece of wadding or cotton wool, which is the traditional tool for applying french polish–by pressing it hard on a piece of card or scrap wood. The level of saturation is correct when the rubber deposits an even smear of polish that is neither wet nor patchy.
When the rubber begins to run out of polish, squeeze it harder to force more polish out of the wadding towards the surface of the pad.

Don't let the sole wear out
Inspect the sole of the rubber–the area of cloth in contact with the surface–frequently; if it wears through, the finish will be spoilt. Rearrange the fabric by opening out the cloth and refolding it (see panel). Make sure you never use a piece of cloth with a seam in it, because this will mark the surface you are working on if it comes into contact with it.

Keep the rubber moving
Never rest the rubber on the surface, or the meths in the wet polish will start to redissolve the previous coat and leave a blotchy patch. Start a sweeping motion before you bring the rubber into contact with the work and don't stop until you lift it away from the surface.

Airtight storage
When you finish working, splash the rubber with meths to keep it soft and store it in an airtight jar.

Hold the rubber steady

Don't allow the rubber to rock from side to side as you use it, otherwise the polished surface will look smeared. Grip the rubber close to the base of the twist and keep your wrist stiff—movement should come from the elbow and shoulder.

Getting rid of drag

If the rubber begins to feel tacky and starts to stick slightly to the surface you are working on, the problem is caused by wet polish in the rubber partly dissolving the previous coat. Stop polishing for a moment and flick a drop or two of linseed oil onto the wood, or rub it onto the sole of the rubber.

The brush method

Thin with meths

You can achieve excellent results by applying french polish with a brush. To reduce brush marks, either thin ordinary french polish with meths to extend the drying time, or use a brushing polish.

Rapid restoration

Use the brush-on method to restore polished furniture without having to strip it back to the bare wood. Use fine-grade wire wool dipped in meths to take off the top layer of the finish, rub it down with fine wet-and-dry abrasive paper, used wet, and brush on the polish.

More coats, extra gloss

Dip just the tip of the brush in the polish and apply the first two coats with quick, light strokes—the first one with the grain, the second at 90° to it. This will leave a satin finish on most woods. To progressively increase the gloss, brush on more coats alternately across and with the grain.

Remember to clean the brush in meths, not in white spirit, when you have finished work.

STAGES IN
MAKING A RUBBER

1 Press a ball of cotton wool into an egg shape and place on pad cut from old cotton shirt or sheeting

2 Make 'fad' by folding four corners of pad together to enclose cotton wool

3 Place one corner of fad on centre of second piece of cotton, then draw material neatly around it

4 Twist ends of cotton round to compress fad and form a tail, which will lie in palm of hand when using rubber

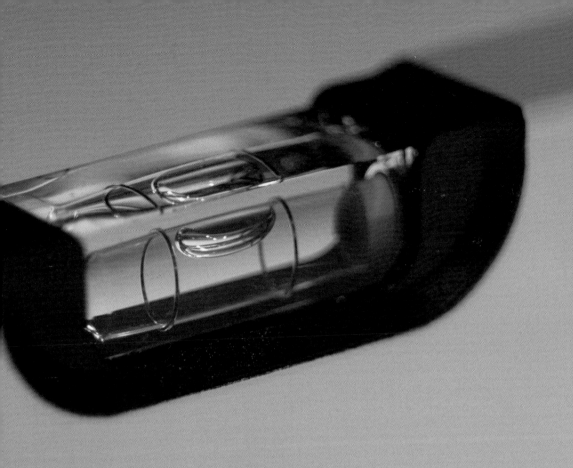

garden

Waterproof windows

Most sheds come with glass or plastic sheet and pre-cut glazing beads for the windows. Make sure you bed the panes in putty or glazing mastic, otherwise rain will get between the beads and glazing.

Batten down the felt

When re-felting a garden shed, lay the felt in horizontal strips, starting at the bottom edge of the roof. Overlap successive strips so the rain can't get underneath, and stick the overlaps down with roofing felt adhesive as protection against wind. Once all the felt is on, nail battens on parallel to the pitch so that they don't form a trap for water.

Winter workshop

If you use your shed as a workshop all year round, it's worth insulating it to make it warmer in winter. Line the walls and roof with rigid polystyrene board, cut to fit between the frame members, then pin on tempered hardboard across the frame. There's usually enough headroom to let you lay a floor of chipboard over a layer of polystyrene slabs on top of the existing shed base.

Security measures

Guard against thieves if you keep valuable equipment or tools in a shed.

Fit a high-security padlock and secure the hasp with nuts and bolts passing through the door and frame. Replace glass with hard-to-break polycarbonate sheet, and fit window locks to opening windows–or simply screw them shut from inside. You could even consider installing a shed alarm.

Germ-free germination

To stop this year's viruses or parasites affecting next year's plants, a greenhouse should be thoroughly cleaned each autumn. Take out the plants and switch off any electricity. Then clean the glass inside and out with a garden hose and a soft brush; dislodge dirt trapped between overlapping panes with a plastic plant label. Treat the glazing bars, staging and floor with a greenhouse disinfectant. Then put back the plants, close the vents and fumigate the building with a smoke cone.

Save the rain

Even a small shed roof can collect worthwhile quantities of rainwater for the garden. Fit small-radius gutters and a downpipe running into a water butt. Set it on a stand that allows you to fit a watering can beneath the tap.

Avoid a poke in the eye

Greenhouses—especially aluminium framed ones—are likely to have sharp corners or window stays at eye level. A few simple preventative measures can avoid anyone getting hurt. An old tennis ball with a slit cut into it makes a soft tip for a window stay (right), while sharp corners of the building can be cushioned with sleeves of pre-formed pipe insulation (below).

tools Keeping a garage in good order

Dirt excluder for up-and-over doors

The wind often blows leaves and dust under up-and-over garage doors. You can easily stop this by screwing a length of proprietary draught excluder for garage doors to the bottom edge of the door. Cut it to length to match the width of your door, drill evenly-spaced holes and screw it in place. Use self-tapping screws if the door is made of metal or glass fibre.

Beat the burglar

A connecting door between the garage and the house is a secluded point of entry, popular with burglars. If you are going on holiday, you can temporarily burglar-proof an up-and-over garage door by closing it and fixing a G-cramp onto each track immediately behind the door wheels. It will then be impossible to open the door from outside, even if the lock is successfully forced.

Smooth operation

To keep an up-and-over garage door operating smoothly and quietly, brush some light machine oil onto the springs. This will also help to keep rust at bay. Apply the oil when the door is open so that the springs are extended, allowing the oil to penetrate them.

Seal the floor

A concrete garage floor may be porous, so oil spills from the car will soak in and stain it. The best solution is to sweep the floor and then seal it with diluted PVA adhesive or a proprietary concrete sealer. Then apply one or two coats of garage floor paint. This heavy-duty gloss paint is impervious to liquids and allows you to wipe up oil and other spills. Non-slip floor paint is good for garages too.

Asbestos safety

Contact your local authority for advice before attempting to dismantle and dispose of a corrugated asbestos roof on a garage or other outbuilding. If the panels can be taken down intact, it may be safe to do the job yourself, provided you wear protective clothing, including a dust mask. Soak the roof first to damp down any fibres that get loose if a corner breaks off a sheet. If they start to break up badly, stop and arrange for professional disposal.

Don't go off the rails

An up-and-over door can run off its tracks if it is pulled open too far. This could bring the door crashing down, injuring someone or damaging the car if it's in the garage. **You can prevent this** by crimping the C-shaped open ends of the tracks with pliers to close them. Alternatively, drill a hole through the end of each track and insert a nut and bolt to arrest the door.

Regular care ensures good performance

Getting the handle out

If a wooden handle snaps off flush with the shaft of a garden spade or fork, it can be extracted with a little brute force. First remove the rivets, drilling them out if necessary. Then drive a large woodscrew into the broken shaft. Grip the screw head in a vice, hold an offcut of wood against the shoulder of the tool and strike it off with a heavy hammer.

Protect feet from bruising

To cushion the sole of your foot as you dig the garden, split short pieces of old garden hose lengthways and slip them over both the shoulders of the spade or fork. Stick them on with epoxy-resin adhesive if they will not stay put.

Thwart a thief

Use a long cable lock to tie expensive garden power tools together and stop them being stolen from your shed or garage even if a burglar breaks in. Fix two metal brackets securely to the shed or garage wall. Anchor the fixed end of the cable to one bracket and the padlock end to the other.

Good sense with garden shears

Cutting hedges blunts shears more quickly than clipping round the edge of the lawn, so buy a pair of shears for each job—short handled ones for the hedge, and long-handled ones for the lawn edges. Sharpen the hedge shears regularly to keep them in top cutting condition.

Test the adjustment of garden shears by holding them by one handle and letting the other hang down. When the weight of the unsupported blade is just heavy enough for the jaws to open, the pivot adjusting screw is correctly tightened.

tools Regular care ensures good performance

A softer grip stops blisters
Raking up a lot of garden leaves can blister your hands. A simple solution is to pad the rake handle with a length of slip-on foam pipe insulation. Use the size designed for 22 mm copper pipe, fixing it in place with insulating tape if necessary.

Crack concrete with a hammer
Don't strike the edge of a spade or shovel on a hard surface to remove mortar or concrete that's set on the blade. Instead, whack the back of the blade sharply with a heavy hammer; the concrete should then break away cleanly.

Sweep water away
If you don't have a broom for clearing standing water from hard surfaces, slit one side of a length of garden hose and slip it over the tines of a rake. This will sweep the water away.

Scouring sand for cleaning tools

Fill a bucket with sharp sand soaked in old engine oil and use it to clean and protect spades and forks. After gardening, stab the tool in and out of the mixture to get rid of any soil stuck to it. The roughness of the sand will make blades and tines shiny and smooth; the oil will protect them from rust and help to stop soil from sticking the next time you use them.

Oil stops rust and splits

Wipe metal parts of tools with an oily rag before putting them away, to stop rust developing. Prevent wooden handles from splitting by rubbing in linseed oil from time to time.

Cleaning sticky teeth

A quick and easy way to clean sap from a pruning saw's teeth is to spray a little oven cleaner onto the sticky area and scrub it off with an old toothbrush. Afterwards, rinse thoroughly with water, dry, and spray with lubricating oil.

Disinfect cutting tools

Wipe the blades of secateurs or saws with diluted household bleach to disinfect them if they have been used to cut away diseased plant growth. This will stop them infecting other plants.

Using power in the garden

Hire a cultivator

Take the hard work out of a large-scale digging job by hiring a power digger or cultivator. Most cultivators are petrol-driven, making them a powerful tool that can quickly lift, separate and blend the soil prior to sowing and planting. They will save you hours of digging.

Start with care

Before you start using an electric hedge-trimmer, always check that its flex is well away from the blades. A lead can easily become entangled if it is hidden under a pile of hedge cuttings.

For additional safety, plug the tool into a socket outlet or adaptor containing a residual current device (RCD). This will switch off the electricity supply instantly if you accidentally sever the flex and then touch the cut ends.

Keep blades moving

It's almost impossible to lubricate hedge-trimmer blades too often. Stop the machine regularly and use an aerosol spray grease or silicone lubricant, or brush the stationary blade with the same oil-and-paraffin mixture recommended for stopping grass from sticking to lawnmower blades (see page 300).

lawnmowers Take safety seriously

Go cordless
If you like the cleanness of electricity, but find the lead a hindrance, consider buying a cordless mower. You'll have the freedom to roam beyond the reach of an extension lead, and no worries about cutting or tripping over cable.

Walk the course
Inspect the lawn before mowing, and remove any sticks, stones or metal items that could fly up and hit someone and also damage the mower's blades.

Solitary but safe
Keep small children and family pets well away when you're mowing the lawn. The combination of long leads, sharp blades and their unpredictable movements is a recipe for accidents.

A firm grip
Wear stout shoes or boots with a good grip when mowing—an old pair of spiked golf shoes is ideal —as lawns can be slippery. Never be tempted to mow in light shoes or sandals, whatever the weather; they will offer little protection should you slip and get your foot caught in the blade.

Behind you
Before you start mowing, unwind and untangle any kinks or knots in the stored flex so it lies flat on the ground. **Always drape the cable** over one shoulder so that it trails behind you while using the mower. As you walk up and down, let it fall onto the area you've just mowed; then you won't have to keep on moving it out of harm's way after each pass.

Insurance against shocks

Always use an RCD (residual current device) with an electric mower. It switches the power off instantly and stops you getting a shock if you cut the flex and touch one of the conductors inside. Some houses have a special RCD socket outlet installed for use with garden power tools. If yours doesn't, plug an RCD adaptor (below) into any socket outlet and plug the tool into that.

Cross with care

Protect the blades (and yourself) from loose flying stones by always switching off a power mower before pushing it across a path, drive or patio. If it's a hover mower, disconnect it from the mains before you pick it up.

Use your ears

Be alert to the sound an electric mower makes, even if it has an automatic cut-out. Its rising pitch will tell you if you're overloading it by trying to cut too much grass at once. Stop, switch off and disconnect it, then adjust the blade to a higher setting. Cutting the grass in two or three stages rather than trying to do it in one go will considerably reduce the risk of burning out the motor.

Control on a bank

Always mow across a slope, never up and down it. Then the mower won't run away with you on the downhill sections. Keep a firm grip on a hover mower on a slope; its lack of wheels means that only your strength will prevent it from drifting down the slope. Don't attempt to use the mower on any slope steeper than the maximum recommended by the mower manufacturer.

Faultfinding

Clean the plug

If the spark-plug lead and ignition are not faulty, the next possible cause of non-starting to investigate is a dirty spark-plug. Make sure there's no carbon lodged between the insulator nose and the outer shell when you clean and reset the plug gap.

A better start

Spray a petrol-driven mower's ignition mechanism with WD-40 or a similar water-repellent aerosol if the machine proves difficult to start. Check the spark-plug lead for damage if the motor still refuses to fire.

Unclog air filters

Black smoke coming from the exhaust of a petrol mower probably indicates a blocked air filter. Wash a sponge filter clean with petrol; replace a paper one.

lawnmowers
Basic maintenance and storage

Scrape the blade with a spatula

An old wooden or plastic kitchen spatula makes an ideal tool for scraping grass clippings off a blade. Always check that the engine is disabled, even if the mower has an OPC (operator presence control) lever before touching the cutting blades. Disconnect the spark-plug lead on petrol mowers and make sure that electric mowers are unplugged from the mains.

Paper test for cylinder mowers

Check whether a cylinder mower's blades are correctly aligned by slipping a sheet of paper between the cylinder

and the bottom blade and rotating the cylinder by hand. Disconnect the spark-plug first on a petrol mower to make sure that a spin of the cylinder cannot start the engine, and unplug an electric one from the mains. If the mower does not slice the paper cleanly, adjust the position of the bottom blade.

The right oil

Always be sure you know the grade of oil your motor mower needs. If it has a 4-stroke engine, or is a side-valve Japanese make, use SAE30; with OHV engines, use a multigrade oil (10W/40, 20W/50). The only time to depart from the recommended petrol-oil ratio for a 2-stroke engine is when using a synthetic oil requiring a different ratio.
Dispose of old oil by taking it to a local recycling point. Alternatively, you could use it to make a scouring cleaner for other garden tools (see page 297).

Winter fuel

Leave a little fuel in the tank over winter if the mower is fitted with a fuel tap so that the cork in the tap won't dry out and need replacing. Then close the tap and run the engine dry to empty the carburettor. When spring comes, drain the tank and refill it with fresh fuel.

Maintaining blade balance

Check the balance of a rotary blade while you sharpen it. Hang the blade by its central bolt hole and if one side hangs lower than the other, file more metal from that side until the balance is perfect. Don't try to remove deep nicks in one session, or the blade is bound to end up out of balance.

Protect from sticky petrol

Old fuel can gum up the carburettor, so if you're leaving any petrol in the can or mower for more than a month, add a fuel stabiliser recommended by the engine manufacturer.

Flood damage

Avoid tipping a mower powered by a 4-stroke engine onto its nose (spark-plug end) or onto its exhaust. In both cases, you'll flood the engine with oil, possibly landing yourself with a costly repair bill. You will also probably spill oil onto the ground where you're working.

Bad vibrations

Vibration on a rotary mower is a sure sign that the blade needs balancing. Re-grind and sharpen it as soon as possible or you'll loosen its fixings and wear out the bearings.

Make surfaces easy to clean

Stop grass cuttings caking up the underside of a mower by spraying the clean surface with a mixture of two parts paraffin to one part engine oil. The cuttings will stick to the coating but come off easily if you wipe the mower straight after using it.

fences How to place the posts

Clearly level

On flat ground, make sure the tops of fence posts are the same height by using a water level—a long length of clear plastic tubing filled with water. With the aid of a helper, drive in the two end posts and hold the ends of the tubing against them. Set the tops of the posts level with the water. Then stretch a string line between the end posts to act as a guide for setting the remaining posts to the right height. **Alternatively, you can hire a spirit level** with a laser beam and use this to get the top of the far end post exactly level with the top of the near one.

A lever for an old post

If an old post won't come out, use a strong piece of wood—the longer the better—as a lever. Lash it to the post and use a low pile of old bricks as a fulcrum. Then push down on the lever. A wood block, nailed to the post to trap the top of the lever, could be used instead of the lashing.

Step this way

If you are putting up fence panels on a steep slope, you will have to 'step' them and then install gravel boards to close off the gaps between the bottom of the panels and the ground. **Use a spirit level and a wooden spacer block** to achieve a uniform height difference at each post. Fix the first post at the top of the slope to the required height. Then drive the second one part way in and place the spacer block on top of it. Rest a plank on the top post and the spacer block, and place the spirit level on it. Tap in the second post until the level is true. Follow the same method to drive in the rest of the posts.

Prospect for pipes

Before putting up the fence, try to discover whether any drains run under its proposed route. Then go over the ground with a hired cable and pipe locator. This senses cables and pipes concealed at a depth of up to 3 m (10 ft) below the surface. If you detect any buried services, stay at least 600 mm (2 ft) away from them.

A quarter underground

At least a quarter of a fence post's length should be below ground level, even if it is going to be concreted in place. For example, if you want to put up a fence that's 1.8 m high, you will need to buy posts which are 2.4 m long.

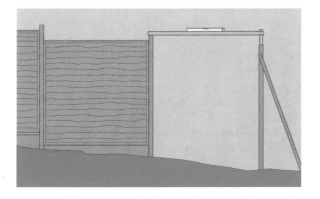

Tailor gaps to fit

Fence panels can vary slightly in width, so don't use just one as a pattern when placing the posts, or you could end up with some spaces that are either slightly too wide or too narrow.

fences Making fixings fast and true

Movable screen

If you are likely to need to remove a section of fencing occasionally—perhaps it is screening a caravan, boat or trailer, for example—use proprietary spikes or bolt-down bases with a clamp-type post grip (above). These allow the fence posts and panels to be lifted out easily.

Bolt-down bases are ideal when you have to erect a fence across an existing concrete surface. Position the bases where you want them, then mark and drill fixing holes for expanding bolts.

Long post spikes are designed to be hammered into the ground. Shorter metal spikes are made for setting in wet concrete—check the size of foundation hole required before choosing this type of base for your posts.

Bring on the heavyweight

A hire tool called a post driver, consisting of a long metal tube with two handles, is better than a sledgehammer for driving sharpened wooden stakes into the ground. Its design helps to keep the post vertical and minimises damage to the top of the post. Because its effectiveness depends on its weight, this type of post driver works best if two people use it.

Concrete craft

Buy a bag of dry ready-mixed concrete if you've got just a couple of posts to erect. For bigger jobs, buy the materials separately at a builders' merchant and mix your own, using 1 part of cement to 2 parts of sharp sand and 3 parts of gravel. Just dampen the mix—it will absorb moisture from the ground—then ram it down around the post to compress it. Form a slope on the concrete around the post at ground level, so rain is deflected and does not gather in a puddle.

Rubble for drainage

Line the bottom of post holes with rubble before back-filling them with soil or concrete. It helps to drain water away from the ends of wooden posts and prolong their life, especially in heavy, poorly drained clay ground.

Boring beats digging

A hire tool called a post-hole borer (below) uses the auger principle to make short work of a long job, if you have a lot of posts to place. On hard stony ground, hire the powered version, driven by a small petrol engine; this is heavier but much more effective, and there's less risk that you will twist your back.

Spikes for speed

Proprietary metal post spikes have two major advantages. Unlike the sharpened end of a wooden post, the point of the spike is more likely to split stones that get in the way than be split by them. Secondly, because the post fits in the top of the spike, above ground level, it is much less prone to rot.

Buy a driving tool (called a 'dolly') when you are shopping for the spikes; this fits in the socket and protects it from being damaged by the hammer as you drive in the spike.

1 Brace fence panel with props, then saw through post above rot and treat cut end with wood preservative

2 Dig hole next to post and place concrete spur in hole. Mark bolt positions on post through pre-formed holes in spur. Then drill through post

3 Bolt post to spur, back-fill hole with concrete and tamp down. Brace post upright for 48 hours while concrete sets

fences

303

Self-closing gates

A garden gate that closes automatically will help to prevent toddlers and pets from straying. You can keep small path gates closed by screwing a spring or bar closer to the hanging post. For larger drive gates, the cheapest solution is to position the hinges slightly out of line so the gates swing shut gently when they are released from their catches. The expensive option is to go for remote-control electric operation.

A pair of braces

Gateposts must be truly vertical if the gate is to hang properly. Get a helper to hold each post upright while you check it with a spirit level. Then nail on two braces at right angles to hold it in place.

Braced for strength

When you are hanging a cross-braced gate, make sure that the bottom end of its diagonal brace is located on the hinged edge of the gate. This will help to prevent the gate from sagging. If you're buying this type of gate, choose one that's braced on the correct diagonal for your opening. On large driveway gates, the ends of the brace should fit into notches cut in the cross-rails.

Add a concrete collar

For a solid anchorage, pack the post holes with crushed rubble or hardcore to within 100 mm (4 in) of the top. Fill the hole with a collar of quick-setting concrete, and slope the top of it away from the post to shed rainwater. Let it set for a week, then remove the braces and hang the gate.

Gatepost guidelines

Small lightweight gates need posts 100 mm square, and at least 600 mm longer than the gate height. Gates that are more than 1.2 m high or wide need sturdier posts; these should be 150 mm or even 200 mm square, and at least 750 mm longer than the gate height. This additional length allows the posts to be securely bedded into the ground.

Stop twin gates from sagging

When hanging a pair of gates, cramp them together with two G-cramps. Sandwich a strip of wood packing about 12 mm (½ in) thick between them to set the clearance gap. Pack the top of the gap with a second sliver about 6 mm (¼ in) thick, so it is wider at the top than the bottom. This allows for settlement of the new gates and for initial wear on the hinges, which could cause the gates to sag and bind.

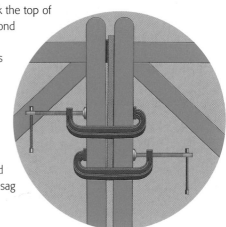

Proof against theft and rust

Keep corrosion at bay

Regularly protect wrought-iron and steel gates from corrosion by using a wire brush to remove rust and loose paint; the small 'cup' wire brushes for electric drills are especially good for this job. Then treat the gate with a rust-inhibiting primer and coat it with a paint suitable for exterior metal.

Avoid plain steel

It's a good idea to make sure that all the nails, screws and bolts used for fencing and wooden gates are rustproof, and to use only galvanised or black-japanned metal brackets, hinges and other fixings. Plain steel fixings quickly corrode and become weak. Rusted metal also stains the wood.

Hang onto your property

To prevent a thief lifting your gate off its hinges, drill a hole through one hinge pin and fit a small nut and bolt through it once the gate is hung. Alternatively, fit threaded hinge pins which take a lock nut (below right), or invert the top hinge pin if you'll never need to take the gate of its hinges.

1 Put blocks between gate-posts and stand gate on them so one face of gate is flush with the backs of the posts

2 Wedge gate in place, allow clearance for hinges and fittings, and check that it is level

3 Mark holes for T-hinges on gate and post, and drill pilot holes for the screws

4 Fix hinges, remove wedges and blocks, and test that gate swings properly. Then fit bolt and catch

fences

305

fences Tricks and treatments that keep rot at bay

Spray away for fast results

To keep your fences in tiptop condition, apply a fresh coat of preservative every couple of years. If you have a lot of fencing to treat, it is well worth hiring (or even buying) a small spray gun. This will speed up the process dramatically and will also ensure even coverage and good penetration.

Use the gun on a still dry day, and take care to avoid spraying any one area for too long; this can lead to excess preservative trickling down between the fence slats and spoiling its appearance from your neighbour's side.

Steep in preservative

When buying timber for fencing, make sure that it has been pressure treated with preservative. Even then, it's a good idea to stand new posts in a container of preservative for half a day or so–long enough for the preservative to soak well into the porous end grain and provide the best protection against rot.

The cheapest preservative is creosote, but it needs renewing every year, smells strongly for several weeks and is very toxic when wet. Modern preservatives are available in a wide range of colours and, unlike creosote, you can paint over them.

Pick a safe chemical

If you have plants immediately in front of a fence, use a preservative that won't harm them if they brush against it. Hold them away from the fence with loops of rope or garden twine while you apply the preservative.

Cap the posts

Fix wooden or decorative plastic caps to the tops of posts to prevent rain soaking into the end grain. Alternatively, shape the post tops so they will shed rain, or fit homemade lead caps.

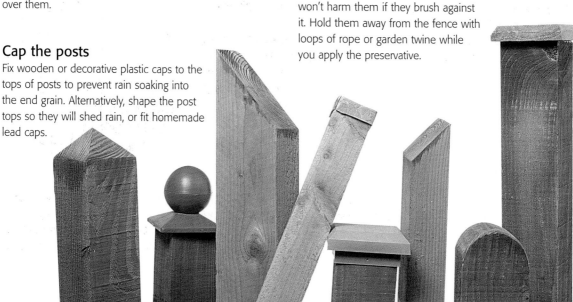

walls Building with bricks

Are you coping?

Brick garden walls need a 'roof' (called a coping) to keep the rain out. This can be created with concrete coping stones (left), walling bricks set on edge or on end, a row of shaped coping bricks or a layer of roof tiles laid with a slope.

How many bricks?

A standard brick is 215 mm long and 65 mm high. To work out how many bricks you'll need for a small wall, use the length plus 10 mm for each mortar joint to work out the number of bricks in each course, and multiply that figure by the number of courses the wall will have. For larger walls, work out the face area in square metres. Then multiply this by 60 for walls one brick thick, and by 120 for walls two bricks thick. Add 5 per cent extra to allow for breakages.

Strong support

Any wall needs concrete footings (also called foundations) that are wide and deep enough to support it and prevent subsidence. For a simple brick wall up to about 1 m (3 ft) high and one brick thick, you need a footing 300 mm (12 in) wide and 150 mm (6 in) deep. For a 1 m high wall two bricks thick, increase the footing size to 450 mm (18 in) wide and 225 mm (9 in) deep.

Mixing mortar

Always mix mortar ingredients by volume, using a bucket rather than a shovel, to ensure that each batch has exactly the same proportion of sand to cement. For garden walls, mix 1 part of cement to 6 parts of soft sand. One 50 kg sack of cement mixed with 300 kg of sand will make up enough mortar to lay about 400 bricks.

Handy stacks

Place bricks in low stacks at intervals along the line of the wall before you start building it, so you don't have to stretch too far for them as you work.

Sound footings on slopes

For walls built on sloping ground, lay footings in steps that are multiples of a single brick in length and height to ensure perfectly level brickwork.

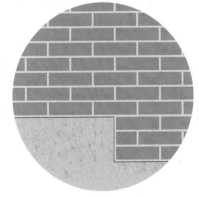

Ways out for water

If you build a low retaining wall or an enclosed planter, leave all the vertical joints in the first course of brickwork open, so water can drain through the masonry. Without these gaps, the wall will act as a dam and the soil behind it will become waterlogged. This could eventually cause the wall to collapse.

walls
Building with bricks

Keep the joints even
Make a wooden gauge rod marked with lines equal to the thickness of a brick plus a 10 mm joint. Hold it against the face of the wall to help you to keep all your joints the same thickness as you build the wall up course by course.

Fill the frog
Most bricks have a hollow recess in one face. It's called the frog, and is created during the manufacturing process. To give the wall some extra lateral strength, lay all the bricks with their frogs facing upwards and fill them with mortar as you bed the next course in place.

Use a mortarboard
To avoid staining your patio or drive, mix mortar and concrete on an offcut of plywood or chipboard. Rest each corner on a brick so the weight of the mix makes the board sag in the middle. This ensures that water doesn't spill over the edges.

Beat the clock
Keep mortar batches small until experience tells you how much you can use in about 2 hours. After that time it will have become too dry to use, especially in hot weather. Load the mortar onto a spot board—an offcut of board about 600 mm (2 ft) square —set on bricks close to where you're working.

Avoid mortar stains
If any wet mortar gets on the face of a wall it can stain it. Don't try to wipe it off immediately. Instead, allow it to dry (but not harden), then remove it with a stiff-bristled brush.

Keep it low
Don't try to build single brick walls higher than about 1 m (15 courses). Above that height, you need to include piers to strengthen the wall, which will also need to have deeper foundations. Leave higher walls to professional bricklayers.

Bed of sand
Sand makes a useful shock absorber when cutting half bricks (called bats). Mark the cutting line on each side of the brick, lay it frog side down on some sand, place a brick bolster on the line and strike it firmly with a club hammer. Repeat this on the other faces, then on the top, until the brick splits.

Cut the suction
Bone-dry bricks will suck water out of the mortar too quickly, causing it to crack. To avoid the problem, dunk each brick in a bucket of water for a few seconds before you lay it. Wet your spot board, too, before you load it up with mortar.

Sealed against salts

Retaining walls and planters often develop ugly white staining called efflorescence. It's caused by water dissolving mineral salts within the bricks and carrying them to the wall surface, where they are deposited as the water evaporates. You can prevent these stains by brushing some bituminous emulsion onto the inner face of the wall before back-filling with soil.

Options with blockwork

Easier to lay

If you prefer the look of stone in your garden, choose reconstituted stone blocks rather than natural stone. They come in a range of colours and sizes and look very realistic, but their top and bottom faces are flat so they can be laid easily in level courses just like brickwork.

Render blender

If your house has rendered outside walls, you can build garden walls in lightweight blockwork–faster to erect than brickwork–and then render and decorate the masonry so it matches the look of the house walls.

Mesh for reinforcement

Walls built with pierced concrete walling blocks more than two courses high need reinforcement. Include a strip of expanded metal mesh in the mortar bed after every two courses. Extend it into any piers you are building too. Without this, the wall is prone to collapse.

1 Lay mortar on footing. Then bed first brick in place, tamp down and check that it is level

2 Spread mortar on end of next brick and butt this end up against first brick. Lay more bricks to finish first course

3 Lay following courses with vertical joints staggered by half a brick length. Trim off any excess mortar

4 As wall rises, use spirit level to check that face and end are truly vertical. Then finish all joints neatly

walls

309

paths Creating new walkways

Room to manoeuvre
When planning a new path, make it at least 1.2 m (4 ft) wide. This allows two people to walk along it side by side, and provides ample space for pushing barrows and lawnmowers. If you plan to use slabs or blocks, set the width to match a whole number of paving units.

Concrete for economy
If performance is more important than looks, use concrete. It's cheap, needs no permanent edging once laid, lasts well and is easy to repair. It can even imitate paving slabs or crazy paving if joint lines are tooled into the surface.

Lay bay by bay
Don't lay a concrete garden path as a continuous strip, or it will crack. Divide it up into bays by tapping 50 mm (2 in) wide strips of hardboard on edge into the wet concrete every 2 m (6 ft) or so to act as a series of expansion joints.

Handy leveller
To get a sand bed level between edge restraints ready for block pavers, tailor-make a spreader. Cut one batten long enough to span the path, and a second to a length that matches the path width. Fix them together edge to edge with offcuts. The depth of the bottom batten should match the thickness of a block.

Edge the bed
You will need to construct a timber framework to contain the wet concrete until it sets. Nail lengths of sawn timber to pegs for straight paths, and cut strips of thin exterior-grade plywood to edge curved sections.

A face-lift for a tired old path

Give old tarmacadam paths a face-lift by treating them with a coat of bituminous emulsion, scattering some small stone chippings over the surface and rolling them into the wet emulsion with a garden roller. Leave the dressing to harden for a week, then sweep off any surplus chippings.

Kill the weeds

Once you have excavated the route of the path water on some long-lasting weedkiller to stop deep-rooted weeds from sprouting through the surface. As an added precaution, spread black polythene sheeting over the subsoil.

Make accurate shopping lists

To estimate how many paving slabs a path needs, count how many will fit across the width and along the length.
Block pavers are usually 200 x 100 mm in size, so you will need 50 blocks to cover a square metre.
For a concrete path 75 mm thick, work out the volume of the path in cubic metres (0.075 x length x width, in metres). Then for each cubic metre of concrete required, order nine 50 kg bags of cement and one cubic metre of all-in aggregate.

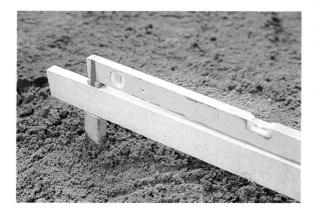

Sloping off

On level ground, a path needs a slight slope of about 10 mm per metre across its width to encourage rainwater to run off. Tape a 10 mm thick offcut to a long spirit level and use this to set the slope.

Watch the levels

When a path crosses or adjoins a lawn, make sure its surface will be just below soil level, so a lawnmower can cut the grass without the blades catching on the path edge and being damaged.

STAGES IN LAYING A CRAZY PAVING PATH

1 Excavate route of path. Lay sand bed, allowing room for a fraction more than the thickness of a slab below the turf

2 Place large slabs with one straight edge at sides of path, and tamp down into sand bed. Add large slabs in centre

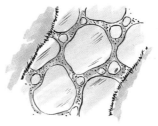

3 Fill in centre of path with smaller irregular pieces, and check they are lying level with edge slabs

4 Fill remaining gaps with small pieces. Then brush sand or dry mortar mix (6 parts soft sand to 1 part of cement) into all joints

311

paths Creating new walkways

Cover up the sand

Place and level only as much sand as you can cover with paving in a day, and keep the sand pile covered overnight with a tarpaulin or heavy-duty plastic sheeting, weighted down with blocks. Uncovered sand will be disturbed by wind, rain and children, and also by cats imagining they have found the world's biggest litter tray.

Three-way split

Sort the broken paving slabs used for crazy paving into three piles. The first should contain large pieces with one or more straight edges, the second large irregular pieces and the third smaller pieces. The straight-edged pieces from the first pile will go along the path edges, other large pieces in the middle and small pieces in the gaps.

Get help to cut blocks

Some block paver patterns involve cutting blocks, which is hard to do accurately with a brick bolster and club hammer. If you have a lot of blocks to cut, lay all the whole blocks first. Then hire a hydraulic block splitter for half a day and use it to prepare all the cut-to-size pieces you need.

Trimming to fit

If you have to cut a paving slab to a particular shape, place a paper template on the slab and mark round it with chalk. Then score the chalk line with your brick bolster, place the slab over another with the line 25 mm beyond its edge and carefully chip off the waste section bit by bit.

Settling down

Bed large paving slabs on a layer of dry sand if they are being placed across a lawn. Excavate a trench deep enough for the surface of the slabs to finish up just below soil level. Once slabs are laid, the turf beside the path will keep the sand bed in place. If the path crosses an area of ungrassed soil, compact the subsoil thoroughly and bed each slab on five blobs of wet mortar instead.

Do not disturb

As you excavate the ground on which your path will be laid, do not dig any deeper than you have to. Undisturbed subsoil will be compacted well enough to support a path without the need for further reinforcement. As you work, shovel the soil straight into a barrow for using elsewhere in the garden.

steps Measuring up

High risers

The height of brick-and-slab steps depends on how the bricks are laid. Bricks are 65 mm high laid flat, and 100 mm high laid on edge; pavers are commonly 38 mm thick. Both are laid on a 10 mm mortar bed, so a brick-and-slab step will be either 123 mm (brick laid flat, plus paver, plus two beds of mortar) or 158 mm high if the brick is laid on edge.

Safe dimensions

For safety, all the steps in a flight should have the same tread and the same riser dimensions. The minimum practical width for a flight is about 600 mm (2 ft), but you need a width of about 1.5 m (5 ft) to allow two people to walk side by side.

Protect the lawn

If steps link two areas of lawn, it's a good idea to set a tread into the ground in front of the bottom riser, to minimise wear and tear on the area of lawn at the foot of the flight.
The top tread usually forms part of the surface on the upper level. Remember to take this into account when you are working out the overall dimensions of a flight of steps.

Counting treads

The number of steps in a flight depends on the height and horizontal distance it has to cover. To work this out, set a peg in line with the face of the proposed first riser. Drive it into the ground until its top is level with the planned top tread, using a board and spirit level to verify this. Then measure the height of the peg and the distance from the top of it to the back edge of the planned top tread. Divide the total height by the height of a brick-and-slab step (above far left) to work out the number of risers; lastly, divide the horizontal distance the flight covers by the number of risers to work out the tread lengths.

Steep or shallow?

Steps work best with either deep treads (the flat surfaces) and low risers (the vertical ones), or shallow treads and high risers. Use the first combination on shallow slopes, and the second on steep slopes. As a general rule, the tread depth plus twice the riser height should add up to about 650 mm (2 ft 2 in).

Choose matching materials

If your steps link paths at the upper and lower levels, it looks best if you use the path paving material for the step treads too. Similarly, where there is a retaining wall, the risers should match the wall masonry.

steps Firm footholds on slopes

Use the slope to support the flight

So long as the soil forming the slope has not been disturbed, you can cut the shape of the steps into it and minimise the amount of back-filling that will be needed. Peg string lines down the slope to mark the sides of the flight, then start cutting out the step shapes one by one, working from the bottom up the slope. As you cut the shape, protect the edge of each tread with a timber offcut.

A level resting place

On flights of ten steps or more, it's a good idea to incorporate a level landing, at least as deep as the flight width. This makes the steps safer, provides a place to pause, and can be a useful device if you want the flight to change direction.

Tilt treads forward

Water will lie on absolutely level treads, creating a hazard if it freezes. Use a spirit level to lay the treads with a very slight fall towards the front edge, so that water drains away.

Create a sharp shadow

It's important to make sure that step edges are clearly visible for safety's sake. If you place each tread slab so that its front edge slightly overlaps the riser below, you'll create a conspicuous shadow beneath the overhang that will make the treads easy to see.

Create a solid base

Make a firm foundation for a flight of steps in a bank by laying a concrete strip beneath the lowest tread and riser. Without it the steps will slowly collapse. **Make the strip** the same size as the bottom tread and about 100 mm (4 in) deep, and leave it to set hard for 48 hours before building on it.

Non-slip treads

If you plan to use paving slabs as step treads, choose textured rather than smooth ones. It is important to keep garden steps free from algae–which become very slippery when wet–by treating them regularly with a proprietary fungicide. You can make timber steps slip-proof by stapling strips of chicken wire across the surface of the treads.

Building a flight of steps against a wall

Two lines of approach

A flight of steps up against a wall can either run parallel to it–so that the wall encloses the flight on one side–or can meet it head-on, at 90°. The first option usually saves space because the flight will only project from the face of the wall by just its width, no matter how many steps there are.

Build up from a firm base

Head-on flights consisting of four steps or more need a solid concrete base slab to support the entire flight, each riser being built up from the slab.

All you need for a shorter flight is a foundation strip placed beneath each side and the front edge. The treads rest on the hardcore infill, and risers on the rear edge of the tread below.

Tie the structure to its support

A flight of steps needs to be tied into the wall against which it is built. The easiest way to do this is with metal profile strips, which are fixed to the wall face and then bonded into the mortar courses of the step brickwork.

STAGES IN PATCHING CONCRETE STEPS

1 Cut back damaged edge of tread with a cold chisel and club hammer

2 Brush exposed surface with diluted PVA adhesive to help to bond the repair

3 Cut a piece of board to match the step height and jam it against the face of the riser with bricks

4 Fill hole with fine mortar, tamp down and smooth off. Leave the repair to set for 48 hours before removing board

315

drives Making an entrance

Face-lift for old concrete

Paving slabs need a continuous mortar bed if laid as a drive surface; they will crack under the weight of the car if you lay them on sand. An old concrete drive provides the perfect base, so long as the new drive surface will still be well below the house's damp-proof course.

Obtain crossover consent

If you are constructing a drive where none existed before, you must apply to your local authority for planning permission. You also need the consent of the highways department, who will install a lowered kerb and pavement section for a fee.

Good as new

Many existing drive surfaces need nothing more than a wash and brush up to remove surface dirt, algae and other stains. Hire or borrow a high-pressure sprayer for a couple of hours and use it to blast away the grime. You will be amazed at the transformation.

Don't let rain splash up

A drive should be at least 150 mm (6 in) below the damp-proof course (DPC) in the house wall, to stop rain splashing up and soaking the wall above the DPC. If this is impossible to achieve, stop the drive surface about 600 mm (2 ft) from the house wall and fill the resulting gap with gravel to act as a soakaway.

Tipped on the spot

A concrete drive is likely to need several cubic metres of concrete–far too much to mix yourself. Order a load of ready-mixed concrete from a local supplier and have the sub-base and formwork prepared, so that it can be tipped into place from the mixer truck. You'll need help to spread and level it before it sets.

Watch the run-off

If your drive slopes towards the house or garage, heavy rain will run down it and will either form pools against the house wall or flood the garage. Lay a drainage gully across the drive to divert the water off it and into a soakaway dug beneath the garden.

On level ground, allow a fall of about 1 in 50 across or along the drive to encourage rainwater to run off it.

No room to pass

When planning a new drive, aim to make it at least 3 m wide so that people can walk past a parked car and passengers can step out onto the drive surface. If you wish to park a caravan or a boat, you will need to allow even more width.

Provide a firm base

The best material to use for a sub-base beneath a new drive is called roadbase. It consists of finely crushed rock and can be compacted much more evenly and solidly than traditional hardcore. Laid to a depth of 100 mm, 1 ton of roadbase will cover an area of about 6 m² (7 sq yd). If you are laying paving blocks on a sand bed, you need 1 m³ of sand for every 15 m² of drive area.

Hiring forms

Timber formwork for a big concrete drive could be expensive. An alternative is to hire steel 'road forms' from a plant hire firm. Both straight and flexible sections are available. Just peg them in place round the area you're concreting.

Patching potholes

On tarmac drives, use cold-roll asphalt to fill potholes and repair crumbling edges. Store it indoors the day before you want to use it, so it is warm and easier to work. Rake out loose material, brush on some bituminous emulsion and then ram in the asphalt with a hired tamper or a length of fence post. Place a board over the patch and drive the car over it to compact it further.

Cat litter poultice

Cover fresh oil spots on a concrete or tarmac drive with ground-up cat litter or baking soda. Grind litter into a fine powder with a brick. Leave the litter or soda for a day or so to absorb the spillage, then sweep it away. **Proprietary stain removers** for oil, petrol and diesel are also available. Pick a biodegradable type that doesn't contain any harmful solvents.

Raising the covers

House drains often run beneath drives, and there may be inspection chambers with metal covers sited within your drive area. If you are altering the level of the drive surface, lift each cover and prise up the frame in which it fits. Bed the frame in mortar at the new drive level and replace the cover.

STAGES IN LAYING A BLOCKWORK DRIVE

1 Place edge restraints along drive perimeter. Then lay and compact sub-base to a thickness of about 100 mm (4 in)

2 Spread layer of sharp sand 60 mm (2½ in) thick and level with rake and straightedge. Compact with plate vibrator

3 Lay all whole blocks, then cut and fit part blocks and tamp down level. Run plate vibrator over the blocks

4 Brush fine dry sand into joints. Vibrate surface again to settle sand into joints and lock blocks together

drives

317

drives Using blocks

Hire shop essentials

Two tools are essential for laying a block drive: a hydraulic block splitter to cut the blocks easily and accurately, and a plate vibrator (below) to compact the base and settle the blocks into their sand bed. Both can be hired.

Herringbone is best

You can lay paving blocks in a number of different patterns. A herringbone pattern is the best one for drives, as the interlocked blocks won't shift under the wheels of cars manoeuvring over them.

Use a kneeler board

When laying blocks, keep off the sand bed and ensure that your weight is evenly distributed over the blocks already laid by using a kneeler board.

Laying gravel

Hear visitors coming

Gravel is cheap, easy and quick to lay, and a useful security measure as you can hear people approaching. However, it is hard work to walk over or push wheeled equipment across. For large areas, buy gravel in 1 ton bulk bags which can be emptied straight onto the drive area on delivery. One ton of gravel will cover about 16 m² (19 sq yd) at a depth of 25 mm.

Big is better

Pea gravel is more rounded than standard gravel and is commonly sold in 10 mm or 20 mm diameter stones. The larger size is less likely to get stuck in tyre treads or shoe soles.

Rake and roll

It is a good idea to spread the gravel in two layers. Using a rake, cover the drive to a depth of about 12 mm (½ in) and roll it with a garden roller. Spread a second layer the same depth and roll it again. The surface will need regular raking to keep it tidy, and an occasional dose of weedkiller.

ponds Siting and lining a pond

Points to ponder

A pond should, ideally, be set into level ground that gets direct sunlight for most of the day: aquatic plants do not like shade. However, these requirements may conflict with your desire to see the pond from inside the house—and to hear it if there's a fountain or waterfall.

Avoid overhanging trees and bushes: any leaves that fall will foul the water as they decay. The foliage of some shrubs may even poison the water for fish. Growing roots from nearby trees can also puncture flexible pond liners.

Seal for concrete

It's a good idea to apply a flexible waterproofing sealant to a new concrete pond before you fill it for the first time. The sealant is simply painted on and, once it's dry, it will prevent chemicals in the concrete from leaching into the water, where they could harm fish or plants. You can use the same product to seal hairline cracks if an old concrete pond starts to leak.

No need to dig

Glass-fibre pond liners are rigid and sturdy enough not to require sinking into the ground, so you can stand one on the surface and create a rockery around it. This saves a lot of digging, especially if your garden is on a slope.

Plastic liners are semi-rigid; they cost less than glass-fibre ones but must be sunk into the ground for support.

Creating irregular shapes

Use a flexible liner if you want to create your own shape and size of pond. These liners vary in quality and price. The strongest and most expensive liners are made of butyl rubber; the cheapest are of laminated PVC, which may stay waterproof for only a few years.

Getting the line right

Use a length of garden hosepipe to design a random shape with smoothly rounded curves on your chosen site, then peg the hose in place.

Keep the shape simple because the more intricate it is the more liner you will need, and the more chance there is that the lining material will crease.

ponds Golden rules for water in the garden

The sound of running water

A waterfall or fountain will help to oxygenate the water in the pond. You can buy mains or low-voltage pumps but the latter are easier to install and safer to use. Different sizes of pump generate different volumes of flow and pressure. Ask your supplier for advice about the pump rating you'll need for the feature you plan to incorporate.

Filters need cleaning regularly, so position a submerged pump where it can be easily reached from the side of the pond. Keeping an eye on how well the waterfall or fountain is working will alert you if a blockage starts to develop.

Stand the pump on a couple of bricks to prevent sediment from the bottom of the pond constantly clogging the filter.

Nearby water and power

For filling or topping up the pond, it's useful to be within hose reach of the garden tap. If you plan to install lighting or a pump for a fountain you'll need a power supply, so the pond should not be too far from the power source, whether this is the house or garage.

Patience pays off

Once you have filled the pond, wait for a week or so to allow chemicals in the water supply to disperse before adding any plants. Then leave the plants for a month to oxygenate the water before you introduce the fish. Check the acidity of the water with a pH test kit first.

Water lights

You can enhance a pond at night by installing low-voltage (12 or 24 volt) garden lights. Their spikes hold them in the ground, so you can place them around the edge of the pond. Low-voltage submersible and floating lights are also available. Because they pose no danger, low-voltage cables can be laid on the surface–hidden in undergrowth, for example.

Job for an expert

Water and electricity are a dangerous combination. Ask an electrician to wire up a pump or pond light unless you are absolutely sure you can do the work safely. Make sure that an RCD (see page 202) is fitted to the supply; it will shut off instantly if there is a fault.

Animal ramp

Gently sloping sides are friendlier to wildlife as well as being more stable. Make an earth ramp stabilised with plants, so that small creatures such as frogs can crawl in and out, and try to arrange perimeter slabs so they don't overhang the edge.

Keep small children away

Fence off the pond securely or cover it with a strong metal mesh to protect young children. It is as easy to drown in a shallow fish pond as in a swimming pool, so never leave babies or young children playing alone near one.

Protecting fish

Fish need a pond with a surface area of at least 4 m² (about 45 sq ft) if they are to thrive. They also need to retreat to deeper water if the surface freezes over. Ponds up to 10 m² (110 sq ft) should be at least 500 mm (20 in) deep; those up to 20 m² (220 sq ft), at least 600 mm (2 ft) deep; larger still, and you'll need a depth of around 800 mm (2 ft 8 in).

Excavating for a rigid liner

The right shaped hole

If the liner is symmetrical, turn it upside down and mark all round the rim. An irregular liner may be supplied with a template. If not, transfer the shape of the top to the ground using a spirit level and pegs. Mark the outline of the base straight onto the ground. Excavate to the full depth inside the base line, then form sloping sides back to the peg line at ground level.

A little earth, a little water

Fill any gaps around the sides with some of the soil you dig out. Riddle it first to make sure it contains no sharp stones, and start to shovel it in all round the liner. Tamp it down with a timber offcut, not a metal object. Then put a little water in the pond.
Alternate between tamping a little more soil in round the liner and running some more water into it until the gaps are all filled and the pond is full too. Let the soil settle for a week, and top it up as necessary with more soil before laying any fixed edging round the pond.

Level sides

Whether you are excavating for a rigid or a flexible liner, the top of the pond must be level, otherwise water will spill over the side. After digging the hole, lay a plank and a spirit level across it to check the level. If one side is higher, dig this away; don't build up the lower edge as the earth will only settle.

Dig too deep

For both flexible and rigid liners, dig the hole about 50 mm (2 in) deeper than necessary so that you can put in a layer of sand. This will prevent the liner being punctured by stones in the subsoil. For extra protection, you can put special pond underlay over the sand.

ponds

ponds Using pond-on-a-roll for unique designs

Estimating the amount of liner

Flexible liner is cut to length from long rolls, and comes in several widths. The length you need is the maximum overall length of the pond plus twice its maximum depth. The width is the pond's maximum overall width plus twice its maximum depth. Suppliers can bond two lengths together if necessary to line a very large pond.

Mowing made easy

If the pond edging is set slightly below the surface of the lawn, you will be able to run the mower right up to the edge. Keep the grass-box on the mower so you don't get clippings in the pond.

Calculating volumes

You may need to work out how much water your pond holds, such as when treating it with something to control algae. Multiply together the average length, width and depth to calculate the volume. Work in metric units: there are 1000 litres in a cubic metre.

The water makes the shape

Drape the liner over the hole so that it touches the bottom and the edges of any plant shelves. Weigh down the edge with bricks and begin filling it slowly. As the weight of the water stretches the liner to the shape of the hole, lift the bricks and form the liner into neat folds.

Create shelves for the plants

Make a template from plywood or other board so you can check the accuracy of your excavation. The sloping sides are cut at about 20° from the vertical, and the plant shelf is about 225 mm (9 in) below the surface and 225 mm (9 in) wide.

Find a use for the soil

Excavating even a small pond creates a mountain of soil. As an alternative to loading it into a skip for removal from the site, you can turn it into a garden feature such as a raised bed supporting a waterfall mould and a surrounding rockery. You will need a pump to circulate water from the pond through a length of concealed hosepipe to the top of the waterfall.

Dealing with leaks and overflows

Preparing to repair

Evaporation causes water levels to drop by as much as about 12 mm (½ in) a month in the summer. If the level is falling faster, the pond probably has a leak. To mend it, you need to know what the liner is made of because different materials need different repairs. Keep the details when you buy a liner. If you move into a house with a pond, ask the vendors what the liner is made of.

Before making a repair, transfer plants and fish from the pond into temporary accommodation (a child's paddling pool, for example). Hire a pump or use buckets to empty the pond.

Picking the right kit

Glass-fibre repair kits, available from car accessory shops, can be used to mend holes in rigid liners. Make sure the liner is dry, and follow the instructions supplied with the kit.

Puncture repair kits are sold by the makers of flexible liners. Usually, the area needs to be clean and dry. Use a wallpaper seam roller to smooth down self-adhesive patches.

Escape for high water

Once you have installed the pond liner, and before laying edging slabs, you could fit an overflow pipe. Use a short length of plastic waste pipe. Fix a mesh cover over one end to stop blockages–a piece of expanded metal mesh or the leaf guard designed to stop gutter blockages is ideal. You can fit a second pipe without a guard to admit a hose for filling the pond, and also the cable for the pump and lights.

1 Mark out the pond shape, remove turf and excavate hole to required depth

2 Check that perimeter is level, remove stones projecting from sides and bottom, and line with sand

3 Drape liner over hole and weigh edge down. Fill slowly, forming neat folds and releasing weights as water rises

4 Trim liner, allowing a 150 mm (6 in) overlap, then lay edging around perimeter

ponds

323

equipment

selecting Make the right choices when you shop for tools

Hire before you buy

It's often difficult to assess how useful and versatile a tool will be until you start using it. Hire—or borrow—whatever you're considering buying, so that you can try it out and then decide whether the purchase will be worth while. Bear in mind that the hire tools will usually be of professional quality, and so will be more robust than those designed for DIY use.

It always makes sense to hire tools or equipment that you'll use very infrequently—a post-hole borer or a steam wallpaper stripper, for instance.

Beware of rust

Secondhand tool shops, craft fairs and car boot sales are good sources for tools, but inspect them carefully before buying. If handles are loose, check whether they can be replaced. Never buy tools with rusty blades. A nicked blade can be ground flat on a grindstone, but if it is pitted with rust you'll never be able to sharpen it to a keen edge. Inspect the flexes and casings of power tools closely for signs of damage.

Choosing a workbench

Always buy the sturdiest workcentre with the biggest worktop that you can find and will fit in the space you have—but unless it is being delivered, make sure it will fit in the car. If you don't have space for a permanent workcentre, pick a foldaway workbench. The most versatile have a section of the top that can be detached and reversed to give extra vice capacity.

If storage space is very limited, a workbox with integral opening jaws on the top is a useful alternative.

Table mount heavy tools

Power tools must feel comfortable to use, so pick up and handle new tools in the shop before you buy. It's not always necessary to select the highest-rated tool. Think about where you'll be using it; a lightweight one won't have the same cutting or drilling capacity, but you'll be able to use it one-handed in awkward situations.

Select heavy-duty saws, routers and other cutting and shaping tools if you have the room to mount them in a workcentre. Then you can use them as fixed tools rather than portable ones.

selecting Drilling holes and driving screws

Drill torque
A drill with a 600–700 watt motor is adequate for most DIY jobs. Pick one with a keyless chuck for quick drill changeovers, variable speed control, and also hammer action for drilling into masonry. If it has torque control, you can use it as a power screwdriver too.

The versatile bradawl
Select a bradawl with a tapered point (left) for marking the starting point for a drill bit. Switch to one with a chisel point (right) for making pilot holes in wood; these prevent the wood from splitting when you're driving in nails or small screws (up to gauge 6).
Don't use a chisel-point bradawl to drive small screws; its blade is not hardened as a screwdriver's is, and it will become damaged very quickly.

Quick change drill-and-drive
A snap-on adaptor eliminates the bother of slackening off and retightening the chuck of your power drill every time you want to exchange a drill bit for a screwdriver one. A shank at one end of the adaptor fits in the chuck, while at the other end there is a sprung collet to hold the bit.

Match the screw pattern
You can sometimes undo a crosshead screw with a slot-head screwdriver if it isn't too tight, and a Phillips screwdriver will loosen a Pozidriv or Supadriv screw. But for real torque you need individual screwdrivers for the many different types of screw around, or a driver that takes interchangeable bits.
Powder coatings give the bits a better purchase on the heads of screws, while rubberised handles give you a more comfortable grip on the driver.

Tools for nails, nuts and bolts

Hammers for maximum impact

A claw hammer (top left), a pin hammer (middle left) and a club hammer (bottom left) will cater for most household jobs, from tapping in a nail to giving a bolster chisel a hefty blow.

If you want a traditional claw hammer with a hickory wood handle, check that the head is securely fixed to it with steel wedges. If you prefer a hammer that's virtually indestructible, choose one with a steel or glass-fibre shaft. Whichever you pick, check whether you can cope with its weight by holding it close to the end of the shaft and swinging it with a smooth, controlled action. It should feel comfortable to use.

Load a pin push

Holding a tiny moulding pin upright while tapping it in with a pin hammer can be really fiddly. An age-old tip is to push the pin through a strip of paper and hold the paper, not the pin, while you tap it down. Even easier is to use a tool called a pin push (right).

Feed a pin into the barrel of the tool, where it is held in place by a magnet, then push down on the spring-loaded handle to locate and insert the pin in one go. You can push it fully home in softwood, but on hardwood the tool will just locate it, ready to be driven home with your pin hammer.

selecting

Turning power

Combination spanners are ideal for working with nuts and bolts. The ring head offers maximum purchase on a tight nut, which can then be removed quickly with the easy-to-locate open jaw. Both ends of each spanner fit the same size nut and bolt.

Beware of cheap spanners, which are likely to burr or snap in use. Look for the words 'chrome alloy steel' or 'chrome vanadium' stamped on the tool.

selecting Tools for nails, nuts and bolts

Hammering home

A nail punch (right) lets you drive in nail heads flush with or below the wood surface without marking the wood with your hammer. Its tip is hollowed out to fit over the nail head. Choose one with a knurled finish for a good grip. A punch with a square head gives you a larger striking surface than a rounded head and is less likely to roll off the edge of your workbench.

Spanners for plumbing

Equip yourself with a pair of adjustable spanners so you can tackle a variety of plumbing jobs. You need a size that will grip the nuts on compression fittings and tap connectors. Add a pipe wrench—also known as a Stillson wrench—for tackling damaged nuts, and a strap wrench (see page 139) for undoing the large nuts on plastic traps beneath fittings.

Taking the right measurements

Perfectly level every time

Choose a long spirit level for maximum accuracy. Brass-edged hardwood levels look beautiful, but lightweight aluminium ones are more practical and durable for the assortment of building and woodworking jobs that are tackled by most do-it-yourselfers.

A level with adjustable vials can be reset if it isn't providing an accurate reading. You'll need to use a known level surface (established with a second spirit level) to do this. Put the level on the surface and adjust the vial position very slightly until the bubble is dead centre. Then turn the level horizontally through 180° and make sure that the bubble still settles precisely in the centre. Finally replace the retaining ring over the vial. With this type of level, you can also replace vials if they are damaged in use.

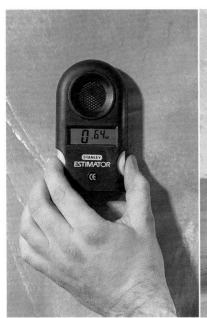

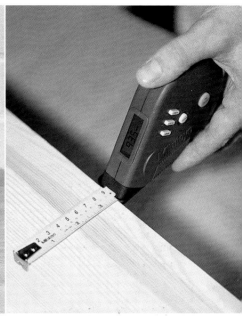

Rule out inaccuracies

An ultrasonic estimator (left) measures distances by emitting an ultrasound beam and then picking up the echo. It's ideal for room dimensions.

State-of-the-art laser levels (centre) fire a laser light beam, enabling guide lines to be marked quickly and accurately round a room or down the garden.

A digital tape measure (far right) looks just like a standard one, but has an electronic display. It includes the width of the case for internal measurements.

Getting to grips

Holding firm

Deep-throated G-cramps enable you to secure items farther from an edge than ordinary ones can reach. They can also secure veneers (see page 276) and edge trims if you don't have proper edge cramps. Oil the threads lightly so the screw moves easily, and set the cramp to roughly the jaw separation you need before fitting it in place.

Comfort and safety

Combination pliers are versatile tools, good for all sorts of gripping jobs and for cutting and crimping wire. Choose a pair with PVC-insulated handles for a safe and comfortable grip.

Buy the heads only

Sash cramps are expensive. You can save money by buying pairs of cramp heads instead. They fit on bars of planed hardwood such as beech, so you'll need to drill holes in the bars for the pegs, which hold the heads at various positions (above). The spaces between the holes must not exceed the maximum travel of the screw on the adjustable head.

selecting
Saws, chisels and angle grinders

Ideal pairing

The two most useful handsaws for the amateur woodworker are a panel saw and a tenon saw. A panel saw is excellent for crosscutting, general joinery, and cutting sheet material. Look for one about 500 mm (20 in) long with 10 teeth per 25 mm (sometimes labelled 10 ppi–points per inch).

With its stiffened back, a tenon saw is used for finer joinery work needing accurate joint cutting. Choose one about 350 mm (14 in) long with 12–14 points per 25 mm.

Opt for saws with wooden handles. You'll pay more, but they're much more comfortable to use than plastic ones.

Some throwaway advice

A traditional handsaw is worth buying if you intend doing a lot of woodwork, but for infrequent use and one-off carpentry projects an inexpensive hardpoint saw is a better choice. It is also ideal if you cut a lot of manufactured boards, because the adhesives used to make them won't blunt the toughened teeth as quickly as those of an ordinary saw. The teeth can't be sharpened, so throw the saw away when it becomes blunt.

Look for a saw with a mitre on the handle–useful for marking a 45° cutting angle (above), if you don't have a mitre square or combination square handy.

Protect the teeth

If your panel or tenon saw was not supplied with a blade guard, use plastic document binder strip (available from office suppliers and some tool shops) or lengths of rigid foam pipe insulation to protect the teeth from damage caused by the saw knocking against other items in your tool bag.

How much power?

A jigsaw powered by a 400–500 watt motor is adequate for most DIY tasks but, as with many power tools, you may find yourself wanting extra power when you discover how useful it is.

Light-duty models should cut through timber around 50 mm (2 in) thick and steel up to 3 mm (⅛ in) thick. More powerful 600 watt models can deal with 100 mm (4 in) thick timber and 10 mm (½ in) thick steel.

Shake the blade

Check the tension of a rip or crosscut saw—stiffness in the blade which stops it from wandering off the cutting line as you work. You can test the tension by holding the saw flat by its handle and shaking it. The blade should rapidly return to standstill, and it should not flop or droop at all.

Choosing a power saw

A 600–900 watt portable circular saw is the best tool for cutting sheet materials such as plywood and MDF, and for general carpentry around the home. It will cut straight lines in wood up to about 50 mm (2 in) thick. **Pick one with a vacuum hose connector** for dust extraction if you're likely to use the saw a lot. Tungsten carbide tipped blades last up to 50 times longer than ordinary steel ones and are a much better buy if you're going to be cutting a lot of sheet materials.

Sandwich to stop vibration

When you're using a jigsaw to cut thin sheet metal or plastic laminate, you will not get a clean cut if the sheet can vibrate in time with the saw blade. To prevent this, lay the sheet on a board offcut with the cutting line a fraction beyond its edge. Then cramp the sheet to the board with another timber offcut, positioned out of the way of the saw body, and make the cut.

selecting
Saws, chisels and angle grinders

New angles on grinders

The range of rigid and flexible grinding discs available makes an angle grinder a versatile tool. It can be used for shaping car body repairs, as well as cutting chases in plaster for electric cables, cutting roof tiles, raking out mortar joints, and grinding an edge on tools like cold chisels. Pick a model with a chunky on/off switch that can be operated through thick work gloves.

Best value in a box

Bevelled-edge chisels can be used to clean out mortises after the bulk of the waste has been drilled out, as well as to carry out fine paring work and to make dovetails. A boxed set of four is likely to represent the best value; look for one containing 6, 12, 18 and 25 mm sizes.

In praise of plastic

Choose chisels with high-impact plastic handles (left). Unlike wooden-handled ones they won't be damaged if you have to tap them with a hammer rather than a mallet. Their only disadvantage is that they can be slippery to hold.

Features to look for

There are three useful features to look for on a jigsaw. Variable speed control enables you to start cuts slowly and then speed up. A sliding sole plate that can be pushed back allows the blade to cut right up to a vertical surface such as a skirting board. Pendulum action, in which the blade swings from front to back while rising and falling, clears the kerf (the cut made by the saw) of sawdust and gives a splinter-free cutting line on the underside of the material.

Routers to shape and mould

Take the work to the router

With some of the latest light-duty models, you have the option of removing the motor unit from the carriage and clamping it in a drill stand (below). You can then push the length of wood being moulded past the revolving cutter as an alternative to fixing the wood in place and passing the router over it.

Distinguishing characteristics

Choose a router with a 600–900 watt motor. A ¼ in collet (the adjustable sleeve that grips the cutters) will cope with light woodworking, but a ½ in one will grip bigger cutters and cope with heavier work. Check that the handles feel comfortable and that the on/off switch is within easy reach. An electronic 'soft' start means you get no kick when you turn the router on. Check too that the cutter depth and fence position are easy to set accurately. The fence controls the distance of the cutter from the edge of the wood.

Tungsten carbide-tipped cutters cost more than high-speed steel ones but are worth it. They keep their edge far longer, especially when used on manufactured products such as chipboard and plywood.

selecting

selecting
Sanders and planers for effortless finishing

Sanding without scratches

Buy a random orbital sander with variable speed control if you want to turn out highly finished work. Its action is designed to leave no scratch marks on the surface of the wood when used with a fine grade abrasive paper.

Reaching awkward areas

For sanding internal corners, a delta sander is the answer. The triangular abrasive sheets are held on with Velcro, and you simply peel them off and reposition them when one point of the triangle becomes worn. Some models have a rotating head which you turn to bring an unused corner into use.

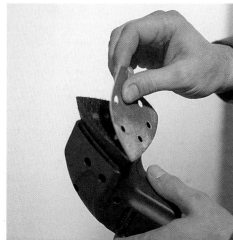

The economy option

Pre-cut perforated sanding sheets for finishing sanders are quite expensive. Save money by cutting up your own from standard sheets of abrasive paper. Sheets for sanders are either a third or a half the size of a standard sheet.

Transfer the pattern of the perforations onto a piece of thin plywood and use it as a template to punch out the holes.

Collect the dust

Make sure any power sander you buy has a dust collection facility. Some have a dust bag, others a nozzle to which you can attach the hose from a vacuum cleaner. This is a more effective way of removing dust from the air but the vacuum cleaner will amplify the sound of the sander, so it is a good idea to wear ear defenders.

Protect yourself

Always wear a dust mask and safety goggles when power sanding, even if the tool has a dust bag or vacuum cleaner connection. This is especially important if you are working on MDF, as there is concern over the health risk of inhaling the very fine dust produced when this board is sanded.

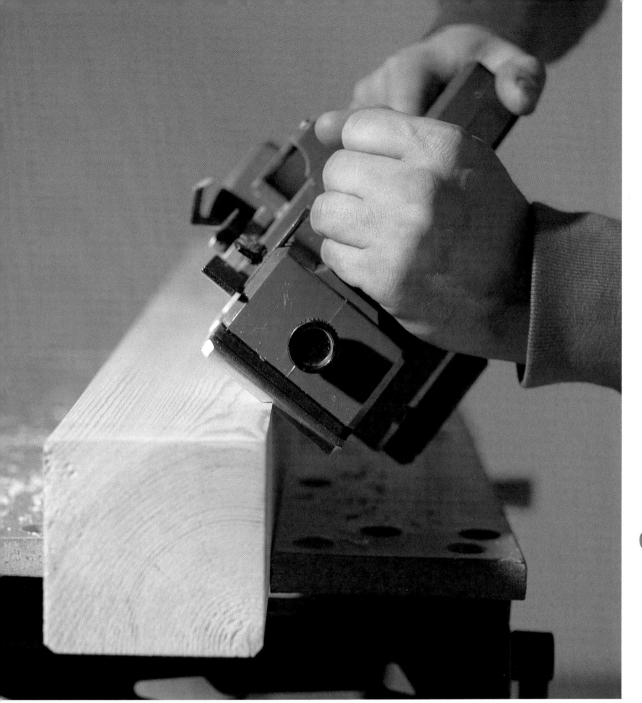

Planing power

An electric planer isn't an essential tool in the same way as a power drill or even a router is, but it does make short work of planing down an oversize piece of wood and it is the ideal tool for trimming oversize doors. If you decide to buy one, look out for the following useful features.

A V-groove running down the centre of the sole plate enables you to chamfer (take the sharp edge or arris off) the edge of doors and other fixtures with one pass of the planer (above).

A flip-down guard prevents the blades from being damaged by contact with any surface on which the planer is laid.

Control cutting depth

Choose a belt sander with a metal frame attachment. This can be set to control the depth of the cut, so that a consistent thickness of wood is sanded off across a wide workpiece.

A cramp is another useful extra. It enables the sander to be held upside-down at the edge of the workbench so it can be used as a fixed tool.

selecting Hiring tools the professionals use

Carry proof of identity

When you collect a tool from a hire shop you will probably need to show them some proof of identity with your address on it–a current insurance document or a telephone bill, for example. A credit card by itself won't be enough.

Pay the extra for insurance against damage, especially if you haven't used the tool before. It is unlikely to add more than 10 per cent to the hire charge, and could save you a hefty bill.

Stock up on the extras

You can buy extras such as 'biscuits' for biscuit jointers (above), router cutters and grinding discs from most hire shops on a sale-or-return basis. Always take more than you'll need, then you won't have to go back for more during the job.

Read leaflets immediately

Hire shops supply an instruction and safety leaflet with many tools, especially powered ones. Read it in the shop, and ask for a demonstration if you're unfamiliar with the tool.

Look for a tag on the tool, stating that it has been serviced and tested since it was last returned to the shop.

Check the catalogue

Pick up a catalogue when you're in your local hire shop–you'll be amazed at the range of tools and equipment available. In fact, you'll often discover the best way to tackle a job is by spotting a tool or a piece of equipment you didn't know existed, such as this right-angled drill for getting into restricted spaces.

Choosing and handling materials

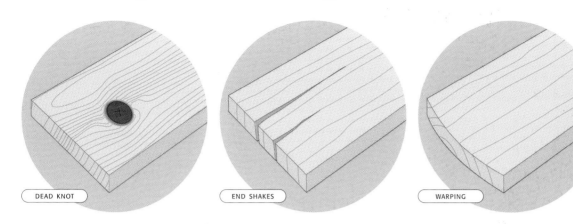

DEAD KNOT

END SHAKES

WARPING

Look out for timber defects
When buying timber, always look for defects caused by poor seasoning and storage. Sight across the surface and along the edges of every piece, and don't buy any that are warped or bowed. Also avoid any with dead knots or splits (end shakes).

Test doors for flatness
Factory-made doors often warp when improperly stored. Lay them flat on the floor of the store, and reject any with a corner raised off the floor.

A ready reckoner for timber
Timber is sold in metric lengths, rising in increments of 0.3 m. Minimise wastage by bearing this in mind when calculating your needs. For example, if you want to clad a wall 2.3 m high in matchboarding, you will need to buy boards 2.4 m long (0.3 m x 8).

If you prefer to use imperial measurements, 0.3 m (300 mm) is very slightly less than 1 ft (305 mm), and is close enough to provide a rough-and-ready conversion factor. Just divide the metric length by 3–thus, 2.4 m is approximately 8 ft.

selecting

selecting Hiring tools the professionals use

Stock or special order

Try to base the design of woodworking projects on the stock sizes of timber stored on the racks and shelves of your timber merchant or DIY store.

If you have to use non-stock sizes, ask for a quotation from a timber merchant with a machine shop where the wood can be cut on a band saw (right) or circular saw, then planed to your specifications. You will probably have to wait a few days before the order is ready to collect.

Look after your back

Take care when lifting heavy bags, or items such as large paving slabs. So you don't injure yourself, stand close to whatever you're lifting with your feet apart and your back straight. Squat down so you can grip the load. Then straighten your legs and stand up as you lift the load, keeping it as close to your body as possible. If something is too heavy or awkward to lift alone, get help or look into the range of lifting equipment that can be hired. This includes such items as panel lifters (see page 76), barrows for carting flagstones around the garden, and manual grabs for handling bricks.

Buy building supplies in bulk

If you have a large job to do involving bricklaying or concreting, buy sand and coarse aggregate (gravel) in bulk. It is cheaper than buying by the 50 kg sack. If your local council forbids delivery of loose materials to the kerb side, ask about delivery in bulk bags. You pay a deposit for these, and get a refund when you return the empty bags.

In planed language

Some DIY stores label planed timber with its finished cross-sectional size, but timber merchants always list by the original sawn size of the timber, whether it is planed or not. So a length of planed timber labelled by a timber merchant as 75 x 50 mm (3 x 2 in) will actually measure 71 x 46 mm because about 2 mm (just under 1/8 in) has been removed from each of the four faces during planing. Planed timber is often abbreviated to PAR (planed all round).

Working with nails and drilling holes

Get a grip

It is often difficult to remove round-head nails without damaging the wood. Unless the head of the nail protrudes well above the surface, the jaws of a claw hammer are too blunt to get a good grip. Try filing a pair of pincers so the jaws are flat on the outside (below) with a shallow bevel on the inside. Then press them flat on the wood and close them under the head of the nail (right).

Use a try square

Drilling holes in wood at right angles to the surface takes practice. The trick is to sight along the axis of the tool, whether you're using a power drill or a brace and bit, and hold a try square against the surface, to check that the drill bit is actually at 90°.

If the workpiece is lying flat, stand the try square next to the drill position so that you can check at a glance whether you're holding the drill upright.

Avoid injuries with a cramp

Always cramp a small workpiece to the bench before drilling it. If you try to hold it down by hand, the power of the drill may snatch it from your grasp, and the fast-spinning 'propeller blade' of wood could give you a nasty injury.

Make an accurate mark

Twist and masonry drill bits tend to wander slightly off centre when you start making a hole with them, especially if they're blunt or the material you're drilling is hard. Avoid this by using a centre punch to mark the hole position accurately. Then you can locate the tip of the drill in the mark.

Improvise a twist drill

A panel pin or small nail can be used instead of a small twist drill to make pilot holes for nails and screws in hardwood. Nip off the nail head with pincers, then insert this end in the chuck of a power or hand drill. Press the point into the wood to make a starter hole, then drill the hole slowly and steadily.

techniques
Working with nails and drilling holes

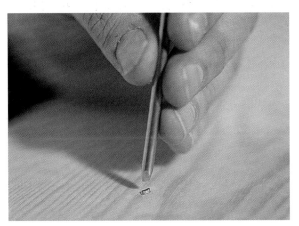

Avoid splintering
When you're drilling holes with a flat wood bit and a power drill, the blades of the bit can splinter the wood surface as they emerge. Avoid this problem by cramping a piece of scrap wood under the workpiece, then drill through into that.

Punch substitute
If you don't have a nail punch, a round-head nail makes a good substitute. File back the point to suit the size of the nail that needs sinking. Your make-do punch will be more likely to slip off the nail head than a real punch, so hold it square and don't hit it too hard.

When space is restricted
A hand brace is useful for making holes in corners and in other restricted places where the body of a power drill gets in the way. Make a starter hole for the tip of the bit, engage the ratchet and start operating the brace through a 90° arc. Repeat as necessary to finish the hole.

Three holes in one
When you're joining wood to wood with countersunk screws, you need to drill three holes—a clearance hole and a countersink for the screw's shaft and head in the first piece, and a pilot hole for the screw thread in the second. You can speed up the job—by avoiding having to keep changing the bit—if you use a combined drill and countersink bit, which makes all three holes in one go. Use the bit size that matches the gauge of the screws you're driving.

Lubricate the drill bit

Keep the speed of the drill down when drilling through metal, to stop the twist drill bit from overheating.
On horizontal workpieces, surround the point at which you're drilling with a small ring of putty, and pour some white spirit into it to act as a lubricant. Use the same trick when drilling mirrors, too (see page 254).

Speedy combination

Continually changing the bit in a power drill or screwdriver is time-consuming, even if it has a keyless chuck—one that you can tighten and loosen by hand. Buy a spring-loaded collar that fits in the drill chuck, and you'll be able to switch backwards and forwards between drills and screwdriver bits in seconds.

Drilling around corners

If the drill body gets in the way when drilling holes in tight spaces, fit a flexible drive shaft to your power drill. You can fit rotary rasps and files as well as drill bits, which will turn your drill into a versatile shaping tool.

Carry on drilling

If you're drilling a deep hole with an auger bit, withdraw it from the hole every now and again so you can clear the waste from the spiral flutes. The bit will jam if the flutes are blocked.

Tightening and releasing screws

Resort to force

Screws in wood can seize fast in time, especially if they have rusted. Hold the screwdriver in the slot and give the end of its handle a sharp blow with a mallet. If this doesn't free the screw, hold the screwdriver in the slot at a slight angle and then strike it with the mallet once again to turn the screw a fraction in the clockwise (tightening) direction.
Lastly, try heating the head of the screw with a soldering iron, so that the metal expands and contracts; this may break the thread's grip in the wood.

Drive steel before brass

Brass screws look good, but they're soft and driving them in often damages the heads, spoiling their appearance. You can avoid this by driving a same-size steel screw in first of all, then replacing it with the brass one. Make an added feature of brass screws by aligning the slots in the heads.

Keeping control of the tool

Pump-action screwdrivers have largely been replaced by powered types, but they're still effective and fast for tightening or removing screws, especially the cross-head type. Grip the collar above the bit to stop the blade from jumping off the head of the screw. If there's much resistance, lock the ratchet and use it like a conventional screwdriver.

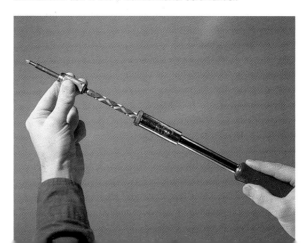

techniques Measuring and marking

Ensuring accuracy

Set a wooden rule on edge when you're using it to mark measurements on a workpiece. Then the graduations on the face can be transferred straight onto the workpiece. If you lay the rule flat, the absence of any edge markings makes it difficult to mark the dimensions accurately.

Pick the right pencil

Select the pencil with care when you're marking measurements on wood. One with a hard lead (marked 1H or higher) will score the wood surface surprisingly deeply, leaving a mark that has to be sanded or even planed off. Use an HB pencil instead. You'll have to sharpen it more often, but the marks it leaves can be removed easily with a soft rubber.
A proper carpenter's pencil is the best buy; its flat sides mean it won't roll off the bench, as a round one will. Sharpen it regularly with your trimming knife.

A smooth curve

To mark a perfect circle on any manufactured board, use a batten, a pencil and a nail. Bore a hole at one end of the batten and push in the pencil.
Then measure the exact radius of the circle along the batten from the centre of the hole, and drive a nail through it at that point. Pivot the batten on the nail and draw the required circle.

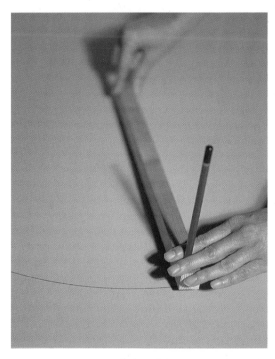

Measure in metric only

Virtually everything you need for DIY, from paint and wallpaper to timber, is sized in metric units nowadays. You can avoid having to make complex conversions by taking measurements in metric only; you'll be a lot more accurate too without those awkward fractions of an inch to worry about. Either ignore the imperial figures on your tape measure, or buy a new one with just metric markings.
Coverage figures using square metres on tins of paint and boxes of tiles will also be much easier to understand if you work in metric measurements only.

Holding and smoothing wood

Keeping frames square

Use a try square to check the squareness of frameworks when you are tightening sash cramps. If the corners are not precisely at right angles, slacken off the cramps and angle them slightly to pull the frame back to a true square.

Alternate the cramps (one above, one below) when using three or more to hold the long edges of boards together while adhesive dries. This counteracts the tendency of the boards to bow under pressure. Place lengths of scrap wood between the boards and the cramps to prevent the boards from being bruised by the cramps.

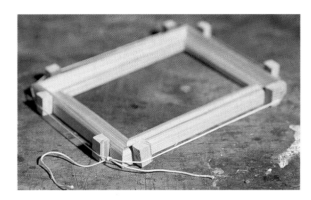

Test for a flat surface

Any true straightedge can be used to check that a surface is flat. Place a spirit level, a metal rule or the sole of a hand plane–with the blade retracted–across the wood and rotate it. Any light visible beneath the edge is a sign that the surface is bowed (raised in the centre) or cupped (hollow).

Diagonal check

Whenever you're assembling a frame or carcass, measure the diagonals with a tape measure as soon as it's cramped up, to check that the assembly is square (see page 94). Alternatively, sharpen one end of a straight stick. Place the point in the angle at one corner, hold the stick diagonally across to the opposite corner and make a mark on the stick in line with that corner. Now check the other diagonal to see if the mark coincides.

Staying in the picture

The mitred corners of picture frames can be held together with a string and block arrangement while the glue sets. Tie a loop of string loosely round the frame, then slip small blocks of wood, two on each side, under the string. Tap each pair towards opposite corners to tighten the string and the joint.

Stop corners splitting

Planing the end grain of a plank always splits the wood as the blade runs off the far edge. One simple solution is to cramp a block of scrap wood hard against this edge so the plane runs off the workpiece and into the scrap. Another is to plane a very shallow chamfer along the far edge first. You can then plane the end grain without any splits until the chamfer disappears.

techniques

345

techniques Holding and smoothing wood

Adjust, then position
Holding an assembly together while you tighten a G-cramp can be fiddly. It is much easier and quicker to adjust the cramp to the approximate depth of the item before putting it in place, leaving just a few turns to be made. Thin scraps of plywood make excellent protective packing.

Wedges work wonders
If you don't have sash cramps, use wooden wedges instead. Screw two parallel battens to your bench top, a little farther apart than the width of what you want to cramp, then push one side of the assembly against one of the battens, and drive a pair of long tapered wedges between the other batten and the assembly to cramp it.

A flat finish
Wrap abrasive paper around a cork sanding block or a small offcut of wood if you're sanding something by hand. This will ensure that the workpiece ends up with a flat surface. A pad of abrasive paper held in the hand will just follow and accentuate any unevenness.

Keep it moving
There are three rules to remember when using a power sander. Let it reach full speed before bringing it into contact with the surface being sanded. Keep it moving steadily across the surface, never letting it remain stationary. Lift it off the surface before switching it off. Stop and check the abrasive at regular intervals. If it's getting clogged with dust, smack it with the palm of your hand.

Cut a guide line

You can eliminate splintering when crosscutting (sawing wood across the grain) by marking the sawing line all the way around with a sharp trimming knife and straightedge. Make the saw cut on the waste side of the line.

Expertise with saws and planes

Support the offcut

As you approach the end of a saw cut, use your free hand to support the end of the wood. Otherwise, it will shear off under its own weight, leaving a ragged and splintered edge. Ask a helper to hold the end, or prop it on a surface, if it's longer or heavier than you can comfortably support by yourself.

Stay on the level

Use a set square to frequently check the squareness of the edge of a board while planing it. You can help to prevent your plane wobbling from side to side by wrapping your hand under the sole of the plane so that your fingertips rest against the side of the board.

Wax away the effort

Rub a candle over the sides of saws and the soles of planes. The wax reduces friction and makes sawing or planing easier, especially if you are working with a resinous timber.

Pointers to sawing

Hold the saw fairly upright to start a cut, pointing the index finger of the hand holding the saw down the blade to help you to keep it on the line. The first few strokes should be made by drawing the saw upwards, pressing your thumb against the side of the blade to steady it. Then cut on the forward stroke and slowly lower the angle of the saw.

techniques

347

techniques
Expertise with saws and planes

Cramp on a saw guide
If you are using a circular saw or jigsaw to make a cut parallel to the edge of a board, which is beyond the reach of the fence supplied with the tool, cramp a straight timber batten in position. Then slide the edge of the sole plate of the power tool along the batten while making the cut.

Wedge long cuts
When you are ripsawing (cutting a board in the same direction as the grain) by hand or with a power saw, tension in the timber can cause the kerf (saw cut) to close and jam the blade of the tool. To prevent this happening, wedge the kerf open by tapping a wooden wedge into it.

Soften the edges then finish with a smoother
Use a smoothing plane to remove the ridge marks left on wide boards by an electric planer, but round off the corners of the blade first or you will simply get a repeat of the problem with the hand tool. To do this, nip the corners of the plane blade under the lid of the oilstone box and stroke them against the edge of the stone once or twice. **Do not do this with the blades** of your electric planer, though; they won't be able to cut square rebates if you do.

Planing end grain
Use a block plane to trim end grain. To prevent the wood splintering on the corners, plane inwards from each corner, lifting the plane off the wood before it runs off the opposite edge.

Avoid surface marks
No matter how sharp a plane blade is, tricky grain will often tear up, marring the surface. The answer is to move the edge of the back iron as close as possible to the edge of the blade (1 mm or even less) so that very fine shavings are taken off.

Tackling hand-tool jobs with a power router

Keep within the lines

Cramp a pair of guide battens across the uprights when you are routing out housings for book shelves. Set the battens apart by a distance equal to the width of the router sole plate plus the housing you want to cut. Then carefully remove the waste by running the router across the workpiece—first against one batten, then against the other. On very wide grooves, finish off by using the router freehand to remove the central part of the waste area.

Don't try to plunge too deep in one go. Several shallow passes will give a more accurate cut and a finer finish than one deep one.

Work across the grain first

When you are cutting edge mouldings around a panel, make the cross-grain mouldings first. Then if the end grain does split at the end of each cut, the blemish will be removed along with the waste when the mouldings are cut along the grain.

Rapid way to cut mortises

Position the router fence close to the body of the router, and you will be able to cut mortises for locks and tenons in next to no time (right). Check your router's maximum plunge depth first.

techniques

fixings
Choosing the right nails and screws

A stock of nails

Make sure you have a supply of the four main nail types in your tool kit, each in a variety of lengths. All are sized in millimetres. You will then be able to cope with a wide range of different fixing jobs; oval wire nails are used for general joinery work; lost-head nails fix panelling to frames; round wire nails are used for rough assembly work; and masonry nails fix timber to masonry.

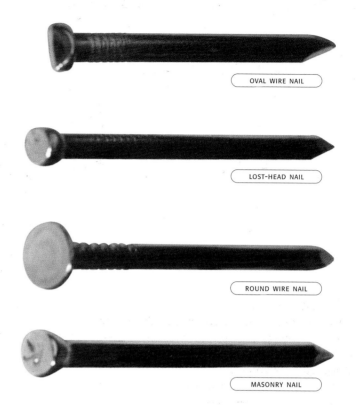

OVAL WIRE NAIL

LOST-HEAD NAIL

ROUND WIRE NAIL

MASONRY NAIL

Extra holding power

Annular (ring) nails have circular barbs around their shanks and are mainly used for nailing down chipboard flooring, which has to be securely fixed to every joist if it is not to squeak. They are driven in with a hammer and are very difficult to pull out.

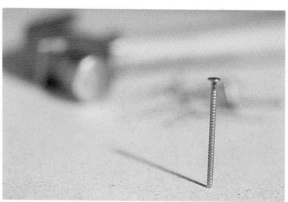

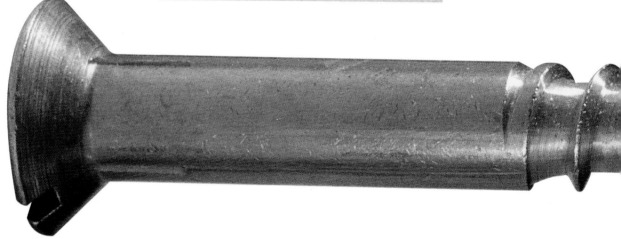

What size screw?

Screws are specified by two dimensions which are printed on the box or pack—the number or gauge (both terms are used) and the length.

The gauge, or number, is the diameter of the screw's shank, and is not a metric or imperial dimension. The higher the gauge, the bigger the screw.

The length of the screw is still usually given as an imperial measurement on boxes of screws manufactured in the UK. For example, the figures '10 x 2' on the label mean that the screws are gauge or No. 10 and are 2 inches (50 mm) long. Screws are also now being sold in a range of metric lengths.

Best choice for power screwdrivers

Cross-head screws are easier to drive than slotted-head types, especially with power screwdrivers. The tip of the screwdriver engages positively in the recess in the screw head, so there's little chance of the tool slipping and marking the work surface.

Use Pozidriv screwdrivers or bits for driving Pozidriv screws (the No. 1 driver or bit for screws up to gauge 4, the No. 2 up to gauge 10, and the No. 3 for 12 and 14 gauge screws).

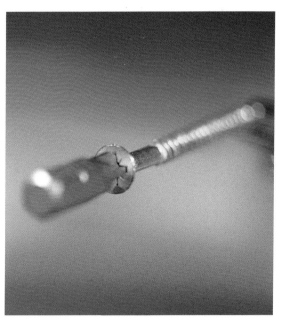

fixings

fixings
A better job with these workshop tips

Screw cups protect surfaces

Removable panels are often secured with screws.
If they're likely to be frequently removed and replaced,
fit matching screw cups under the screw heads to prevent
the surrounding wood being damaged by the screwdriver.
There are two types of screw cup. One rests on the
surface, so the screw head is raised. The other fits in a
countersunk hole, allowing the screw head to sit flush with
the surface. Both types are available in brass, steel and
bright chrome; choose whichever finish matches the screws
you are using.

Fixing into end grain

Reinforce screw fixings
made into weak end
grain by gluing a
length of dowel into a
transverse hole drilled
in the part that will
receive the screw.

Hide the evidence

Make a feature of concealed screw heads by plugging
the counterbored hole with a glued dowel and then
planing and sanding this flush with the surface once the
glue has dried.
If you prefer to disguise the fixings, use a plug cutter
with a power drill to make matching plugs from scrap
wood that resembles the colour and grain of the
workpiece more closely.

Drill clearance and pilot holes

When you're joining two pieces of wood, the
screw shank passes through a clearance hole
drilled in one piece, while its thread goes into
a smaller pilot hole drilled in the other. The
clearance hole must be big enough to prevent
the screw shank from binding, while the pilot
hole must allow the screw thread to bite into
and grip the wood.
For No. 6 screws, drill a 4 mm clearance hole
and a 1.5 mm pilot hole. For No. 8 screws, the
sizes are 4.5 mm and 2 mm; for No. 10 screws,
5 mm and 2 mm, and for No. 12 screws, 6 mm
and 2.5 mm. Increase pilot hole sizes by 0.5 mm
for screws being driven into hardwood. For very
small screws, make the pilot hole with a bradawl.

fixings
Precision application for sealants and adhesives

Keep nozzles clear
Wrap a piece of clingfilm round the end of the nozzle when you've finished using the cartridge. This will save you having to remove a hard plug of sealant from the nozzle before you can use it again. Alternatively, fit a spare uncut nozzle.

A neat finish
Cut the nozzle of a sealant cartridge at a diameter that will deliver a bead a little wider than the gap you are trying to fill. Make the cut at an angle of about 45°. Then cut off the seal on the end of the cartridge, screw on the nozzle and fit the cartridge in the gun.

Squeeze the trigger to start the sealant flow, and begin applying it at one end of the gap. To ensure a neat finish, keep the gun moving steadily as the sealant is extruded. Stop the flow by releasing the locking bar on the piston.

Making a perfect seal
Cartridge sealants come in several varieties; make the right selection for each job.

Frame sealants are used outdoors to fill gaps between frames and the surrounding masonry.

Silicone sealants are mainly used in bathrooms and kitchens to seal the join between the edges of fittings and worktops and walls.

Roof and gutter sealant is a rubberised bitumen specially formulated for repairing gutters, downpipes, flat roofs and flashings.

Decorator's sealant is a gap filler used indoors round doors, windows and ceilings, and along skirting boards.

Instant fixing in a tube
Cartridge adhesives are excellent for sticking mouldings to walls and panels to frames. Simply apply them like a ribbon of toothpaste to the back of whatever you're fixing, and press the item in place. They grab instantly and stick very firmly.

Warm up your tubes
In cold weather dunk a cartridge of sealant or adhesive in a bucket of warm water for half an hour before using it. The heat will make the product much easier to apply smoothly.

fixings
Alternatives to using screws and nails

Light but strong
Use corrugated metal fasteners (above) to secure butt joints in light frameworks. They make a stronger joint than nails with less risk of splitting the wood.

Metal dowels for strength
Reinforce a mortise and tenon joint and peg the tenon in place by driving a metal star dowel through the joint–they are stronger than traditional wood dowels. Take care to strike the dowel squarely with the hammer and to drive it in at 90° to the surface, because the dowels are brittle and break easily.

Teeth for extra bite
Toothed connectors (above) are used in various ways to join timber. If you want to extend one piece of wood by bolting another piece alongside it, for example, sandwich double-sided galvanised connectors between the two pieces. As the nut is tightened on the bolt, the teeth on the connector bite into the wood and lock the two pieces together.

Picking the right plug for wall fixings

Size matters for a firm hold
It is important to drill the right size of hole for a plastic wall plug. If it's too small the plug won't fit; too large, and the plug won't grip. Moulded plugs on plastic 'trees' have the drill size stamped on the tree; loose plugs have it printed on the packet. Some manufacturers make different-size plugs in different colours for instant recognition. This is fine so long as you use the same brand of plug all the time, but beware–colours are not standard across different brands.

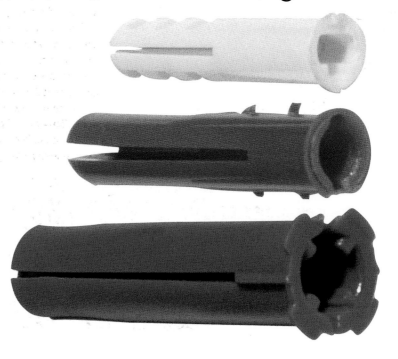

Gripping in plasterboard

If you want to fix something fairly light in weight directly to plasterboard, you can use a plug that's screwed into a pilot hole. The plug has a coarse thread which bites into the core of the board, and is made in metal or plastic.

For heavier-duty fixings, choose a plug with flanges which open out and press against the inner face of the board once they have been inserted through a clearance hole. Use extra fixings if you want to increase their holding power.

The strongest choice

Spring toggles are the strongest type of fixing you can use in plasterboard. The metal arms flip open after the toggle is pushed through a hole in the board. With this version, the toggle is lost if the screw is removed, but some designs have a toggle that remains captive when items are taken down.

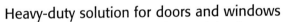

Heavy-duty solution for doors and windows

Use frame fixings to attach a new door or window frame to the masonry, or to secure a loose one. The plain sleeve of the fixing passes through the side of the frame and into the wall behind it.

With the frame in position, use a twist drill to make the clearance hole in the wood. Then replace it with a masonry drill bit of the same size: switch to hammer action, and insert it through the hole in the frame to make the hole in the masonry. Countersink the frame to suit the head of the fixing. Push the fixing in fully, then tighten the screw to expand the fixing and secure the frame. Finally, fill over the countersunk fixing.

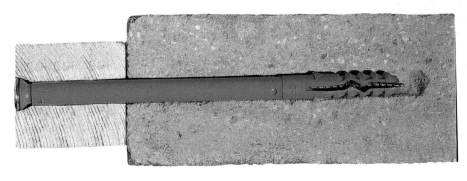

maintenance
Looking after tools

Look for a line of oil

If you don't have a honing guide to help you to keep
the blade that you're sharpening at the correct angle to the
oilstone, pour on some oil and place the honed edge on
the stone with the blade at an angle of about 45° to it.
Reduce the blade angle gradually until a fine line of oil can
just be seen welling up along the honed edge of the blade.
Try to hold that angle as closely as you can while you move
the blade up and down the stone to sharpen it.

Off with the burr

The action of honing a chisel or plane blade on an oilstone
produces a thin burr of metal on the back of the blade.
You can feel it if you run your thumb down the blade and off
the edge. Take this burr off by holding the blade absolutely
flat on the stone, bevel side up. Then rub it along the stone
just once. Keep the blade perfectly flat as you do this.
Remove the machine marks on the back of a new blade
by working it flat on the stone, moving it back and forth until
the back is mirror smooth. You won't be able to get a really
sharp edge until you've done this.

Get a better grip

Tap a few panel pins into the bottom of an oilstone box,
making sure they don't penetrate the stone compartment.
Nip off the heads with pincers to leave the ends slightly
protruding. These will grip any surface and stop the box
sliding about when you're using the stone.

One bevel is enough

Many books say that chisel and plane blades (right) should
have two bevels–a machine-made ground one,
and a steeper one honed on the oilstone.
In fact, it's easier to keep the broad
ground bevel flat on the stone and to
hone that bevel instead. If you use
an oilstone only occasionally, a
honing guide (below) makes it
easy to maintain the correct angle.

Different grades

Buy a carborundum (silicon carbide) combination oilstone for
good all-round performance. It has coarse or medium grit on
one side and fine grit on the other. The coarse face removes
metal quickly and sharpens tools such as shears, while the
fine face puts a cutting edge on chisel and plane blades.
The standard size for an oilstone is 200 x 50 x 25 mm,
but smaller sizes are also available. Buy or make a wooden
box to store the stone.

Finish with a strop

Give a sharpened blade the final touch by stropping it on a
piece of leather glued to a softwood offcut (below).
Draw the blade bevel side down across the leather, then turn
it over, lay it flat and rub it back and forth a couple of times.
Don't be tempted to use the palm of your hand as a strop;
you risk cutting yourself.

The right kind of oil

Never use vegetable oil on an oilstone to sharpen tool blades. The mixture of oil and ground-off metal particles will gum up the stone and create a slippery surface glaze so that the stone is no longer abrasive. **Use a light machine oil** which will float away the tiny particles produced during sharpening. Then rub some sawdust from a non-resinous wood across the stone to completely clean it when you have finished using it. If an oilstone is clogged with oil, soak it overnight in a tin of paraffin or petrol.

Improvise an oilstone

If you're working away from your bench and don't have an oilstone, make one by sticking a piece of fine silicon carbide paper to a wood offcut.

Restoring a plane

An old neglected wooden plane with cracks in its body can often be restored to make an excellent tool. The blade is usually made of top-quality steel and a wooden sole slides more easily than a metal one over wood. Stop up the throat with putty, then pour linseed oil into it. Over the space of a few days the trapped oil will soak through the wood and the cracks will close up.

Sharp investment

Buy a sharpener for restoring the edge to twist-drill bits (above). You will soon recoup the expense in the money you will save by not having to replace blunt bits. Most are powered by an electric drill. **Store drill bits upright** in a block of wood to prevent them from being damaged. For a perfect fit, drill each hole with the bit to be kept in it.

Testing a honed edge

Hold a chisel or plane blade against the light when you think it is sharp. A really keen edge won't reflect the light, but if you see a fine white line of reflected light, the blade needs more work to bring it to a really sharp edge.

Test the blade by stroking it across the edge of a sheet of paper. If the paper slices easily, the blade is ready to use.

Store tools safely

Keep drill bits, saw blades, rotary files and other cutting attachments sharp, by removing them from the tool and storing them in suitable containers when you've finished using them. Alternatively, make sure that they are out of harm's way before setting the tool down; raise the blades of a power planer and the cutter of a router.

index

Main entries in the index are shown in **bold** *type*

a

abrasives 229, 346
  see also sanders, sanding
adhesives
  cartridge 353
  felt 42
  flooring 68
  PVA 40, 54
  safety 68
  tiling 226, 230, 231
  wallpaper 238, 239, 240, 242
aerials
  FM radio 205
  television 205
airbricks 17
alcoves, shelving 248
angle grinders 67, 334
appliance servicing 29
architraves
  doors and windows 85, 88, 89, 257
  mouldings 85
asbestos 294

b

balusters, balustrades 84
basins
  fitting 139, 141
  inset 139
  overflows 134, 135
  pedestal 141
  tap holes 141
  taps 130
bathrooms
  condensation 20
  grab handles 27
  mirrors 254
  painting 26, 217
  safety 27
  showers *see* main entry
  storage 250
  tiling 233
  toilets 145-7
baths 142-4
  boxing in 143
  cast-iron 140, 144
  enamelled 144
  installing 142-3
  limescale 144
  overflows 134, 135, 142
  paint touch-up kits 144
  plastic 142, 144
  removing 140
  restoring 144
  rust spots 144
  scratches and chips 144
  sealing 142, 143, 144
  steel 144
  storage 250
  surface damage 144
  taps 130, 131, 142
bedroom storage 250, 251
blinds 257
blockwork 309, 317, 318
boilers 154-6
  back boilers 154
  blocked gas jets 156
  Building Regulations 154
  combination 154
  condensing 154
  cut-outs 156
  fan-assisted 155
  flues 154
  gas 154, 156
  ignition 154, 155
  limescale 154, 168
  noisy 168
  oil-fired 154
  overheating 156
  pilot lights 154, 156
  safety 156
  sealed systems 156
  stuck switch 155
  thermocouples 155, 156
  thermostats 155, 168
  traditional 154
  water pressure 156
bolts
  cockspur 101
  hinge 103
  rack 101, 103
bookcases 28, 266
bradawls 17, 20, 328
brass furniture fittings 272
  artificial ageing 273
  lacquered 273
  tarnish 272
brickwork 47-49
  bonds 13
  bulging 16
  cavity walls 13
  cleaning 47
  efflorescence 47
  frogs 308
  frost damage 47
  garden walls 307-9
  header bricks 13
  painting 214
  pointing 6, 48-49
  sandblasting 47
  solid walls 13
  steps 313
  stretchers 13
Building Regulations
  boilers 154
  floors 14
  loft insulation 170
  safety glass 105
bulk buying 340

c

cable and pipe detectors 58, 73, 195, 246, 301
cables 183-5
  ceilings, above 184
  chasing in 184, 187
  clips 184
  coaxial cable 205
  concealing 184, 195
  cores 183, 192
  detectors 58, 73, 195, 246, 301
  earthing 186, 188
  gardens, in 297
  insulation 186, 190
  kinks 183
  mounting boxes 184
  outdoor 201, 202, 203
  PVC-sheathed 202
  safety 183, 186
  sizes 183
  spur 195, 196, 197
  stud walls, in 75, 184
  surface-mounted 184, 204
  telephones 204
  on tiling 184
  trunking 184
  underfloor 58, 185
  walls, in 184
car body filler 265
carborundum 356
carpet, paint spills on 222
castors 28
ceilings
  cables above 184
  curtain tracks 257
  false ceiling 71
  joists 74
  light fittings 194
  painting 220
  plasterboard 76
  plastering 71, 72
  polystyrene ceiling tiles 217
  wallpapering 242-3
central heating
  boilers *see* main entry
  condensation 19
  controls 163-5
    flat battery 163
    motorised valves 163
    programmer problems 164
    thermostats 164-5
    updating the programmer 165
    valve problems 163
  draincocks 119
  draining 119, 160
  noises 168
  open system 120, 160
  overheating 168
  pipes *see* main entry
  pump failure 158
  pump speed 168
  radiators *see* main entry
  re-filling 160
  safety 120
  sealed systems 156, 160
chimneys 16
  bulging 16
  capping 35
  damaged chimney stack 16, 35
  flashings 19, 35
  flaunching 16, 35
  flues 16, 35
  pointing 16, 35
  pots 16, 35
  stacks 16, 35
chisels 334
  bevelled-edge 334, 356
  blades 356
  cold 334
  handles 334
  honing 356, 357
circles 344
circuits *see under* electricity
cladding 53-55
  exterior 53-55
  fixing 53-55
  moisture barriers 53
  replacing 54
  splits 54
  warped and bulging boards 53
concrete
  concrete breaker 65
  drives 316, 317
  floors 14, 26, 64-65
  garage floors 294
  garden walls 309
  lintels 256
  paths 310, 311
  pipework in 14
  ponds 319
  roof tiles 12, 35

steps 315
condensation 19, 20, 25
  anti-condensation paint 26
  anti-condensation
    plaster 26
  kitchens 20, 25
  lofts 17, 170
conservatories
  glazing 105, 106
  roofing 106
continuity testers 178, 179
cork tiles 66
cornicing, timber 88
corrosion
  inhibitors 158, 160, 168
  metal gates 305
  radiators 158, 160
corrugated plastic roof 43
cracks *see* subsidence
cramps
  floor 63
  G-cramps 103, 230, 276,
    331, 346
  sash cramps 331, 346
crawl boards 35, 36
curtains 255-6
  automatic closing 256
  bay windows 257
  brackets 255, 256
  cord pulls 255
  hanging 256
  tracks 255, 256, 257
  valances and pelmets 257
  weight 255

d

dado rails 85, 86
damp 18-20
  anti-condensation paint 26
  causes 18-20
  combating 26
  condensation 17, 19, 20,
    25, 170
  damp-proof course (DPC)
    17, 18, 20, 25, 26, 316
  damp-proof membrane
    (DPM) 14, 26
  damp-proof plaster 26
  doors 92
  floors 14, 26, 64
    concrete 14, 26, 64
    suspended 17, 58, 59
  foil test 19
  lofts 17, 19
  rising damp 17, 20, 64
  walls 17, 18
  wet rot 17, 20, 113,
    114, 115

windows 92
Danish oil 213
decorating 208-57
  painting 214-25
  preparation 208-10
  sanding floors 211-13
  tiling 226-34
  wallpapering 235-43
dehumidifiers 25
design tricks 22
diagonals, measuring 345
digital tape measures 331
dishwashers 151, 152, 153
display units 28
doors
  architraves 88, 89
  binding 95
  cupboards 274
  dismantling 94
  door chains 99
  door trimmer 93
  door viewers 99
  double ball catches 274
  drilling 100, 102-3
  exterior, painting 216
  fitting 93
  frame fixings 355
  garage 294
  glass
    obscured 104
    safety 105
  hardware 95-103
  hinges
    fitting 97
    handed hinges 95
    hinge bolts 103
    loose and seized
      screws 96
    packing out 96
    parliament hinges 96
    problems 95-97, 274
    rising butts 94, 95
    security hinges 103
    third hinges 96
  jammed 17, 92-93
  locks 95, 98-100,
    101, 103
    5-lever locks 98
    cylinder nightlatch
      98, 99, 101
    mortise 98, 100, 101
    padlocks 292
    rack bolts 103
    reinforcing 99
    sashlocks 99
  loose joints 94
  magnetic catches 274
  painting 221
  patio doors 27, 103
  rack bolts 103
  rot 17, 92, 115
  sliding doors 250

split frames 97
  stud walls, in 73
  viewers 99
  warped 339
dowel joints 94, 95, 266,
  267
downpipes
  blockages 16, 44
  mesh excluders 44
  painting 216
  plastic 216
  water butts 293
drains
  blocked 137
  inspection chambers
    16, 317
  removing drain cover 138
  rods 138
draught-proofing 20, 25
drilling, drills 328, 341-3
  adaptors 328
  bits
    auger 343
    countersink 342
    flat wood 342
    lubrication 343
    masonry 341
    overheating 343
    safety 357
    sharpening 357
    storage 357
    twist 341
  chucks 343
  clearance holes 352
  corrugated plastic 43
  cramps, using 341, 342
  doors 100, 102-3
  flexible drive shaft 343
  hand braces 342
  hole positions 341, 342
  mirrors 254
  plastic wall plugs 354
  power 343
  right angles to surface 341
  right-angled drill 338
  safety 341
  slates 40
  splinters 342
  spring-loaded collar 343
  stud walls 73, 75
  tiles 231
drives 316-18
  blockwork 317, 318
  cleaning 316
  concrete 316, 317
  DPCs and 316
  drainage 316
  gravel 318
  inspection chambers 317
  oil spots 317
  patching 317
  planning permission 316

sub-bases 316
  tarmac 317
  width 316
dry rot
  floors 17
  lofts 17
  windows 113

ear defenders 28, 211
earth bonding wires 139
earthing 29, 120, 124,
  139, 180, 183, 186,
  188, 191, 198
efflorescence 47, 309
electrics 174-205
  adaptors 190
  aerials 205
  appliance servicing 29
  cables *see* main entry
  circuits 188
    lighting circuits 175,
      176, 192-3, 198
    miniature circuit
      breakers (MCBs)
      174, 175, 176,
      177, 178, 188
    radial power 188
    residual current device
      (RCD) 175, 178,
      299
    ring 188, 191
    sockets 176
    spurs 191
    telephone 204
  continuity testers 178, 179
  earthing 29, 120, 124,
    139, 180, 183, 186,
    188, 191, 198
  emergencies 177
  extension leads 182
  faultfinding 177-9
  flexes *see* main entry
  fuses *see* main entry
  lighting, lights *see* main
    entry
  plugs 176
    fuses 176, 177, 182
    moulded on 180
  power failure 178
  programmers 164
  safety 29, 124, 175,
    186, 202
  shocks 175, 204
  sockets *see* main entry
  switches *see* main entry
  systems 174-7
  telephones 204

index

televisions 205
voltage testers 179
Wiring Regulations 191
equipment
choosing 327-40
hiring 327, 338
lifting 340
maintenance 356-7
safety 327
secondhand 327
see also tools
estimators 331
extractor fans 25

f

fences 16, 301-3, 306
on concrete 302
creosoting 306
movable 302
panels 301
posts
capping 306
concreting 302
holes 302, 303
levelling 301
metal 303
post drivers 302
post spikes 303
reinforcing 303
removing 301
services, avoiding 301
on slopes 301
wood preservatives 306
fire safety 27, 213
fire blankets 27
flammable materials 27
smoke detectors 27
first-aid kit 28
fittings
curtains and blinds 255-7
mirrors 254
pictures 252-3
shelving 246-8
storage 249-51
flashings
chimneys 35
flashing tape 36, 40
roofs 35, 42, 43
flat roofs 41-42
access to 41
blisters 42
'cold' roof 42
felt 41
insulation 42
lead flashings 42
loose seams 42
metal roofs 42
repair kit 41
safety 41

solar-reflective coating 41
splits, taping over 41
stone chippings 41, 42
'warm' roof 42
waterproofing 41
flaunching 16, 35
flexes 180-2
coiled 29
connectors 182, 203
cord grips 182
cores 180, 181, 182
extension leads 182
heat resistant 181
insulation 182
non-kink 181
PVC-sheathed 181
replacing 180, 181
safety 180
sizes 180
stripping 181, 182
floor coverings 66-69
adhesives 68
carpets 222
ceramic tiles 62, 65
cork tiles 66
cutting 67
damaged 67
hardboard 63, 65
joins 67
laying 65, 67-69
lino 67
parquet 68
pipes, around 68
plywood 65
quarry tiles 65, 67, 68
safety 68
sealing 68, 69
slip-resistant 27
terracotta tiles 68
vinyl 65, 66-69
wood strip 68, 69
floor cramps 63
floorboards
ceilings and 63
cramping 63
cutting 61
gaps between 60
hollows 212
knot holes 59
laying 62-63
lifting 61
oiling 213
replacement 212
reversing 212
sanding 211-13
sealing 213
secondhand 212
secret-nailing 63
square-edged 14, 61
squeaking 60
tiling 65
tongue-and-groove

(t & g) 61, 63
varnishing 213
floors 58-69
Building Regulations 14
concrete 14, 64-65
coverings 64-65
damp 14, 26, 64
garage 294
levelling 64
self-levelling
compound 26
cramps 63
garage 294
ground floors 14
painting 221, 294
suspended
access 14, 58
airbricks 17
crawl space 58
damp 17, 58, 59
hardboarding 63
insulation 59
joists 14, 23, 58, 59, 74
rot 14, 17, 59
sagging 59
skirting boards 85
tiling 62
underfloor services
58, 185
ventilation 17, 58
woodworm 19
underfloor draughts 14
flues
balanced 154
capping 35
lining 16
freeze-ups 133, 135
french polish 260, 262,
287-9
brushes 289
carvings and mouldings
288
cloudy 288
colours 287
gloss 287, 289
heat damage 260
holes 263
identifying 260
restoring 289
ring stains 260
rubbers 288-9
satin 287, 289
scratches 262
temperature 288
fungicides
paint 217
tiles 233
wallpaper paste 238
furniture 260-89
blemishes 260-2
burns 260, 262
castor cups 28

catches 274
cleaning 260
cupboards
hinges 274
locks 273, 274
shelving 247
ventilation 19, 20
woodworm 19
dents 261
finishes 278-89
air bubbles 279
applying 278, 279, 280
coloured 280, 281,
283, 284-5, 286
dyes 284-5, 286
french polish 260,
262, 287-9
identifying 260
lacquer 260, 261,
278, 279, 280
limed 283
oil 260, 281
stains 260, 261, 284-5
varnish 260, 261,
278, 279, 280
veneers 275-7
wax 260, 282-3
flatpack 250
garden 281
handles 274
heat damage 260
hinges 274
holes, cracks and gouges
264-5
ink blots 261
joints 266, 267
locks 273, 274
metal fittings 272-4
mouldings 271, 283, 288
repairs 263-8
chairs 268
chests of drawers 267
hot wax treatment 263
inserts 265
joints 266, 267
patching 265
reassembly 267-8
resin reinforcement 264
safety 264, 266
shellac 263
split panels 267
tables 267
wood fillers/stoppers
263, 264, 265, 275
ring stains 260
safety 260, 264, 266,
269, 270, 281, 288
scratches 262
sealing 282
stains 260, 261, 269
stripping 269-71
brushes 271

caustic dips 269
chemical strippers 269, 271
gel strippers 269
mouldings 271
newspaper poultice 271
scourers 269
solvent-based strippers 271
woodworm 263, 264, 279

fuses
blown 175, 176, 177, 178
circuit fuses 175, 176, 177, 179
consumer units 174, 175
fuse boards 174
fuse boxes 174
miniature circuit breakers (MCBs) 174, 175, 176, 177, 178, 188
plug fuses 176, 177
ratings 178
rewirable 176, 177
safety 175
wire 16

g

G-cramps 103, 230, 276, 331, 346
garages 294
asbestos 294
concrete floors 294
integral 23
security 294
up-and-over doors 294
gardens 292-323
cables
buried 202
lighting 201
overhead 202
drains 16, 137, 138
drives 316-18
electricity 201, 202, 297
fences see main entry
fountains 320
furniture 281
garages 294
gates 304-5
greenhouses 293
gullies 138
lawnmowers 298-300
lighting 201-3
paths 310-12
ponds 319-23
power tools 175, 203, 297
rainwater butts 46, 293
safety 306

security 292, 294, 295, 305
sheds 292
steps 313-15
tools 295-7
broken handles 295
cleaning 297
cultivators 297
hedge-trimmers 297
power tools 297
rakes 296
safety 297
security 295
shears 295
spades 295, 296
walls 307-9
blockwork 309
brick 307-8
concrete 309
coping 307
efflorescence 309
footings 307
height 308
mortar 307, 308
retaining walls and planters 307, 309
on slopes 307
stone 309
waterfalls 320, 322
gas
appliance servicing 29, 120, 156
boilers 154, 156
carbon monoxide alarms 120
CORGI 120, 156
pilot lights 154, 156
safety 120, 156
stoptap 16
gates 304-5
corrosion 305
cross-braced 304
hanging 305
metal 305
pairs 304
posts 304
security 305
self-closing 304
wooden 304, 305
glass, glazing 23, 33, 104-9
cleaning 107
cutting glass 106-7
double glazing 106
glazing beads 109
glazing sprigs 108, 109
laminated glass 27
measuring 106
mirrors 254
obscured 104
puttying 108, 109
replacing 109
safety 105, 107

secondary glazing 106
shelves 247
solar-control 105
toughened 27, 104
wired 104
glues see adhesives
goggles 88, 104, 178, 221, 264, 336
greenhouses
cleaning 293
safety 293
gullies, blocked 138
gutters 44-46
blockages 16, 44
brackets 44, 45
cast-iron 45
dislocated joints 46
diverter kits 46
downpipes 16, 44, 216
gutter rake 44
gutter scoop 44
installing 46
leafguards 44
metal 216
painting 216
plastic 32, 45, 46, 216
rubber seals 46
safety 45
sealing 45

h

hammers
claw 329, 341
club 329
pin 329
hand braces 342
handrails 27, 83
hardboard 63, 65
hinges
doors 95-96
fitting 97
furniture 274
handed hinges 95
hinge bolts 103
loose and seized screws 96
packing out 96
parliament hinges 96
problems 95-97, 274
rising butts 94, 95
screw holes 96
security hinges 103
windows 95
honing guide 356
hosepipes 132
hot water cylinder 118
thermostat 120, 165
humidity 25
hygrometers 64

i

immersion heaters 120, 181
insulation 169-71
Building Regulations 170
cables 186, 190
cladding 55
cold water tanks 171
double glazing 106
flat roofs 42
flexes 182
floors 59
foam 59, 169
glass fibre 170
hair felt 169
lofts 170-1
pipes 169, 170
plasterboard 80
roofs 12, 170-1
safety 170
sheds 292
sound insulation 74, 106
stud walls 74
vermiculite granules 171
windows 106

j

joints
butt 354
doors 94
dowel 94, 95, 266, 354
loose furniture joints 266, 267
mortise-and-tenon 95, 266, 349
windows 94
joists
ceilings 74
finding 74
floors 58, 59, 74
rot 17

k

keys, furniture 273
kitchens
breakfast bars 250
carousels 249
condensation 20, 25
painting 26, 217
peninsula units 250
plinths 249
sinks 136-7, 139, 141

index

storage 249
tiling 233
worktops 226, 231, 233, 281
knee pads 36, 212

l

lacquer, lacquering 213, 260, 261, 278, 279, 280
brass 273
brushes 278, 279, 280
cellulose 260, 278, 280
cold-cure (two-part) 213, 261, 278, 280
fittings 279
safety 260
storage 279
ladders 32-34
aluminium 34
climbing 32
extension ladders 33
platforms 34, 37
raising 33
roof ladders 35, 36
safety 32-34
securing 33, 34
stabilisers 37
stand-offs 32, 44
stepladders 34
tools, carrying 34
wooden 34
laser levels 331
lath-and-plaster 70, 71, 72
lawnmowers 298-300
air filters 299
cordless 298
cylinder mowers 300
electric 298, 299
hover mowers 299
maintenance 300
motor mowers 299, 300
rotary blades 300
safety 298, 299
lead
paint 210, 269
pipes 119, 121
safety 210
leafguards 44
levels 301, 330, 331
lifting, lifting equipment 340
lighting, lights 192-203
bulbs
halogen 200
smashed 178
spotlights 200
wattage 178
ceilings 194

pendants 194
recessed 199, 200
roses 186, 192, 193, 194, 199
circuits 175, 176, 192-3, 198
extending 192-3
overloading 195, 198
residual current device (RCD) 202
spurs 192, 193
conduit boxes 193, 194
decorating and 209
earthing 198
gardens 201-3
controls 201
fitting 203
floodlights 201
low-voltage 202
mains 202
passive infra-red (PIR) detector 201
ponds 320
positioning 201
waterproof connections 203
wiring 202
luminaire support couplers (LSCs) 194, 195
portable work lights 209
spotlights 200
strip connectors 194
switches *see* main entry
track 198-9
circuits 198
couplers 198
earthing 198
fitting 198-9
low-voltage 198, 200
mains-powered 199
tube 200
wall 195-7
conduit boxes 197
decorating and 195
height 196
putting up 197
replacement 196
wiring 195, 196, 197
wallpapering and 243
limescale
baths 144
boilers 154, 168
inhibitors 154
removers 144
showers 150
taps 128
toilets 147
valves 133
liming 283
lino 67
linseed oil 108, 213, 278, 281

living room storage 250
locks 95, 98-100, 101, 103
5-lever locks 98
bolts, locking 103
casement stays 102
cylinder nightlatch 98, 99, 101
doors 95, 98-100, 101, 103
fire safety 27
furniture 273, 274
lubricating 274
mortise 98, 100, 101
old cabinet locks 273
padlocks 292
push-button 102
rack bolts 101, 103
reinforcing 99
sashlocks 99
windows 101, 102
lofts 12, 17
condensation 19, 170
conversion 23
damp 17, 19
dry rot 17
hatches 170
inspecting 17
insulation 170-1, 184, 200
roof timbers 17
tanks *see* water tanks
ventilation 17, 170
woodworm 17

m

masks 21, 28, 221, 336
mastic
bituminous 41, 42
roofing 42
mats and rugs 27, 28
measuring
circles 344
diagonals 345
digital tape measures 331
laser levels 331
marking 344
metrication 344
pencils 344
spirit levels 301, 330
ultrasonic estimator 21, 331
medium density fibreboard (MDF) 85, 336
metal dowels 354
metal fasteners 354
metric measurements 344
mirrors 22, 254
drilling 254
fixing 254

mirror clips 254
mirror tiles 254
mitre box 87, 121
mitred angles 86, 87, 332
moisture meters 58
mould
cupboards 20
fungicides 217, 233, 238
grout 233, 234
paintwork 217
tiles 233, 234
wallpaper 238
mouldings 85-89
corners 86-87
cross-grain mouldings 349
fixing 88
furniture 271, 283, 288
joins 87
MDF 85
mitred angles 86, 87
plaster 86
routers 335, 349
wooden 210
multimeters 178

n

nail punch 330, 342
nails
annular (ring) 350
floor brads 62
lost-head 350
masonry 72, 88, 350
plasterboard 78
removing 341
round-head 341, 342
wire 350
noggings 73, 74, 184

o

oil finishes 260, 281
oil-fired boilers 154
oilstone box 348, 356
oilstones 356, 357
overflows 133, 134-5
basins and sinks 134, 135
baths 134, 135, 142
gutters and downpipes 16
overflow pipes 133, 134, 141
ponds 323

p

paint, painting 214-25
  anti-condensation paint 26
  bathrooms 217
  brickwork 214
  bristles, loose 222
  brushes 215, 218, 223, 224
  ceilings 220
  colours 216, 221
  disposal 224
  doors 221
  downpipes 216
  eggshell 217
  equipment, care of 223, 224
  feathering 216
  filtering 225
  flaws 222
  floors 221, 294
  fungicidal 217
  gloss 215, 217
  grit and dust 215, 216, 221, 225
  gutters 216
  insects in 222
  kitchens 217
  lead paint 210, 269
  leftover paint 224, 225
  matt 217
  microporous 215
  outdoor 214-15
  pads 219
  paint kettles 216, 224
  pipes 216
  plaster 208
  power rollers 219
  preparation 208
  primers 217
  protective clothing 220, 221
  radiators 217, 218
  rollers 214, 218, 219, 223, 224
  rubbing down 208
  safety 210, 217, 220, 221
  sags and runs 222
  skin formation 224
  solvent-based 217, 220, 224
  spills 222
  splashes 220
  spray painting 219, 221, 223
  stains, obliterating 217
  staircases 221
  storage 225
  stripper, stripping 210, 222
  textured finishes 218
  top coats 217
  undercoats 217
  volatile organic compounds (VOCs) 217
  wallpaper, over 209
  walls 220
  water-based 217, 224, 225
  white spirit 223, 224, 225
  windows 33, 215, 221
    removing from 222
  woodwork, exterior 215, 216
panel lifters 77
parquet flooring 68
paths 310-12
  block paving 311, 312
  concrete 310, 311
  crazy paving 311, 312
  lawns and 311
  lighting 16, 27
  tarmac 311
  weeds 311
  width 310
patio doors 27, 103
pattresses 190
paving see paths
pebbledash 52
pencils 230, 344
  carpenter's pencil 344
picture rails 85, 86
pictures 252-3
  frames 253, 345
  grouping 252
  hanging
    battens 253
    cord 253
  heavy pictures 253
  hooks 252
  mounting 252, 253
  picture rails 252
  wire 252
pin push 329
pincers 341
pipes
  airlocks 166
  bending 122
  blockages 136-8
  burst 126
  capillary fittings 123
  central-heating 166
  compression fittings 122, 123, 125, 126, 142
  in concrete floors 14
  connecting see joining, joints (below)
  copper 122, 123, 166, 167, 217
  cutting 121
  draining 119, 160
  earthing 120, 124
  flooring around 68
  flushing out 160
  gatevalves 118, 119
  hot-water 166
  insulation 169, 170
  joining, joints 122-5
  lead 119, 121
  leaks 20, 126
  locating 58, 73, 195, 246, 301
  nails in 126
  noisy 166-7, 168
  overflows 16, 133, 134-5
  painting 216
  pipe clamps 126
  pipe-freezing kit 126
  plastic 121, 122, 124, 125
  push-fit joints 122, 125
  shut-off valves 119, 131
  solvent welding 125, 126
  steel 121
  stud walls, in 75
  tilework, in 231
  underfloor 14
  waste pipes 75, 121, 136-7, 152
  water hammer 166
  water pressure 130, 131
planes, planing 337
  bevels 356
  blades 348
  block plane 348
  end grain 348
  guards 337
  honing 356, 357
  planed all round (PAR) 340
  restoring an old plane 357
  safety 357
  smoothing plane 348
  soles 347, 357
  squareness 347
  surface marks 348
  waxing 347
  wooden 357
planning permission
  drives 316
plans 21-3
plaster, plastering 70-72
  anti-condensation plaster 26
  bulging 72
  ceilings 71, 72
  corners 72
  damp-proof plaster 26
  lath-and-plaster 70, 71, 72
  mixing 70, 71
  mouldings 86
  painting 208
  patching 70, 71, 72
  replastering 25, 26
  tiling over 226
  walls 71-72
plasterboard 76-81
  bonding compound 80
  ceilings 76
  corners 79-80
  cutting 77
  edges 80
  filler 79, 80, 81
  fixings 355
  foil-backed boards 76
  frame fixings 81
  handling 76-78
  horizontal fixing 78
  insulation 80
  joints 79-80
  nailing 78
  panel lifters 77
  plasterboard lath 76
  rocking wedges 78
  sealing 79
  sizes 76
  solid walls 80-81
  spring toggles 355
  standard 76
  stud walls 70, 73, 75, 76
  tiling 226
pliers 107, 331
plugs 176, 180, 182
  plug pins 29, 190
plumbing 118-71
  appliances 151-3
  baths see main entry
  blockages 136-8
  boilers see main entry
  draincocks 119
  fittings 139-41
  leaks 20
  noises 166-7, 168
  overflows 16, 133, 134-5
  pipes see main entry
  radiators see main entry
  showers see main entry
  stoptaps 118
  systems 118-20
  taps see main entry
  toilets see main entry
  underfloor, accessing 14
  valves see main entry
plungers 136
plywood 65, 226
pointing 48-49
polycarbonate sheeting 106
ponds 319-23
  concrete 319
  digging 321
  fish 320, 321
  fountains 320
  leaks 323
  lighting 320
  liners 319, 321, 322, 323
  overflows 323

plants 320, 321, 322
pumps 320
safety 321
shapes 319
siting 319
waterfalls 320, 322
wildlife 321
post-hole borers 303
power tools 180, 327, 333, 343, 346
  cordless 32
  garden tools 175, 203, 297
  safety 28
profile gauge 88
putty, puttying 45, 108, 109

q & r

quarry tiles 65, 67, 68
radiators 157-62
  bleeding 158, 159, 168
  blocked air vents 159
  cold 157, 158
  convector 161
  corrosion inhibitor 158
  draining 160
  enamelling 217
  flushing 160
  leaks 157
  noisy 168
  painting 217, 218
  papering behind 241
  positioning 21
  refilling 160
  removing 159
  replacing 160-1
  sludge 158
    valves
      Belmont 157
      fitting 161, 162
      handwheel 157, 162
      jammed 157
      leaking 157, 158
      lockshield 162
      removing 162
      thermostatic radiator
    valves (TRVs) 157, 162, 165
radio aerials 205
rainwater butts 46
rendering 50-52
  DPC 20
  external corners 51
  hairline cracks 50
  patching 50-52
  pebbledash 52
  reinforcing 50

respirators 47, 211, 260
ridge hooks 36
roofs 35-43
  access towers 37
  asbestos 294
  boarded 12
  conservatories 106
  corrugated plastic 43
  crawl boards 35, 36
  felt roofs 41-42
  flashings 35, 42, 43
  flat roofs *see* main entry
  inspecting 35
  insulation 12, 170-1
  ladders 35, 36
  leaks 19
  metal roofs 42
  rafters 12
  safety gear 36
  scaffolding 24
  sheds 292
  slates
    damaged 38-39
    replacing 38-40
    sealing cracked
      slates 40
    secondhand 36
    slipping 35
  surveying 16
  tiles
    clay 12
    concrete 12, 35
    damaged 35, 38-39
    removing 39
    replacing 38-40
    ridge and hip tiles 35, 40
  timbers 12, 17, 19
  traditional timber roof 12
  trusses 12, 23
  valleys 36
  verges 36
  waterproofing 41
  see also chimneys;
    gutters; lofts
rot *see* dry rot; wet rot
routers 335, 349
  tungsten-carbide tipped
    335

s

safety
  accident black spots 27-28
  adhesives 68
  appliance servicing 29
  asbestos 294
  bathrooms 27
  boilers 156

cables 183, 186
central heating 120
clothing 28, 33, 36
drilling 341, 357
dust masks 28
ear defenders 28
electrics 29, 124, 175, 186, 202
fire safety 27, 105, 213
first-aid kits 28
flat roofs 41
flexes 180
floorcoverings 68
furniture 28, 260, 264, 266, 269, 270, 281, 288
fuses 175
garden steps 313, 314, 315
garden tools 297
gas 120, 156
glass 27, 107
goggles 88, 104, 178, 221, 264, 336
greenhouses 293
grouting 233
gutters 45
insulation 170
lacquer, lacquering 260
ladders 32-34
lawnmowers 298, 299
lead 210
lifting 340
lighting 27
masks 21, 28, 221, 336
mats and rugs 27, 28
paint, painting 210, 217, 220, 221
planes 357
ponds 321
risk avoidance 24
roofs 36
safety spectacles 104, 208, 220, 264
sanders, sanding 211, 336
sealants, sealing 213
shelving 28
showers 27, 29, 148
sockets 29
stair gates 27
switches 192
tiling 229
timber preservatives 113
tools 28, 203, 327
water supplies 119
windows 104, 105
sanders, sanding 211-13, 336
  abrasive paper 346
  belt sander 337
  corners 212
  cramps 337

delta sander 336
drum sanders 211, 212
dust 212, 336
edges 212
floors 211-13
hand 346
MDF 336
power 346
random orbital sander
  336
safety 211, 336
sanding sheets 336
sash cramps 331, 346
sawing, saws 332-3
  blade guards 332
  circular saw 61, 348
  coping saw 87
  crosscut saw 333
  crosscutting 347
  floorboard saw 61
  handles 332
  hardpoint 332
  jigsaw 61, 332, 333, 334, 348
  offcuts, supporting 347
  panel saw 332
  power 333
  pruning saw 296
  ripsawing 333, 348
  splintering 347
  techniques 347-8
  teeth 332
  tenon saw 332
  tile saw 67, 229, 230
scaffolding 24, 45
screwdrivers 328
  Phillips 328
  power 351
  Pozidriv 351
  pump-action 343
screws
  brass 97, 343
  clearance holes 352
  countersunk 342
  cross-head screws 351
  in end grain 352
  gauge 351
  hiding 352
  hinges 96
  length 351
  pilot holes 352
  Pozidriv screws 351
  removing 343
  screw cups 352
sealants, sealing
  cartridge 353
  decorator's 353
  floorboards 213
  frame 114, 353
  furniture 282
  gutters 45

lacquers 213, 260, 261, 278, 279, 280
microporous 47
oil polishes 213
pipes 126
plasterboard 79
roof and gutter 40, 353
safety 213
Sealright tool 142
silicone 142, 143, 144, 231, 353
tiles 68, 231, 232
varnishes 213, 260, 261, 278, 279, 280

security
bolts *see* main entry
chains 99
door viewers 99
doors 98-100, 101, 103
garages 294
garden tools 295
gardens 292, 294, 295, 305
gates 305
hinges 103
locks *see* main entry
sheds 292
windows 101, 102, 104, 112

set squares 347
shears 295
sheds
insulating 292
re-felting 292
security 292
windows 292

shelving 246-8
adjustable 28, 248
alcoves 248
battens 246
book shelves 349
brackets 246, 247, 248
cupboards 247
fixed 246-7
glass 247
loads 246, 247
masonry walls 246
materials 246
safety 28
screws 246, 248
single 247
spacing 246
stacks 246
timber-framed walls 246, 247

shims 60, 84
showers 148-50
anti-scald device 148
bath/shower mixer taps 148, 150
clogged shower head 150
cubicles 149, 226

electric 148
heat surges 29
limescale 150
over-bath 148
pressure booster 149
pump filters 150
pumps 148, 149
safety 27, 148
taps 129, 131
thermostats 150
tiling 226
traps 149

sinks
blocked 136-7
fitting 139, 141
inset 139, 141
overflows 134
sizes 141
taps 130
traps 136, 137

skirting boards 85
cutting 87
double-sided 85
fixing 87, 88, 89
mitred angles 86
patching 89
profiles 85
replacing 89
rot 17, 20

slates
battens 39
checking 36
crawl boards 35, 36
cutting 39
damaged 38-39
drilling 40
nailing 35, 38, 39, 40
replacing 38-40
rippers 38, 39
sealing cracked slates 40
secondhand 36
slipping 35
tingles 39, 40

sliding sashes 106, 110-12
catches 112
cords 112
broken 110, 111
fitting 111, 112
locks 101, 102
painting 215
parting beads 111
rattles 112
weights 106, 110, 111, 112

smoke detectors 27
sockets 186, 188, 189-91
adaptors 190
aerials 205
baby-safe 29
blanking off 191
cavity wall boxes 190
circuits 176

double 189
earthing 191
faceplates 191
flush-mounting 190
flying earth link 191
levelling 190
mounting boxes 184, 189, 190, 191, 203
in outbuildings 203
papering around 242
pattresses 190
positioning 21, 191
RCD sockets 202, 299
replacing 186, 188, 190
single 189
socket-outlet tester 178
spur 191
stud walls, in 75
telephone 204
testing 179

soil pipes 152
blocked 138

solar-reflective coating 41
space, illusions of 22
spanners 329, 330
spirit level 301, 330
stains
grout 233, 234
painting over 217
wallpapering over 243

staircases, stairs 82-84
angle blocks 82, 83
broken balusters 84
creaking 82-83
handrails 27, 83
painting 221
risers 82, 83
safety 27
slack joints 83, 84
stair gates 27
strings 84
treads 82, 83, 84

steam *see* condensation
stepladders 34
steps, garden 313-15
brick-and-slab 313
concrete 315
dimensions 313
foundations 314
lawns and 313
paved 315
safety 313, 314, 315
timber 315
treads and risers 313, 314, 315
walls and 315

stoptaps 118
gas 16
indoor 118
locating 16, 118
outdoor 118
T-bar handles 118

testing 118
water 118

storage 249-51, 357
bathrooms 250
bedrooms 250, 251
carousels 249
children's rooms 251
fireplaces, disused 251
kitchens 249
living rooms 250
plinth space 249
wardrobes 249, 250
window seats 251

straightedge 345
strop 356
stud walls 70, 71, 73-75
building 74-75
cables and pipes 75, 184
doors 73
drilling 73, 75
noggings 73, 74, 184
sockets and switches 75
sound insulation 74

subsidence 17, 50
sugar soap 208, 228
surveys, home 15-20
switches 186-8
brass 196
ceiling-mounted 188
dimmer switches 187
faceplates 186, 187, 188
labelling 187
metal 188
mounting boxes 184, 187, 203
in outbuildings 203
papering around 242
positioning 21
pull cords 188
replacing 186, 188
safety 192
spurs 192, 193
stud walls, in 75
testing 179
two-way switches 27, 183, 196
see also lighting, lights

tape measures 331
tapes
flashing tape 36, 40
masking tape 215
plasterboard 72
PTFE tape 123, 129, 158
self-adhesive mesh tape 79

index

t

self-adhesive plastic
  sealing strips 143
self-amalgamating tape
  126
tape dispenser 79
taps 127-32
  basins and sinks 130
  baths 130, 131, 142
  ceramic discs 127, 132
  check valves 132
  connectors 139, 140,
    141, 142
  dismantling 127
  dripping 132
  extenders 131
  handles 127, 128
  leaking 129
  limescale 128
  mixers 129, 130, 131,
    142
    thermostatic 148, 150
  monobloc 130
  O-rings 129, 132
  outside 132
  replacing 130-1
  seating 128
  showers 129, 131
  spluttering 166
  stoptaps 118
  stuck taps 127, 128
  swapping 130
  tails 130, 131, 142
  washers 127, 128
  water pressure 130, 131
telephones 204
  cables 204
  extensions 204
  Ring Equivalence Number
    (REN) 204
  sockets 204
  system overload 204
televisions 205
  aerials 205
  signal, boosting 205
tenon saw 332
terebene 280
terracotta tiles 68
thermostats
  boilers 155, 165
  hot water cylinder 120,
    165
  room 120, 164-5
  showers 148, 150
  thermostatic radiator
    valves (TRVs) 157, 162,
    165
tiles, tiling 226-34
  adhesives 226, 230, 231
  angled tiles 231
  area 226
  bathrooms 233
  bond 226

cables on 184
ceilings 217
ceramic 62, 65
clay tiles 39
cleaning 234
colour variation 227
cork 66
corners 232
cutters, cutting 229, 230
damaged 233
drilling 231
edges 227
fixings in 231
floor-tile stripper 64
floors
  ceramic 62, 65
  cork 66
  cutting 229, 230
  quarry tiles 65, 67, 68
  setting out 65
  suspended floors
    62, 65
  terracotta tiles 68
  vinyl 66
gauges 228
glazed edges 227
grout, grouting 232-3
  adhesive and 233
  cleaning 234
  coloured 234
  discoloured 234
  dried 234
  drilling into 231
  estimating 234
  excess 233
  flush 233
  mouldy 233, 234
  recessing 233
  removing 234
  safety 233
  stains 233, 234
  waterproof 233
kitchens 233
laying 226-9
marking 230
mirror tiles 254
mosaic 230
old tiles, tiling over 228
pipes in 231
placing 230-1
plaster and plasterboard
  226
polishing 234
quarry tiles 65, 67, 68,
  229
roofs 12
  concrete tiles 35
  crawl boards 35, 36
  damaged 38-39
  nailing 38
  removing 39

ridge and hip tiles
  35, 40
safety 229
sealing 231, 232
showers 226
spacers 68, 233
terracotta 68
vinyl 66, 67, 68
walls 227-8
  painted 226
  papered 226
worktops 226, 231, 233
timber
  buying 339
  cladding 53-55
  cornicing 88
  creosoting 306
  defects 339
  doors see main entry
  end grain 345, 348, 352
  fences see main entry
  furniture see main entry
  holding and smoothing
    345-7
  mouldings 210
  planed all round (PAR)
    340
  planing 337
  preservatives 55, 58, 113,
    115, 306
  roofs 12, 17, 19
  sawing see main entry
  sizes 339, 340
  steps 315
  toothed connectors 354
  woodworm 17, 19, 263,
    264, 279
timber partition walls see
  stud walls
timber-framed houses
  13, 53
toilets 145-7
  blocked 138
  cisterns
    close-coupled 145, 147
    flap valves 145, 147
    floats 134
    high-level 140
    leaks 147
    limescale 147
    low-level 140
    overflows 134
    siphon units 145
    valves 134, 167
    water levels 145, 146
  flushing
    action 145-6
    continuous 146
    flush cones 147
    flush lever arm 146
    problems 145-6
    speeds 140

leaks 147
pans, replacing 140
pipe collars 140
tools
  choosing 327-40
  fixed tools 327
  garden 203, 295-7
  hiring 327, 338
  maintenance 356-7
  power 180, 327, 333,
    343, 346
    cordless 32
    garden 297
  safety 28, 203
  secondhand 327
  sharpening 356-7
  techniques 341-9
  tool pouches 36
  see also individual entries
try squares 94, 341, 345

U & V

ultrasonic estimators
  21, 331
valves
  ballvalves 133
  Belmont 157
  brass 167
  check valves 151
  diaphragm valves 133
    replacing 135
  double-check valves 132
  flap 145, 147
  float-operated 119, 134
  gatevalves 118, 119
  handwheel 157, 162
  lockshield 162
  motorised 163
  olives 162
  piston-operated 133, 134
  radiators 157, 158, 161,
    162, 165
  shut-off 119, 131
  thermostatic radiator
    valves (TRVs) 157, 162,
    165
  zone 120
varnish, varnishing 260,
  261, 278, 279, 280
  acrylic 260
  air bubbles 279
  brushes 213, 278, 279,
    280
  coloured 280
  drying 280
  fittings 279
  floors 62, 213
  furniture 279

microporous 215
polyurethane 213, 260, 261, 278
water-based 213, 217, 278
veneers, veneering 275-7
blisters 276-7
cramps 276
filling 275
holes 275
patching 275, 277
repairing 275-7
stripping 271
vinyl flooring 66-69
fitting around pipes 68
laying 67-69
patching 67
sheet 66, 67, 68
tiles 66, 67, 68
voltage testers 179

W

wall plugs 354
wallpaper, wallpapering 235-43
borders 235
bubbles 240
ceilings 242-3
corners 241
creases 242
cutting 236
embossed 235
estimating 236
grease marks 240, 243
hanging 237, 239
lights 243
lining paper 235
marks, avoiding/hiding 240, 243
measuring and marking out 236-7
mould 238
old, papering over 240
painting over 209
paste, pasting
brushes 238
excess paste 238, 239
fungicidal 238
leftover paste 238
overlap adhesive 242
pasting tables 238, 239
soaking time 240
types 238
patching 243
patterns 235
pencil marks 243
positioning 237
radiators, behind 241
ready pasted 239

rust spots 243
seams 241
stains, blocking 243
steam strippers 208
stripping 208
switches and sockets 242
textured 235
tiling over 226
types 235
vinyl 235, 242
wall plugs, marking 237
washable 235, 238
water marks 243
walls
boundary 16
cavity wall construction 13
damp 17, 18
external 13
brick 13
dry-lining 76
garden see under gardens
loadbearing walls 23
painting 220
plastering 71-72
rendering 50-52
repointing 48-49
solid wall construction 13
stud walls see main entry
tiling 227-8
zigzag cracks 17
wardrobes 19, 249, 250
washers, tap 127, 128
washing machines 151-3
anti-flood loops 153
back-siphonage 151, 153
cold fill 151
connectors 151, 152
hoses 151, 152, 153
hot fill 151
installing 151-2
leaks 152
siting 151
waste water 152
waste pipes 75, 136-7, 152
blockages 136-7
cutting 121
disconnecting 139
gurgling 166
joints 125, 136
plastic 121, 124
water
butts 46, 293
conditioners 150
drinking water 119
limescale 144, 147, 150, 154, 168
overflows 16, 133, 134-5
pipes see main entry
pressure 130, 131, 156
soft 119, 121
stoptaps 16, 118

storage tanks
see water tanks
water tanks
bouncing ballvalve 167
bracing plates 167
cold-water storage tank 118, 119, 131, 134, 135, 167, 171
draining 119, 131
feed-and-expansion tank 134, 158, 159, 160, 168
freezing 135
galvanised 119
hot water cylinder 118
insect screens 135
insulation 171
plastic 119
rusting 119
valves 119, 134
wax
'antiquing' wax 283
beeswax 282
colouring 283
furniture finish 260, 282-3
liming wax 283
polish 282
wet rot
doors 17, 115
skirting boards 17, 20
windows 17, 113, 114
white spirit 223, 224, 225, 260, 278
windows
bay 257
blinds 257
casements 92, 95, 101
cockspur bolts 101
cracked 104
curtains 255-7
dismantling 94
external glazing beads 101
flexible frame sealant 114
frame fixings 355
glass, glazing 23, 33, 104-9
coated solar glass 105
cracked 104
double glazing 106
laminated 104, 105
paint spills 222
patterned (obscured) 104
safety wired 104
secondary glazing 106
tinted glass 105
toughened glass 104
hinges 95
jammed 17, 92

leaded 107
lintels 256
locks 101, 102
loose joints 94
louvred 101
painting 33, 215, 216, 221
rack bolts 101
repairs 113-15
safety 104, 105
sash 101, 102, 106, 110-12
broken cords 110, 111
catches 112
cords 110, 111, 112
painting 215
parting beads 111
rattles 112
weights 106, 110, 111, 112
security 101-2, 104, 112
sheds 292
shutters 113
sills
drip grooves 19, 51
patching 115
replacing 113
wet rot 17, 113, 114
window seats 251
window stays 102
wiring see electrics
Wiring Regulations 191
wood see timber
wood dyes 284-5, 286
wood preservatives 55, 58, 113, 115, 306
wood stains 284-5
wood strip flooring 6, 69
woodwork
exterior 215, 216
knots 210
painting
exterior 215, 216
preparation 208
rot 17
sanding 211-13
stripping 210
see also timber
woodworm 17, 19, 263, 264, 279
workbenches/centres 327
wrenches 139, 330

index

Acknowledgments

The publishers wish to give their special thanks to the following organisations for equipment and help given in the preparation of this book.

HSS Hire Shops Mitcham Surrey

Robert Bosch Power Tools Denham, Buckinghamshire

Black & Decker Power Tools Slough, Berkshire

St Johns Street Cycles Bridgwater, Somerset

Thanks also to

Abru Ltd Belper, Derbyshire

Agfa Gevaert Ltd Brentford, Middlesex

Apple Computer Uxbridge, Middlesex

Aqua-Dial Ltd Kingston upon Thames, Surrey

Armitage Shanks Ltd Rugeley, Staffordshire

Bletchley Timber Bletchley, Milton Keynes

Brian Hyde Ltd Solihull, West Midlands

Christopher Wray Lighting Ltd London SW6

Colebrand Ltd London W1

Dewalt Power Tools Slough, Berkshire

Docklands Garden Centre London E14

Epson (UK) Ltd Hemel Hempstead, Hertfordshire

Evode Ltd Stafford, Staffordshire

Flymo Partner Newton Aycliffe, Co Durham

Foxall & James London EC1

Gainsborough Electrical Norwich, Norfolk

Greenwich Interiors London SE10

Grohe Ltd Barking, Essex

Hewlett Packard Bracknell, Berkshire

Hodgson Sealants Beverley, Yorkshire

Hunter Plastics London SE28

J. Crispin & Sons, Veneer Merchants, London EC2

JDB Beadmore London SW1

Kickstop Security Products Ltd London E9

Laybond Products Ltd Chester, Cheshire

Marley Rainwater Products Sevenoaks, Kent

Orpington Caravan Centre Orpington, Kent

Paul Marchant Ravensbourne College, Chislehurst, Kent

Paul Riley Odell & Co Ltd Stony Stratford, Buckinghamshire

Peglers Ltd Doncaster, South Yorkshire

Pilkington Glass St Helens, Merseyside

Redland Roofing Systems Dorking, Surrey

Richard Burbridge Ltd Oswestry, Shropshire

Southern Motor Factors Ltd Bromley, Kent

Stanley Europe Sheffield, South Yorkshire

The Building Centre London WC1

The Sash Window Workshop Windsor, Berkshire

Thule Ltd Roof Carriers, Accessories and Roof Boxes Clevedon, North Somerset

Wednesbury Copper Tube & Fittings Bilston, West Midlands

Picture credits

The position of photographs and illustrations on each page is indicated by letters after the page number: *T* = Top; *B* = Bottom; *L* = Left; *C* = Centre; *R* = Right

12–29 picture frieze from Edifice except **18** *TL* Houses & Interiors by David Copsey *CL* Houses & Interiors by David Markson *BL* Houses & Interiors by Ed Buziak

24 *BL* Houses & Interiors by David Markson

35 *CR* artwork based on photo from Skyscan

66 *T* The Amtico Co Ltd; *BL* Fired Earth; *BC* Crucial Trading; *BR* Mainstream Photography © Ray Main

82 *TL* The Loft Shop Ltd

85 Room setting A.W. Champion

106 *TR* Roehm Ltd

113 *T* Rentokil Initial

131 *R* artworks based on Successful DIY © Eaglemoss Publications Ltd 1994 by Andrew Green

147 *R* artworks 1 & 3 based on Successful DIY © Eaglemoss Publications Ltd 1994 by Maltings Partnership

149 *R* artworks 1 & 2 based on The Which? Book of Plumbing & Central Heating © 1994 Which? Ltd by Tom Cross; artworks 3 & 4 based on Step-by-Step DIY © Guinness Publishing Ltd & Keith Faulkner Publishing Ltd 1994

159, 161, 170 *R* artworks based on Collins Complete DIY Manual © 1993,Harper Collins Publishers

179 *R* artworks based on Step-by-Step DIY © Guinness Publishing Ltd & Keith Faulkner Publishing Ltd 1994

181 *R* artworks 1 & 2 based on a photograph by David Copsey from The Which? Book of Wiring and Lighting © 1997 Which? Ltd; artworks 3 & 4 based on an illustration by Peter Harper from The Which? Book of Wiring and Lighting © 1997 Which? Ltd

197 *R* artworks based on Step-by-Step DIY © Guinness Publishing Ltd

199 *R* artworks based on Successful DIY © Eaglemoss Publications Ltd 1994

201 *TR* Garden Picture Library by John Glover

205 *R* artworks based on Successful DIY © Eaglemoss Publications Ltd 1994

313 *BL* HSC

314 *CL* Garden Picture Library by Christi Carter

Editorial team

Editor Neil Thomson

Art Editor Neal Martin

Consultant Editor Simon J. Gilham

Contributing Editor Mike Lawrence

Assistant Editors Helen Spence Judy Fovargue • Alison Candlin • Celia Coyne

Designers Keith Miller • Jane McKenna Jill Adams

Contributors and Specialist Consultants Roger Bisby • Paul Bloomfield • Kevin Jan Bonner John Durrant • Cliff Forrest • Fred Milson Mark Ramuz • John Ratcliff • Ian Williamson

Researcher Deborah Feldman

Photographers Colin Bowling • Paul Forrester

Illustrators Rosalyn Kennedy • David Ritchie

Studio Ian Atkinson

Indexer Laura Hicks

Proofreaders Barry Gage • Roy Butcher

Technical Assistant John Ireland

Special thanks to Fred Spalding Labeena Ishaque

Additional photography Jon Bouchier David Sheppard • Gene and Katie Hamilton

For this edition (Quick Fix DIY)

Editor Lisa Thomas

Art Editor Julie Bennett

Designer Martin Bennett

Editorial Assistant Katharine Swire

Indexer Marie Lorimer

Proofreaders Ken Vickery • Rosemary Wighton

Readers Digest General Books

Editorial Director Cortina Butler

Art Director Nick Clark

Executive Editor Julian Browne

Managing Editor Alastair Holmes

Picture Research Editor Martin Smith

Style Editor Ron Pankhurst

Reader's Digest Production

Book Production Manager Fiona McIntosh

Pre-press Account Manager Penelope Grose

Origination Colour Systems Limited, London

Printer Tien Wah Press, Singapore

THE READER'S DIGEST QUICK FIX DIY was published by The Reader's Digest Association Limited, London from material first published in 1001 DIY HINTS AND TIPS

First edition Copyright © 2003 The Reader's Digest Association Limited, 11 Westferry Circus, Canary Wharf, London E14 4HE

We are committed to both the quality of our products and the service we provide to our customers. We value your comments, so please feel free to contact us on 08705 113366 or via our web site at **www.readersdigest.co.uk** If you have any comments or suggestions about the content of our books, email us at **gbeditorial@readersdigest.co.uk**

Book code 400–164–01
ISBN 0 276 42807 2
Oracle code 250007909H.00.24